THE NEW MIDDLE AGES

BONNIE WHEELER, *Series Editor*

The New Middle Ages presents transdisciplinary studies of medieval cultures. It includes both scholarly monographs and essay collections.

PUBLISHED BY PALGRAVE MACMILLIAN:

Women in the Medieval Islamic World: Power, Patronage, and Piety
edited by Gavin R. G. Hambly

The Ethics of Nature in the Middle Ages: On Boccaccio's Poetaphysics
by Gregory B. Stone

Presence and Presentation: Women in the Chinese Literati Tradition
by Sherry J. Mou

The Lost Love Letters of Heloise and Abelard: Perceptions of Dialogue in Twelfth-Century France
by Constant J. Mews

Understanding Scholastic Thought with Foucault
by Philipp W. Rosemann

For Her Good Estate: The Life of Elizabeth de Burgh
by Frances Underhill

Constructions of Widowhood and Virginity in the Middle Ages
edited by Cindy L. Carlson and Angela Jane Weisl

Motherhood and Mothering in Anglo-Saxon England
by Mary Dockray-Miller

Listening to Heloise: The Voice of a Twelfth-Century Woman
edited by Bonnie Wheeler

The Postcolonial Middle Ages
edited by Jeffrey Jerome Cohen

Chaucer's Pardoner and Gender Theory: Bodies of Discourse
by Robert S. Sturges

Engaging Words: The Culture of Reading in the Later Middle Ages
by Laurel Amtower

Crossing the Bridge: Comparative Essays on Medieval European and Heian Japanese Women Writers
edited by Barbara Stevenson and Cynthia Ho

Robes and Honor: The Medieval World of Investiture
edited by Stewart Gordon

Representing Rape in Medieval and Early Modern Literature
edited by Elizabeth Robertson and Christine M. Rose

Same Sex Love and Desire Among Women in the Middle Ages
edited by Francesca Canadé Sautman and Pamela Sheingorn

Listen Daughter: The Speculum Virginum and the Formation of Religious Women in the Middle Ages
edited by Constant J. Mews

Science, The Singular, and the Question of Theology
by Richard A. Lee, Jr.

Gender in Debate from the Early Middle Ages to the Renaissance
edited by Thelma S. Fenster and Clare A. Lees

Malory's Morte Darthur: *Remaking Arthurian Tradition*
by Catherine Batt

*The Vernacular Spirit: Essays
on Medieval Religious Literature*
　　edited by Renate Blumenfeld-Kosinski,
　　Duncan Robertson, and
　　Nancy Bradley Warren

Popular Piety and Art in the Late Middle Ages
　　by Kathleen Kamerick

*Absent Narratives, Manuscript Textuality, and
Literary Structure in Late Medieval England*
　　by Elizabeth Scala

*Creating Community with Food and Drink
in Merovingian Gaul*
　　by Bonnie Effros

*Representations of
Early Byzantine Empresses:
Image and Empire*
　　by Anne McClanan

REPRESENTATIONS OF EARLY BYZANTINE EMPRESSES
IMAGE AND EMPIRE

Anne McClanan

REPRESENTATIONS OF EARLY BYZANTINE EMPRESSES
© Anne McClanan, 2002.
All rights reserved. No part of this book may be used or reproduced in any manner whatsoever without written permission except in the case of brief quotations embodied in critical articles or reviews.

First published in 2002 by Palgrave Macmillan
175 Fifth Avenue, New York, N.Y. 10010 and
Houndmills, Basingstoke, Hampshire, England RG21 6XS.
Companies and representatives throughout the world.

PALGRAVE Macmillan is the new global publishing imprint of St. Martin's Press LLC Scholarly and Reference Division and Palgrave Publishers Ltd. (formerly Macmillan Press Ltd.).

ISBN 0–312–29492–1

Library of Congress Cataloging-in-Publication Data
available from the Library of Congress.

Design by Letra Libre, Inc.

First edition: November 2002
10 9 8 7 6 5 4 3 2 1

Printed in the United States of America.

CONTENTS

Series Editor's Foreword — vii
List of Illustrations — ix
Photo Credits — xv
Acknowledgments — xvii

Introduction — 1

1. Historical Prologue: Women of the Houses of Constantine and Theodosios — 13
2. Early Byzantine Steelyard Weights: Potency and Diffusion of the Imperial Image — 29
3. The Empress Ariadne and the Politics of Transition — 65
4. The Patronage of the Empress Theodora and Her Contemporaries — 93
5. Looking at Her: Prokopios Rhetor and the Representation of Empress Theodora — 107
6. The Visual Representation of the Empress Theodora — 121
7. The Empress Sophia: Authority and Image in an Era of Conflict — 149

Conclusion — 179

List of Abbreviations — 189
Notes — 191
Bibliography — 247
Index — 273

SERIES EDITOR'S FOREWORD

The *New Middle Ages* contributes to lively transdisciplinary conversations in medieval cultural studies through its scholarly monographs and essay collections. This series provides focused research in a contemporary idiom about specific but diverse practices, expressions, and ideologies in the Middle Ages; it aims especially to recuperate the histories of medieval women. In her monograph *Representations of Early Byzantine Empresses: Image and Empire,* Anne McClanan considers the production and consumption of images of imperial women in the sixth century from Adriane through Sophia. McClanan analyzes an impressive array of artifacts and materials—from the ordinary to the opulent—to demonstrate how Byzantine culture deployed a specific visual language that crossed the barriers of form to create a discernable typology of "empress." This typology emblazoned "empress" as a public, political identity with whom one could affiliate in distinct ways. One of the most intriguing elements of this study is McClanan's absorbing presentation of the empress Theodora. Using the tools of contemporary gender analysis, she dismantles the "political pornography" of Procopios's *Anekdota,* which overburdens the imperial image with gross corporeality in an anxiety-driven attempt to void the empress's "claim to an imperial essence" and thus to divest Theodora of typological status. In this book we see empress both as subject and object who occupies a cultural space distinct from that of emperor. McClanan's study is rooted in a forceful understanding of the registers of Byzantine culture, and her study gives us fresh vantage points from which we can approach the mosaic of imperial life and discourse.

Bonnie Wheeler
Southern Methodist University

LIST OF ILLUSTRATIONS

Chapter 1: Historical Prologue

fig. 1.1.	Gold pendant, fourth century, Dumbarton Oaks, Washington, D.C. (70.37).	18
fig. 1.2.	Reliquary procession ivory, early Byzantine period, Landesmuseum, Trier.	23
fig. 1.3.	Solidus commemorating the marriage of Licinia Eudoxia to Valentinian III, gold, Obverse: armored bust of Theodosios II, Reverse: Theodosios II (center), Valentinian (left), Licinia Eudoxia (right), A.D. 437, Constantinople mint, Dumbarton Oaks, Washington, D.C. (LRC 395).	27

Chapter 2: Early Byzantine Steelyard Weights: Potency and Diffusion of the Imperial Image

fig. 2.1.	Drawing of a typical early Byzantine steelyard apparatus with an empress counterweight.	31
fig. 2.2.	Photograph of modern counterbalance in use, Izmir, Turkey, 1996.	32
fig. 2.3.	Empress steelyard counterweight possibly from Latakia, Syria, early Byzantine period, Dumbarton Oaks, Washington, D.C. (50.25).	34
fig. 2.4.	Empress steelyard counterweight excavated from Philippi, Greece, early Byzantine period, Twelfth Ephorate of Byzantine Antiquities, Kavala, exhibited at the White Tower, Thessaloniki.	35
fig. 2.5.	Front view, empress steelyard counterweight from Yalova, Turkey, early Byzantine period, Istanbul Archeological Museum (5940).	36

fig. 2.6. Side view, empress steelyard counterweight from Yalova, Turkey, early Byzantine period, Istanbul Archeological Museum (5940). 37

fig. 2.7. Empress steelyard counterweight, early Byzantine period, Kunsthistorisches Museum, Vienna, Austria (AS VI 3142 C). 38

fig. 2.8. Empress steelyard counterweight from Kayseri, Turkey, early Byzantine period, Istanbul Archeological Museum (1333). 39

fig. 2.9. Licinia Eudoxia solidus, gold, Obverse: facing bust, Reverse: enthroned empress holding globus cruciger and cross scepter, A.D. 439, Ravenna mint, Dumbarton Oaks, Washington, D.C. (LRC 870). 40

fig. 2.10. Licinia Eudoxia solidus, gold, Obverse: bust facing right with *Manus Dei*, Reverse: Constantinopolis enthroned facing left, A.D. 442/3, Constantinople mint, Dumbarton Oaks, Washington, D.C. (LRC 872). 41

fig. 2.11. Front view, empress steelyard counterweight, early Byzantine period, Malcove Collection, University of Toronto (M82.395a). 42

fig. 2.12. Back view, empress steelyard counterweight, early Byzantine period, Malcove Collection, University of Toronto (M82.395a). 43

fig. 2.13. Empress steelyard counterweight, early Byzantine period, The Metropolitan Museum of Art, New York (1980.416a). 44

fig. 2.14. Marble bust of a woman holding a scroll, sixth century, The Metropolitan Museum of Art, New York (66.25). 46

fig. 2.15. Athena steelyard counterweight from Anemourion, Turkey, early Byzantine period, Anemourion Excavation(AN70/133). 48

fig. 2.16. "Hybrid" empress steelyard counterweight, early Byzantine period, The British Museum, London, UK (1870.3–15.15). 49

fig. 2.17. Corbridge lanx, found near Corbridge, Northumberland, fourth century, The British Museum, London, UK (1993.4–1.1). 51

fig. 2.18. Gold bracelet with the image of Athena of personification, fifth century, The Metropolitan Museum of Art, New York (17.190.2053). 52

LIST OF ILLUSTRATIONS   xi

fig. 2.19. Athena steelyard counterweight, early Byzantine period, The Metropolitan Museum of Art, New York (61.112).   53
fig. 2.20. Front view, Athena steelyard counterweight, early Byzantine period, Virginia Museum of Fine Arts, Richmond (66.15.1).   54
fig. 2.21. Side view, Athena steelyard counterweight, early Byzantine period, Virginia Museum of Fine Arts, Richmond (66.15.1).   56
fig. 2.22. Silver pepperpot, found in Hoxne, Suffolk, before A.D. 407, The British Museum, London, UK (1994.4–1.33).   59
fig. 2.23. Male steelyard counterweight, perhaps Constantine the Great, early Byzantine period, The Art Museum, Princeton University (y1955–3257).   61
fig. 2.24. Male steelyard counterweight, Late Roman period, excavated in Corinth, 1920, Corinth Excavations, Greece.   62

Chapter 3:
The Empress Ariadne and the Politics of Transition

fig. 3.1. Consular diptych of Clementinus, A.D. 513, Liverpool Merseyside County Museum, UK.   72
fig. 3.2. Drawing of destroyed consular diptych once in Limoges, A.D. 515 (diptych date).   73
fig. 3.3. Consular diptych of Anastasios, A.D. 517 (other panel destroyed), Victoria and Albert Museum, London, UK (368–1871).   75
fig. 3.4. Consular diptych of Anastasios, A.D. 517, Bibliothèque nationale de France, Paris.   77
fig. 3.5. Diptych of Orestes, A.D. 513/530, Victoria and Albert Museum, London, UK (139–1866).   79
fig. 3.6. Marble head of an early Byzantine empress, perhaps Ariadne, ca. 500, Musée du Louvre, Paris, France (R. F. 1525).   84
fig. 3.7. Front view, marble head of an early Byzantine empress, perhaps Ariadne, ca. 500, Lateran Museum, Rome, Italy.   85

fig. 3.8. Side view, marble head of an early Byzantine empress, perhaps Ariadne, ca. 500, Lateran Museum, Rome, Italy. 86

fig. 3.9. Marble head of an early Byzantine empress, perhaps Ariadne, ca. 500, Capitoline Museum, Rome, Italy. 88

fig. 3.10. Bronze head of an early Byzantine empress, perhaps Ariadne, excavated in Balajnac, ca. 500, Niš Archeological Museum, Serbia, Yugoslavia. 89

fig. 3.11. Ariadne tremissis, gold, Obverse: Diademed bust facing right, Reverse: Cross in wreath, A.D. 474–515, Constantinople mint, Dumbarton Oaks, Washington, D.C. (LRC 606). 90

fig. 3.12. Verina solidus, gold, Obverse: Diademed bust facing right with *Manus Dei,* Reverse: personification of Victory standing facing left, holds long cross, Harvard University Art Museums, Whittemore Collection, Cambridge, MA. (LRC 593). 91

Chapter 4: The Patronage of the Empress Theodora and Her Contemporaries

fig. 4.1. Fragment from the Church of Saint Polyeuktos, A.D. 524–27, originally in Istanbul/Constantinople, now by the Church of San Marco, Venice, Italy. 95

fig. 4.2. Vienna Dioskorides, Anicia Juliana, before A.D. 512, Österreichische Nationalbibliothek, Vienna, Austria (cod. med. gr. 1, fol. 6v). 97

Chapter 5: Looking at Her: Prokopios Rhetor and the Representation of Empress Theodora

fig. 5.1. Hillary Rodham Clinton cover, composite photo, *Spy* magazine, February 1993. 115

Chapter 6: The Visual Representation of the Empress Theodora

fig. 6.1. View toward apse, Church of Saint Vitale, A.D. 526–547, Ravenna, Italy. 122

LIST OF ILLUSTRATIONS

fig. 6.2.	Empress Theodora and Court, Church of Saint Vitale, mosaics ca. A.D. 537–544, Ravenna, Italy.	124
fig. 6.3.	Emperor Justinian and Court, Church of Saint Vitale, mosaics ca. A.D. 537–544, Ravenna, Italy.	126
fig. 6.4.	South gallery, mosaic of Emperor John II Komnenos and Empress Irene with the Virgin Mary and Child, A.D. 1118–34 Church of Hagia Sophia, Istanbul, Turkey.	138
fig 6.5.	Front view, marble head, early Byzantine empress, found in Milan, Castello Sforzesco, Milan, Italy.	141
fig. 6.6.	Side view, marble head, early Byzantine empress, found in Milan, Castello Sforzesco, Milan, Italy.	142
fig. 6.7.	Overstruck follis, bronze, Obverse: Heraklios (center), Heraklios Constantine (right), and Martina (left), Reverse: Denomination mark M, A.D. 615–24, Constantinople mint, Dumbarton Oaks, Washington, D.C. (DOC II, 1.96).	145
fig. 6.8.	Follis, bronze, Obverse: bust images of Heraklios (center), Heraklios Constantine (right), and Martina (left), Reverse: Denomination mark M, A.D. 616/7, Ravenna mint, Dumbarton Oaks, Washington, D.C. (DOC II, 1.289a2).	146
fig. 6.9.	Consular diptych of Justinus, A.D. 540, Staatliche Museen zu Berlin, Germany (6367).	147

Chapter 7:
The Empress Sophia: Authority and Image

fig. 7.1.	Justin II solidus, gold, Obverse: facing bust of Justin II, Reverse: personification of Constantinople seated looking right, holds globus cruciger, A.D. 566, Constantinople mint, Dumbarton Oaks, Washington, D.C. (DOC I, 1.1).	159
fig. 7.2.	Justin II and Sophia follis, bronze, Obverse: Justin II and Sophia enthroned, Justin holds globus cruciger, Sophia holds cruciform scepter, Reverse: Denomination mark M, A.D. 567/8, Constantinople mint, Dumbarton Oaks, Washington, D.C. (DOC I 24c).	160
fig. 7.3.	Justin I and Justinian solidus, gold, Obverse: Justin I (left) and Justinian (right), Reverse:	

	angel, A.D. 4 April–1 August 527, Constantinople mint, Harvard University Art Museums, Cambridge, MA, Dumbarton Oaks, Washington, D.C. (DOC I 1a).	161
fig. 7.4.	Front, Crux Vaticana, gilt silver and precious stones, sixth century, Sancta Sanctorum, Vatican, Italy.	164
fig. 7.5.	Back, Crux Vaticana, sixth century, repousée silver, Sancta Sanctorum, Vatican, Italy.	165
fig. 7.6.	Enthroned empress, perhaps Sophia, ivory panel, early Byzantine period, Kunsthistorisches Museum, Vienna, Austria (ANSA X 39).	169
fig. 7.7.	Standing empress, perhaps Sophia, ivory panel, early Byzantine period, Bargello, Florence, Italy.	170
fig. 7.8.	Barberini Diptych, ivory panels, early sixth century, Louvre, Paris, France (OA. 9063).	174
fig. 7.9.	Gold belt of twelve solidi and four medallions, consular issues, A.D. 583 or 602, Metropolitan Museum of Art, New York (17.190.147).	177

PHOTO CREDITS

Note on the illustrations: All coins are reproduced at actual size

figs. 1.1, 1.3, 2.3, 2.9, 2.10, 3.11, 6.7, 6.8, 7.1, 7.2 : Byzantine Collection, Dumbarton Oaks, Washington, D.C.
fig. 1.2: Photo by Ann Münchow, Amt für kirchliche Denkmalpflege, Trier
fig. 2.1: Drawing by Catherine S. Alexander
figs. 2.2, 3.7, 3.8, 4.1, 6.5, 6.6: Photo by author
fig. 2.4: Twelfth Ephorate of Byzantine Antiquities, Kavala, Greece
figs. 2.5, 2.6, 2.8: Istanbul Archeological Museum, Istanbul, Turkey
figs. 2.7, 7.6: Kunsthistorisches Museum, Vienna, Austria
figs. 2.11, 2.12: Malcove Collection, University of Toronto, Canada
figs. 2.13, 2.14, 2.18, 2.19, 7.9: All rights reserved, The Metropolitan Museum of Art, New York
fig. 2.15: Photo by Hector Williams, Anemourion Excavation, Turkey
figs. 2.16, 2.17, 2.22: Copyright The British Museum, London, UK
figs. 2.20, 2.21: Photo by Ron Jennings, Copyright Virginia Museum of Fine Arts, Richmond, Virginia
fig. 2.23: Photo by Clem Fiori, Copyright The Art Museum, Princeton University, Princeton, New Jersey
fig. 2.24: The Corinth Excavations, Corinth, Greece
fig. 3.1: Copyright Liverpool Merseyside County Museum, UK
fig. 3.2: author after Richard Delbrueck, *Die Consulardiptychen und verwandte Denkmäler* (Berlin: Walter de Gruyter, 1929), vol. 2, no. 17
figs. 3.3, 3.35: V & A Picture Library, London, UK
fig. 3.4: Cliché Bibliothèque nationale de France, Paris
figs. 3.6, 7.8: Musée du Louvre, Paris, France
figs. 3.9, 6.3, 7.7: Deutsches Archäologisches Institut, Rome, Italy
fig. 3.10: Niš Archeological Museum, Serbia, Yugoslavia
figs. 3.12, 7.3: Harvard University Art Museums, Whittemore Collection, Cambridge, MA. Photo: Dumbarton Oaks, Washington, D.C.
fig. 4.2: Bildarchiv d. ÖNB, Vienna, Austria
fig. 5.1: Photo courtesy of *Spy* Magazine, Sussex Publishing

figs. 6.1, 6.2, 6.4: Photo courtesy of Dumbarton Oaks Byzantine Photograph/ Fieldwork Archives, Washington, D.C.
fig. 6.9: Staatliche Museen zu Berlin, Germany
figs. 7.4, 7.5: Museo Tesori della Basilica Vaticano, Italy

ACKNOWLEDGMENTS

It is a pleasure to thank now the people who have been so generous in assisting my work on this project. While working on my doctoral dissertation on the topic, the members of my committee, Ioli Kalavrezou, Sarolta Takács, and Norman Bryson, helped shape its initial incarnation with patience and intelligence. Katy Park, Bettina Bergmann, Michael McCormick, and David Mitten also gave prescient advice on portions of the thesis.

Subsequent revision has gone through many phases. I owe thanks to Glenn Peers and Kriszta Kotsis as well as anonymous press readers for invaluable correctives, although the remaining flaws remain my responsibility, of course. Elizabeth Mae Marlowe, student assistant Jamie Joanou, and my colleagues in the Portland Late Antique, Medieval, and Renaissance Society assiduously commented on portions of the manuscript. Many other scholars have contributed to the project, especially the editor of the New Middle Ages series, Bonnie Wheeler, whose ongoing encouragement and support made this book possible. Amanda Johnson and Meg Weaver at Palgrave likewise marshaled the manuscript through editing and production with dispatch. A crucial subvention from Portland State University's Office of Graduate and Research Studies funded many of the illustrations.

My family and friends have sustained me with their belief both in me and my work. This book is dedicated with gratitude and joy to Ben Hadad.

INTRODUCTION

One day a Byzantine emperor decided to test the security of his palace. Dressed in rags, he slipped out under cover of darkness onto the streets of medieval Constantinople. When the emperor returned to the Great Palace, he was stopped at the first two guard posts. He handily bribed the guards and moved on. At the third post, however, with his bribe refused, the disguised ruler was dispatched to jail. And the story continues, "when the soldiers had gone away the Emperor called to the jailer and said, 'My friend—do you know the Emperor Leo?'" "How could I know him?" replied the man, "when I do not remember ever having seen him properly? Certainly I gazed at a distance once or twice, when he appeared in public, but I could not get close, and it seemed to me then that I was looking at a wonder of nature rather than at a human being. It would be more to the purpose for you to be thinking how to get out of here with a whole skin rather than to ask such questions as that . . . You lie in prison, he sits upon his golden throne . . ."

Emperor Leo's mischief related in this tenth-century traveler's account then ends happily, for the emperor convinced his recalcitrant jailer to go with him into the palace the next day where his vigilance was rewarded.

—Liutprand of Cremona, Antapodosis, *11*.[1]

The emperor and empress stood at the apex of the Byzantine state. Even when their very persons were unrecognizable to the functionaries who circled the periphery of the court, the imperial image was replicated endlessly throughout the Empire in their stead. Although Liutprand's anecdote concerns an emperor, we will see that the same conundrums apply to empresses when we look earlier in Byzantine history at the imperial women of the late fifth and sixth centuries. At once accessible and remote, their representations circulated everywhere at the same time that the individuals receded into the infinity of the concept of divine rule. To their medieval audience, the multiple meanings of imperial images rested on a foundation of visual, political, and cultural traditions that buttressed the institutions of authority. The early Byzantine period presents the chance to study the nascent form of these practices as we see the transition from Roman imperial norms to new paradigms. The role and representation of imperial women demonstrates how those traditions diverged and coincided on the basis of gender.

This book examines the visual representation of early Byzantine empresses. These depictions appeared across multiple registers of consumption, and the interpretations of these differing modes inform one another. One of the main goals of this book is to assess the full range of images, in order to balance our sense of female imperial representation. Too often, imperial art has been elided into a study of work befitting an imperial milieu. The glittering spectacle of works such as Ravenna's mosaics present only a tiny portion of what people then actually saw; historians and art historians have based their conclusions largely on luxury goods.

The full spectrum of extant female imperial representations includes modest coins and commercial weights, as well as sumptuous mosaics and architecture. The omniform evidence has been neglected, and each kind of material calls for different strategies of interpretation. Although relevant case studies of specific images and historical problems exist for the women considered here, no attempt to understand the images' roles within a broader cultural context has been undertaken until recently. Because of the fractured view of the place and image of these women, the strongly typological nature of the literary and visual representations of the empress has been neglected in favor of an illusory sense of one or two colorful individuals.[2] The term "typological" is used in this book more generally, as it denotes forms strongly based on a normative type, as opposed to its theological meaning of interpreting the Hebrew Bible as a prefiguration of the New Testament. Here we will investigate how typological forms are strongly shaped by preexisting dictates and structures in the visual rendering of early Byzantine empresses. The implications of this way of thinking are often hard to reconcile with modern ideas of individuality and even of celebrity. Markers such as insignia constituted an empress' identity in a way that grates against sensibilities shaped by a more disposable consumer culture. Clothing, of course, used to carry a far higher relative value than it does today. A general feature of medieval society was the basis of a public persona in items of clothing; even in early modern Europe, "Wanted" circulars would often list clothing rather than facial features.[3]

The rarefied existence of empresses does not particularly illuminate the lives of women in society in general; this study instead explores an important subset of Byzantine imperial art.[4] The intersection of class and gender in the representations of these institutions remains pertinent, for in many ways the experience of these individuals as members of the imperial house shaped their lives more than the social practices for being a woman in the fifth through seventh centuries.[5] Empresses' most distinctive attribute in the public eye was the fact of their imperial, not their feminine, identity. If anything, the prominence of women underscores aristocratic or imperial power as against the power of the people in the ancient Greek tradition. The portrayal of empresses, however, diverged in significant ways from that of emperors, as we will see by chapter two when we consider commercial weights.

The term "portrait" must be used here advisedly, for the images at the heart of the discussion are not attempts at mimetic representations but renderings of idealized types. The early importance of numismatics for establishing our ideas of ancient portraiture carry over to how we view the early Byzantine material under consideration here.[6] Because our medieval sources are voluble, they beguile us into a false sense of familiarity. The upcoming chapters will show that what we might consider "empress-looking" today cannot be taken for granted as we grapple with Byzantine sources.

The elision between the imperial image and personal identity is crucial for understanding the manner in which early Byzantine imperial representations functioned. Modern notions of portraiture based on likeness are irrelevant here, for they do not accommodate the public role these images had. Empresses' public identities were constituted not only from being part of the imperial house, and thus the embodiment of state authority, but also from being women. Thus even the appearance of a woman possessing independent power, such as Cleopatra, assimilated with that of her husband on their numismatic depictions.[7] In Roman society women were viewed not so much as individuals but as part of a biological class, as seen in women's omission from the explorations of personal character in ancient physiognomic manuals.[8] This sense is perpetuated to some degree in the early Byzantine period. Just as most of the textual sources that we have from the period were written and transmitted by men, the visual record that survives seems a largely masculine realm of production.

The "normalized" status of imperial women's representations depends on this notion. The anecdote from Liutprand of Cremona that begins this introduction renders a world in which the appearance of the imperial person is unknown, and indeed irrelevant, even to palace staff. Discussed later in more detail, the motif of bride shows is another way that the typological force of empresses' images can be shown.[9] In accounts such as the *Vita* of Saint Philaretos' bride show, potential candidates for marriage to the heir apparent were gathered in Constantinople on the basis of how closely they approximated a set of measures and a picture (*lauraton*) of the ideal future empress.

A cliché such as the feminine beauty of empresses offers an obvious example of the way stock formulae have beguiled some scholars such as Garland, who makes the mysterious assertion that one sixth-century empress "was worth looking at."[10] While I too think these empresses are worth looking at, it is more for what they can tell us about how early Byzantine public identity was created through images and words. Convention dictated that imperial women must be represented both in texts and visual depictions as beautiful by medieval standards. It is simply nonsensical to determine their "real" appearance based on the highly filtered images that survive. The original audience would hardly have expected a faithful replication of every blemish. This convention already had a venerable heritage by the early Byzantine period, for throughout antiquity the notion of physical beauty and moral perfection were interlinked so that outer appearance reflected virtue or its absence (an idea known in its early Greek form as καλοκἀγαθός). Just as modern notions of beauty often relate to symmetry, so too does the regularizing force of public representation put these women into a predictable mold of acceptable contours.[11] Rigorously grounded in the methodology of ancient art history, museum curators have dutifully sought out identifications with individual historical figures for those objects in their care, but this approach is strained past its limitations by some of the works we will consider.

The current work follows a loosely continuous art historical narrative in an attempt to correct some of these imbalances. The three empresses discussed in the main chapters—Ariadne, Theodora, and Sophia—reigned in the fifth and sixth centuries A.D. Their predecessors, women of the Houses of Constantine and Theodosios, offer important antecedents in the transformation of Roman institutions, and their immediate successors following the Empress Sophia often have only oblique mentions in that period's scarce sources. Focusing tightly on this period allows enough depth of analysis to look at the complex layering of visual culture. Both the continuities and innovations in the role and image of imperial women during this period require understanding the milieu in which they operated. For example, the Empress Theodora's place within this sequence establishes the very conventional nature of both the positive and negative rhetoric that represented her. Understanding the representation and role of these women removes them from isolation, for imperial women need to be seen in comparison with emperors.

The first chapter quickly surveys the representation and patronage of late Roman imperial women in order to provide a historical framework for the period addressed in the main chapters of the book. The second chapter establishes the strongly typological nature of the imperial image by looking at a body of material that is largely unfamiliar to many art historians. The empress was the favored form on steelyard weights used in routine commerce in the fifth to seventh centuries. Such unimpressive objects exposed a wide range of citizens of the Byzantine Empire to representations of the empress, yet they have been largely overlooked in discussions of Byzantine imperial art. These weights have been often buried in the research of metrology and archeology. Their dating, place of origin, and varying meanings all require reassessment as part of the broader study of visual culture. Her presence also validated ordinary commercial exchanges at the edge of the Empire, just as the image of the empress prominently marked widely circulated coinage during this period. Throughout this book we will see how important coinage is as a medium for the imperial image.

Even in the realm of mass-produced, utilitarian objects, past scholars have resisted accepting the typological nature of imperial representation. The bronze counterpoises of steelyard scales represent an empress clumsily; differences among this cluster of objects arise from minor irregularities among the multiple workshops that cranked out these guarantors of trade. The trivial fluctuations in form that exist—some have a necklace, some do not—are seized upon as the necessary marks of personal difference to create an identification with a specific empress. When scrutinized as a group, these rather generic emblems of imperial authority cannot be reckoned as portraits in a more modern sense. This tension between typological and individual representations poses specific problems when applied to imperial art. The "empress-ness" or "emperor-ness" of an effigy overrode individual appearance in these official representations; this necessity imbues Byzantine imperial art with a strong typological aspect. The balance between the two elements had shifted even by the early Byzantine period, which comes up against our assumptions formed by the remarkably apposite requirements of Roman imperial art.

The third chapter chronicles the Empress Ariadne (d. 513/15), who reigned in the last decades of the fifth century and first years of the sixth. To an unprecedented extent, Ariadne's representation was emblazoned throughout the Empire on official diptychs, coinage, and statuary. The way typologies shape images on luxury goods is profoundly different from the way it operates in more mundane spheres such as commercial weights. Ariadne's power was considerable, and at the death of her first husband she selected the next emperor—the civil servant Anastasios—through her marriage to him. The imperial couple reformed coinage with a new system of denominations and iconographic conventions that survived for centuries, until the Middle Byzantine period. Bronze and gold coinage reinforced at both ends of the spectrum the ubiquity of the imperial presence, for silver is not used much until later in Byzantium.

The next three chapters reassess the visual and textual representations of the Empress Theodora (ca. 497–548). Because Theodora has so often been discussed in the scandalous terms of Prokopios' *Anekdota*, a work popularly called the *Secret History*, her artistic and religious patronage has been neglected. She is, remarkably, the subject of more modern biographies than any other Byzantine figure, but these works, often for a general audience, gullibly cast her as one of history's great sexual adventurers. This book's revision shifts the terms of discussion about two of the most well-known images of Byzantine art, the portraits of Justinian and Theodora in the Church of San Vitale, Ravenna. Although not a sponsor of the building, the Empress' inclusion in this political message conveys her importance as a beneficent head of state. The topos of empress-as-founder recurs as a defining theme in the construction of female imperial identity. Yet the image of Theodora and her attendants also portrays the *sekreton ton gynaikon*, the female court surrounding the empress. The empress was clearly defined in these Byzantine sources as the leader of a female court structured by a subtly nuanced hierarchy.

Prokopios' political pornography in the *Anekdota* can be understood in terms of late antique rhetoric, but also parallels more recent manifestations of anxiety toward female rulers. Within patriarchal societies, such maneuvers remain ever-popular means of diminishing the male ruler.[12] Using methodological strategies that have been applied with success to verbal and visual rhetoric about powerful women as disparate as Marie Antoinette and Jacqueline Kennedy Onassis, this project explores further problems and paradoxes in Theodora's depiction. Prokopios' rhetoric incisively manipulated the terms of regnal identity in such a way that he negates Theodora's claim to an imperial essence, in the terms of the ruler's "two bodies" delineated by Ernst Kantorowicz.[13] Theodora's almost palpable corporeality in the *Anekdota* thus becomes the crux of our understanding of her representation in this source. The fascinating vixen of such works as *Theodora, She-Bitch of Byzantium* turns out to be a mirage that melts away under closer examination.

The visual representation of Theodora's niece, the Empress Sophia, is the focus of the final chapter. In the late sixth century, powerful figures such as the Empress Sophia (d. after 600) emerged in the Byzantine political arena. This period begins what is called the "Dark Ages" in Byzantium because of the paucity of contemporary textual sources, but it also produces compelling evidence for the importance of an exceptional empress such as Sophia. When Sophia's husband, Justin II, succumbed to mental illness, she in effect ruled the Empire, an authority registered in her prominent image on coinage and also naming substantial imperial projects after the empress. The most abundant currency denomination—the bronze follis—proclaimed Sophia's status by rendering her seated on the throne beside the emperor in a manner previously used only for coemperors.

As Angeliki Laiou has noted in her research on the later Byzantine period, representations of women particularly lean on conventions, making an assessment of specific historical circumstances all the more vexed.[14] Looking at the formative period of Byzantine culture, this book asks how power was represented and implemented by imperial women. Dynamics of continuity and change shape the narrative of imperial representation, and empresses' roles both as subjects in art and as patrons of art are significant. In the past, Byzantine empresses have been studied in isolated historical investigations, which fragmented our image of their role in the functioning of the Byzantine state. Charles Diehl's *Byzantine Empresses* exemplifies this approach; Donald Nicol's more recent book, *The Byzantine Lady: Ten Portraits*, continues this trend.[15] Slighting important individuals such as Ariadne, whose "story" does not exude the tantalizing aroma of scandal, this method, structured as a string of vignettes, dwelled on more flamboyant figures.[16] The sixth-century Empress Theodora, whose histories best exemplify the distortions of this phenomenon, has had inordinate attention lavished on her of a rather peculiar kind, and these speculations warrant historiographic study in a later chapter. Once returned to the traditions of early Byzantine imperial women, Theodora suddenly seems a far more ordinary empress than before, but the way these norms are applied will prove quite interesting.

The specific qualities of empresses' representations are lost when empresses are subsumed into a larger study of imperial art, such as the foundational work by André Grabar, *L'empereur dans l'art byzantin*, or its predecessors such as Lampros' Λεύχωμα Βυζαντινῶν Αὐτοκρατόρων.[17] Grabar's monograph became the fulcrum for ensuing discussions of imperial art and he characterizes imperial art of the fourth through sixth centuries as a thin veneer of Christian forms imposed onto an underlying stratum of ancient types.[18] A little over thirty years ago, a Grabar student, Maria Delivorria, wrote a diachronic study of the visual representation of empresses as her unpublished dissertation.[19] Delivorria's thesis proffers a sometimes very insightful assemblage of the early Byzantine material, but its iconographic methodology and focus on luxury goods now allows further questions to be asked. She enhances the iconographic work of Delbrueck with the study of textual sources such as acclamations.[20]

The present work, though, is only possible because of the careful work of these and other scholars who created a foundation for this work. For example, Lynda Garland produced a more synthetic history of Byzantine Empresses from A.D. 527–1204.[21] Her diachronic study offers a helpful introduction to the topic, but follows the well-baited path laid by previous studies in its ready acceptance of several of the rhetorical tropes found in the medieval sources. She is more successful in the wide array of evidence she has managed to collect from folk songs to church histories. Visual evidence is assiduously interwoven into Garland's account, and this evidence will be discussed more extensively in the following chapters. Liz James recently analyzed specifically the power of early Byzantine empresses during the period from the Theodosian empresses through Iconoclasm.[22] Her book uses images to substantiate arguments that are based largely on texts about the institutional role of imperial women. In many ways, its work is complementary to the undertaking here, though I will discuss a few points of disagreement in the following chapters.

The visual representation of Byzantine imperial women appears in other noteworthy recent studies, such as Henry Maguire's intriguing work that posits a theory of modes in the visual representation of the imperial house.[23] His theory will be discussed in depth later, for it contributes an important insight to our understanding of this domain of Byzantine visual culture. Leslie Brubaker pursued these notions further, and—looking at Late Byzantine portraiture—broadens this analysis of visual modes to distinguish formal differences between depictions of men and women.[24]

Part of exploring the complex meanings of different kinds of imperial imagery entails the study of Byzantine concepts of gender. The particular functions of imperial women in early Byzantine visual culture make this book potentially relevant to understanding other means by which gender can be a useful parameter for research. As Susan Bordo noted, there is a "new skepticism about the use of gender as analytical category," but imperial women's image is different enough from that of emperors that this sliver of early Byzantine visual culture yields insights into broader questions.[25] Imperial women were sometimes elided from the more recent wave of revisionist scholarship that sought to understand the lives of ordinary people.[26] A good recent monograph adheres to this mold: Gillian Clark's *Women in Late Antiquity* probes the everyday life of women, bringing fascinating detail to matters of dress and medical care, but mentioning imperial women only incidentally.[27] Likewise Irmgard Hutter's brief article on the representation of women over a broad spectrum of Byzantine history, "Das Bild der Frau in der byzantinischen Kunst," tries to analyze visual representation as documentation of social practices.[28] Empresses possessed a distinct role and representation in early medieval art, and by looking at the variations of the imperial image their meaning becomes more clear. New work, including a nicely balanced anthology edited by Liz James, represents a deeper involvement in historicizing the representation of gender.[29] Judith Herrin and Barbara Hill's recent books on imperial women of the Iconoclast and Komnenian periods respectively also map out important later terrain.[30]

Barbara Hill, in her monograph, provides an intelligent discussion of how the heritage of feminist scholarship can inform the study of Byzantine women, and her arguments need not be replicated here.[31] The ways in which gender shaped the identity of both the male and female members of the Byzantine imperial house are distinct yet inextricably bound. The definition of this project is based on the assumption that the study of one informs the other, just as gender is taken here as "a social category imposed on a sexed body" in a well-known formulation of this distinction central to feminism and gender studies.[32] As Jill Dubisch noted, "The female anthropologist's identification with women of other societies, despite differences of culture and power, is often taken for granted (by women as well as men) in a way that a male anthropologist's identification with men is not."[33] A preponderance of recent work on women in Byzantium has been pursued by female scholars, replicating a pattern well familiar from other fields. The alterity of the medieval world can slip away under the illusion of a unifying sameness of women's experience, and facile transhistorical comparisons must be used with caution. The creativity of some of these ahistorical juxtapositions can be entertaining, such as Fischer-Papp's book that delineates the supposedly uncanny parallels between Theodora and Evita Peron, apparently linked across time as sister femme fatales, "Theodora died on June 28, 548. Even the date bears a significant similarity with the date of Evita's death, July 26, 1952."[34] The beloved theme of eternal woman rests on a notion of masculine and feminine gender that is a fixed binary opposition.[35] Just a reminder of the challenges to this idea posed by Byzantine eunuchs, potentially a third gender, illustrates how problematic that tidy divide is.

These polysemous imperial representations confound the static interpretations given in the past to imperial images on media as diverse as those on commercial weights or gold mosaic. As Gilbert Dagron argued in a discussion of the narthex mosaic of Leo the Wise (emp. 886–912) in the Church of Hagia Sophia, Byzantine art historians have shied away from the potential ambiguities of the objects under inquiry.[36] These mosaic figures communicated many meanings to the diverse people who encountered the assembly of imperial effigies populating the urban space. The categories of representations natural to us diverge from medieval perceptions, so we cannot take for granted what "empress-looking" meant to the first audience of the imperial panels in the Church of San Vitale. There remain, too, the questions of what power looks like at a particular time and place. The alterity of medieval visual experience, a very interesting topic in its own right, figures in the reappraisal made here of the imagery of Byzantine steelyard weights.

Ignoring these ambiguities, previous research on these empresses sometimes sought immutable rules by which they functioned within Byzantine society. Maslev exemplifies this phenomenon in his study, "Die staatsrechtliche Stellung der byzantinischen Kaiserinnen," which assembles examples that span from the late Roman period through the Komnenian Dynasty.[37] His approach implies that the Byzantine state was operated for a millennium by a secret constitution that scholars can deduce from its plenitude of manifestations. In this vein Maslev's influential article is riddled with judgments about matters such as whether the sixth-century Empress Theodora can be considered a "co-ruler in a constitutional sense" ("Mitherrscherin im konstitutionellen Sinne").[38] Part of the strength of the thousand-year long Byzantine state resided in the flexibility of its institutions, and this monograph will demonstrate the fluidity of the roles played by imperial women within the reigns of Ariadne, Theodora, and Sophia as Augustae. The numismatic record illustrates the strongly typological nature of their depiction, yet reveals the somewhat improvised manner in which practices were reinvented to fit new circumstances. I would argue that the reason scholars such as Garland conclude that the "empress's constitutional importance was never defined," was because there was no Byzantine constitution to define it, and that its specter only misleads us into speculations about timeless institutions that disappear under scrutiny.[39]

Likewise the titulature of imperial women changed. Returning to the Roman origins of the institution, Augusta was first used when Augustus willed it to his wife Livia by adopting her into his family.[40] The title Augusta was occasionally bestowed by the Augustus during the early Roman Imperial period, and in the period following the reign of Domitian was used more frequently.[41] The emperor typically crowned the empress before her marriage ceremony, which suggests a precedence of her new identity as empress over her identity as wife.[42] In the fifth and sixth centuries conventions in titulature shifted to a readier use of Augusta, and conservative sources such as Prokopios register alarm at innovations in Roman institutional traditions.[43] Only in the late eighth century, as part of the shift to the use of Greek for official documents and titulature, did the Greek title *basilissa* become standard for the empress when it was taken on by Irene.[44] The rank of Augusta was normally a singular role held by one woman, and this singularity was often defined by officiating over the many activities at court. In chapter seven, the controversy of the Empress Sophia and her successor to the role of Augusta will demonstrate that the empress' role of the *sekreton ton gynaikon,* the imperial court of women, was highly coveted. When the new Caesar wished to make his wife Augusta, the dowager Sophia strenuously opposed this infringement on her prerogatives. By the tenth century, the female court included at least a thousand women in its ranks.[45]

An examination of the empress' court shows how palatial institutions could function as ordinary Byzantine domestic structures writ large. As during the Roman Imperial period, a theme of almost down-home goodness plays out in the public styling of imperial women. An ambivalence about the appropriate role and status of imperial women is evident from the founding of the Empire.[46] For example, the Roman biographer Suetonius tells us that Augustus wore clothes woven by the women of the imperial family.[47] Eve D'Ambra explores at some length the motif in both art and literature of the Roman matron assiduously spinning.[48] Spinning and weaving persist as the quintessential female activities even through the Middle and Late Byzantine periods.[49] To cite a well-known example, popular legend relates that the Empress Irene supported herself by spinning after her exile to Lesbos.[50] In the same vein, late antique imperial women were typically praised for traditional female virtues, now amplified onto the grander scale of state. Specific patronage practices connected to these female stereotypes evolved for imperial women that are distinct from those of the emperor. As we will see, female imperial patronage often gravitated toward charity that specifically benefited women, such as the convents established by the Empress Theodora.

The ways women such as Ariadne, Theodora, and Sophia worked within these frameworks communicate the resilience of the norms and the possibilities contained within them. The next chapter, an overview, sets the historical stage for the book's questions; early Byzantine imperial women's representations are shaped by a rich context of tradition and conventional expectations.

A note on spelling:

I have used the spellings of the *Oxford Dictionary of Byzantium* for consistency and cross reference common alternate spellings in the index.

CHAPTER 1

HISTORICAL PROLOGUE:
WOMEN OF THE HOUSES OF
CONSTANTINE AND THEODOSIOS

The first centuries of the Roman Empire witnessed important developments in the role and representation of the empress, but the powerful empresses of the Houses of Constantine and Theodosios during the fourth and fifth centuries provide the precedents most relevant to early Byzantine women's patronage and other public displays of authority. Livia (58 B.C.–A.D. 29), the wife of the first Augustus, looms large as a paradigm for Roman women, whether imperial or not. Livia's patronage in Rome inspired women's patronage throughout the Empire, such as that of Eumachia of Pompeii.[1] The very presence of women in public monuments is constitutive of the imperial period, for in the Republican era only Cornelia, as the mother of the Gracchi, had a public statue.[2] Domitia offers another important first-century example of a Roman empress who wielded authority quite independent of her husband. Eric Varner recently demonstrated that a new diademed portrait type was introduced a mere two weeks after her husband's accession to the throne. This portrait type continued to be promulgated after her banishment on charges of adultery. After perhaps hastening Domitian's demise, Domitia escaped the ignominy of her husband's *damnatio memoriae* and continued to be represented during the reign of Trajan.[3]

Late antique antecedents also show consistent patterns in the patronage and self-representation of imperial women. They gravitated toward traditional Christian *philanthropia,* often establishing poorhouses, hospitals, and religious establishments. These projects were perhaps seen as extensions of typical Byzantine women's interest in their families and immediate communities. In addition to these charitable enterprises, some of the period's most remarkable buildings were funded by Augustae.

Elements of the representation of the imperial family also depend on the heritage of the Roman imperial ruler cults. Simon Price discusses the phenomenon of the ruler cult in Asia Minor using cross-cultural comparisons, and provides several pertinent antecedents for the use of imperial images in the early Byzantine era. Whereas the Hellenistic ruler cults depended on royal initiative, the Augustan era cults rose up in the provinces from a broader base of support.[4] After Augustus, extravagant individual imperial cults evolved into general cults of the Sebastoi. In the Latin West, the focus centered on specific deified deceased rulers; in contrast, the ruler cults of the Roman East lavished their attention on the living members of the imperial house. Thus the public celebration of the ruler's family was more acceptable in the East in this early period.[5] Local Roman officials sometimes imposed the Latin model on their local subjects, so the governor in Ephesus altered the choir of Livia to reflect her apotheosis.[6] One of the most useful aspects of Price's work is that he goes beyond strict dichotomies once posed both between popular and elite as well as public and private domains. The supposed skepticism of educated Roman society distorts our notion of the audience of the imperial cults in a way that also colors how we commonly understand the reception of the medieval imperial house. The image of imperial women in turn accrues meaning from multiple contexts in medieval society.

The Christianization of the imperial cult was gradual. The first Christian emperor, Constantine the Great, granted several Umbrian towns their request to hold games and build a temple to his family, though as a nod to the newly accepted religion, he added a new stipulation—no sacrifices could occur in the temple.[7] These imperial images seem almost ubiquitous. The imperial cult in a very familiar form continued to thrive under the first Christian rulers; for example, Theodosios issued laws forbidding pictures of actors and charioteers in the public places where imperial images were consecrated. The law codes repeatedly reinforce the notion of the singular respect owed to the imperial person and representation.[8] The fifth-century *Vita* of Saint Thekla provides further evidence for the diffusion of the imperial image in the thriving imperial cult in Asia Minor.[9] When assaulted by a priest in the imperial cult, young Thekla wrenched away so violently that the emperor's image on his crown was damaged. That accidental slight to the imperial cult was seen as so egregious that it served as the grounds for her martyrdom. This almost incredible prestige attached to the imperial image takes another aspect in the reverence with which imperial women such as Helena were held.

Helena (d. between A.D. 330–336), the mother of Constantine the Great, stands as the first, and arguably most revered, Christian imperial woman. While even her most famous act—the discovery of the True

Cross—no doubt derives from legend, this unearthing was an undisputed truth during the early Byzantine period.[10] Western medieval sources, too, such as Liutprand of Cremona, assume she performed this archeological feat.[11] By the time of her death in the early 330s, Helena's renown as a patron of the most important monuments in the Christendom was considerable, since she had built in Rome, Bethlehem, and Jerusalem.[12] Michael McCormick tentatively links the elevation of Helena and Fausta to Augusta status to Constantine the Great's victory celebration for the annexation of the East and the defeat of Licinius in 324.[13]

After domestic unrest in the imperial court that possibly implicated her in the murder of her daughter-in-law Fausta, Helena seems to have made a voyage to the eastern part of the Empire that included the Holy Land.[14] As we will see, too, in the discussion of textual sources for the sixth-century Empress Theodora, slander filtered into the mix of Helena's otherwise beatific depiction, and she was alleged to have been a prostitute when she conceived Constantine the Great.[15]

Helena's individual patronage in the Holy Land remains a murky issue. Her visit overlapped the Emperor Constantine's main phase of building in the area, and the activities of Helena and her son are not demarcated very strongly in most sources.[16] That confusion is also manifest in the discrepancy between Paulinus of Nola, who indicates that Helena was the more enthusiastic Christian, and Eusebios, who suggests that her son persuaded Helena to convert to Christianity.[17] Kate Cooper's analysis of the trope of womanly influence in the Christianization of men suggests why Paulinus' narrative would be appealing, for it made sense in the patriarchal society of the time as a means of coming to terms with such conversions.[18]

Eusebios cites the churches on the Mount of Olives and in Bethlehem as Helena's initiatives.[19] The magnitude of her patronage was gradually exaggerated to the point that she was said to have built over thirty churches throughout the Holy Land, and later empresses were routinely eulogized as the "new Helena."[20] Brubaker comments on the zeal with which her model was followed by subsequent Augustae.[21] Ambrose goes so far as to say that "Mary was visited to liberate Eve; Helena was visited that emperors might be redeemed."[22] The ninth-century source, the *Epistola synodica patriarcharum orientalium*, likewise reveals the legendary proportions of Helena's patronage in later sources.[23] It anachronistically ascribed to her the later church at Bethlehem, which is typical of the way in which miscellaneous Holy Land religious foundations accrued to her memory over time. The many fifth-century basilical churches in Constantinople commissioned by imperial women were probably inspired by the widely held idea that Helena had founded the Church of the Holy Sepulcher.[24] Helena's ongoing stature has led to many unlikely appropriations, from the scholarly ascription to her of a Jewish past to the fond literary representation of her as a British princess by Waugh.[25] Within the Byzantine world, her story received further adornments over time. Sources such as an anonymous *Life of Constantine* found in an eleventh-century menologion bedecks a rather sordid narrative outline of Constantine's conception with niceties such as miraculous visions of light.[26]

The foundation of this later acclaim was laid during her lifetime. One of the most prominent public areas of Constantinople, the Augustaion, probably received its name from a statue of the Empress Helena.[27] Constantine the Great, while restructuring the urban fabric of his new capital, placed a statue of his mother Helena on a porphyry column in the area opposite the Senate and south of the Hagia Sophia. This name persisted throughout the space's existence in Byzantine Constantinople, through several reconfigurations over the centuries. From its origins as a capital, the tradition existed of prominently depicting imperial women in the public space of Constantinople. The *Parastaseis Syntomoi Chronikai*, an anonymous ninth-century text, describes a profusion of figures of Helena carpeting the city five centuries after her death.[28] This text comprises part of the larger gathering of *Patria* of Constantinople, which chronicle the local monuments and legends of Constantinople. The *Parastaseis* tells that when Justinian dispersed the sculpture of the Hagia Sophia in the sixth century, three of the statues represented Helena in sumptuous materials: "one of porphyry and (other) marbles, another with silver inlay on a bronze column and the other of ivory given by Cypros the rhetor."[29] In the Forum, statues of Helena and her son flanked depictions of angels, just as in the Milion Helena and Constantine's statues also perched above the arch with a cross having a Tyche, a personification of a city, in the middle.[30] In other instances, Constantine appears with both his wife and mother: "Constantine and his wife were made of cast bronze and partly of stone, but Helena was of porphyry all over."[31] The statue of Helena probably joined the couple later, since it seems unlikely that a set would be originally produced of different materials. Fausta seems underrepresented compared to her mother-in-law, for the rest of the *Parastaseis* lists almost *ad nauseam* the many statues of Constantine and Helena littering the cityscape: "In the same Forum Bovis a silver gilt cross was set up, and likenesses of Constantine and Helena, the hands of both the slaves of God holding the cross."[32] The imperial mother and son present an interesting parallel in another construction: "Constantine . . . built a church of the Theotokos . . . portraying himself and his mother and Jesus and the Virgin. . . ."[33] Helena functions in lieu of the imperial wife Fausta, even slipping into place with Constantine and his sons at the gate of the Philadelphion.[34] The preeminence of Helena at Fausta's expense may not represent the ratio of images while both women lived, for we know of one instance in which Fausta's statue in Surrentum (Sorrento) was reinscribed to render Helena following Fausta's *damnatio memoriae*.[35]

The indissoluble bond between Helena and her son may have been displayed in the personal adornment of the dowager empress. Dumbarton Oaks owns a gold pendant, thought to have once belonged to Helena, which includes a double solidus from Sirmium encircled by six imperial heads boldly projecting from the pendant surface in high relief (see figure 1.1).[36] The coin chosen for such exquisite treatment pictures Constantine the Great in profile on the obverse with Crispus and Constantine II, the Caesars, on the reverse. Her own numismatic depiction at times reached as much as 20 percent of the issues, we learn from the analysis of coin hoards.[37] Thus Helena presents a new array of possibilities for imperial women in both her depiction and patronage.

The son of Constantine I and Fausta, the Emperor Constantius II, married three times. One wife, Eusebia, seems to have been an early literary patroness, for Julian's fulsome panegyric to her stands in contrast to the half-hearted exercise he wrote to her husband the emperor. She protected Julian at court after the demise of his rebellious brother, and his gratitude is reflected in warm praise that compares her to Penelope.[38]

In addition to supporting literature, empresses had a consistent, and occasionally vexed, patronage of the visual arts. One cliché in the representation of imperial women begins in the House of Constantine, for the letter of Eusebios to Constantia offers evidence early in the Christian era that women's devotions were deeply intertwined with image use. Eusebios chides Constantia, the sister of Constantine the Great, who apparently had requested an icon of Christ from him.[39] Eusebios goes on to relate how an anonymous woman once brought him an icon depicting Paul and Christ, which he confiscated as an idol. Sister Charles Murray, though, disputes the authenticity of this document as part of her broader critique of early Christian sources hostile to images.[40] A consistent *topos* associates women with particularly intense devotion to religious images, and this theme recurs throughout the rhetoric in the debates surrounding Iconoclasm in later centuries. The *Vita* of Saint Stephen, for example, recounts women taking to the streets of Constantinople and killing a man sent to remove the Chalke icon at the Emperor Leo III's order at the beginning of Iconoclasm. This evidence must be used with care, though, for Marie-France Auzépy has shown that, not only was the howling mob of female iconodules a convenient ninth-century fiction, but the Chalke icon did not exist at that time for any variety of mob to destroy.[41] The image of female iconophiles recurs in the writing of a nun of the Iconoclastic period, Kassia. In her hymn to the martyr Christina, Kassia writes,

fig. 1.1. Gold pendant, fourth century, Dumbarton Oaks, Washington, D.C. (70.37).

"We praise your great mercy, Oh Christ,
and your goodness to us,
because even women have abandoned the
error of idol-mania."[42]

This persistent social construction of woman as iconophile is ratcheted up in intensity when applied to empresses, just as we will see other ongoing themes in the representation of imperial women exaggerate prevailing feminine stereotypes in Byzantine culture.

Like her predecessors in the House of Constantine, Aelia Flavia Flaccilla fulfills all of the traditional ideals of female *basileía* (imperial dominion), a concept Kenneth Holum explores in his study of Theodosian empresses.[43] As the first wife of Theodosios I and a descendant of Spanish aristocracy, Flaccilla's historical position at the beginning of the Theodosian Period enhanced the importance of her example for subsequent imperial women. In his *oratio consolatoria* upon her death in about 387, Gregory of Nyssa sets forth her fundamental attributes, one of the most prominent being her *philanthropia,* manifest in her generous largess to the poor.[44] The terms for the description of imperial women become conventionalized, so that the same *topoi* frame the charitable deeds and foundations of later empresses. Galla Placidia, the daughter of Theodosios I, built a palace that was still under imperial domain during the reign of the Emperor Justinian, referred to in a poem by Agathias in the *Greek Anthology*.[45]

The Empress Eudoxia (d. A.D. 404), the wife of Arkadios, is probably best known for her public battle with the Church Father, Saint John Chrysostom. This battle lingered in the memory of Byzantine writers as "a classic conflict between good and evil," that the twelfth-century Cypriote Saint Neophytos belabored in his homily of Chrysostom.[46] Neophytos grimly viewed Eudoxia as manifestly evil, ascribing to her the negative tropes of ancient rhetoric attached to women: conspiracy, sexuality, and witchcraft.[47] Byzantine writers on the attack consistently marshal these themes; we will see them expertly deployed by Prokopios against the Empress Theodora.

Eudoxia picks up the thread of traditional imperial women's patronage, an important example of her work being mentioned in Mark the Deacon's *Life of Porphyry*. After the Temple of Zeus Marnas in Gaza burnt down, the local bishop decided to build a cathedral on its site. The Empress Eudoxia agreed to fund this project, and a debate ensued over the appropriate design, for a contingent wanted to follow the circular contours of the familiar landmark, the Marneion. Eudoxia reportedly resolved the dilemma, perhaps unknowingly, by sending to Gaza a document with a cruciform plan.[48] This new plan required that the area be entirely cleared, particularly of the debris and marble cladding of the pagan sacred precinct for which "access was forbidden, especially to women." The new Christian building reused the temple's revetments to pave the open courtyard in front of the cathedral "so that they might be trodden on not only by men, but also by women, and dogs, and pigs, and cattle. . . ."[49] To enhance the new construction, the empress promised to dispatch expensive building materials such as columns and pieces of imported marble.[50] Eudoxia also featured prominently in public monuments; in 400 Arkadios erected a triumphal column that depicts her by his side.[51] The *Parastaseis Syntomoi Chronikai* reports several statues in Constantinople that spotlight imperial women: "A very large (statue) of Eudoxia, the wife of Arcadius (395–408), and of her daughter Pulcheria and two other daughters, all in silver. Another of the same Eudoxia in bronze on a pillar and one more at the Augustaion, on account of which arose the machinations against Chrysostom."[52] With unparalleled status, the Augusta traveled in the provinces basking in ceremonial usually reserved for an emperor.[53] Once in the Holy Land, Eudoxia visited Saint Melania the Younger, herself an aristocratic woman who had cultivated a following through asceticism and piety.[54]

The patronage of the wife of Theodosios II, Aelia Eudokia Augusta (d. A.D. 460), followed in the path laid by Eudoxia, albeit inflected by her personal interests and background. In Constantinople, the prolific Eudokia built the original Church of Saint Polyeuktos, later sumptuously reestablished in the sixth century by her descendant, Anicia Juliana. When she made her first pilgrimage to the Holy Land in 438 she stopped in Antioch, where she delivered an encomium on this city. Perhaps to establish kinship she states, "I boast that I am of your race and blood."[55] She was originally called Athenaïs, but, as was commonly done, upon marriage to the emperor she assumed a more regal name, Eudokia. Eudokia's name change parallels another Byzantine practice of shifting identities, whereby on entering a monastery or convent a person assumed a new name that often began with the same letter as their secular one. Holum's hypothetical Antiochene birthplace for Eudokia is by no means certain, for the name Athenaïs could evidence Athenian origins. Both Antioch and Athens fell within the borders of the Empire at the time, so she would be considered a proper Roman with either birthplace, which seems to have been one precondition in the early Byzantine period for becoming an empress. In contrast, in the later Byzantine period, a number of women, such as the string of Latin princesses, came into the imperial family from abroad. Only the dire circumstances in 703 forced the deposed emperor Justinian II to accept a foreign wife when he married a Khazar, despite deep-seated prejudice against such unions. The tenth-century *De administrando imperio* written by Constantine Porphyrogennetos forbids imperial marriage to all outsiders but the Franks, claiming authority going back to Constantine the Great.[56]

On the same visit to Antioch, Eudokia endowed the city's corn supply and paid for the restoration of the burned Bath of Valens.[57] The grateful citizens commemorated her generosity with a bronze statue in the Mouseion that was still standing when Malalas wrote almost a century later.[58] Eudokia also may have extended Antioch's city walls to include the suburbs.[59] The *Parastaseis Syntomoi Chronikai* mentions one sculpture of Eudokia in the forest of imperial statuary at the Palace Tribunal: "In the Tribunal of the palace (a statue) of Eudocia, the wife of Theodosius (II, 408–50) . . . here many ceremonial dances of the Blues and Greens took place up to the reign of Heraclius (610–41)."[60]

In 441 or 442, Eudokia acrimoniously parted from her husband Theodosios, yet managed to retain many prerogatives of *basileía* while living in Jerusalem until her death in 460. The reason for her removal from court in domestic unrest resembles the equally inauspicious inspiration for Helena's acclaimed pilgrimage. John Malalas reports an unlikely story that centers on a misunderstanding about an apple, a traditional love token.[61] Theodosios II gave a exceptionally large apple to Eudokia, who then bestowed the fruit on the favored courtier Paulinus. Unwittingly Paulinus returned the apple to the emperor, provoking Theodosios' fury at Eudokia's apparent infidelity.

In almost two decades, the Augusta reshaped the sacred landscape of Palestine. Eudokia's impressive list of foundations in the Holy Land includes Saint Stephen's Church, Saint Peter's Church, several hospices, and a tower on Mount Muntar. Eventually she was buried in this Church of Saint Stephen near the martyr, a common practice in the period for the elite. She rebuilt the south wall of Jerusalem, reportedly saying, "It was for me that the prophet David spoke when he said, 'In thy good pleasure [eudokia], O Lord, the walls of Jerusalem shall be built.'"[62] The allusion to David effectively reinforces her connection to *basileía*. The scale of her patronage in the Holy Land puts her in the ranks of its greatest builders, surpassing even the earlier female patrons of ancient Palestine, Flaccilla and Helena.[63] The expansion of the cult of the Virgin Mary, the recently declared Theotokos at the Council of Ephesus in 431, perhaps received an additional boost by Eudokia's discovery of an icon of the Virgin Mary purportedly painted by Saint Luke, though the impetus for this find may have sprung from the same preoccupations.[64] In addition to her momentous works of Christian philanthropy, the Empress Eudokia may also have influenced the enlargement and reorganization of the "university" in Constantinople.[65] Her training in classical literature was extensive, and she is sometimes considered the impetus behind reforms made by Theodosios II. Several of the changes include a sharp increase in the status of senior professors as well as the expansion of facilities. Even well-known pagans received these new distinctions, such as the grammarian Helladios, who boasted of killing nine Christians in a religious clash in Alexandria.[66] Eudokia's personal inclinations are evident in the literary project she sponsored while in Palestine, the *Homeric Centos*, which were Bible stories retold in the Homeric idiom.[67] She also wrote a Life of Saint Kiprian of Antioch in verse form, of which 801 lines are extant, and an inscription from the baths at Hammat Gader.[68]

Eudokia's rival in court politics was Pulcheria (d. A.D. ca. 453), the sister of Theodosios II. The conflict between the two Augustae seems somewhat ironic, for Pulcheria had initially brought Eudokia to the attention of her brother, in a story styled much in the way that later, somewhat fanciful accounts of eighth- and ninth-century bride shows orchestrated by the dowager empress were framed.[69] The sister, Pulcheria, avowed celibacy early in life ostensibly to express her piety, but abstinence proved an effective tool to solidify her personal power at court.[70] One of the primary means that Pulcheria employed for the display of her carefully cultivated authority was patronage. A series of well-chosen projects strategically emphasized aspects of her public identity. Her foundations reflect the predictable range of ventures, including churches, poorhouses, hospitals, and hostels.[71] Fashioning herself a "bride of Christ," she underscored this affinity by a series of foundations dedicated to the Virgin Mary: the Churches of the Virgin of the Blachernai, the Virgin of the Hodegetria, and the Virgin of the Chalkoprateia.[72] Pulcheria also built the Church of Saint Lawrence to house the relics that her sister-in-law Eudokia had brought back from the Holy Land. Judith Herrin has recently suggested that these carefully timed acts by Pulcheria speeded the replacement of the Tyche with the Virgin Mary as patron of the capital.[73] In addition, she initiated the Church of the Prophet Isaiah and the Chapel of Saint Stephen. Pulcheria was also prominently represented with a statue set up near the Theodosian porticoes of Constantinople by Leo the Great. Leo's devotion to her memory was noted by the anonymous author of the *Parastaseis Syntomoi Chronikai*: "accordingly he observed the commemoration of her death and on her tomb he represented her image. And in the imperial palace when he looked on her picture he would deem her whole life blessed."[74] Likewise the same source describes a statue of Pulcheria near the Chalke Gate, which was "like the one in the Peripatos in front of the palace."[75]

The heated controversy between Pulcheria and Nestorios in the midfifth century, and moreover Pulcheria's ultimate victory in this power struggle, centered on her identification with the Virgin Mary. This battle between the Augusta and the churchman has been discussed at length elsewhere, so the details need not be rehearsed here.[76] The virulent conflict indicates her authority, for she directly confronted the bishop of Constantinople. The connection Pulcheria drew between herself and the *Theotokos* is evident both in the imperial imagery replete in the Akathistos hymn and Proklos' hymn to her written in response to Nestorios.[77] Kate Cooper has demonstrated that Pulcheria's claim derived from a series of rituals and beliefs connected with late antique devotion to the Virgin Mary in general, and Nativity in particular.[78] These displays of singular privilege solidified Pulcheria's position of strength, and gave her a very visible edge in her controversial maneuvers for influence at court. After the death of her brother Theodosios in 450, Pulcheria as Augusta next transmitted imperial authority. This capacity demonstrates the flexibility of these institutions, which Pulcheria now molded to her purposes. The fact that she had not married earlier, for a husband would have displaced Pulcheria from her immediate proximity to the ruling emperor, her brother, empowered her to designate the next emperor. She chose Marcian as her consort and by

fig. 1.2. Reliquary procession ivory, early Byzantine period, Landesmuseum, Trier.

her selection he became the next emperor, although the union was brief. Marcian mourned her death in 453, honoring her with a porphyry sarcophagus in the mausoleum of Constantine the Great.

The Empress Pulcheria is perhaps represented on an exquisitely carved ivory now in the Cathedral Treasury in Trier (see figure 1.2). The identification of this scene has been hotly debated, for the individuals represented, the type of ceremony, and the date and location of carving are all in question. Because it opens up some of the interpretive questions important to the rest of the book, the discussion of the Trier Ivory bears further scrutiny now.

There are three main components to the image: the two churchmen coming from the left on their horse-drawn carriage, the architectural setting inhabited by anonymous rows of attentive spectators, and the empress and the cluster of officials who fill the center of pictorial narrative. The architectural setting structures the image and focuses attention on the action unrolling in the foreground. Stretching across as the background is a three-tiered colonnaded arcade with a gateway on the left end. This gateway—perhaps the Chalke Gate—is bordered by two Corinthian columns with a haloed image of Christ in the tympanum, carved in relatively high relief, with his head and gaze turned slightly toward the activity on the right side of the ivory. The way that a triangular pediment is represented above the semi-circular niche—but carved flat across the top edge of the ivory—exemplifies the flexible sense of space that shapes this image. A crowd has gathered to witness the transportation of these relics. The upper tier is filled by two rows of spectators. The scrupulous detail of the carving is manifest in the fact that even these ancillary figures are individually carved down to the waist level, with the spectators' arms crossed across their laps. The lower levels of the colonnade each has a row of curious onlookers. On the right side of the ivory plaque cluster a strange triad of building units, which represents a church under construction. The fractured spatial representation of the church shows the east-end apse seemingly detached and unfolded onto the same angle as the south side of the building. The same laborious carving details the church as the arcade, and four men agilely moider on the roof.[79] The two churchmen share on their laps the precious burden of a casket reliquary, with a peaked dome similar to the buildings on the right side of the ivory. Their chariot resembles a throne. Like the men standing beside the empress, the horseman wears a chlamys, in contrast to the ecclesiastical garments of the two bearded men holding the reliquary. The side of the chariot is decorated with the image of three standing togate figures.

The center foreground of the Trier Ivory depicts an empress standing in front of the west end of the church as she meets the cluster of men approaching from the left. She is set off—the angle of her body and her feet counter the direction of the men and horses processing toward the church.

She wears a bejeweled ceremonial cloak, a chlamys, and carries a long cross, perhaps evoking associations with the Empress Helena.[80] An elegantly dressed man stands in front of her and offers her a scroll, which the empress reaches out to hold with her outstretched right hand.

A body of scholars as noteworthy as Strzygowski, Wiegand, and Grabar believed the ivory represents Theodora translating the relics of the Forty Martyrs to Hagia Sophia in 544.[81] In this sixth-century scenario, the two churchmen on the chariot would be the Patriarch Menas of Constantinople and the Patriarch Apollinarios of Alexandria. An alternative is Grümel's hypothesis of an identification of the figures on the ivory with Leo and Verina, in which case the relic being moved is the girdle of the Virgin. Suzanne Spain argued for an attribution of the ivory to a Syro-Palestinian workshop in the late sixth or early seventh century immediately preceding the explosion of Islamic armies into that region.[82] Gary Vikan and Kenneth Holum argue that the translation of the relics is better understood within the typology of an *adventus* scene, and offer a hypothesis of a specific historical moment that it commemorates.[83] As they point out, the lack of any comparable artworks limits the certainty of any identification of this uninscribed piece of ivory, but they attribute the ivory as a representation of Pulcheria, translating the relics of Saint Stephen Protomartyr in 421 without committing to a date of manufacture. Calling upon a textual tradition that includes Theophanes the Confessor, George Kedrenos, and Nikephoros Kallistos, the ivory might render the final phase of the ceremonial sequence when the procession has reached the imperial palace, where the Augusta had founded a chapel to house the relics.[84] Laurie Wilson offered an interpretation of this scene that runs counter to the prevailing interpretation offered by Vikan and Holum.[85] Wilson argues that the Trier Ivory renders Eudoxia in the act of participating in the transportation of the relics to the shrine of Saint Thomas at Drypia, which was described by Saint John Chrysostom.[86] In contrast, Spain views the assembly as a funeral procession. Leslie Brubaker has recently developed the Holum/Vikan thesis to say that the Trier Ivory depicts a ninth- or early tenth-century version of the fifth century event with the Empress Pulcheria.[87] She suggests that either the Empress Irene or Theodora's reigns may have been particularly auspicious times for such a precious image of an earlier Byzantine empress. Although Holum and Vikan's suggestion is widely accepted, the enthusiastic chorus of alternatives, each with its own considered basis, bespeaks the ambiguities of the scene. James is right to point out that evidence for such religious patronage by empresses is even more abundant than that for their artistic patronage.[88] Imperial donation formed a central component of an empress' public identity, so these ostentatious displays of generosity recur in the textual accounts of Augustae, and thus offer a rich mine for art historians looking for the perfect verbal corollary to the Trier Ivory. The sense of typology and convention seem central to understanding this range of possibilities.

Throughout the Late Roman period, imperial women also maintained an important role in numismatic iconography. The power of coinage as propaganda was taken seriously by their original audience; a Roman text warns of the consequences of debasing coinage, for it "diminishes the prestige of the Sovereign's links in that coins are repudiated through the fault of the Mint."[89] Eusebios' *Life of Constantine* draws a correlation between numismatic and sculpted imperial portraits. The church historian offers as proof of the emperor's Christian devotion the pious appearance he chose for his public image,

> He had his image portrayed on gold coins in such a manner that he appeared to be gazing fixedly upward as if praying to God. These effigies he circulated throughout the Roman world. Furthermore, at the palaces of certain cities, the statues placed high up over the entrance represented him standing upright, gazing up to heaven and stretching out his arms in the manner of a man praying.[90]

The passage is interesting not only for the ready parallel Eusebios draws between different media, but also for his implication that the emperor, or those close to him, determined the manner in which he was depicted on his coinage.

Knowing this significance, it is all the more important that women early in the Roman Imperial period took a place on coinage, and Octavia was likely the first Augusta to be represented in her own right.[91] Imperial women's ongoing prominence in the fourth and fifth centuries followed a consistent pattern of representation, in which they issued a distinct series of coins upon being granted Augusta status. Although in the Roman Imperial period the emperor and empress could be depicted together, such as the jugate image of Claudius and Agrippina the Younger, in the Late Roman period imperial women were shown by themselves on the obverse face of their coins. Thus Eudoxia, Eudokia, Licinia Eudoxia, and Verina all issued coins individually. One limitation to this prerogative of women was that the co-emperor would not recognize the Augusta of his fellow emperor with a coin series; so Leo, for example, did not issue any coins of Euphemia.[92] The coins of imperial women followed a consistent iconography tightly interwoven with that of emperors. Their standardized representation on coinage during this period has led to some confusion in the scholarship amongst some of their issues, for example, the coins of Eudokia and Eudoxia have been muddled.[93]

fig. 1.3. Solidus commemorating the marriage of Licinia Eudoxia to Valentinian III, gold, Obverse: armored bust of Theodosios II, Reverse: Theodosios II (center), Valentinian (left), Licinia Eudoxia (right), A.D. 437, Constantinople mint, Dumbarton Oaks, Washington, D.C. (LRC 395).

The coins of Eudoxia in gold, silver, and bronze typify the numismatic iconography of this period.[94] On the obverse, the Empress Eudoxia appears in a bust length portrait in profile facing to the right. The *Manus Dei* descends to crown the empress with a wreath. The inscription on the coin continues the tradition of Theodosian imperial women taking on "Aelia" as part of their name, for it reads "AELEVDO XIAAVG." The reverse depicts a personification of Victory seated on a cuirass as she writes Chi-Rho on a shield (see figure 1.3).

Not only wives of the emperor but also sisters, such as both Pulcheria and Valentinian III's older sister Honoria, were elevated to Augusta status and subsequently issued their own coinage. This anomaly undercuts the generalization made by Grierson and Mays that Augusta rank was normally a prize allotted a woman who had produced an heir.[95] Both this premise and their alternate explanation, that gaps in the series of imperial women's coin issues can be explained by personal scandals, will be addressed further in chapter seven's analysis of the numismatic depiction of Sophia. The representation in the Theodosian era of the emperor's sisters—such as Pulcheria or Honoria—on coinage hardly lacked precedents, for the first representation of living women identified by name on Roman coinage came with the sestertius issued by Caligula that rendered his three sisters as Concordia, Fortuna, and Securitas.[96]

The precedents of imperial women in this earlier period will inform how we look at Ariadne, Theodora, and Sophia. A pervasive visual and verbal language represented these women of the Houses of Constantine and Theodosios, and this communication was then transformed with the ascendancy of the Empress Ariadne. The upcoming chapters interpret a range of media that includes objects often left out of the discussion of imperial art, such as bronze coins and commercial weights, and we will attempt to understand their significance to their many audiences. Just as the Trier Ivory, an exquisite product in a rarefied medium, challenges scholars with its ambiguities, so, we will see, do lowly steelyard weights evince some of the same conundrums.

CHAPTER 2

EARLY BYZANTINE STEELYARD WEIGHTS: POTENCY AND DIFFUSION OF THE IMPERIAL IMAGE

> The woman seated on a bronze chair in the hippodrome . . . Herodian told me is Verina, (the wife) of Leo the Great; but as I myself have heard from many people, it is instead the statue of Athena from Hellas, and this I believed.
>
> Parastaseis syntomoi chronikai, *trans. and eds.*
> *Averil Cameron and Judith Herrin, Sect. 61, p. 139*

The image of the empress was broadly disseminated throughout early Byzantine visual culture. Modest bearers of the imperial sign offer a new way of understanding the meaning and distribution of the rulers' symbolic presence throughout the Empire. The resplendent images of the emperor and empress on luxury goods such as gold mosaic or ivory preoccupy art historians, but—as tantalizing as these objects are in their visual richness—they represent only a narrow sampling of the varied imperial image of this time. The study of the imperial image has gravitated toward the opulent things that we imagine befit the imperial milieu, but has neglected the imperial image as it was constituted on the objects of everyday life. In contrast with the empresses' images on luxury goods, ordinary objects such as steelyard weights and bronze coinage represented imperial rule to a much wider audience. This chapter will show that the identification of empress steelyard weights as portraits of specific historical figures is no longer tenable, and offers a counterpoint to the "cult of personality" that swirls around our discussion of the individual historical figures represented on luxury goods. The distribution and chronology of these weighing implements also needs reassessment.

The term "steelyard" in English somewhat misrepresents the Byzantine objects. "Steelyard" derives from the area on the north bank of the Thames where steel was sold until 1597, where similar crossbeam weights were used. In contrast, these Byzantine scales measured a range of bulk goods in commercial transactions.[1] The ruler's form also served as a standard commercial measure later; the English distance measurement of the yard was supposedly based on the circumference of the king's midsection! Steelyard balances still measure out transactions today in rural marketplaces in Turkey and elsewhere, with a top crosspiece that is poised between a sliding weight on one end and the commercial goods on the other (see figures 2.1 and 2.2).

The history of scholarship concerning these weights consists largely of the progressive accumulation of examples rather than successive waves of interpretation. In 1933, Delbrueck first identified the counterpoises with specific empresses, classifying them as portraits of fifth-century imperial women.[2] The Empress Ariadne (d. 513/515) became *de facto* the latest possibility in this series of attributions, deriving from tidy comparisons made to numismatic renderings, as her reign marks the termination of Late Roman coinage. This reliance on coin portraits assumes that when portraits of empresses stopped regularly appearing on coins, their rendering on commercial weights simultaneously halted. Even if one puts aside the question of whether the empress counterpoises in fact depict individuals, this contrived system of correlation skews the dating.[3] Part of the confusion may arise from the fact that there are a few, very rare examples of later Byzantine weights identified with specific empresses, but they take an entirely different form.[4]

Recently, Norbert Franken began to address the problems of the weights' disparate treatment, producing a useful catalog of these objects that begins to reappraise earlier assumptions.[5] Franken's Bonn dissertation catalogs seventy-two empress and fifty-five Athena weights and includes what little information we have available on these early Byzantine counterpoises. He also discusses Roman imperial weights and the much smaller class of Byzantine counterpoises that depict a seated emperor. The prevalence of female figures on steelyard counterpoises is striking, especially given the preference for the emperor's figure on other units of measurement, such as glass or bronze weights, and on silver stamps. The main *lacunae* in Franken's study arise from the lamentable lack of archaeological context for these steelyard counterpoises, so that find spots, if indicated at all, often remain vague and speculative. Unfortunately, almost all of the published examples of the steelyard weights have filtered into museum collections from the art market.

The few excavated examples of weights from northern Greece, Cilicia, and the coast of modern Turkey hardly justify sweeping claims, but they do

fig. 2.1. Drawing of a typical early Byzantine steelyard apparatus with an empress counterweight.

contravene another common assumption made by scholars such as Ross about these steelyard weights: that they can be situated in Constantinople both in production and use. In reaction to scholarship earlier in the twentieth century that concentrated artistic production in classical cultural centers, namely Antioch and Alexandria, the following tide of research sought Constantinopolitan provenances. Ross presents this view in his catalog entry of one empress weight (see figure 2.3), "Although the Dumbarton Oaks piece is said to have been found at Latakia (Syria), these weights, in the form of imperial busts, seem related to Constantinopolitan statuary and may well have been made for export. Many have been found in or near

fig. 2.2. Photograph of modern counterbalance in use, Izmir, Turkey, 1996.

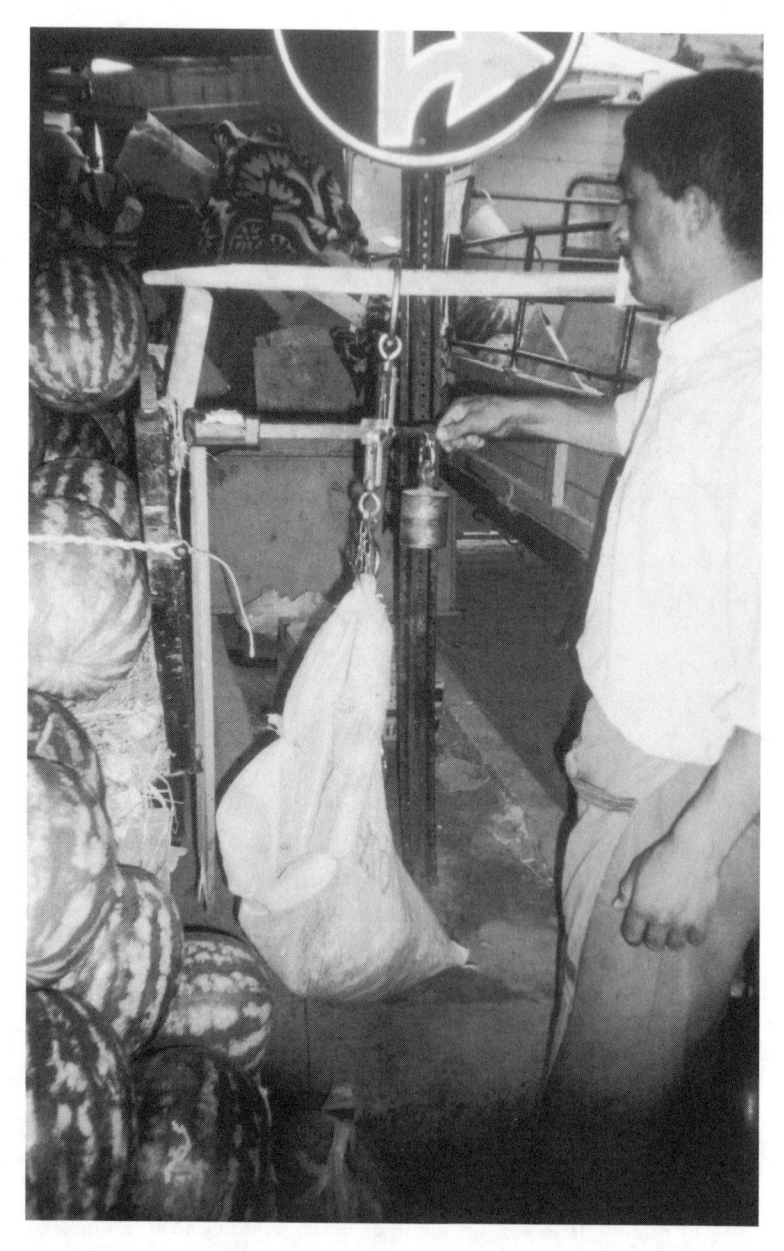

Constantinople, and, in fact, the largest extant collection is located in the Museum in Istanbul."[6] The empress steelyard weights now housed in the Istanbul Archeological Museum actually undermine Ross' claim. Fourteen examples from the collection are published, of which five are given a provenance: only two were found in Istanbul. The other three originate in Adana, Kayseri, and Çanakkale. Similarly, the empress weight about which Ross made this claim for Constantinopolitan origins came from a modern Syrian port town, which seems like a reasonable location for their commercial use. The large Athena weight in the Metropolitan Museum, discussed later, was probably found in the sea near the Dardanelles, which seems in keeping with the other maritime findspots such as the Yassi Ada shipwreck.[7]

One empress weight was retrieved in excavation, and this example from Philippi neatly represents the standard type (see figure 2.4).[8] She is minimally adorned with only the most basic markers of her status, the crown and a scroll or mappa. The reports of the find identify the figure as either Eudokia or Pulcheria primarily on the basis of the same attribution given to other steelyard weights.[9] Beyond the information that the weight was found in the Octagon at Philippi, the analysis by Georgios Gounaris does not reveal details about the stratigraphy of the object's find spot. The suggested identification is further complicated by the fact that the Octagon was built ca. A.D. 500, decades after either Eudokia or Pulcheria lived.

The find spots and manufacture of the two main groups of early Byzantine steelyard counterpoises follow slightly different patterns. To the extent that we know these objects' origins, the locations of the empress and Athena weights seem concentrated in Asia Minor. While no empress weights come from the western reaches of the early Byzantine Empire, a few Athena weights may come from the West. These locations are putative; no western examples were legally excavated, but Franken nevertheless speculates that their manufacture began there before shifting to the eastern part of the empire.[10] A western origin may explain idiosyncratic differences in the craftsmanship between empress and Athena weights. The opposing orientations of the upper loop, for example, might derive from these divergent workshop traditions.[11] The upper loop, with which the figure would be attached to the steelyard weighing instrument, was aligned in one of two different ways. The loop on the empress busts ran front-to-back, so that the narrow profile pokes up from the top of the diadem as one views the counterpoise directly from the front. The Athena figurines, in contrast, rotate that alignment ninety degrees, for the top loop presents a circular face to the viewer in front of the piece. The Athena weights furthermore possess rectangular socles; the empress weights, oval socles. This variation suggests different workshops

fig. 2.3. Empress steelyard counterweight possibly from Latakia, Syria, early Byzantine period, Dumbarton Oaks, Washington, D.C. (50.25).

or at least different streams of production, but given that no objects with this feature definitely come from the West, it is not clear why Franken supposes the rectangular socle indicates a specifically Western origin.[12] The eastern-oriented distribution reflects the relative prosperity of the region compared to the western regions riddled by upheaval. The Romans initiated the use of these weights in the eastern Mediterranean; the

fig. 2.4. Empress steelyard counterweight excavated from Philippi, Greece, early Byzantine period, Twelfth Ephorate of Byzantine Antiquities, Kavala, exhibited at the White Tower, Thessaloniki.

Greeks preferred other types of weights.[13] Franken's survey of the ancient and late antique written sources for manufacturing methods of these specific objects yielded no concrete information.[14] His hypothesis of their production seems reasonable, and well in keeping with our notions of how other small ancient bronzes were made. Probably artisans used the lost wax process to form the basic shape, then subtler details were worked at cooler temperatures. The hollow interior cavity was filled with lead to achieve an exact weight, then a thin bronze sheet was used to cap the lower opening.[15]

After the empress, the goddess Athena was the second most popular type of steelyard weight used in the early Byzantine era (see figures 2.15 and 2.19), and these two types diverge perceptibly in form, size, and weight. The

fig. 2.5. Front view, empress steelyard counterweight from Yalova, Turkey, early Byzantine period, Istanbul Archeological Museum (5940).

Athena figures are in general bigger than their empress counterparts. Whereas the Athena weights range in length from 12.4 to 28 cm., the empress busts measure only 13 to 24.2 cm. The weight of the objects follows this difference in size. Athena's effigies vary widely, ranging from 1,070 g to 11,200 g in their extant condition. Empress counterpoises fall within a more narrow, generally lighter band of weight at 1,402 to 5,945 g.[16]

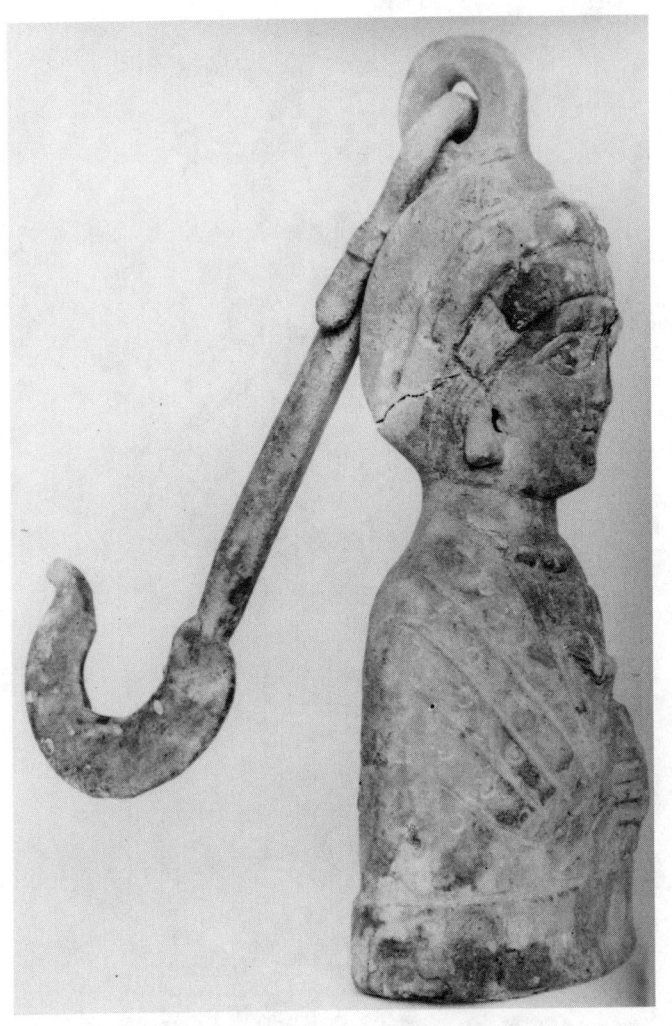

fig. 2.6. Side view, empress steelyard counterweight from Yalova, Turkey, early Byzantine period, Istanbul Archeological Museum (5940).

A representative example of the empress steelyard weights is the well-preserved counterpoise from Yalova, in the Istanbul Archeological Museum (see figures 2.5 and 2.6).[17] The female figure terminates mid-torso; the body is swathed to cover all but the hands and the neck and face. This counterpoise is identified as an empress primarily because of its diadem. While the earrings and necklace bespeak wealth, any aristocratic woman could wear them. Many of the empress weights show jewelry, such as a

fig. 2.7. Empress steelyard counterweight, early Byzantine period, Kunsthistorisches Museum, Vienna, Austria (AS VI 3142 C).

fig. 2.8. Empress steelyard counterweight from Kayseri, Turkey, early Byzantine period, Istanbul Archeological Museum (1333).

fig. 2.9. Licinia Eudoxia solidus, gold, Obverse: facing bust, Reverse: enthroned empress holding globus cruciger and cross scepter, A.D. 439, Ravenna mint, Dumbarton Oaks, Washington, D.C. (LRC 870).

necklace, but examples without these accessories prove that these status symbols were not necessary in order to render the type. One, now in the Kunsthistorisches Museum in Vienna depicts a rather plainly garbed empress with only a speckled decoration on the hem of her chiton for adornment (see figure 2.7).[18] Encircling the bottom of the Vienna weight is a plain, slightly concave band. Rising up from this oval base, the form tapers to the top, where a solid loop provides the connection for the hook linking the counterpoise to the rest of the balance weight. In profile the flat body reveals very little additional detail, and the back is relatively smooth.

The cursory catalog of early Byzantine empress weights produced by the Istanbul Archeological Museum follows the usual practice of identifying each object with a specific historical figure.[19] Only three of the fourteen counterpoises are listed as anonymous; the others are identified with Aelia Eudokia, Licinia Eudoxia, Galla Placidia, and Aelia Pulcheria.[20] The earlier catalog of these objects refrained from identifying the Kayseri steelyard weight with a specific empress, labeling it merely a diademed woman (see figure 2.8).[21] The justification for each attribution in the later Istanbul catalog forces each weight into the category of a Theodosian numismatic portrait type; for example, one is explained with "a coin struck in the name of L. Eudoxia bears the same features, a plumpish oval face, pendant and pendules (medallions), a necklace of three rows of pearls. This latter is a feature of representations of L. Eudoxia only."[22] In fact, Licinia Eudoxia, the wife of Emperor Valentinian III, was represented on coins with a three-

fig. 2.10. Licinia Eudoxia solidus, gold, Obverse: bust facing right with *Manus Dei*, Reverse: Constantinopolis enthroned facing left, A.D. 442/3, Constantinople mint, Dumbarton Oaks, Washington, D.C. (LRC 872).

strand necklace only on the solidus minted in Ravenna (see figure 2.9). On the western issue tremissis and both gold denominations of the Constantinopolitan mint she wears only two rows of pearls (see figure 2.10). The comforting surety of the cataloger's assertions, then, does not really work out in practice, for the three rows of this figure's necklace are only one of several slight variations possible for the typological representations. The facial features, which would seem a more reliable indicator of an attempt at portraiture, do not stray from the appearance iterated on other counterpoise weights. Even when considering the elite realm of marble statuary of the Theodosian era, Bente Kiilerich came to the conclusion that the facial features and marks of office were so standardized at that time that "the identity of sculpted heads cannot be based on coin images only."[23] This discussion of one particular weight illustrates the tenuous basis for these attributions to an individual historical figure.

This stretch is not unusual. In the 1985 catalog of the Malcove Collection, written by Sheila Campbell, a steelyard weight is identified as a portrait of the Empress Licinia Eudoxia (see figures 2.11 and 2.12).[24] Campbell sensibly asserts that the bronze figure is an empress on the basis of her well-preserved accouterments of rank: the jeweled diadem, the single-row necklace, the prependoulia of her headdress, and the scroll or *mappa* in her left hand. She continues, though, by asserting that these mass-produced commercial weights attempt individual portraiture, and identifies the object with the ever-popular Licinia Eudoxia.[25] Likewise, even a recent notice by the Metropolitan Museum identifies one of its examples as a specific empress (see figure 2.13).[26]

fig. 2.11. Front view, empress steelyard counterweight, early Byzantine period, Malcove Collection, University of Toronto (M82.395a).

The dress worn is not distinctively imperial. Most examples depict a dalmatic covered by a palla draped over both shoulders. On some weights the lower garment is decorated with circles, but the upper garment, the palla, has only lines marking the drapery folds breaking up the surface. In addition to the occasional inelegant necklace or earrings, some carry a

fig. 2.12. Back view, empress steelyard counterweight, early Byzantine period, Malcove Collection, University of Toronto (M82.395a).

long cylindrical object in their left hand. Perhaps this is a *mappa,* a traditional late antique badge of consular authority, which will be discussed at more length in the next chapter. In the sixth century, the emperor took over the function of the consul. More likely, however, the object is a scroll,

fig. 2.13. Empress steelyard counterweight, early Byzantine period, The Metropolitan Museum of Art, New York (1980.416a).

which has ample parallels in other sculpture representing early Byzantine aristocratic women. The Metropolitan Museum possesses a beautiful marble bust of such a woman from the sixth century, proudly holding a scroll in her right hand (see figure 2.14).[27] The scroll denotes erudition of the bearer, and images of women with a scroll possess a venerable lineage. Ancient depictions of the Muse Polymnia included a scroll, and on later sarcophagi and coins women such as the Empress Sophia appropriate this attribute.[28]

The right hand on the empress weights assumes two different positions. On most—fifty-two of the seventy-two catalogued by Franken—the hand is outstretched to follow the line of the bent arm. The palm rests against the body on the lower chest. In contrast to this rather neutral gesture, the other examples hold a more active, engaged pose. Here the right hand is poised in a traditional gesture of speaking; the palm is forward and two or three fingers point upward as the thumb crosses the front of the hand.

The identification of these weights as empresses hinges on the diadems that are almost uniformly present. Their simplicity precludes a very detailed analysis of their type, but certain features consistently emerge. Above the forehead sits a rectangular plaque with a circle in the middle. This ornament tops a band encircling the head, sometimes demarcated into rectangular or oblong units that likely represent pearls. A parted border of hair falls in front, with plain incisions indicating plaits. The head is covered in different ways. On a few examples, such as CA5 and CA13 in the Franken catalog, the top of the headpiece rises into two points similar to those in the marble representations of Ariadne. The suspension loop determines the upper profile of most pieces, so a rounded block, sometimes decorated with lines or dots, mediates between the loop and the diadem band. This upper piece may depict a stylized hair covering, such as a snood, which seems very popular for women in the early Byzantine era.

While the diadem certainly betokens imperial status, the meaning of these modest bronze figures remains debatable. The temptation to identify the steelyard weights with individuals should be resisted, because when studied as a group they appear to be mass-produced renditions of the Empress as a type, rather than portraits of individual imperial women. In a similar way, the generic trope of "Empress" recurs in Byzantine literature, for the βασίλισσα personifies the highest love in John Klimax as well as the Church of Hagia Sophia itself in Paul Silentiarios.[29] Implicit in the representation of an official entity is that, as observed by Richard Brilliant, "the typological representation of royalty predetermined the viewer's cognitive response to the individual ruler portrayed. Thus the general propositional attitude took precedence over the particular, even if the king or

fig. 2.14. Marble bust of a woman holding a scroll, sixth century, The Metropolitan Museum of Art, New York (66.25).

queen had a face that could be recognized."[30] The generic nature of the weights' representations best serves their purpose.

The most common interpretation holds that these figures represent specific historical entities, the famous imperial women of the Theodosian house or perhaps their successors. The second viewpoint, the one taken by Franken, ascribes to these figures a more general imperial status. The steelyard weights according to this line of thought depict an empress as a generic type and do not show a specific empress. The next and final step along this path of generalization is the position taken in one of the first discussions of the objects. As Volbach argued in 1932, the counterpoise weights could represent Tyches, the personifications of cities also included in the consular diptychs.[31] While the second, typological interpretation has merit, Volbach discovered an important area of associations that contributes to how we understand the Athena-shaped counterpoises considered next. A related object type illustrates the use of imperial features in the personifications of cities. This modest square lead weight, or token, was recently published and identified as a Tyche figure. Traces of the prependoulia on both sides of her face were misinterpreted by a cataloger as "curly hair, rendered as a series of knobs on either side of her head."[32]

Another important aspect that affects our interpretation is the dating of this material. The Athena type weights excavated from Anemourion and the seventh-century shipwreck of Yassi Ada push the use of these weights into the sixth and seventh centuries, undermining the standard fourth- and fifth-century dating of these pieces. In the archeological excavation of Anemourion in Cilicia, the Canadian team found the steelyard weight in the half meter of fill above the mosaic in the area of the palaestra (see figure 2.15). Based on numismatic evidence and stylistic comparison, C. W. J. Eliot contends that the weight was from the fifth or sixth century.[33] The fill layer in which the weight was found, however, was disturbed, and correlates to the more than two-hundred-year-span of habitation of the area before its abandonment in about A.D. 660. The directors' summaries from the year of discovery, 1970, simply place the weight as being "of Byzantine date."[34] Given the disturbed state of the fill, the object could have found its way into the debris as late as the seventh century, and the finds of the shipwreck Yassi Ada also support the viability of a later dating. Eliot, in fact, allows for this possibility in the final words of his publication of the piece, "For how long Athena and the steelyard for which she was designed had performed useful service at Anemourion before this end (about A.D. 660), we cannot tell."[35] The solidity of the seventh-century date of the Yassi Ada weight casts even further doubt onto the attributions of many early Byzantine weights to Theodosian empresses.[36] No certain evidence, then, places the empress figures in that earlier era, and the following discussion of the

fig. 2.15. Athena steelyard counterweight from Anemourion, Turkey, early Byzantine period, Anemourion Excavation(AN70/133).

Athena weights may better place these objects in their original context. Franken speculates that an empress steelyard weight now in the British Museum betrays features that relate it to the Athena example (such as its oddly thickened neck where the helmet would terminate on an Athena weight), which would indicate the two types were at least partially coeval (see figure 2.16).[37] Since only one of the 127 empress and Athena weights shows this formal hybridization, the two types seem distinct, though we will see that their meanings could overlap.

An overview of the ancient usage of mythological images on steelyard weights will help to clarify the potential import of these pagan figures in a Christian milieu. Ancient Mediterranean steelyard counterpoises present a

fig. 2.16. "Hybrid" empress steelyard counterweight, early Byzantine period, The British Museum, London, UK (1870.3–15.15).

much more diverse assemblage of iconographic types than the early medieval group. The heterogeneous mythological figures represented in antiquity include Apollo, Attis, Bakchos, Herakles, Jupiter, Mars, and Mercury. Just two of the Roman counterpoises in the Franken catalog depict Minerva, countering James' claim that the goddess was a popular type.[38] Another category of interest in terms of later developments is the small group of weights ascribed to individual historical figures, such as Ptolemy XII Auletes, who ruled Egypt from 80–51 B.C.[39] Given the range of forms deployed on weights at that time, this one object seems unlikely to constitute an attempt at individual portraiture when it does not possess any particularly distinctive traits. The tentative attribution of another weight to Augustus seems more viable, for it fits within the widely dispersed images of Rome's first emperor and broader patterns of rendering public imagery at the time.[40] The most curious identification is the final item in Franken's catalog of ancient bust type weights; an object in the Dumbarton Oaks Collection supposedly portrays a "Portraitbüste eines Mannes als Merkur."[41] Whereas Richter's earlier catalog entry on the object makes the more straightforward attribution to Hermes, god of commerce, Franken needlessly complicates matters by suggesting the figure represents an individual in the guise of a god.[42] The contemporary Tiberian hairstyle combined with divine attributes more likely is a modified representation of the god, given the absence of other human/divine admixtures in ancient weights.

Imperial Roman steelyards present Minerva with the distinctive trappings of her mythological identity: a crested helmet, armor, and an aegis all make this attribution fairly certain. The early Byzantine steelyard counterpoises that are the focus of our attention here share these traits, but archaeological evidence anchors them in a later time when their pagan meaning cannot be taken for granted. E. B. Thomas suggested that these weights might depict personifications such as Roma, Constantinopolis, or even Sophia (Wisdom).[43] In this context it is worth remembering that the personification of Roma assumed two forms. The amazon type used to depict Roma on the consular diptychs competed with the representation of Roma as Athena, known from Roman imperial gems.[44] It was in the Greek eastern part of the Roman Empire that Roma often assumed the guise of Athena/Minerva.[45] In specifically imperial contexts, Roma appeared as Athena both on a chalcedony cameo and the Gemma Augustea, both in Vienna, stalwartly at the side of the Emperor Augustus.[46] The Gemma Augustea, usually dated after the Dalmatian War in A.D. 10, renders opaque figures of Augustus and Livia/Roma swathed in exquisitely translucent drapery. On both gems Roma wears a helmet and bears a shield, although on the chalcedony piece the face of Roma is more rounded.[47] These personifications remained important in imperial art, for

fig. 2.17. Corbridge lanx, found near Corbridge, Northumberland, fourth century, The British Museum, London, UK (1993.4–1.1).

fig. 2.18. Gold bracelet with the image of Athena or personifictaion, fifth century, The Metropolitan Museum of Art, New York (17.190.2053).

Constantinopolis was carefully crafted to match Roma in a pair of dedications in temples to Roma and Constantinopolis made by Constantine. The two Tyches appear enthroned together in 343 on a coin reverse, and share a place on the base on Arkadios' column erected in Istanbul in 401/2.[48] Furthermore, personifications of Constantinople and Victory were depicted on Byzantine coinage until the seventh century.

Earlier scholarship attributed the Athena-shaped steelyard counterpoises to the second and third centuries, for clearly these little effigies of the goddess must belong safely in the pagan past.[49] The speculation offered by Dalton that the Athena type might be the result of the short-lived revival of paganism under the fourth-century Julian the Apostate seems highly unlikely.[50] Archeological discoveries, particularly the shipwreck of Yassi Ada, overturned these initial assumptions. Numismatic evidence places the cargo squarely in the early seventh century, yet it contained an Athena-shaped steelyard counterpoise amongst its assembly of weighing instruments. Rather than reevaluate earlier premises, Franken simply attenuates the production of the Athena weights. Thus the Yassi Ada weight marks the end of a dwindling series according to his reasoning, although he never explains why the most firmly dated example would also happen to represent the death knell of its type. Franken theorizes that the Athena steelyard counterpoises were manufactured from the early fifth through the early seventh centuries.[51] The initial date seems plausible, but their manufacture may extend later in the seventh century and possibly even

fig. 2.19. Athena steelyard counterweight, early Byzantine period, The Metropolitan Museum of Art, New York (61.112).

fig. 2.20. Front view, Athena steelyard counterweight, early Byzantine period, Virginia Museum of Fine Arts, Richmond (66.15.1).

into the eighth century. The poorer textual record of the seventh and eighth centuries pushes scholars away from attributing objects of material culture to that era, the Byzantine "Dark Ages." As the conclusion will consider, this preconception is also based on the habit of looking at imperial art as individual portraits, rather than as typological images. Given the clear archeological evidence, a later date seems reasonable for this specific class of commercial implements.

As in the case in Franken's study of the empress counterpoises, he places the Athena counterpoises into a linear sequence of stylistic development.[52] The beginning of his series in the early fifth century is based on a correlation to empress weights, which he thinks began slightly earlier.[53] Predictably he orders the disparate grouping into a range that begins with the most naturalistic modeling. Full faces, big eyes, and high cheekbones earn a coveted place in the start of the lineage before its descent into medieval abstraction.[54] Because of the paucity of examples dated by external criteria, this sequence remains untenable. This period of stylistic transition at the end of antiquity is notoriously eclectic, a confusion sometimes understood by art historians as successive waves of classicism riding over the rising tide of abstraction. The time span from which these objects originate, then, remains speculative, and their rough-hewn typological representations do not lend themselves to a meaningful sequential ordering.

With the chronology expanded, the meanings held by this pagan goddess for the Christian merchants using the balances pose several intriguing questions. The two most popular categories of representation on these weights—the empress and Athena—may not be so disparate.[55] The imperial Roman cult of individual empresses often assimilated with long-standing goddess cults. Athena Polias was paired with these new cults, although the goddess' virgin status would not seem to offer the most obvious association for these women whose primary public role was procreation. A late second-century example linked the worship of Athena and an empress in a fragmentary inscription from Athens indicating that sacrifices for Athena Polias simultaneously expressed devotion to Julia Domna.[56] James Oliver, in his reconstruction of this important inscription from Athens, concludes that in the relationship of Julia Domna to Athena Polias: "Julia Domna was not associated but identified with Athena Polias. The piety toward Julia Domna could have been partly expressed in the sacrifices to Athena Polias only if Athena Polias represented one aspect of Julia Domna. Sacrifices, accordingly, were made to the latter as μήτηρ στρατοπέδων and again as Athena Polias."[57] This inscription entailed many provisions for the syncretic cult, including the addition of a cult statue of Julia Domna as Athena Polias to the sanctuary beside the earlier statue of Athena.[58] A gold statue of Julia Domna was ordered installed in

fig. 2.21. Side view, Athena steelyard counterweight, early Byzantine period, Virginia Museum of Fine Arts, Richmond (66.15.1).

the Parthenon, too.[59] At Kyzikos, an aristocratic woman likewise dedicated a cult statue of Livia to Athena Polias during the reign of her son Tiberios.[60] This kind of linked dedication may well provide a context for the later iconographic types of the steelyard weight counterpoises. The statue of the empress Livia prominently displayed in the Temple of Athena could be one step toward the early Byzantine connection made between the empress and Athena.

Athena in her Roman form, Minerva, also possessed multiple manifestations, which imbued her image with shifting and nuanced meanings during antiquity. Athena Ergane, the goddess of work, exemplifies industriousness by spinning like any good Roman matron. Rome's Forum Transitorium juxtaposed this domestic representation with one of Athena as the warrior.[61] Suetonius' *Life of Caligula* suggests, in addition, a maternal aspect of Minerva: "This babe, who [Caligula] called Julia Drusilla, he carried to the temples of all the goddesses, finally placing her in the lap of Minerva and commending to her the child's nurturing and training."[62] Objects then as diverse as the Corbridge silver lanx from the late fourth or early fifth century and the early fifth-century gold bracelet now in the Metropolitan Museum render Athena in lavish style (see figures 2.17 and 2.18), but what is their relevance to the modest renditions of Athena on commercial steelyards from two centuries later?[63]

Athena/Minerva seems to have been a pervasive cultural symbol in this period. Because Athena was the goddess of wisdom, she also symbolized good balance and accurate measure. The North African Bishop Fulgentius—who probably lived in the fifth or sixth century—is not unusual for his lively interest in paganism, recounting several myths involving Athena/Minerva. Fulgentius suggests her core attributes, " . . . the Gorgon, worn on her breast as a symbol of fear. . . . They give her a plume and helmet . . . and Minerva in Greek is called Athene, for *athanate parthene,* that is, immortal virgin, because wisdom cannot die or be seduced."[64]

The polysemous nature of these classical mythological symbols in late antiquity is reflected, too, even in the pagan name of the Christian Empress Ariadne discussed in the next chapter. Names and identities redolent with paganism to the modern audience clearly possessed broader connotations for their Byzantine audience. There is a rich stratum of precedents for such ambiguities in visual representation in the Roman imperial period. Henning Wrede's work, for example, masterfully surveys the topic of private individuals who chose to represent themselves in a deified form, and the imperial house's assimilation and association with divinity is a commonplace.[65] Augustae often assumed the guise of goddesses, as seen throughout Roman Imperial coinage.[66] Thus two distinct phenomena occurred in this earlier period: women took on the attributes of a goddess, and empresses were represented as the deified imperial figure, the *Diva Augusta*.[67] Minerva does not seem to have been a particularly popular goddess to appropriate, although a Flavian statue of a matron takes on the goddess' helmet.[68]

A fine example of an early Byzantine Athena weight now in the Metropolitan Museum in New York points to these images' complexity (see figure 2.19).[69] The details are well-preserved and crisply delineate her aegis with a gorgon surrounded by four snakes. The partially preserved Christian inscription along the base begins, "ΚΥΡΙΕ ΒΟΗΘ (Ε) Ι...," (Lord protect me . . .), a standard evocation for holy protection, which is particularly interesting given the ostensibly pagan shape of the weight.[70] This strange conflation of a Christian inscription with a pagan deity initially seems paradoxical, yet the cross incised onto the arm of the Richmond Athena echoes the sentiment of the words (see figures 2.20 and 2.21).[71] Further exploration might offer a surprising insight into what these objects meant to their sixth- and seventh-century audience. The inscription contributes a tantalizing clue to the multivalent nature of these banal objects.

A modern viewer sees a Christian empress and a pagan goddess as distinct within our tidy taxonomies of iconography, but an early Byzantine work on Constantinople overturns these anachronistic categories of visual representation. The anonymous *Parastaseis Syntomoi Chronikai* offers insight into how these two classes of objects may have been understood to the Byzantine viewer in his account of Constantinople. The writer of this work rambles through Constantinople stopping at a statue in one of the public arcades, "the woman seated on a bronze chair in the hippodrome—she too is above (the imperial seat) as we mentioned before—Herodian told me is Verina, (the wife) of Leo the Great (474–91); but as I myself have heard from many people, it is instead the statue of Athena from Hellas, and this I believed."[72] A thirty-foot-high statue of Athena dominated the Forum of Constantine in Constantinople until 1204, so perhaps prominent local figures of the goddess inspired his confusion. The *Parastaseis'* statement suggests that "empress-looking" and "Athena-looking" were not such distinct categories of visual representation at the time. These figures probably signified central authority and just measure to the merchants using them throughout the Empire. These tokens convey the authority of empire to routine business transactions, and that an empress signified this authority bespeaks her viability as an emblem of imperial power.

In this realm of possibilities, the female figures of the counterpoises defy precise classification. The confusion of the *Parastaseis* author raises important questions about the value of the semiotic meaning we attach to these forms. As Dan Sperber proposed in his work *Rethinking Symbolism*, "symbolic interpretation is not a matter of decoding, but an improvisation that rests on an implicit knowledge and obeys unconscious rules."[73] Our inter-

fig. 2.22. Silver pepperpot, found in Hoxne, Suffolk, before A.D. 407, The British Museum, London, UK (1994.4–1.33).

pretation of the elusive iconography of these steelyard weights falters because the traditional attribution, premised on static signification, does not in the end seem appropriate to this material. Their meanings shifted and fulfilled different roles for their numerous medieval spectators, who used these objects as part of everyday life. Even the inscriptions detailing the sculpture of the Erectheum in classical Athens merely denote each piece, not as a mythological figure, but more generically, such as "the man leaning on a staff."[74]

Very often these weights must have been as unobtrusive as a pattern on wallpaper, the diffusion of the imperial image weakening the impact of individual manifestations. At times, though, the force of these images may have suddenly "switched on" again, such as when the measure of the weight was double-checked with official metrological standards and the quotidian object's power as an imperial emblem was revived.

Based on a vague similarity to empress steelyard weights, several household objects have been labeled as empresses. The Museum of Fine Arts in Boston has a late Roman bronze lamp in its collection that it claimed represents an empress. This attribution seems tenuous because the headdress does not appear particularly imperial, although the curator hazards that it may depict Ariadne.[75] The modeling and triangular face also differ substantially from the appearance of the empress-type steelyard weights. Curators dated this object to the fifth or sixth century, which is also problematic. Another unlikely example of the female imperial image is one of the four small pepper pots found in the Hoxne treasure in England (see figure 2.22). The stunning assemblage of hoarded wealth included 15,244 coins and roughly 200 silver and gold objects, which places the pepper pot at a vastly more ostentatious level of consumption than the steelyards. Now kept in the British Museum, this object was discovered in 1992 in a sealed archeological context that has a *terminus ante quem* of ca. A.D. 407–450 from numismatic evidence.[76] The hollow figure gilt with silver has "a simple but ingenious device in the base that can be turned to close the container, to fill it with ground pepper, or to reveal groups of small perforations which allow the contents to be sprinkled."[77] As intriguing as this piece of Late Roman workmanship is, the image's imperial identity is dubious, for no diadem of a known empress resembles this head covering. The scroll in her hand certainly marks affluence and education, but not necessarily the rarefied status of the imperial family. A sense of how these splendid silver things may have appeared can be gleaned from the tomb painting of Storias Priscus at Pompeii, in which a nineteen-piece silver set gleams on the table. The Hoxne figure more resembles Roman weights than their Byzantine counterparts.

The few counterpoise weights of male figures in the early Byzantine period are so varied that it is hard to generalize what their meaning might

fig. 2.23. Male steelyard counterweight, perhaps Constantine the Great, early Byzantine period, The Art Museum, Princeton University (y1955–3257).

have been. An idiosyncratic male steelyard counterpoise appears in the collection of the Museum of Fine Arts in Richmond, Virginia. This simple hooded form may represent a city eparch.[78] A seated male type, which survives in several examples, has been unconvincingly identified as an image

fig. 2.24. Male steelyard counterweight, Late Roman period, excavated in Corinth, 1920, the Corinth Excavations, Greece.

of the enthroned Emperor Constantine the Great.[79] The Princeton University Art Museum's seated male weight, once in the Gréau Collection, has been dated to the fourth to sixth centuries, and was "said to have been found in Gaul"(see figure 2.23).[80] The excavation of ancient and medieval Corinth uncovered another male steelyard figure (see figure 2.24). In 1920 this object was found in the area of the West Shops in a fill with no recorded stratification, as you would expect for archeological practice at the time. Waagé speculates that this man is an emperor, viewing the armor as a direct descendant of the accouterments on pagan imperial busts such as the one of Titus in the Louvre and the two of Caracalla in the Bibliothèque Nationale. A unique example of another "imperial" type, found in Haifa, is now in the British Museum.[81] In keeping with the methodology used by curators cataloging the empress figures, O. M. Dalton dutifully sought out a numismatic corollary to his steelyard weight, and a 1994 museum catalog entry on this piece likewise maintains the attribution to Phokas on the basis of numismatic corollaries to insignia type: "The best parallels for the style of the beard and the circular type of fibula with three prependoulia are all found on the emperor's coins."[82] Although the limited remains make any conclusion difficult, it seems unlikely that the male figures represent specific historical figures when it is clear that the female counterweights do not.

What meanings did the image of the emperor and empress have as it was encountered in the course of daily life? Imperial statuary populated the urban streets, coins endlessly replicated their semblance, and empress-shaped steelyard counterpoises measured out the transactions of everyday commerce. The startling range of media demonstrates the flexibility and range of imperial imagery. Just as a porphyry statuette of an empress, planted in a main thoroughfare of Constantinople, evoked traditions specific to imperial statuary of costly materials, the weights used on steelyards parceling out bulk goods drew from a disparate realm of visual culture. As illustrated by the overlapping signification of the Athena- and the empress-shaped weights, these objects require different interpretative tools than those applied to the exquisite renderings of Ariadne in ivory discussed in the upcoming chapter.

The imperial image on the commercial weights throughout the Empire effectively disseminated this emblem of authority. This far-flung distribution parallels practice in low-value contemporary Byzantine coinage. As will be discussed in chapter seven, the Empress Sophia, wife of Justin II, assumed the unprecedented honor of being jointly enthroned with the emperor on the primary bronze coin, the follis, which passed through many more hands than other, more valuable denominations. This profusion of the imperial image contravenes our initial assumptions about imperial art, which are often based on the exclusivity of luxury goods. These rarefied items represent only a limited range within the whole spectrum of early Byzantine visual culture. Looking at cake molds in the shape of the emperor from the Roman Imperial period, Richard Gordon sketched a compelling image of this prevalence of the imperial image:

> To think of participants at festivals as far from Rome as Britain or Pannonia nibbling at the head of the sacrificant emperor on their way home suggests a quite extraordinary degree of banalization of what at the time of Augustus had been a solemn, original and difficult motif, mediating the centre and periphery of the Roman world through the image of the emperor engaged in an (erstwhile) peculiarly Roman ritual: what had been a new image of domination is here seen not only as *accepted,* but also as *banal.* [Gordon's italics][83]

The steelyard weights similarly illustrate this proliferation of the imperial form in the early Byzantine era. The boundaries amongst the categories of female representations used on the steelyards were fluid and confound our modern taxonomies. City personifications assumed elements of imperial dress and sometimes shared the accouterments of Athena. An early Byzantine viewer, a man of passable literary aspirations, articulated the confusion between figures of Athena and an empress in his time. The empress weights draw upon this wellspring of visual traditions that for centuries had signified the vitality and permanence of the Empire.

CHAPTER 3

THE EMPRESS ARIADNE AND THE POLITICS OF TRANSITION

> Ariadne the queen, the wife of Zeno, was allied to this Anastasius after the death of her husband, and she made him king, and she held the kingdom for many years, as many as forty. . . .
>
> —*Zacharias of Mitylene, Syriac Chronicle, VII.13*

The Empress Ariadne (d. 513/515)—whose period in power stretched between the fifth and sixth centuries—transformed the Late Roman traditions that imperial women such as Helena, Eudokia, and Pulcheria had so successfully developed. Her reign marks the transition to the altered conception of the imperial woman that emerged in the early Byzantine period. Theodosian predecessors had mostly elaborated Roman imperial imagery, but with Ariadne a new sensibility starts to materialize. Her identity is conveyed through normative visual language, and Ariadne's images carved out of luxury materials do not even bear her name, so strongly does her imperial identity override any individual meaning. The eldest daughter of the Emperor Leo I and Verina, Ariadne had no brother to follow Leo to the throne. The Empire now without a male heir, Ariadne became the transmitter of imperial rule. The Empress Ariadne assumed an unprecedented level of authority in the nebulous moments between emperors, and this chapter will focus on how these dynamics are reflected in the official ivories. She determined a sequence of three emperors in her roles as mother and wife, for after her son ruled, Ariadne's two husbands, Zeno and Anastasios, reigned in succession. Fundamental changes made in coinage during her rule with Anastasios also impart a sense of rupture in the official imagery of her reign. This flux sets the backdrop for arguments later in this book, for the numismatic record has too often been confined to the narrow domain of specialist studies, and its importance within broader visual culture neglected.

Art historians and historians have overlooked the accomplishments and public status of the Empress Ariadne; glamorous figures such as the Empress Theodora captivate our imagination. Charles Diehl's *Byzantine Empresses* omits Ariadne altogether from his pantheon of *femmes fatales,* and she falls just beyond the chronological span of both the end of Kenneth Holum's *Theodosian Empresses* and the start of Lynda Garland's *Byzantine Empresses.* A careful review of the early medieval textual and visual record will correct this oversight; Ariadne emerges as a central figure in sources such as the *Chronicon Paschale* and Zacharias of Mitylene. Extant visual representations flaunt her preeminence. Ariadne's image emblazoned part of the coinage that circulated throughout the Empire, as well as the ivory consular diptychs now scattered through Europe from Liverpool to Verona. The consular diptychs document her authority within a series of medallion portraits. The identification with Ariadne of the two imperial ivories in Florence and Vienna, however, will be reassessed in chapter seven's look at the Empress Sophia's images.

A survey of the historical context will help clarify our understanding of the visual representation of Ariadne. Because the Emperor Leo I had no son, his daughter Ariadne assumed a crucial role in the transition of power. While her father ruled, Ariadne married Zeno in 466 or 467.[1] Ariadne soon bore a son and named him Leo II to honor his grandfather. The young grandchild, not the son-in-law Zeno, was designated the next ruler by the aging Emperor Leo. Ariadne's prominent depictions illustrate her dynastic significance, for a tenth-century manuscript describes a votive image commissioned by her parents that visually marks their grandson, Leo II, as heir:

> The same emperors (Leo and Verina) beloved of God and Christ set up . . . an image, all of gold and precious stones, in which image [is represented] Our Lady the immaculate Mother of God seated on a throne and on either side of her Leo and Veronica, the latter holding her own son, the younger emperor Leo, as she falls before Our Lady the Mother of God, and also their daughter Ariadne. This image has stood from that time onward above the bema of the holy soros. . . .[2]

Cyril Mango is no doubt correct in his explanation of the text's reference to the son Leo as a reference to Ariadne's son Leo, and therefore the boy who was the grandson of Leo I and Verina.[3] The image likely was fashioned for the ciborium above the reliquary of the Virgin in the Church of

Hagia Sophia, for Her relics were reputedly brought to Constantinople in 473 by the elder Emperor Leo. These traditions of depicting the imperial family as a group portrait in state-supported religious foundations extend back to the Roman world and earlier. At the Temple of Artemis at Ephesus, for example, stood statues of the Emperor Marcus Aurelius, his wife, son and five daughters.[4]

Theophanes the Confessor relates that the Emperor Leo crowned and proclaimed co-emperor his grandson, Leo II, who then ruled as a child emperor briefly after the death of his grandfather Leo I in 474.[5] The fleeting reign of Leo II was entirely elided from otherwise diligent accounts such as that of Zacharias of Mitylene.[6] The thirteenth-century Syriac chronicle of Gregory Abu'l-Faraj, also known as Bar Hebraeus and based on the ninth-century Michael the Syrian, attests to the peculiar situation: "During the one year in which he reigned his father Zaynôn himself used to pay homage to him."[7] This late chronicle speculates that Ariadne fanned the flames of the imperial ambitions in her husband, Zeno, who seized power leaving the son "to exercise the chief authority as Consul."[8] The boy Leo II died after only months on the throne amid speculation of murder.

At the death of his son, Zeno became emperor and ruled from 474–491, though Leo and Verina had clearly marked their grandson as their favored successor. Contenders heavily disputed Zeno's status, and his mother-in-law Verina orchestrated a coup by her brother Basiliskos in 475. The *Chronicon Paschale* speculates that Verina bore a grudge against Zeno, for "Zeno the emperor had some matter requested of him by his mother-in-law Verina, and since he did not grant it was the object of intrigue by her."[9] According to the *Chronicon Paschale* and Gregory Abu'l-Faraj, the Emperor fled and Ariadne sought out her husband in Isauria, where they lived in exile for two years while Verina's brother, Basiliskos, ruled in Constantinople. Basiliskos was eventually overthrown, and he and his wife Zenodia took refuge with their children in a church before their exile to Cappadocia.[10] Zeno imprisoned Verina in an Isaurian fort, yet his mother-in-law's scheming continued.[11] Eventually the dowager queen was released following an illness and died; Ariadne then returned her mother's remains to the capital after a discreet interval.[12] Marcian attempted another revolt, claiming his legitimacy on the basis of his wife, Leontia's, status, since she bore the dual honor of being closely related to two imperial women as the daughter of Verina and sister of Ariadne. After fierce fighting, Zeno won out, but a distinctly negative tone is voiced in Zeno's portrayal in Byzantine sources, "Zeno administered the Empire harmfully . . . [and] spent his time on wicked pleasures and unjust deeds."[13] Zeno's death on 9 April 491, of an epileptic seizure gains the same sinister edge in our texts, for the Emperor expired "while continually repeating the name of Pelagios whom he had murdered unjustly."[14] With dazzling alacrity, Ariadne moved to designate a new ruler.

The unassuming, elderly Anastasios became the new emperor five days after Zeno's death.[15] Ariadne then married the civil-servant-crowned-emperor when only another six days had passed. On the face of it, Anastasios in some ways posed a surprising choice for Ariadne. He held the title of *decuriones* of the silentiarioi, which meant that he was one of three leaders of the thirty-man schola of the marshals and personal attendants for the emperor. The sixth-century *Vita* of Saint Sabas illustrates the prosaic role of these functionaries: "As they all entered the palace . . . the silentiarioi at the doors, while admitting all the rest, repelled this great luminary [Sabas] who through humility of spirit judged himself the last, they did not admit him since he looked like a beggar."[16] In addition, being about sixty years old on his ascent to the throne, Anastasios hardly promised a long-term solution to the question of succession. Who would guess that he would go on to rule almost another thirty years? The *Chronicon Paschale* hints at the unlikely nature of this arrangement. The Emperor Zeno had consulted the *comes* Maurianus, "who knew certain mysteries," to have his fortune told, only to receive the unpleasant news that "a certain former silentiary would inherit his rule and his wife."[17] Rashly misguessing the prophecy's meaning, Zeno had another man, Pelagius, arrested and killed, and so it seems Anastasios did not loom large as an imperial rival to his predecessor.[18]

Another factor predisposed Ariadne toward Anastasios, friendship. The sixth-century *Syriac Chronicle* of Zacharias of Mitylene relates that Anastasios enjoyed a long-standing, close association with Ariadne: "When he was a soldier he had a confidential friendship with Ariadne the queen, who desired and agreed to make him king."[19] This personal tie outweighed concern for her friend's Monophysite beliefs. Anastasios' orthodoxy was suspect from the beginning; before he became emperor he was impelled to give "a written declaration not to upset any part of the Church or the creed; [for the patriarch Euphemios] described him as unworthy of the Christians and of the Empire. With the empress Ariadne putting pressure on him and also the Senate, he gave his signature to a statement that he accepted the decisions of the synod at Chalcedon as the definition of faith."[20] These precautions did not prevent Ariadne's second husband from exploiting his new status to appoint Monophysite bishops, "which greatly saddened both Ariadne and the members of the Senate."[21] Anastasios' prudent fiscal administration, however, created a stockpile of 320,000 pounds of gold by the time of his death in 518.

Ariadne's influence on governmental affairs during Anastasios' reign was indirect, and our evidence derives from chance anecdotes. John Lydos' *On Powers* relates the tug-of-war between the imperial couple over the appointment of a magistrate. The empress pressed for the position to go to Anthemios, a man from an illustrious family, but the emperor resisted with another candidate in mind.[22] Another glimpse of court life appears in the *Vita* of Saint Sabas, which relates that Sabas upon "Leaving the emperor's presence . . . went to see the Augusta Ariadne and, after blessing her, exhorted her to hold firmly onto the faith. . . ."[23] This brief reference conveys several points. The Empress Ariadne had a distinct official presence from that of her husband the emperor, for the hagiographer makes clear that the couple performed their official duties in separate locations within the palace. The institution of the empress' court, the *sekreton ton gynaikon*, will be discussed more fully in chapter six. Furthermore, the text contrasts the tenor of the religious discussions that the holy man had with the emperor and then with the empress, which may allude to the couple's differing religious beliefs.[24] Acclamations also articulate the widespread perception of Ariadne's importance, for the public accolades of the Empress Ariadne take the form usually associated with those of the emperor, and the emperor and empress are likewise paired on ivory diptychs.[25]

The history of these political vicissitudes illuminate the visual traces of Ariadne's eminence. The proliferation of Ariadne's image throughout the empire marks her importance, for she appeared on numerous ivory and marble official images. Medallion portraits of Ariadne adorn five ivory consular diptychs. Life-size heads of both marble and bronze are identified with her, based on similarity to these miniature images. Ariadne appeared on her own coins as well as on issues that commemorated her second marriage. Texts also record sculptural monuments to the empress throughout Constantinople. We will see that the sense of typology plays out somewhat differently in these luxury goods than it did in the steelyard weights.

The five consular diptychs with Ariadne's portrait were first discussed in depth in Richard Delbrueck's definitive study of 1929, *Die Consulardiptychen und verwandte Denkmäler*.[26] This project, which was begun by Graeven, offers cogent formal and iconographic analysis of the entire group of early Byzantine ivories known at the time. Delbrueck brings together much of the comparanda of surviving ivory carving, and W. F. Volbach augments this research.[27] A long-standing tradition persisted in the Roman world of dramatically marking the accession of a new consul, an impressive title that carried with it the responsibility for staging elaborate public games. In fact, by the time the Emperor Justinian terminated the office in A.D. 541 amidst jealous squabbling, the office of consul by traditional reckoning had lasted over a thousand years since the first consul, L. Junius Brutus, in 509 B.C.[28] The Emperor Justin II revived the consulship for himself, with the precedent since Vespasian that new Augusti and Caesars would serve as consul beginning on the January 1st after their elevation.[29]

Corippus, who admittedly was writing a panegyric, effuses later in the sixth century about the Emperor Justin II's decision to become consul.[30]

In the mid-fourth century AD, the issue of consular coinages and medallions stopped, and a series of consular solidi began.[31] The first extant consular diptych belongs to Felix, the consul of 428, but we can only safely say that the manufacture of consular diptychs began sometime in the early fifth century. The consul probably distributed these diptychs, like the previous commemorative medallions, on the day of his accession to office to an elite circle of dignitaries.[32] These diptychs only hint at the extravagant generosity that new consuls were expected to display through gifts on accession.[33] Corippus' description of the inauguration of the Emperor Justin II as consul emphasizes his philanthropy: "the emperor would come out in his trabea from the holy palace and distribute riches to the people with his right hand, giving them his ritual donation and scattering it like snow. . . ."[34] The prestige of a consul was unparalleled amongst Byzantine offices of the time. John Lydos notes that although consuls did not actually possess the most power, they warranted more honors than any other office holder.[35]

Our extant body of consular diptychs does not evenly represent the run of consuls, and some consuls may not have issued diptychs. The largesse of a few of these officials, notably Areobindus, the consul of 506, reached a profligate scale—seven of his diptychs exist. If the range of surviving ivories roughly represents the proportionate numbers produced, personal wealth probably determined the volume of these flourishes of new prestige.[36] The modern museum display of these diptychs, however, creates a misleading sense of their late antique use and appearance. Today the pairs of ivory plaques are splayed open like a dissected animal for view, but originally the two pieces of ivory nestled together like book covers. The richly carved sides faced outward. The plain inner surfaces received a layer of wax that was then inscribed. Like on a coin, the opposing sides of the ivory plaques were not seen simultaneously.

The earliest consular diptych depicting the Empress Ariadne, now in the Liverpool Merseyside County Museum, celebrated the consulship of Clementinus in 513 (see figure 3.1).[37] The pair of panels repeats the same composition and iconography with trivial differences in details, such as the pattern on footstools and the assortment of gifts at the bottom of the panels, for below two of the consul's flunkies dutifully distribute largesse from sacks. Clementinus was an eastern consul, whose family tree likely included previous consuls.[38] On the Liverpool ivories, the front *tabula ansata* records the consul's name; the rear panel, his Latin titles. The medallion above his head on both panels reiterates in Greek letters the monogram of Clementinus. The consul proudly bears the tokens of his new office: the long, purple cloth wrapped around his body, a distinctively consular item at this time known as the *trabea triumphalis* or *toga picta*, and the requisite mappa rests in his hand.[39] At the top of both sides of the diptych of Clementinus sit two medallions separated by an elegantly formed cross; Ariadne's image is on the viewer's right, and both plaques replicate the same imperial insignia for the empress.[40] The emperor is shown on the left, so these conjoined portraits explicitly link the emperor and empress as joint rulers. The negotiations of Justinian and the Ostrogothic leader Theodatus a few decades later articulate the significance of paired ruler portraits: "No statue of bronze or of any other material should ever be set up to Theodatus alone, but statues must always be made for both, and they must stand thus: on the right that of the emperor, and on the other side that of Theodatus."[41] On coins, likewise, the emperor would assume the position to the viewer's left, and the secondary male ruler or Augusta would stand on the right, just as in Byzantine art the Virgin Mary appears to the right of Christ. Jeffrey Anderson speculates that the clipeate portraits on consular diptychs render real portraits that hung above the consul, but our knowledge of the consul boxes is too flimsy to make this correlation certain, although we do know imperial images hung in law courts.[42] In any event, these *imagines clipeatae* show the potential role of the Augusta as co-ruler and not merely the consort of the emperor.[43]

The central figure of the consul Clementinus enthroned on his curule chair is flanked by vivid personifications of Constantinople and Rome that match the new official in size.[44] The two personifications often appeared on fourth- and fifth-century coins as equals, analogous to the co-ruling emperors of the eastern and western parts of the Empire.[45] Roma and Constantinopolis initially assume consular associations in the Missorium of Apar Ardabur from 434 now in Florence, in which the Tyches carry *fasces*, the traditional bundle of rods.[46] Cutler is right to point out that by the Justinianic period, the two personifications were barely differentiated, and Delbrueck in fact mistakenly switched the two in his reading of the Clementinus diptych.[47]

The *mappa*, which is clutched so visibly by the consul in the diptych, is a folded piece of cloth whose ceremonial function began with the Emperor Nero. As the Roman crowds restlessly awaited the games, the Emperor Nero rose from his banquet and signaled the start of the festivities by tossing down his napkin. The ongoing popular appeal of Nero as the founder of games such as the Juvenilia and the Noreen is reflected in his ever-present image on the mass-produced Kontorniate medallions in the Late Roman period. The mappa falls as the final, and perhaps most distinctive item in the sixth-century writer John Lydos' careful delineation of

fig. 3.1. Consular diptych of Clementinus, A.D. 513, Liverpool Merseyside County Museum, UK.

the appropriate dress for a consul in his work *On Powers:* "White, ankle length paenulae; broad, purple-striped colobi... white shoes... and a white napkin of linen on the right hand... were the insignia of the consuls."[48] Furthermore, on Byzantine coinage starting in the late sixth century when emperors subsumed the consulship, emperors such as Tiberios II chose to depict themselves in consul's dress on the widely circulated bronze coins, but refrained from this popularizing depiction on normal

fig. 3.2. Drawing of destroyed consular diptych once in Limoges, A.D. 515 (diptych date).

gold issues.[49] The origins of this symbolism express how intimately the consular and imperial identities were interwoven.

Our understanding of the next diptych that represented Ariadne relies on an eighteenth-century drawing of this ivory, for this panel once in Limoges no longer exists (see figure 3.2).[50] Discounting the stylistic adaptations of the Rococo draftsman, the drawing's rendition of iconography and text seems quite plausible. Anthemios ascended as the new eastern consul in 515, with a predictably august lineage as the scion of the fifth-century western emperor Anthemios.[51] Corinthian columns frame the consul's head and three medallion portraits—not the two of the Clementinus diptych—dominate the upper section. Anastasios commands the central place, flanked by Anthemios on the left and Ariadne on the right.

The other three consular diptychs with Ariadne's image date from 517, for they celebrate the ascent of the consul Anastasios. The eastern consul Anastasios was the great-nephew of his namesake, the Emperor Anastasios.[52] Museums in Verona, London, and Paris now house these ivory plaques that follow the same composition, although their manner of carving varies.[53] All three diptychs depict the enthroned consul flanked by Corinthian columns supporting a pediment. Three clipeate portraits surmount the pediment, with the central image of the emperor flanked by the consul on the viewer's left and the empress on the right. As with the two medallions on the Clementinus diptych, these three diptychs follow later numismatic conventions of precedence for three figures depicted on one coin face: the emperor assumes the central place, with the secondary figure on the viewer's right and the tertiary person on the left side of the coin.[54] By this reckoning, Ariadne has the second place in the hierarchy on the diptychs of 515 and 517.

The single panel of a consular diptych in the Biblioteca Capitolare in Verona follows this general form.[55] The loros-clad consul fills the central space on a throne flanked by the accouterments of rank: lion heads, Victory personifications, and scenes of the games. In the riotous place below, two men each lead a feather-plumed horse above a group of performers. The highest part of the relief shows a wonderful figure in profile juggling an arc of balls, while others play the organ and pipes. The hippodrome images constitute an important element of consular identity, for these men often paid for races and other proletarian entertainments.

Another consular diptych of Anastasios from 517 had been divided between Berlin and the Victoria and Albert Museum in London (see figure 3.3), but the ivory panel in Germany was regrettably destroyed during World War II.[56] The basic composition of the two panels resembles that of the lost diptych panel in Limoges: Corinthian columns flank an enthroned consul. Games—bankrolled by the consul—transpire below, and personifications of

fig. 3.3. Consular diptych of Anastasios, A.D. 517 (other panel destroyed), Victoria and Albert Museum, London, UK (368–1871).

Victory frame him. The end panels of his curule chair depicted the bust of the consul Pompeius in the Berlin panel, and gorgoneia in the London panel. Both plaques show another image inset at this middle level on the chair: personifications with mural crowns fill round medallions on each side. Roman Augustae sometimes wore a crown of this type based ultimately on the mural crown of the Tyche of Antioch.[57] The interchange between the worlds of imagery used to denote empresses and city personifications was explored further in the previous chapter's discussion of empress-shaped steelyard weights. The co-consul or Pompeius, a relative of Anastasios, on the left balances Ariadne's medallion portrait placed on the other side of the emperor.

The diptych from 517 in Paris portrays the same confrontation of serene authority and ribald sport. This work, in the Cabinet des Médailles of the Bibliothèque Nationale, was once ensconced in the treasury of Saint Etienne of Bourges, and its reverse side lists past bishops of Bourges (see figure 3.4).[58] The detail and carving seem less fine than on the ivory panel in the Victoria and Albert Museum, for the pair of Paris ivories have greater surface wear. There are traces of red paint on these ivories, which was the case for most of the thirteen consular diptychs examined by Carolyn Connor.[59] The figure of the consul sits on his throne with a lively tableau of circus games filling the lower portion of both plaques. The personifications with mural crowns represented in the square panels at each end of the curule chair probably depict something like the silver Tyche furniture fittings of the Esquiline treasure.[60] Three medallions are at the top of the composition above the pediment, with Anastasios at the pinnacle above his wife and the consul.

Although the upper section of the two panels of the Cabinet des Médailles diptych share most iconographic details, their lower portions depict entirely different images. The right panel represents a particularly animated circus scene. Single and paired men valiantly provoke, coax, and ride beasts. The left panel renders two registers below the curule chair. The upper register shows a horse on each side being led to the center, each animal gaily decorated with a feather. The horsemen wear short tunics and carry poles with a banner. While this simple scene of two horses easily fits within circus life, the meaning of the lower register's scene seems more enigmatic. Its odd assortment of characters—including both a trio of women reminiscent of classical groupings and a hunchback—lacks parallels on other diptychs and may show the hippodrome's theatrical performances.

The medallions of Ariadne vary in details amongst the diptychs, both in the portrayal of the empress' face and her regalia, but a basic formula pervades her image. On the earliest diptych, that of Clementinus, her crown has long double strands of pearls hanging on each side and a heavy jewel-

fig. 3.4. Consular diptych of Anastasios, A.D. 517, Bibliothèque nationale de France, Paris.

encrusted collar with hanging jewels that differs only slightly in the two panels. In the Limoges drawing, her diadem assumes its familiar form. Large gems or pearls ornament her bifurcated jeweled collar, and a trace of the circular pattern of her chlamys peaks below the collar. Ariadne's medallion portrait on the Verona plaque lacks the rich detail of other ivories, but the basic contours remain clear. Her diadem protrudes from the top and prependoulia hang down beside her face. A heavy collar encircles her neck with two rows of large stones. In both halves of the Berlin/London diptych, Ariadne wears a spherical hairstyle with two braids disappearing under the diadem.[61] Strands of pearls cross over the front of her hair. The wide diadem that Ariadne wears is set with large pearls, with a giant rectangular gem planted on her forehead as on the crown of Anastasios. Similarly, her collar is set with gems placed between crosspieces, with distinct patterns on each side of the diptych. The sculptors of the Berlin and London panels also carved somewhat different facial shapes. The depiction of Ariadne on the destroyed *verso* panel, known from photographs, renders her with a narrower, more oval face. The diadem and hair covering overwhelm the delicate features and the earrings loom out of proportion with the finely balanced facial forms. On the *recto* plaque in the Victoria and Albert, the face of Ariadne takes a plumper form that solidly anchors the impressive imperial headgear. This variant mirrors the other figures represented in the two pieces of the consular diptych; the slender, attenuated faces of the Berlin panel contrast the solid, round visages on the London diptych. Ariadne's portrait medallion again assumes the right side on the Cabinet des Médailles example, and the *verso* panel in particular is rather crudely wrought. Her spherical hairstyle is decorated with five double strands of pearls. Her diadem consists of two strands of pearls surmounted by a sphere between two points, and the jeweled collar is patterned simply in neat rectangular pieces. The top of her garment peeks out in the *verso* medallion, in which Delbrueck identified a toga with balteus.[62] Ariadne's diadem differs even between the two sides of the Paris diptych, which illustrates the generous parameters within which the ivory carvers produced these images. Unlike some instances in the medieval West, the Byzantine court did not develop a single crown that designated imperial office, and the emperor or empress would possess several crowns. The regalia of Ariadne on the ivories shows fairly simple interpretations of the key components within the small medallion: a bejeweled diadem and collar. Of course, it is difficult to assess to what extent these renderings of costume correspond to court practice. The minor variations in the diptychs' style and iconography suggest that multiple carvers, if not workshops, produced the ivories.

While these descriptions register variations in matters such as diadem types and circus scenes, we have seen that a fairly standardized visual language accompanied the office of consul at this time. Just as the empress' identity was denoted primarily by her diadem, the consul's official identity required the mappa and the curule chair. To illustrate the relative homogeneity of the cluster of consular diptychs depicting Ariadne, the diptych

fig. 3.5. Diptych of Orestes, A.D. 513/530, Victoria and Albert Museum, London, UK (139–1866).

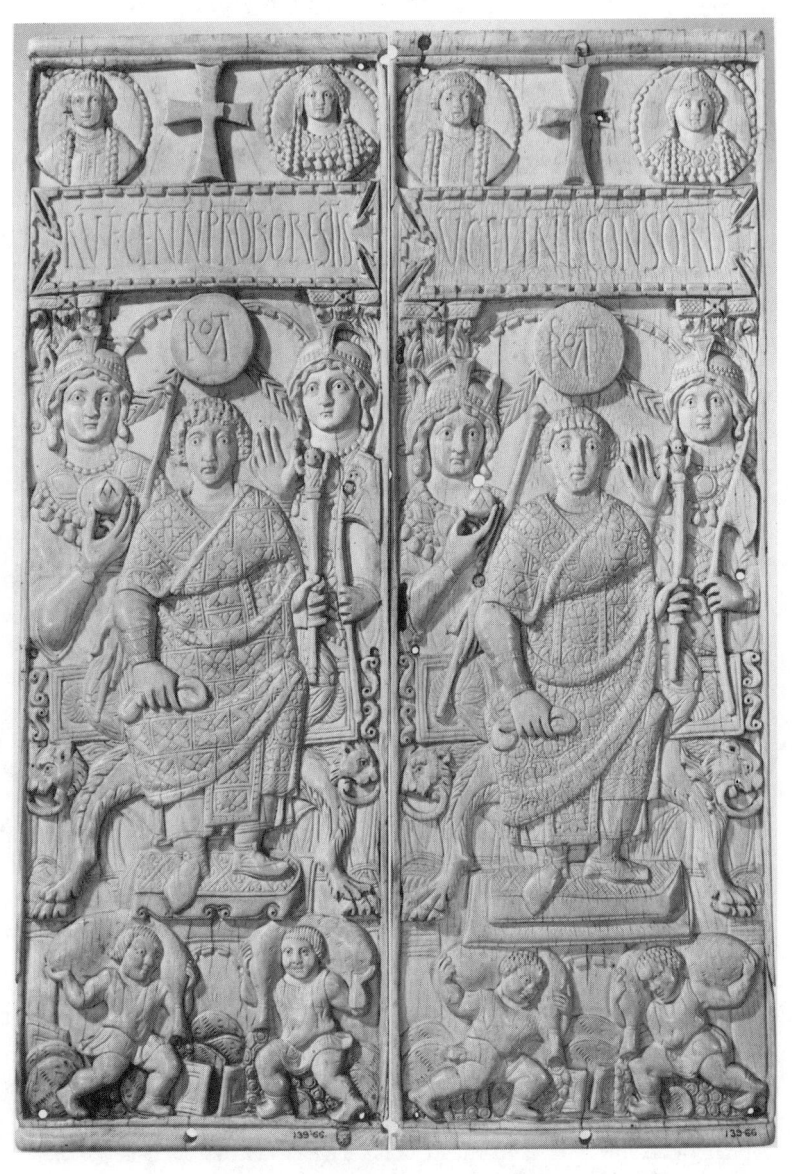

of Orestes, with its depictions of the Gothic elite, affords a useful contrast (see figure 3.5). This ivory issued in 530 is now in the Victoria and Albert Museum in London and is displayed beside the consular diptych panel from 517 just mentioned.[63] As the last surviving consular diptych from Rome, it concludes the western line of this tradition of "ostentatious greeting cards" in ivory, and tightly follows the diptych of Clementinus of 513 discussed previously.[64] Of the two medallions in the upper zone, the Gothic Queen Amalasuntha takes the right position. The left head represents her adolescent son Atalarich. The widowed queen had sought a classical education for Atalarich, but the Gothic warrior-leaders of the court in Italy insisted on military training for the boy. This conflict in the identity of the Goths between assimilation and resistance to Roman traditions plays out in the diptych, which reshapes the consular diptych's iconography in Gothic terms. The main departure on the Orestes diptych in the woman's depiction is the Phrygian cap worn by the Ostrogothic queen.[65] The tip of the cap flops over in the front, and two crossed braids decorate the surface. The common terminology "Phrygian cap" is misleading, for we have no evidence that this simple headcovering was considered distinctively Phrygian, and thus somehow obliquely referring to the distant roots of the Goths.[66] Just as a Byzantine empress could assume accouterments of rule usually born by men, this cap, if anything, alludes to the more typically male dress for Goths that Amalasuntha's exalted status as Queen entitled her to wear.[67] Like her Byzantine counterparts, the Ostrogothic female ruler is costumed with a heavy bejeweled neckpiece. Rows of pearls edge the round, worked stones in the middle of her collar, and a patterned textile peeks out from below.

The representation of Amalasuntha on the diptych of Orestes literally as well as symbolically reinscribes the Gothic Queen over the typology of a Byzantine empress. Nancy Netzer strongly argued that the new consul, Orestes, appropriated a diptych of one of his predecessors, Clementinus, and had the inscriptions and portraits recut for his own consulship.[68] Thus the image of Amalasuntha was crafted out of an image of Ariadne, with the face left largely untouched in this identity transformation. The jeweled collar served well for both female rulers, just as the facial features of an official image were not expected to capture the nuances of individual likeness. The faces are so generalized that the ivory cutter does not even differentiate the men and the woman. The crown denoted the imperial identity of Ariadne, so a suitably Gothic attribute substitute needed to be found, and the Phrygian cap securely shifted the meaning of the portrait to new terms that reflected the balance of power in the western part of the Empire. The Gothic leaders participated in the appointment of the new consuls for the western half of the Byzantine Empire, so Atalarich and

Amalasuntha easily occluded the images of Anastasios and Ariadne on the consular diptychs.[69] The consequences of this reworking of the Orestes diptych are twofold. The Orestes diptych results from a recutting of an Ariadne diptych, but the chance preservation of a lone two-medallion plaque from 513 does not mean that it was the only year such a dual portrait type was issued, so it could have originally been a consular diptych from another year of Emperor Anastasios' reign. On a more general level, Netzer's thesis opens the door to reconsideration of other diptychs, for further scrupulous physical analysis may overturn some of the assumptions that have underpinned the discussion of these objects since Delbrueck.[70]

Another important element of the diptychs' chronology has been neglected in preceding scholarship. The five surviving consular diptychs with Ariadne celebrated the ascendancy of consuls who took office on January 1 of 513, 515 and, in three cases, 517. These years mostly follow the death of Ariadne, but a discrepancy in our sources records two different years for Ariadne's demise. Zacharias of Mitylene puts the event in 513, whereas Marcellinus, Victor Tonnensis, and Theophanes the Confessor locate her death in 515, so a brief consideration of these sources may help grapple with the disparity. The text now called Zacharias' *Ecclesiastical History* comes to us substantially altered from what we can reconstruct of the sixth-century text. The original Greek history of Zacharias comprises only chapters three through six of today's Syriac text, which was compiled by an anonymous mid sixth-century monk in Amida. The section that concerns the death of Ariadne falls in the seventh chapter for which the Syriac monk used disparate sources.[71] The *Chronicle* of Marcellinus cryptically notes the death of Ariadne during the period between 1 September 514, and 31 August 515: "Ariadne Augusta died in the palace, after completing sixty years."[72] This Latin text written by one of Justinian's courtiers only covered the period to 518 in its original form, and its chronology tends to be fairly sound. Victor Tonnensis wrote a Latin chronicle that extended to 567, which survives in part from the year 444. Victor's chronology often falters, so his allocation of Ariadne's death to 515 does not lend much credence to that date.[73] Theophanes the Confessor composed his *Chronographia* from multiple sources, and the nature of the composite has been the subject of recent scholarly debate.[74] His source in the ninth century for the statement that Ariadne died in 515 is unknown, leaving its credibility difficult to assess. The visual evidence suggests, in its change in 515 from two to three medallions, that date, which is corroborated by the texts.

What did the image of Ariadne mean on the consular diptychs that appeared before and after her death? She was not included on the imagery of the consular diptychs while she ruled with Zeno, just as no preceding empresses had appeared on the consuls' ivory plaques. Perhaps the diptychs' change from two upper medallions to three in 515 signals her death. The five diptychs commemorate a woman who choreographed the ascendancy of three successive emperors—her son, Leo II, and two husbands, Zeno and Anastasios. Thus Anastasios strove to solidify his legitimacy with this reminder of his connection to earlier rulers. The meaning of these early Byzantine images of the empress can be clarified when we contrast it with a very old tradition from the Roman Imperial period. The sudden emergence of women in public arts in the Imperial period after their virtual absence from representation in the Roman Republican period has been noted, but an interesting feature of this new prominence was that Roman imperial women often found a more conspicuous place in official imagery following their death.[75] For example, the safely deceased Faustina the Elder and Sabina were deified, and each cult received lavish honors. In many ways, the clipeate portraits on the consular diptychs hearken back to earlier numismatic imagery, and the emperor and empress were jointly represented on coins as early as the reign of Claudius and Agrippina the Younger.[76] Whereas Ariadne on the ivories proclaimed the Byzantine *Realpolitik*—serving as the necessary justification for Anastasios' rule—the Roman women in their image posthumously joined the ranks of these worshipped in the imperial cult. The frontal rendering used in the clipeate portraits on the diptychs mimics the frontal type utilized on contemporary coins of the early sixth century. Preceding empresses were not represented on consular diptychs, but Ariadne's inclusion would be emulated on the consular diptych of Justinus in Berlin discussed in chapter six, which represents the Empress Theodora in a clipeate portrait (see figure 6.9). Therefore, although centuries earlier in Imperial Rome women had seemingly presaged some aspects of Ariadne's depiction, the affect was now entirely different. A similar inventiveness within the structures of tradition appears later in the sixth century in the coinage of Justin II and Sophia considered in chapter seven.

In addition to the ivory images of Ariadne, large-scale sculpture also represented her throughout the Empire. Textual sources describe numerous public statues of Ariadne and her husbands, and these sculptures tangibly represented the imperial house across Byzantium. The *Chronicle* of Marcellinus, for example, illustrates insurgency by citing the abuse of imperial statuary: "Civil strife occurred at Constantinople against the rule of Anastasios. Statues of the emperor and empress were bound with ropes and dragged through the city."[77] The mob's visceral rejection of the new emperor extended to include the empress in other attacks on imperial authority. The early medieval imperial image palpably served as an imperial presence. Likewise, in the Hellenistic and Roman periods, statues honoring imperial couples, such as cult statues of Antiochos and Laodike III, arose in the temple of Dionysos in Teos in 204/3 B.C.[78] In the third century A.D., the arrival of the imperial image inspired festivals, such as the one recorded in an inscription in the provincial town of Termessus Minor.[79]

Just as a statue served as the simulacrum for the body of the ruler, the public persona of the ruler conversely was expected to be frozen into the repose of a sculpture. Eusebios extols Constantine the Great's statue-like bearing—in this sense, the person of the Byzantine emperor was regarded as a likeness.[80] The actual emperor or empress was perceived as embodying the imperial image. The *Vita* of Saint Philaretos gives an engaging account of the bride show initiated by Empress Irene in the eighth century. Although the account is two centuries after Ariadne's rule, it illustrates the overriding sense of type that colors imperial representation.[81]

The first step in a bride show was the gathering of candidates. To this end, imperial agents were sent throughout the kingdom in search of wellbred young women who fit extremely precise physical specifications. The emissaries bore with them as the tools of their quest a strange assemblage of measures: not only a foot and height measurement, but an image (*lauraton*) of the ideal of an empress as well. The editors and translators of the text of the *Vita* of Saint Philaretos translate *lauraton* as a bust measurement, but the author agrees with Hunger's correction of the translation to "portrait" as more likely. As Gilbert Dagron describes, "ce portrait de l'impératrice souhaitée devait être assez général pour correspondre à de multiples jeunes filles répondant aux normes, et il suffisait sans doute d'y ajouter quelques touches décisives pour transformer ensuite ce portrait-type en 'icône' de l'impératrice réelee."[82] This generalized mode of representation indicated by the story of the bride show further demonstrates the difficulties of attribution of empresses' images.

The three marble sculptures identified as Ariadne now in the Lateran Museum in Rome, the Palazzo dei Conservatori in Rome, and in the Musée du Louvre in Paris have this standardized quality. These works share the same round face and headpiece that strongly resembles those of Ariadne on consular diptychs. The lack of subtlety in the comfortable solidity of their sculptural forms led Elisabeth Alföldi-Rosenbaum to disparage this group of sculptures as "lifeless masks, summary and coarse in the execution of detail."[83]

The marble head of an empress in the Louvre has a restored nose, but the sculpture otherwise preserves fine surface quality (see figure 3.6). The plump face is modeled most carefully around the features, with delicate nuances shaping the marble beneath the lower lip and the corner of the mouth. The wide eyes are drilled and resemble those on contemporary male imperial sculpture.[84] As in the ivory representations, a snood covers the empress' hair, and only the bottom of her ears peak out from beneath

fig. 3.6. Marble head of an early Byzantine empress, perhaps Ariadne, ca. 500, Musée du Louvre, Paris, France (R. F. 1525).

the fabric. This sculpture, now in Paris, was allegedly found in Rome, and came to the Louvre as part of the bequest of Isaac de Camondo. Likewise, the head in the Lateran shares many of the same, almost genderless conventions of imperial portraiture at the time (see figures 3.7 and 3.8). The

fig. 3.7. Front view, marble head of an early Byzantine empress, perhaps Ariadne, ca. 500, Lateran Museum, Rome, Italy.

fig. 3.8. Side view, marble head of an early Byzantine empress, perhaps Ariadne, ca. 500, Lateran Museum, Rome, Italy.

head in the Palazzo dei Conservatori was found in 1887 near S. Maria dei Monti (see figure 3.9).[85] The Roman findspot of all three of the marble heads posited as Ariadne led Siri Sande to speculate that the three were of Roman manufacture, but Breckenridge countered that there is little other evidence for this type of high-quality imperial marble sculpture production in Rome around 500.[86] Both scholars agree on a Constantinopolitan model for these empress heads. The general dating in the late fifth century and even the attribution to Ariadne seems plausible enough. The importance, though, of the individual identification seems overemphasized given the ambiguities of imperial representation.

In addition, a bronze head in Niš in former Yugoslavia, discovered in Balajnac in 1958, was identified by Dagmar Stutzinger as Ariadne (see figure 3.10).[87] Her argument militates both stylistic and iconographic arguments to posit that the head represents the young Ariadne. The figure compares stylistically with others placed in the final two decades of the fifth century, for the head presents a mixture of naturalistic and abstracting details that link it strongly to the three marble heads identified with Ariadne in Rome and Paris.[88] Stutzinger's careful assessment of the Niš sculpture usefully delineates some of the problematic issues of understanding the crowns of imperial women in the fifth century. The basic covering envelopes all but the hair nearest the forehead; these snoods were fashionable for all aristocratic women and are not specifically imperial.[89]

No doubt many representations of Ariadne have been destroyed over time, for textual references describe other public images that testified to her importance. Zeno and Ariadne were prominently depicted on pedestals near the Chalke Gate, according to a peculiar text that mentions monuments in Constantinople, the *Parastaseis Syntomoi Chronikai*. This sculptural pair was inscribed with epigrams of the philosopher Secundus.[90] One odd element of the second *Parastaseis* mention of the statuary pair is the phrase applied to the Empress Ariadne, "eventually chaste but earlier shameless," which the editors Cameron and Herrin explain as a confusion of the Empress Ariadne with her successor Theodora by the author. As we have seen and will discuss further in chapter five, the imputation of past sexual transgressions to imperial women has a venerable tradition, including Julia from the beginning of the Roman Empire and Helena at the start of the Christendom, so that statement is not necessarily an elision of Ariadne with Theodora. The *Parastaseis'* small slip repeats a telling pattern that we will see in other references to imperial women, in which medieval sources muddle their identities.

The main streets of Constantinople must have seemed thickly littered with imperial statues, for even relatively inconsequential imperial figures were so glorified. For example, Anastasios' successor had a wife, Euphemia,

fig. 3.9. Marble head of an early Byzantine empress, perhaps Ariadne, ca. 500, Capitoline Museum, Rome, Italy.

who barely exists in the historical record, and no visual representations of her survive. Yet the *Parastaseis Syntomoi Chronikai* mentions an inconspicuous public statue of Euphemia once extant: "a very small gilt statue of Euphemia . . . on a plinth in the quarter of Olybrius, near S. Euphemia, a church she founded herself."[91]

fig. 3.10. Bronze head of an early Byzantine empress, perhaps Ariadne, excavated in Balajnac, ca. 500, Niš Archeological Museum, Serbia, Yugoslavia.

fig. 3.11. Ariadne tremissis, gold, Obverse: Diademed bust facing right, Reverse: Cross in wreath, A.D. 474–515, Constantinople mint, Dumbarton Oaks, Washington, D.C. (LRC 606).

As a corollary to Ariadne's statues placed throughout the capital city, her image also marked official coinage. A marriage solidus may honor Ariadne's union with Anastasios, but the coin's attribution remains uncertain.[92] This gold coin renders the emperor on the obverse in three-quarters view. The reverse depicts the imperial couple arrayed on each side of the standing figure of Christ, which, with the marriage solidus of Marcian, constitutes the first representations of Christ on coinage. The iconography resembles that on a gold marriage ring in Dumbarton Oaks, which also shows a central figure of Christ joining the hands of a couple. The coin inscription reads CONOB for Constantinople in the exergue and FELICITER NUbTIIS around the standing figures. This main reverse inscription misspells *Feliciter Nuptiis,* which can be roughly translated as "best wishes to the newly-weds."[93] The importance of Ariadne for bolstering the legitimacy of Anastasios may have inspired such an issue, a historical situation that repeats many aspects of Marcian's need to emphasize his association with Pulcheria by producing a marriage medallion.[94] It seems significant, too, that it was the previous wedding medallion's iconography that was duplicated, instead of other types, such as the paired frontal busts on the Rothschild cameo of Honorius and Maria.[95]

Ariadne also issued solidi and tremisses in small numbers, for both types of her gold coinage are now quite rare (see figure 3.11). The dating of Ariadne's coinage poses problems, and is generally placed at the very beginning of Zeno's reign in 474–5. This early dating derives from its similarity to the coinage of her mother Verina, which is in turn dated by numismatists to the end of Verina's reign because of its resemblance to that of her daughter (see figure 3.12).[96] The coinage of Verina includes joint images with her husband Leo, but the sole issues depict her in a manner predictable from other late Roman numismatic issues of imperial women. On the obverse of her solidus issue, the bust of Verina bears a diadem and the *Manus Dei* descends to crown her; the reverse side renders a standing Victory with a long cross.[97] Ioli Kalavrezou pointed out that the *Manus Dei* on the coins of imperial women of the Theodosian House might render an element of the imperial palace, the portico of the Golden Hand.[98]

fig. 3.12. Verina solidus, gold, Obverse: Diademed bust facing right with *Manus Dei*, Reverse: personification of Victory standing facing left, holds long cross, Harvard University Art Museums, Whittemore Collection, Cambridge, MA. (LRC 593).

Ariadne's tremissis, of which only about ten exist, conforms to a large extent to issues by earlier Augustae.[99] The obverse depicts a bust of Ariadne facing right with the customary diadem; the reverse, a cross encircled by a wreath with the exergue CONOB that abbreviates Constantinople and a star below. Wolfgang Hahn completed the fullest study of Ariadne's numismatic issues, and carefully analyzed her solidi, of which three are known.[100] These solidi show the empress in a profile portrait, wearing a chlamys clinched over the shoulder facing the viewer and a jeweled diadem and necklace.[101] The reverse of one solidus of Ariadne shares an image and perhaps even die used by Zeno, with a winged Victory bearing a staff facing left and the legend CONOB in the exergue.[102] Because of this similarity, Hahn proposes this solidus of Ariadne was issued in the second reign of Zeno, 476–491. The second solidus does not offer such a tidy correlation with a better dated coin, but comes from early in the second reign of Zeno based on comparison of letter types in the inscription.[103] The wife of the usurper Basiliskos, Zenonis, likewise issued at least solidi and nummi, which follow the portrait type of Verina closely.[104] Ariadne's numismatic portrait types, therefore, resemble those of the coins of preceding imperial women to such an extent that it does not seem necessary to cluster the sole issues of Verina and Ariadne to the end of the mother's reign and the beginning of the daughter's.

The era of careful fiscal management under Anastasios is connected with the beginning of a distinctively Byzantine coinage, and so the scholarship of Byzantine numismatics typically begins with his reign. In 498, Anastasios introduced into circulation the follis, the large bronze coin then issued for many subsequent centuries in the Empire (see figures 6.7, 6.8, and 7.2). Ariadne was not depicted on these new coins. This new bronze denomination filled a real need, since the inflation of the Late

Roman period had left the plentiful low-value bronze coins virtually worthless. Another change connected with Anastasios' reign was the end of the line of western rulers, and their separate line of coins, at the death of Julius Nepos in 480. Some coin hoard evidence contravenes the standard account of the Anastasian coin reforms, in which the plentiful small bronze issues of the Late Roman period were demonetized. Adelson's work on the Zacha hoard of 1,179 coins from the Peloponnesos, for instance, indicates that minimi were issued surprisingly late during the reign of Justinian in the 540s.[105] This evidence begins to blur the sharp demarcation drawn by earlier scholars between late Roman and Byzantine coinage. As seen from the overview of Ariadne's numismatic images, her coinage largely mirrors preceding types of Late Roman imperial women such as her mother Verina.

The numismatic record bespeaks the broader terms in which the representation of Ariadne both maintains and transfigures the preexisting traditions of imperial women. Consular diptychs existed a century before Ariadne made her appearance on the ivories as the first empress to be included there. Her posthumous portraits on the ivory diptychs confirmed Anastasios' legitimacy, which hedged on his wife's birthright. Ironically, our most certain representations are from liminal moments in Ariadne's influence—on the early votive image with her parents and then on the ivory consular diptychs following her death. She managed to designate the next emperor after the death of her first husband Zeno, and ultimately, as the chronicler Zacharias noted on her death, "she had held the kingdom for many years, as many as forty."[106] Ariadne's centrality in the chain of succession also perpetuates the tradition established by her predecessors in the Houses of Constantine and Theodosios. The imperial identity of her husbands and son depended on their connection to Ariadne, who extended the notion of female *basileía* developed earlier.

The paucity of the visual and textual records for this period confronts us with a dilemma. Our most securely dated images of Ariadne are the consular diptychs' clipeate portraits, which mostly render the empress after her death as co-ruler with Anastasios. Both the identity and chronology of the ivory imperial diptychs and marble heads remain vexed issues, and their very ambiguity demonstrates the level of consistency amongst imperial representations at this time. As the recut Orestes diptych shows, the identity could shift with changed headgear for the face rendered a fairly generic type. Likewise the numismatic images of Ariadne shirk firm dating precisely because of their seamless continuance of Late Roman norms for imperial women. When we now consider the Empress Theodora, we will see how strongly her rendering in both image and word was also colored by preexisting forms.

CHAPTER 4

THE PATRONAGE OF THE EMPRESS THEODORA
AND HER CONTEMPORARIES

> *The believing queen also would regularly once in every two or three days come down to them to be blessed by them, being amazed at their community and their practices, and admiring their honoured old age, and going round among them and making obeisance to them, and regularly being blessed by each one of them.*
>
> —*John of Ephesus*, Lives of the Eastern Saints, p. 680

Because of the peculiar inflection of Prokopios' *Anekdota*, evidence of Theodora's (d. 548) patronage has been neglected in scholarly literature, although contemporary sources demonstrate its variety and extent. Theodora's patronage affords the chance to see how typical, indeed banal, her fulfillment of the expectations of her role was. Records of the beneficence of the Emperor Justinian's wife appear in several sixth-century sources, the best known being those by Prokopios, namely the *Buildings* and the *Anekdota*. We are not, however, compelled to rely on Prokopios alone. Other contemporary writings, typically relegated to a subordinate position, provide valuable information that augments our understanding of the empress's patronage and importance. The Syriac historians John of Ephesus and John Malalas diverge from Prokopios' account of this time. Other more limited sources include the *Chronicon Paschale,* Zacharias of Mitylene, and Victor Tonnensis. John Lydos, another courtier in Constantinople, offers perhaps the most direct corrective to Prokopios.[1] To this wealth of resources can be added epigraphic traces, which comprise monograms and inscriptions that once emblazoned major buildings of the era. For example, a series of inscriptions from North Africa collected by

Durliat testify to the ubiquity of the Empress Theodora's name in the Empire's urban spaces.[2] Acclamations show another way the imperial pair was yoked together in public address. Even in the tumult of the Nika Riot, the crowds chanted "Lord, preserve Justinian and Theodora."[3] Inscriptions found on walls at Bostra and Cyrrhus commemorate Theodora along with Justinian in the border territories.[4] John Malalas tells of a fortress' elevation to city status and subsequent renaming to "Anasarthon Theodorias" in honor of Theodora.[5]

The conventional nature of this patronage comprises only a portion of representation of an early Byzantine empress in words and monuments, for there was a complex verbal system for registering approval and dismay at the imperial house, which was redolent with centuries of antecedents and associations. This rhetorical rubric shaped the utterances of Prokopios, and the vilification of a celebrated woman via sexual slander was hardly a new phenomenon in the sixth century. This chapter "unpacks" these structures to regain a more balanced understanding of the Empress Theodora, and lays the groundwork for the analysis of the political pornography by Prokopios in the next chapter.

Earlier female imperial patrons determined the patterns that represent Theodora's patronage and elucidate her individual significance. Theodora's patronage emulates aristocratic models set by women in her immediate circle and by the Theodosian empresses of the preceding two centuries. In keeping with this illustrious tradition, she extended her charity to poorhouses, convents, and new churches. One particular woman in Constantinople in the early sixth century set a high standard for Theodora to emulate. Anicia Juliana (d. A.D. 527 or 529) had personally funded one of the most impressive buildings in Byzantine Constantinople, the now-destroyed Church of Saint Polyeuktos (see figure 4.1). This building was just completed at the time of Justinian's ascent to sole rulership and Theodora's coronation. Located in the heart of the capital city in the Constantianae quarter, Saint Polyeuktos was constructed from 524–527.

Anicia's venerable lineage offers a strong contrast to that of the illiterate former peasant, the Emperor Justin I, who had managed to acquire the Byzantine throne in 518 instead of Anicia Juliana's son, Flavius Anicius Olybrius. Because of this rivalry, Anicia's patronage requires scrutiny; it could not have escaped the attention of her contemporary, the Empress Theodora. Anicia Juliana was the sole heir to wealthy and illustrious parents, Anicius Olybrius and Placidia the Younger. Her father, one of the last emperors of the western portion of the Byzantine Empire, traced his family back through seven centuries of Roman statesmen. Both of her mother's grandparents furthermore were the descendants of Theodosios I.[6] John of Nikiu relates that Anicia Juliana's husband was once briefly pro-

fig. 4.1. Fragment from the Church of Saint Polyeuktos, A.D. 524–27, originally in Istanbul/ Constantinople, now by the Church of San Marco, Venice, Italy.

claimed emperor, but he fled when contenders challenged him.[7] The wealth and power of Anicia's husband, Areobindus, is displayed in the extravagance of his consular diptych issues, for the unparalleled number represents no doubt only a portion of his gift giving on accession to consulship in 506.[8]

Anicia clearly possessed vast resources as well as the accompanying strong inclination to demonstrate both this wealth and her lineage. The lavish decoration of the Church of Saint Polyeuktos, therefore, illustrates her imperial prerogative. Archeological excavation by Martin Harrison has revealed a great deal about this building. The main plan was square, with the standard eastern apse and western narthex. A side aisle along the north and south walls further divided the interior. Based on the size and arrangement of the foundations, the structure probably had a large dome, in keeping with the grandiose nature of Anicia's church.[9] Marble revetments adorned the interior, accented by elaborately carved and inscribed architectural ornament.

This decoration identified the church to its modern excavators, for fragments contained a few pieces from the dedicatory inscription of Saint Polyeuktos preserved in the *Greek Anthology*, a collection of ancient and Byzantine epigrams.[10] This poem offers a revealing image of female aristocratic patronage, for Anicia Juliana's church continues the tradition of her female forebears. With encomiastic flourish, the text reads:

> Eudokia the empress, eager to honour God, first built here a temple of Polyeuctus the servant of God. But she did not make it as great and as beautiful as it is, not from any economy or lack of possessions—what doth a queen lack?—but because her prophetic soul told her that she should leave a family well knowing how better to adorn it. Whence Juliana, the glory of her blessed parents, inheriting their royal blood in the fourth generation, did not defeat the hopes of the Queen, the mother of a noble race, but raised this from a small temple to its present size and beauty, increasing the glory of her many-sceptered ancestors. . . .[11]

The patronage of Anicia is thus carefully shown in the light of her rarefied ancestry, tacitly commenting by force of contrast on the parvenu Emperor Justin I. Leslie Brubaker has carefully established similar patterns in fifth-century female architectural patronage by looking at the work of Galla Placidia amongst others.[12] While the inscription artfully casts a look to the past, it in turn may have influenced future descriptions of buildings such as that by Prokopios of Hagia Sophia.[13]

An allusion to Solomon further deepens the imperial potency of Anicia's patronage, "She alone did violence to Time and surpassed the wisdom of

fig. 4.2. Vienna Dioskorides, Anicia Juliana, before A.D. 512, Österreichische Nationalbibliothek, Vienna, Austria (cod. med. gr. 1, fol. 6v).

renowned Solomon by raising a habitation for God."[14] Measured out by the "royal" cubit equivalent to 0.518 meters, the church was built to be a hundred royal cubits square, emulating in size and grandeur Ezekiel's Temple.[15] The decoration of the church derives from descriptions of Solomon's more richly embellished temple, including palm trees, lilies, and vines. In scale and costliness, Anicia's church exceeded any other church in the capital at the time of construction; Hagia Sophia, built shortly thereafter, might seem like one-upmanship, especially in view of Justinian's apocryphal remark on entering his church for the first time, "Solomon, I have outdone thee!"[16]

The *Greek Anthology* provides other examples of Anicia's patronage, such as the Church of Saint Euphemia at Olybrius. As in the case of the Church of Saint Polyeuktos, here she also constitutes her *philanthropia* in terms of her female ancestors. The building was founded by the Empress Eudokia, adorned by Galla Placidia, then further enhanced by Anicia.[17] Likewise the *Vita* of Saint Sabas speaks of her devotion to the holy man in several passages.[18] Even the ninth-century chronicle of Theophanes the Confessor mentions Anicia's piety, further illustrating her prominence and how effectual her patronage was in its aims.[19]

The most well-known artwork associated with Anicia Juliana's munificence, though, is a luxurious manuscript that was probably originally a gift (see figure 4.2).[20] One of the finest surviving late antique manuscripts, the Vienna Dioskorides, portrays Anicia Juliana in "the oldest dedication miniature in existence."[21] Significantly, her image in the manuscript alludes to her architectural patronage by surrounding her with an eight-pointed star, with putti at work building. Seated between classically inspired personifications of Prudence and Magnanimity, she powerfully vaunts her cultivated background. The manuscript's dedicatory inscription reads, "Hail o Princess, the people of Honoratae (a suburb of Constantinople for whose inhabitants she had erected the church) extol and glorify you with all fine praises; for Magnanimity allows (you) to be mentioned all over the world. You belong to the family of the Anikiai, and you have built the temple of the Lord raised high and beautiful."[22] Cutler thus asserts the manuscript's status as a token of "social exchange," for the Vienna Dioskorides probably served as a return-gift to Anicia for her patronage.[23]

Our evidence for the Empress Theodora's patronage is likewise both textual and epigraphic. Prokopios' *Buildings* provides the most detailed and geographically comprehensive account of the imperial patronage of Justinian and Theodora.[24] It records an extensive program of building throughout the empire, the magnitude of which notoriously emptied the imperial treasuries. The work as a whole is uneven and incomplete; for instance, it omits all of Italy. The later sections of *Buildings* seem skeletal and in place of stock encomia merely list public works. Book One, however, appears substantially more complete and polished; its entirety is devoted to Theodora's and Justinian's patronage in Constantinople. It differs to such an extent from the later books that Glanville Downey concluded that Book One of *Buildings* might well have been written as "a literary showpiece designed to be presented orally before the Emperor and the Court."[25] It describes the efforts of Theodora and Justinian to rebuild Constantinople after the devastating Nika Riot of 532. The burden that this extensive construction placed on the people of the city, the recent rioters, was immense. The almost punitive pace of construction hints at a rather brutal side to this rich phase of Byzantine patronage. Other Byzantine sources corroborate the magnitude of the era's building program. Even in the twelfth century, Michael the Syrian made a point of enumerating the constructions of Justinian.[26]

In addition to rebuilding what had been destroyed, Theodora supported entirely new foundations. The Church of Hagia Irene and its neighboring hospice were lavishly rebuilt after the riots, on a substantially grander scale than the original structures. The empress co-sponsored the House of Isidoros and the House of Arkadios, two hospices next to Hagia Irene.[27] At the end of Book One of the *Buildings,* Prokopios mentions that she also helped found another "very large" hospice specifically for the destitute who had come to Constantinople to petition the imperial court and those "led to come either by some errand of business or by some hope or by chance."[28] These projects parallel the patronage of the Theodosian empresses who demonstrated their *philanthropia* as discussed in chapter one. Theodora's patronage almost duplicates a list of the Theodosian Augusta Pulcheria's good works, including churches, hospices, and hostels. Funds for these projects came in part from the income of estates in Asia Minor, which Justinian gave her upon their marriage and later augmented.[29]

Many appraisals fixated on the salacious aspect of the empress' representation neglect other contemporary evidence that balances the image of Theodora, by informing our knowledge of her patronage. John of Ephesus' Syriac text, *Lives of Eastern Saints,* compiles a wide range of lives of holy men, women, and Christian communities. The fact that John of Ephesus included Theodora in his predominantly male hagiographic compilation is exceptional. In his account of the "blessed virgin" Susan, he prefaces his history with a justification for her presence, "The strong power of Christ . . . is wont to display its operation not only through men of great size or mighty strength, but also in weak, feeble, powerless women."[30] These statements iterate the Early Christian stereotype of female weakness.[31]

The third part of John of Ephesus' *Ecclesiastical History* begins with the declaration that "During the reign of Justinian, the empress Theodora, a devoted member of the Monophysite party, had built and endowed at Constantinople numerous monasteries, in which she placed bodies of monks drawn chiefly from the Asiatic provinces of the Roman empire."[32] Their geographic origin represents the heartland of Monophysite belief, covering much of the eastern Byzantine territories.[33] Monophysitism, which emphasized the divine nature of Christ, began in early fifth-century Egypt, and was declared heretical at the Council of Chalcedon in 451. John of Ephesus' *Lives* records the sanctuary for Monophysites in the

Hormisdas palace by Theodora, "the believing queen."[34] Justinian had been a particularly vigorous persecutor of many groups deviating from Chalcedonian orthodoxy, including Manicheans, Jews, homosexuals, and above all the Monophysites who were so popular in Egypt and the Levant. Theodora's family may well have originated in the Levant, and the sources agree that for whatever reason she was very protective of the Monophysites.[35] John of Ephesus, whose account might exaggerate, describes the haven she created within the Great Palace for over five hundred former stylites, heads of convents, and desert solitaries.[36]

Once established in Constantinople, the holy men organized themselves on a monastic model, including an archimandrite and a steward. According to John of Ephesus, our only source mentioning this palatial asylum, the Monophysites filled every area of the Palace, "their marvelous canticles and their melancholy voices . . . were performed and uttered in all the chambers and courts (πλατεῖα) and cells and halls (τρίκλινος) of that palace (παλάτιον)."[37] In addition to the description of this Monophysite community given in the forty-seventh section of the *Lives of the Eastern Saints,* John of Ephesus alludes to it within other lives included in his collection of the Egyptian Bishop John from Hephaestu, the Edessene Monk Hala, and the holy man Mare.[38]

Having a sizable presence of Monophysites in the Palace threatened the Chalcedonian community both in the capital city and the imperial household. John of Ephesus claims that some orthodox believers were so impressed by the holy men that they converted to Monophysitism and took communion with them. If we follow our eastern sources, resentment mounted at the active support that the Empress showed for the heretics: "The believing queen also would regularly once in every two or three days come down to them to be blessed by them, being amazed at their community and their practices, and admiring their honoured old age, and going round among them and making obeisance to them, and regularly being blessed by each one of them."[39] In return for these spiritual favors, Theodora "provided the expenses required for them liberally in every thing."[40] Other Monophysite texts, such as Zacharias of Mitylene, often repeat that Theodora shielded the persecuted group.[41] Zacharias describes the hardship of the Monophysite Severos, but "the Christ-worshipping queen was sufficient protection."[42]

Cyril Mango has convincingly argued that Theodora's patronage of the Monophysite community extended even to the construction of a lavish church within the Hormisdas Palace in the heart of Constantinople, the Church of Saints Sergios and Bakchos. The Hormisdas Palace is where Justinian and Theodora lived until 527, when Justin I died and the couple moved to the Great Palace. The refuge and building happened close to the time that the Persians destroyed the tombs of these saints: "The Persians ... carried away the bones of Mâr Bakchos the martyr, and the gold which was on the sarcophagus of Mâr Sargîs."[43] Theodora's power was sufficiently great for her to build this church for the holy men, perhaps during the period of reconciliation with the Monophysites from 530 to 536 and after a fire had wrecked their shrines.[44] While the inscription engraved inside the church mentions Justinian as well as Theodora, the empress is eulogized to a greater extent within the standard phrasing for appropriate *philanthropia:* "God-crowned Theodora whose mind is adorned with piety, whose constant toil lies in unsparing efforts to nourish the destitute."[45] Since both Sergios and Bakchos were Syrian saints, they posed suitable choices for serving the Monophysite community. If Mango's theory is correct, then the church is contemporary with Hagia Sophia and was not its prototype.[46] The simultaneous construction of the two churches created an intriguing pair, and for good reason the Church of Saints Sergios and Bakchos has the name "Little Hagia Sophia" in Turkish (Küçük Aya Sofya Camii). With similar plans but vastly different scales, the smaller church parallels Justinian's grandiose endeavor. Theodora's monogram appears on column capitals of Sergios and Bakchos, as well as on other important Justinianic commissions, such as Hagia Sophia in Constantinople and the Church of Saint John in Selçuk near Ephesus.[47] She is also tied to the Constantinopolitan Church of Saint Panteleemon by a suspect patriographic source that claims the church was built on the site where the empress had once lived and spun wool while poor.[48]

The Chalcedonian Justinian must have been more ambivalent about the horde of former stylites encamped in the palace, although he, too, occasionally sought their blessings.[49] Before Theodora died in 548, she commanded the continued support of the Monophysite community, but the *Lives of the Eastern Saints* hedges on whether Justinian perpetuated her patronage. While one passage of John of Ephesus states that Justinian continued their special protection, another says that the emperor was persuaded by their adversaries to transfer the holy men to a less prominent location.[50] The introduction of married couples and "others who were not chaste" into their midst further diluted the Monophysite community. In response, the hagiographer tells how God showed his anger at this defilement by setting some of the women and the building on fire.[51]

John of Nikiu also presents Theodora as the loyal champion of Monophysites. Her protection temporarily cloaked them from the worst of Justinian's Chalcedonian fervor: "his wife besought him on behalf of Timothy, patriarch of Alexandria, (and) he permitted him on her account."[52] Gregory Abu'l-Faraj spins a tale in which Justinian sought out Theodora's hand, in which she was the sheltered daughter of a Monophysite priest, a story line also taken up in a twentieth-century Coptic play performed in Cairo. He was only allowed to marry her on the condition that she not be forced to accept the tenets of the Council of Chalcedon.[53] The twelfth-century Michael the Syrian, the Jacobite Patriarch of Antioch, fits into this tradition in his representation of Theodora. His account is interesting for the alternative past it ascribes to Theodora:

> This prince [Justin] sensing his end approaching, named Caesar his nephew [son of his sister], called like him Justin [Justinian], and he sent him against the Persians. Arriving at Membedj, there he heard discussion of a young woman born to a priest, and he sought her hand in marriage. The priest asked him to declare orthodoxy and the prince promised with an oath that [his fiancée] would remain free to profess her faith.... Then the priest gave him his daughter named Theodora who lightened greatly the sufferings of the Church.[54]

Once ensconced in Constantinople, Theodora seemingly remained Monophysite, "The Empress Theodora emplored the emperor for the re-establishment of orthodoxy...."[55] Theodora's ability to sustain this Monophysite community within the Hormisdas Palace and the construction of the Church of Saints Sergios and Bakchos testifies to her status as an independent patron, and must have fueled Prokopios' rancor. While some of her projects were joint foundations with Justinian, she pursued a distinct agenda of building and cultural support. Her sanctuary for the heretical holy men, if John of Ephesus is to be believed at all, contravenes directly her husband's policies.[56]

Theodora's public role extended into the political sphere as well. John Malalas relates that Theodora participated in diplomatic gift giving with the Persian Empire: "Gifts were sent from the emperor of the Romans to the emperor of the Persians. Likewise the Augusta sent gifts to the Persian empress."[57] In negotiations with Byzantium, the Gothic Queen Amalasuntha wrote an effusive letter to Theodora as empress, suggesting her political clout.[58] Likewise Lydos' work *On Powers* stiffly rehearses Theodora's virtues, depicting her as the savior of the Byzantine state through her animosity to John of Cappadocia: "Only his co-reigning spouse, being more strongly vigilant than such as have never at any time been endowed with understanding and sympathy towards those wronged ... went to the emperor and informed him...."[59]

Women's participation in public life, however, was often covert, and Prokopios' tactics in describing Justin I's wife, Euphemia, afford a prime example. Prokopios writes approvingly of the former Empress Euphemia, for "she was quite unable to take part in government, but continued to be wholly unacquainted with affairs of State."[60] This seclusion is used as evidence that she was "far removed from wickedness."[61] Although Euphemia serves as an exemplary foil to his negative portrayal of Theodora, here it is only another convenient turnaround for the historian. Earlier in the *Anekdota*, he claimed that Euphemia was previously a concubine, "Justinus . . . had a wife named Lupicina (Euphemia) who, as being a slave and barbarian, had been concubine of the man who had previously bought her."[62]

Theodora exerted her influence through patronage and indirect action, and Liz James' recent work on power and early Byzantine imperial women illuminates this topic. Resenting her power, Prokopios militates the old stereotypes of feminine conniving and willfulness, "This woman claimed the right to administer everything in the State by her own arbitrary judgment."[63] The well-rehearsed contours of this accusation have been discussed insightfully by scholars such as Fischler and Cooper, who remind us that the point of such charges against a woman was to denounce the character of a man, her husband or father, indirectly.[64] Prokopios speculated that when Theodora and Justinian seemed to disagree, it was merely in order manipulate and deceive the people around them. Prokopios alludes to the conflict between Theodora's and Justinian's religious views in *Anekdota*: "They set the Christians at variance with one another, and by pretending to go opposite ways from each other in matters under dispute, they succeeded in rending them all asunder."[65] Other sources, such as Zacharias of Mitylene, on the other hand, indicate that substantive differences of opinion did exist between Justinian and Theodora—the handling of the Nika Riot is an obvious example.[66] Prokopios indicates that the discrepancy in their views on Christian orthodoxy posed merely a misleading front, and the imperial couple's enthusiasm for different circus factions was considered yet another instance of dissembling.[67]

Whereas Prokopios' positive rhetoric emphasizes the couple's harmony and common faith, the necessary opposite is discord: "Now in all this trickery they were always in full accord with each other, but openly they pretended to be at variance and thus succeeded in dividing their subjects and in fortifying their tyranny most firmly."[68] This reversal of representation inverts the traditional values of marital and social harmony described by Kenneth Holum in his work on the Theodosian empresses: "the potency of *basileía*, and with it peace and order in the Empire, depended on the fiction that all holders of dominion, female as well as male, acted from a single imperial will."[69] Thus in a typical panegyric of the *Buildings*, Prokopios describes the imperial couple, "who always shared a common piety in all that they did," carefully planning together their projects.[70]

The *Chronicle* of John Malalas enumerates rather blandly the pious acts of Justinian and Theodora, citing their patronage, and specifically mentions the work of the empress that was directed toward helping other women.[71] The practice continued in sixth-century Byzantium that young girls from poor families could be sold by their parents to brothel keepers as prostitutes. A standard act of charity lauded by Christian sources was to buy the women back from the brothel keepers and provide them with bridal dowries. In Malalas' *Chronicle,* Theodora freed many prostitutes of Constantinople from "the yoke of their wretched slavery."[72] Such glimpses reveal the grim realities of prostitution in the sixth-century capital city. This gesture by Theodora resonated with centuries of imperial beneficence by women. In the second century B.C., Laodike III, the wife of Antiochos, provided the dowries for impoverished young women. To honor her generosity, the office of an unmarried priestess of "Aphrodite Laodike" arose; Laodike's birthday inspired processions, and newlyweds would sacrifice to the new cult of Laodike now conflated with the goddess of love.[73] The Hellenistic empress furthermore was commemorated with a fountain used for the ritual bathing of brides.[74]

Prokopios mentions another example of Theodora's patronage in both the *Anekdota* and the *Buildings,* and a comparison of the two depictions affords a prime example of the malleable nature of his rhetoric. Theodora built the Convent of Repentance as a refuge for former prostitutes of the Constantinopolitan marketplace, who would sell their services for the pittance of three folles.[75] Located on the Asian shore of the Bosporos, the convent accommodated over five hundred women. In the *Anekdota,* the foundation is described by Prokopios as a sadistic move to punish the women "for sins against the body."[76] The motivation in the *Buildings* is, as one would expect for its rhetorical genre, much more innocuous. Lavishing money on the institution, she "added many buildings most remarkable for their beauty and costliness, to serve as a consolation to the women, so that they should never be compelled to depart from the practice of virtue."[77] The two accounts likewise invert the moral status of the prostitutes. Whereas the *Anekdota* indicated that the women had to be forcibly compelled to leave prostitution and live in the convent, the *Buildings* describes Byzantine prostitution as a form of slavery entered "not of their own free will, but under force of [the patrons'] lust."[78] John of Nikiu understands Theodora's initiatives in a more general way, "she put an end to the prostitution of women, and gave orders for their expulsion from every place."[79]

Malalas briefly mentions other philanthropy by Theodora in his chronicle, such as "a very costly cross, set with pearls" sent to Jerusalem.[80] Further good works are described, such as an excursion she made to the mineral springs of Pythia Therma in which she and her "4,000...." companions made donations to the churches, poorhouses, and monasteries en route.[81] Theophanes the Confessor embroiders this description, "Theodora, the most pious Augusta, journeyed to the hot springs at Pythia to take the waters. She was accompanied by the patrician Menas, the patrician Helas, who was comes largitionum, and other patricians, cubicularii, and satraps, a total of 4,000 . . ." These displays of the sixth-century empress' *philanthropia* mirror the actions of the Theodosian Empresses.

Theodora's patronage extended to Antioch. Throughout antiquity one of the most culturally and economically important cities of the Mediterranean, in the second quarter of the sixth century it experienced a sequence of disasters from which it never fully recovered. A ravaging fire in 525, two earthquakes in 526 and 528, then the Persian sack in 540 nullified any hope of recovery.[82] The *Chronicle* of Malalas enumerates Theodora's acts as a patron: "the most devout Theodora also provided much for the city [Antioch]." She built "what is known as the basilica of Anatolios, for which the columns were sent from Constantinople."[83] The prestige of imported materials marked the building as a noteworthy foundation. She also founded a church dedicated to Saint Michael in Antioch. Both buildings were started in 527, the year that Justinian became co-emperor in April and then sole ruler in August upon the death of his uncle, the Emperor Justin I. Perhaps these examples of Theodora's patronage marked this occasion, although the earthquake of 526 that devastated Antioch may well also have been a factor. Malalas' description of her activity centers on Antioch, because of the writer's hometown bias.

Prokopios' eulogy in the *Buildings* of Justinian's construction in Antioch diverges from Malalas' account. The *Buildings* only speaks of the patronage of the emperor as he rebuilt the walls, cleared debris, and had the city center rebuilt after its destruction by Chosroes; it omits Theodora's patronage within Antioch.[84] Prokopios' description of Antioch, though, must be viewed as a set piece, much like his rhetorical recital of Justinian's heroically proportioned building program at Daras.[85] The most thorough commentator on this passage concluded that Prokopios lacks even the minimal accuracy or "circumstantial information" that one might reasonably expect from a panegyric that would customize the routine rhetorical tropes to the particular subject at hand.[86] Prokopios not only misrepresents features of Antioch in *Buildings,* but he even contradicts the account he gave of Antioch in his *Wars*.[87] Malalas, therefore, is a more reliable source than Prokopios for evaluating Theodora's patronage in Antioch, where the chronicler lived until 532, and saw her Antiochene building projects' completion.

Although Prokopios is routinely privileged as the most dependable source for the Justinianic Period, the case of Theodora's patronage in Antioch is but one instance when an alternate source such as Malalas should be favored. Each document presents its own problems and strengths; in particular circumstances Malalas offers the best source we have. Detailed analysis of Prokopios' and Malalas' treatments of Arethas, King of the Ghassanids, for example, led Kawar to rely on Malalas and not Prokopios for portions of his account.[88]

Traditions of rhetoric and female imperial patronage shaped the representation of Theodora's *philanthropia*. The active patronage of Helena, the Theodosian empresses, and Anicia Juliana set an impressive standard by which to judge the public generosity of Theodora. Her protection and building for the heretical Monophysites inside an imperial palace in Constantinople demonstrate that she could pursue policies that conflicted with those of the Emperor Justinian. Her building projects both within the capital city and at the borders of the Byzantine Empire show considerable command of resources. The type of *philanthropia* in which she engaged, moreover, evidenced a shrewd awareness of the practices and precedents of aristocratic female patronage. Her capabilities as a cultural patron have therefore often been underrated, primarily because of scholars' overdependence on Prokopios as a source for the period. Once we recognize Theodora's achievements, her patronage offers a fascinating example of the display of female *basileía* in early Byzantium.

CHAPTER 5

LOOKING AT HER: PROKOPIOS RHETOR AND THE REPRESENTATION OF EMPRESS THEODORA

> Her murmurs, her pleasures, and her arts must be veiled in the obscurity of a learned language. . . .
> —Edward Gibbon, The Decline and Fall of the Roman Empire, ed. J. B. Bury, vol. 4 (London: Methuen, 1909), p. 228.

The medieval textual record of the Empress Theodora voices many perspectives, yet the work of the sixth-century historian Prokopios overwhelms our contemporary image of her, as the quote by Gibbon illustrates. Prokopios wrote an account of Justinianic building and military history, but his most widely read work is the so-called *Secret History*, the *Anekdota* in Greek. Even its tantalizing modern name, the *Secret History*, bespeaks the special status of this text, which now must be balanced against a fuller consideration of other sources for the period.

Our fragmented contemporary image of the Empress Theodora arises out of the disparate representations created during her own time. Today, Theodora is most often viewed through the lens of the *Anekdota*, which has focused our attention on the invective's strange tale of sexual exploits. The Greek title, *Anekdota*, simply means "unpublished things," but even this workaday label may have accrued to the work after the sixth century. The title *The Secret History*, adopted for English translations of the text, has naively sensationalistic overtones, with the implicit assumption that the scandalous "secret" history must be more truthful than more easily recognized rhetoric of the *Buildings* or *Wars*. Because so much discussion of Theodora has relied on a misunderstanding of the *Anekdota* as the "real story," we should now consider how this text fits within the rhetorical genres of its time. The point of this chapter is not so much to ascertain the sexual virtue of Theodora, a dubious historical enterprise at best, but to look at how this negative rhetoric was itself one typology of an early Byzantine empress.

Training in rhetoric allowed Prokopios to write with dazzling facility both a stately encomium of Theodora and a withering invective. Understanding this contradictory rhetoric requires consideration of its original intellectual context. Prokopios' invective, or antiencomium, is surely a classic within the genre of the character assassination.[1] In contrast to the image of the empress formulated from the personal attacks of the *Anekdota*, other representations frame her in terms of her idealized public persona. In the *Buildings* and *Wars*, Prokopios praises Theodora, and other Byzantine authors, such as John of Ephesus and Malalas, corroborate this image. Theodora's representation in the Church of San Vitale proves that she had a viable role in official images of imperial authority. Likewise, the preceeding chapter's account of Theodora's patronage serves to "normalize" our understanding of her within the tradition of practices of early Byzantine imperial women.

The flattering depictions conform to a typology, of course, just as the invective does. While numerous accounts of the Byzantine and Classical imperial milieux survive in this aggrandizing propagandistic mode, the rhetorical type represented by the *Anekdota* is more rare. There are commonsense reasons for this scarcity. Authoring a document that incriminates the current rulers is risky, whatever the accuracy of its contents. More often these indictments were penned after the death of their subject to legitimate the new regime. Prokopios begins the *Anekdota* by justifying it within a rather venerable heritage of invective: "For what men of later times would have learned of the licentious life of Semiramis or of the madness of Sardanapalus and of Nero, if the records of these things had not been left behind by the writers of their times?"[2] With the same clichés, the contemporary Lydos also names Sardanapalus as a shameful antecedent for the depravity of John of Cappadocia's tax-collecting excesses.[3] By claiming to assume the truth of these previous alternate histories, Prokopios implies that his is also trustworthy.[4] Feigning great reluctance at performing such an unsavory task, he thereupon dives into his exposé with relish.

The *Anekdota* masterfully exemplifies its rhetorical mode, but the specific circumstances surrounding its composition remain mysterious. Internal evidence led J. A. S. Evans to posit a date of composition of 550, for Prokopios places the work at thirty-two years after Justinian's rule, which seems to have encompassed the reign of Justin I in the Byzantine historian's mind.[5] Because the *Anekdota* was read only after some of its main characters were dead, that check on the veracity of his speculations is lost. Prokopios' basis was at best merely hearsay, Theodora's childhood and adolescence preceded by a number of years the historian's arrival in 531/32 in Constantinople. Once inculcated into the highest echelons of Byzantine society and established in a position to record for posterity his speculation, decades separated Prokopios from the most flagrant deeds of Theodora's youth that he relates.[6] His stated intention in writing his invective was for it to poison the opinion of later times, as indeed it has. In the *Buildings,* he claims that "History . . . transmits to future generations the memory of those who have gone before, and resists the steady effort of time to bury events in oblivion; and while it incites to virtue those who from time to time may read it by the praise it bestows, it constantly assails vice by repelling its influence."[7] The abrupt change of Prokopios' tone and content between the two modes of representation evokes the moment of shift in Suetonius' account of Caligula: "So much for the Emperor; the rest of this history must deal with the Monster."[8]

We have no evidence that Byzantine contemporaries read Prokopios' invective, and no other work that has content that significantly corresponds to his scabrous account of Theodora's activities. Nothing within the *Anekdota* indicates that Prokopios intended for his contemporaries to have access to the work, removing an important check to its truthfulness. We actually have no references to the work before the tenth century.[9] This Middle Byzantine citation was the gossipy Souda lexicon, which is laden with other salacious tidbits.[10] This absence of early references to the *Anekdota*'s contents contrasts with the fame Prokopios' other work enjoyed. John of Nikiu, for example, offers respect for the monumental *Wars:* "These great victories have been carefully recorded by . . . a learned man named Procopius the patrician. He was a man of intelligence and a prefect, whose work is well known."[11]

Another reason to think that the *Anekdota* did not have a broad readership in Byzantium is that only one manuscript survives. Interestingly, it surfaced during the seventeenth century in the Vatican, where Theodora's support for the heretical Monophysites had hardly made her beloved.[12] In the medieval West, a tradition of criticism of her different from that of Prokopios persisted based on these religious differences, so it is perhaps not coincidental that the Vatican harbored the one copy in existence.[13] Initially its authenticity was questioned because of its extraordinary reversal from the known flattering texts by the courtier, but philologists now accept the *Anekdota* as the work of Prokopios.[14] His education gave Prokopios the capacity to manipulate any fact into the desired framework, be it encomium or invective. This inversion premises his treatments of many figures; thus the one version's depiction of Belisarios as the brave general reconfigures him into an alter-image, the henpecked husband.[15]

Our modern valorization of artistic originality makes us predisposed to underestimate the weight of convention in classical oratory. Rhetoric provided writers such as Prokopios an acceptable framework by which to structure their representation of a chosen subject.[16] The education of Prokopios grounded him firmly in these stylized patterns, and his work is the product of a system that instructed its pupils in how to argue with equal conviction both sides of an argument.[17] The long-standing critique of rhetoric focused on its disregard for the truth, since even some of its earliest proponents were accused of being uninterested in "what is really just, but what would seem just to the multitude who are to pass judgement, and not what is really good or noble, but what would seem so."[18] By the Second Sophistic, the rhetorical tradition as exemplified by the third-century A.D. Menander Rhetor was fossilized into a set of formulaic descriptions. Thus Menander's handbook of rhetoric, widely utilized in Byzantine education, delineates the form and content of genres such as the encomium.[19] He teaches how to praise one set of features as well as to vilify its inverse set; the aspiring Byzantine writer and statesman thus learned to transform facilely any fact.[20] This well-oiled rhetorical machine depends on the shared assumptions and background of the audience and literary performer. Stanley Fish's notion of a "community of interpreters" offers a helpful way of understanding this relationship, for Fish emphasizes the significance of the reader's suppositions.[21] The educated Byzantines who comprised Prokopios' initial audience could richly savor his piquant literary forms, but possessed the sophistication from shared cultural assumptions to value the *Anekdota* not as reportage but as literature. A whole series of habits of thought conditioned by rhetorical forms such as *synkrisis* made this preparation complete, so the extremely conventional nature of the *Anekdota* dilutes its status as documentation. Nevertheless, the overwhelming bulk of scholarship is based on a reading of Prokopios that dramatically undervalues the weight of rhetorical tradition. Standard works on the era, such as John Barker's *Justinian,* swallow Prokopios' allegations about Theodora whole, primly asserting that "It was, at any rate, only after a highly unsavory youth that her path finally crossed that of Justinian."[22] Even feminist scholar Judith Herrin sustains the *Anekdota*'s speculations, "after all, Justinian first noticed her in a popular entertainment connected with the Hippodrome . . ."[23] Lynda Garland opens her recent study of Byzantine empresses with a lengthy catalog, on the book's first page, of Theodora's wicked deeds, concluding that Theodora had in all likelihood worked as a prostitute.[24]

Analysis of the *Anekdota* illuminates how overdetermined some of its rhetorical flourishes were. Empresses are typically extolled for their great beauty, and Prokopios duly enthuses in the *Buildings* that "to express her [Theodora's] loveliness in words or to portray it in a statue would be, for a mere human being, altogether impossible."[25] Stock comparisons of the beauty of an empress to that of a statue linger into the Middle Byzantine period, demonstrating the tenacity of this convention.[26] With deadening regularity empresses are described as beautiful. Prokopios must then reverse his opinion of the empress' looks expressed in the *Buildings*. Conceding in the *Anekdota* that she was fairly attractive, he goes on to elaborate her flaws in this regard, manufactured or otherwise—informing the reader that she is short, sallow-complexioned, and apparently always transfixed by an intense expression with contracted brows.[27]

The conventional virtue of motherhood is likewise turned inside out, for a good Byzantine empress is fecund. The Middle Byzantine imperial author, Anna Komnene, continues the early Byzantine standards by lingering over the maternal qualities of her mother, the Empress Irene, describing at length Anna's own birth, with the implication that it was somehow divinely delayed to accommodate the travel plans of the emperor. Through the contorted twists of the antiencomium, though, Theodora becomes the aborter rather than the mother: "And though she was pregnant many times, yet practically always she was able to contrive to bring about an abortion immediately."[28] The image of a woman-as-aborter would have been repugnant, for the identification of Byzantine women with their role as mother applies even more stringently to empresses.[29] The accusation was loaded in the early Byzantine period, when abortion was associated with lower-class women. Prokopios goes on to recount in the *Anekdota* that Theodora had a son, John, raised by his father. After his father died, John went to Constantinople only to disappear ominously, with the assumption by the historian that Theodora murdered her son to conceal his existence from Justinian.[30] Based on her public recognition of the daughter whom she had before marrying Justinian, this story of her automatic and ruthless murder of her son seems unlikely.[31] The disappointment that Justinian and Theodora's marriage did not produce children sharpens these speculations, for, as Peggy McCracken noted in her study of the courtly love tradition, "the queen's barren body becomes the subject of secrets and rumors, or tests and judgements. . . ."[32]

Other laudable qualities of an empress, beneficence and temperance, are in a similar manner inverted and exaggerated into inhumanly proportioned cruelty and excess. According to the *Anekdota,* Theodora dispensed punishments arbitrarily and tortured to promulgate her political agenda. These descriptions have a particularly formulaic quality. The torture is inflicted upon innocents, their treatment exceptionally harsh, and their final fate always mysterious, "For first she tortured certain intimates of Belisarios and Photios, alleging against them only the fact that they were on friendly terms with these two men, and then so disposed of them that up to this day we do not yet know what their final fate was."[33]

The magnitude of Theodora's cruelty depicted by Prokopios matches the indulgence he describes in her daily regime. Prokopios fixates on minutia of the empress' body. The degradation of Theodora's youth acquires spectacular proportions through the lenses of exaggeration and fabrication.[34] But the same preoccupation with her physicality is evident in his description of her toilette:

> Her body she treated with more care than was necessary, yet less than she herself could have wished. For instance, she used to enter the bath very early and quit it very late, and after finishing her bathing, she would go thence to her breakfast. After partaking of breakfast she would rest. At luncheon, however, and dinner she partook of all manner of foods and drinks; and sleep for long stretches of time would constantly lay hold of her, both in the daytime up to nightfall and at night up to sunrise.[35]

This image of Theodora's gluttony fashioned by Prokopios is matched by the contemporary attack by Lydos on his rival, John of Cappadocia. Like Prokopios, Lydos interweaves the tropes of sexual excess and gluttony: "Harlots were wont to entice him . . . with lascivious kisses that impelled him to sexual intercourse; and, after he had been worn out, he used to taste of both the delicacies and drinks offered him by other catamites."[36] In contrast, in a later period Anna Komnene glorifies her father's stoicism set against those debased rulers who "enjoyed a life of ease and took pleasure in the baths (like some emperors who prefer and usually follow an animal existence)."[37] A key contradistinction between Prokopios' public and private history is the status of Theodora's body, the most contested aspect of her imperial identity. The corporeality of Prokopios' invective taps into a tradition of invective against women seen earlier in Horatian Epodes. Prokopios depicts Theodora in terms opposite from those he used in his public encomium, ascribing to her a grotesque, emphatically un-imperial physicality. The unwavering focus on Theodora's body in the *Anekdota* was meant to undermine her viability as an emblem of imperial power. No other character in the negative text is so consistently described in terms of body and physical excess.

The palpably visible role of the *Anekdota* Theodora was a calculated divergence from acceptable norms of the public behavior of empresses. Imperial women were expected to lead a secluded lifestyle, with only limited forays into public. An adulatory description of a Middle Byzantine empress by Anna Komnene eulogizes an almost pathological shyness:

> Her natural inclination would have been to shun public life altogether. Most of her time was devoted to household duties and . . . reading the books of saints. . . . Whenever she had to appear in public as empress at some important ceremony, she was overcome with modesty and a blush at once suffused her cheeks . . . [and was] so far from being pleased to reveal to the common gaze an arm or her eyes, was unwilling that even her voice should be heard by strangers.[38]

Prokopios' louche imputations against Theodora are just as predictable: "For the girl had not a particle of modesty, nor did any man ever see her embarrassed . . . she would undress and exhibit to any who happened along both her front and rear naked . . ."[39] By accentuating her visibility, her real presence in public, Prokopios implicates Theodora's physicality in his strongest criticism.

The central theme of Prokopios' calumny is Theodora's wanton display of her body. What space in Justinianic Constantinople was more public than the Hippodrome, where Theodora allegedly spent her youth as a lewd performer? Her level of self-display radically contrasted the veiled seclusion of aristocratic women: he claims that for certain performances she would wear only a loincloth in front of the hippodrome audience estimated to include at least 50,000 people.[40] By stating that Theodora was a hippodrome performer, Prokopios locates her with deadening accuracy in an irredeemably base location on the social topography of Constantinople.[41] While this display of her body certainly undercuts any sense of imperial presence, in more general terms Prokopios' accusations place her in a much lower social sphere.[42] To similar effect, the first-century writer Seneca claims Julia, the first emperor's daughter, worked as a prostitute in the Roman Forum.[43]

Recent examples in the United States reveal presidential first ladies being debased in similar ways. The perceived authority of Hillary Rodham Clinton is hypersexualized and undercut on the cover of the satirical magazine, *Spy* (see figure 5.1). The image of Clinton in S & M gear materializes in a composite photograph the time's anxieties about a woman having undue influence in the White House. As Laura Kipnis has remarked in her recent cultural study based on the topless photographs of Jacqueline Kennedy Onassis illicitly published in *Hustler* magazine during the 1970s, "The very highness of high culture is structured through the obsessive banishment of the low, and through the labor of suppressing the grotesque body . . . in favor of what Bakhtin refers to as 'the classical body.'"[44] This orifice-less classical body is exactly what Theodora is not in the *Anekdota*, if we think only of the quote Prokopios attributes to her, "Three orifices are not enough to satisfy my sexual desire . . . ," which has turned into her signature attribute in more popular modern representations.[45] Prokopios' obsessive disquisition on Theodora's youth is thus highly class-coded within Byzantine social norms that resonate today. Thus we see tensions not only between visibility and invisibility but also the classical and the grotesque. Such slander inverts gender roles by having John adopt sexual practices coded feminine, just as the *Anekdota*'s Theodora was made to subvert gender norms in the opposite direction. These shocking images of the Byzantine ruling elite fit a tidy pattern. As Bakhtin observed in his study of Rabelais, "Debasement is the fundamental artistic principle of grotesque realism; all that is sacred and exalted is rethought on the level of material bodily stratum . . ."[46] The representation of the imperial presence affords no middle ground, therefore the rhetoric of encomium and invective parallel the "king's two bodies." Prokopios' representation of Justinian's court is molded both by classical rhetorical formulae as well as the ascendant ideology of kingship discussed by Kantorowicz in *The King's Two Bodies*. As will be described in the next chapter, Theodora's haloed image in San Vitale sustains the fiction of a dual imperial identity; she appears at once as a specific woman and a representation of the divine nature of imperial rule. The degradation of Theodora's body in the *Anekdota* undermined her credibility as a divine imperial presence.

Though the *Anekdota* renders other characters as debauched, none possess Theodora's vivid physicality. As Pauline Allen notes in her study of Prokopios' invective, "exaggeration is a first desideratum in invective."[47] Lynn Hunt identified more contemporary examples of such strategies in her study of political pornography written about Marie Antoinette: "The queen's body, then, was of interest, not because of its connection to the sacred and divine, but because it represented the opposite principle—namely, the possible profanation of everything that the nation held sacred."[48] Having married into the imperial family, Theodora's identity as an incorporeal representative of imperial rule was more vulnerable, so Prokopios emphasized all-too-human details such as her toilette and sexual history. His rhetoric incisively manipulated the terms of regnal identity to negate her claim to an imperial essence.

Prokopios' sexual history of Theodora needs this context. Sherry Ortner has argued that female purity is particularly valued in societies in which hypergamy, marriage amongst classes, occurs.[49] Women become the guardians of propriety, so these imputations against Theodora would carry a sharper sting. Again Prokopios asserts the typology of a good empress, "that woman who, of all the women in the world, was in the highest de-

fig. 5.1. Hillary Rodham Clinton cover, composite photo, *Spy* magazine, February 1993.

gree both well-born and blessed with a nurture sheltered from the public eye, a woman who had not been unpracticed in modesty, and had dwelt with chastity, who not only surpassingly beautiful but also still a maiden and, as the expression runs, erect of breast."[50] To establish that Theodora embodies the opposite set of traits, Prokopios recounts an incredible biography of her life before marriage to Justinian that, predictably, depicts her as the most lascivious creature imaginable, claiming "there was never such a slave to pleasure in all forms."[51]

A standard strategy in the tradition of antique rhetoric was to accuse one's opponent of embarrassing origins whenever this humiliating maneuver was possible. The case of Demosthenes and Aeschines exemplifies this practice, and the rhetoric of Demosthenes served as a model in the most popular rhetorical manual in the Byzantine period, Hermogenes' *On Types of Style*. An early fifth-century source, Asterios of Amaseia, recounts his enthusiasm for the classical orator's vitriolic prose, "The other day, gentlemen, I was studying that marvelous author Demosthenes—I mean the work of Demosthenes in which he assails Aeschines with vehement arguments. Having spent a long time on this speech, I became congested in my mind and had need of recreation . . ."[52] In *De Falsa Legatione,* Aeschines claims that his father was an athlete and soldier, and his wife likewise was from a solidly respectable family. Demosthenes in contrast imputes that Aeschines' father was an ex-slave and his mother an infamous *hetaira*. When the ancient biographer Pseudo-Plutarch confronted this disparity, he placed Aeschines' background somewhere between the two extremes, neither especially wealthy and illustrious nor poor and disreputable. Pseudo-Plutarch's compromise seems well-justified, and it is "all the more worth taking note of because ancient scholars were more familiar with the conventions of classical invective than we are."[53] In other ancient epitomes, however, the more lurid background created by his enemy survived to the exclusion of the respectable one.[54] A comprehensive study of these rhetorical practices led Janet Fairweather to conclude: "When we study ancient biographies we have to be on the look-out for stories reminiscent of the conventional topics of invective. It will be seen that we have to call into question a wide range of assertions: any statements, indeed, imputing to (the) famous . . . low birth or disgraceful morals."[55]

The conformity of Prokopios' rhetoric in the *Anekdota* to traditional models of invective undermines its credibility.[56] Prokopios states that in Theodora's youth "all the more respectable people who chanced upon her in the market-place would turn aside and retreat in haste, lest they should touch any of the woman's garments and so seem to have partaken of this pollution. For she was, to those who saw her, particularly early in the day, a bird of foul omen."[57] This moment suspiciously echoes an example from Demosthenes given in Hermogenes' *On Types of Style* to illustrate vehemence as a rhetorical style, "this man . . . the public pest, whom anyone when he saw him would shun as a bad omen rather than address him."[58] Slandering the empress by extension defamed the emperor, and this was largely the point of the exercise.[59]

The preoccupation of modern historians with the hypersexualized identity of Theodora is distortive.[60] This focus illustrates the phenomenon discussed by Michel Foucault in the first volume of his *History of Sexuality:* "What is peculiar to modern societies, in fact, is not that they consigned sex to a shadow existence, but that they dedicated themselves to speak of it *ad infinitum,* while exploiting it as *the* secret (Foucault's italics)."[61] The notion of secrecy colors the reception of this text following its rediscovery in the Vatican in the seventeenth century. The first printed edition of this work of Prokopios invested the text with the allure of the forbidden, for Alemmanus' 1623 edition was entitled *Historia Arcana* (Secret History). From the High Middle Ages, secrets were particularly associated with women and, ultimately, the uterus, and Alemmanus' choice of title may hint at these associations.[62] Likewise, although Byzantine sources such as the *Souda* refer to the text as the *Anekdota,* the unpublished things, the allure of the secret persists, and the *Secret History* remains the consistently preferred title for translations. The Prokopian text's status as a secret, the private dirty tale available for the delectation of generations of scholars, has prevailed over rigorous standards of historical evaluation.

The Theodora Legend

By looking at the handling of the "Theodora legend" by two seminal figures in Byzantine studies—Edward Gibbon and Charles Diehl—our modern quandaries in dealing with this material may be clarified. Our skewed contemporary image of Theodora now requires that we try to unpeel from it successive layers of interpretation. The Enlightenment historian Edward Gibbon in his monumental *Decline and Fall of the Roman Empire* established the terms of later treatment of Theodora. He unquestioningly reiterates the outlines of Prokopios' narrative, giving gullible assent to the sixth-century historian's incriminations. Gibbon introduces her onto the historical stage as "the famous Theodora, whose strange elevation cannot be applauded as the triumph of female virtue."[63] The historian then recounts the most damning of the *Anekdota*'s imputations about Theodora's past, rehearsing Prokopios' clichés about her lowly origins, needlessly interesting adolescence, and tyrannical presence in the court. Coyly Gibbon refrains from repeating just a few details, for these "must be veiled in the obscurity of a learned language."[64] The logic of inversion that creates the invective gives the *Anekdota* a certain coherence of representation. When the formulaic structure is not acknowledged, however, this accord—that is, the homogeneously bad character of Theodora—becomes evidence of veracity. Not wanting to recognize the force of rhetorical convention in this text, Gibbon claims that "even the most disgraceful facts . . . are established by their internal evidence."[65] This false assumption allows him to linger over Theodora's "venal charms," which he seems to have found so fascinating.[66] The marked contrast in Gibbon's assessment of the Middle Byzantine historian Anna Komnene with his appraisal of Prokopios illustrates his consistent bias against the women included in his purview. The alternate model exemplified by Anna Komnene in the *Alexiad* makes the rhetoric of the *Anekdota* more apparent by force of the disparity. The magnanimous, virtuous creatures inhabiting the official discourse of the *Alexiad* or Prokopios' *Buildings* and *Wars* are just as conventionalized as the bawdy hippodrome performer conjured up by Prokopios. It was exactly Anna Komnene's adulatory praise that aroused the suspicions of Gibbon, who had found Prokopios' slander credible: "Yet instead of the simplicity of style and narrative which wins our belief, an elaborate affectation of rhetoric and science betrays in every page the vanity of a female author."[67] The *Anekdota* representations slide into the comfortable forms established by centuries of ancient invective, yet the Enlightenment writer possessed a blindspot to the conventional nature of the accusations, for they dovetailed with eighteenth-century gender stereotypes. Thus her positive forms collapse as literary confections for—ironically—the typological nature of her rhetoric aroused Gibbon's suspicion where Prokopios' did not, thus "the genuine character of Alexius is lost in a vague constellation of virtues."[68] The Emperor Alexios is described by Gibbon with positive, presumably masculine words such as "bold," "dexterity," "improve," and "patient," whereas Anna Komnene is associated with the words "tender," "mournful," "affection," and "vanity." For Gibbon, Anna fell outside of the golden triad of historians worthy of emulation for their manly, objective stance: Tacitus, Ammianus, and Prokopios.[69] Another validation for Prokopios in Gibbon's eyes came in his reliance on Thucydides, a credible classical lineage, in contrast to the suspect ecclesiastical sources that counter Prokopios' incriminations.[70]

Charles Diehl, the eminent Byzantinist active a century ago, was fascinated enough by the *Anekdota* Theodora that he wrote her biography with ironically entitled chapters such as "La vertu de Théodora" and "Le féminisme de Théodora." He even takes it upon himself to evaluate the likelihood of Theodora having had affairs with several men at court, though adultery is one of the few vices that Prokopios does not impute to her in the *Anekdota*.[71] This bizarre exercise may be a response to the popular play about Theodora by Victorien Sardou in 1884 starring Sarah Bernhardt as the empress, which includes such dalliances.[72] Diehl's perspective is infused with aspects of the Orientalism that characterized Byzantine studies at the time, constructing its feminized subject as a dissolute and voluptuous foil to the West's self-image.

Just as the Enlightenment biases of Gibbon predisposed him to trust Prokopios over his clerical contemporaries, the intellectual climate of late nineteenth-century Paris led Diehl to cast Theodora within the Orientalist fantasies of the *femme fatale*. Theodora must prop up a contrast to the asceticism of her husband Justinian in these terms, "While Justinian, born in the rough mountains of Macedonia, was profoundly penetrated with the Roman spirit, Theodora remained always a pure Oriental, full of all of the ideas, beliefs and prejudices of her race."[73] Diehl reconstructs her psychology from the tropes of Prokopios, usually reconfigured along the lines of modern clichés of feminine behavior.[74]

Charles Diehl's representation of Theodora conforms neatly to preoccupations of fin-de-siècle Paris, in which the sixth-century Byzantine empress seamlessly assumed the attributes of other *femme fatales*. Flaubert satirized the banality of this rendering with his *Dictionary of Received Ideas*' definition: "EMPRESSES. Always Beautiful."[75] The parallel with Salome is particularly striking, for Theodora, rendered as a decadent Oriental beauty by Diehl and Rimbaud, was like Salome an object of such fascination. Conflating stereotypes of women and "degenerate races" into one potent amalgam, the Semitic origins of both women magnified the threat they posed.[76] This aspect of Salome's identity emerged prominently in both literature and art, for French painters of the late nineteenth-century such as Jules Lefebvre were complimented by their contemporaries for painting Salome as the Semitic "tigress rather than the woman."[77] For Oscar Wilde, Salome served as Everywoman, combining many of the stock female attributes of late Victorian literary culture, for she is likened to the moon, vampirism, death, as well as, of course, possessing a rapacious appetite for the souls and minds of men.[78] As in the Prokopian assault on Theodora, a primary attribute of Salome in Wilde is her pronounced visibility.[79]

The decadence of Theodora stands for the depravity of the Byzantine Empire, an ongoing theme that was part of broader Orientalist impulses. The *Anekdota* has yielded a series of popular biographies, making Theodora one of the best-known figures from Byzantine history, albeit in a form warped by the anti-encomium. Their titles, such as *Empress of the Dusk* (1940), *The Female* (1953), and *The Bearkeeper's Daughter* (1987), divulge the ready acceptance of Prokopios' slander.[80]

The tawdry innuendoes sharply contrast with Theodora's respectable rendering in the majority of Byzantine sources. Theodora was admired precisely for her careful fulfillment of her imperial role, and this respect is demonstrated by the emulation of her successors striving to associate themselves with an era of greatness. Admiration for the mother of Constantine the Great led later Byzantine empresses to seek the label "the new Helens." Theodora's name was likewise adopted later by new empresses.

Michael the Syrian gives an account of Justinian II's marriage to the Khazar wife who took the name Theodora.[81] No doubt she wanted to emulate the wife of her husband's namesake, Justinian I, whose status loomed large during the subsequent troubled generations in the Byzantine Empire. This choice also indicated that the name of the sixth-century Empress Theodora had positive connotations for Byzantines about 150 years after her death, which supports the argument made previously that her *Anekdota* representation did not dominate medieval perceptions of her. Theodora remained a popular name for imperial women, and in the ninth century the wife of the Emperor Theophilos assumed the name Theodora. Perhaps chosen in a bride show, this Theodora achieved sainthood for her role in reestablishing the use of icons in the wake of Iconoclasm in 843.[82] The name Theodora reappears, too, with the eleventh-century daughter of Constantine VIII, who ruled briefly with her sister Zoë as well as alone. In the centuries following Prokopios, Theodora enjoyed great prestige.

The unraveling of the rhetorical fabric woven by Prokopios returns us to his audience, whose education provided the tools to interpret both his extravagant praise and condemnations. The modern question of "did she or didn't she" distorts the Byzantine material, for the shared assumptions of Prokopios' original community of interpreters attuned them to the predictable drum of the rumors. The schooled Byzantine reader would not assume the appropriate dyad was true versus false (i.e., by asking whether it is the *Anekdota* or *Buildings* and *Wars* that tells the real story), but would instead recognize the two discourses as different modes of speech. Gibbon's assertion of the *Anekdota*'s reliability, embraced even today by historians such as J. A. S. Evans, unduly emphasizes Prokopian political pornography.

Perhaps the greatest distortion in our records is the preponderance of material that we have about the Empress Theodora compared to other early Byzantine imperial women. Theodora's fame (or infamy) is something of a historical fluke—her prominent representations in both word and image overshadow those of her immediate predecessors and successors holding Augusta rank. Had the San Vitale mosaics or the one manuscript of the *Anekdota* been destroyed, her lasting repute would be merely as the consort of the empire-building Justinian.

CHAPTER 6

THE VISUAL REPRESENTATION OF THE EMPRESS THEODORA

Typologies also shape the visual record of the sixth-century Empress Theodora. Her representation provides both continuity and rupture with the traditions of depicting imperial women. Glorious messages of imperial might such as the mosaics in the Church of San Vitale in Ravenna can mislead us into overestimating Theodora's importance in her era. The Empress Theodora wielded less power than both her predecessor Ariadne and her successor Sophia, but several factors contribute to the disproportionate attention that she has received since the seventeenth century. An accident of preservation has left us the lavish mosaic portrait in the Church of San Vitale (see figures 6.1 and 6.2). While we can enumerate a few examples of Theodora's image scattered across the Empire, her visual record comes short of that of the Empresses Ariadne and Sophia in quantity. Both her predecessors and successors warranted inclusion on coinage, but Theodora was absent from any coins, one of the core vehicles of the imperial image. The San Vitale portrait carefully crafts Theodora and her cohort's likeness through the standard imperial iconography; it interests us here for its ordinariness in those official terms. The era of Justinian and Theodora was furthermore documented by a historian of the stature of Prokopios, who looms over the chroniclers of the following two centuries of the Byzantine "Dark Ages." The contrast of her stately image in Ravenna with the scandalous incriminations of Prokopios serves only to further pique interest in her.

This and the previous two chapters explore both dimensions of Theodora's depiction, and return her to the context of other early Byzantine imperial women. Her portrayal at Ravenna, a stock image in the American university art history survey, will be considered in terms of sixth-century patterns of imperial iconography and patronage, just as the

fig. 6.1. View toward apse, Church of Saint Vitale, A.D. 526–547, Ravenna, Italy.

depictions by Prokopios were seen to conform to late antique rhetorical conventions. Much as specific, established language described imperial women, empresses and their court possessed a distinct institutional history, reflected in the image of Theodora and her court, the *sekreton ton gynaikon*. The group portrait in the Church of San Vitale depicts the Empress Theodora and her retinue making a resplendent entrance, in tandem with the Emperor Justinian and his court (see figure 6.3). Christ the Redeemer dominates the center of the church's apse, with the emperor privileged on Christ's right and the empress on His left, so that the two groups face each other squarely across the apse. The portraits' general offertory nature is obvious; the precise kind of offering, however, is debated in modern scholarship. Furthermore, the sixth-century political situation also frames the image. Robin Cormack's proposal that the dual mosaic portraits betoken an "Age of Theodora" must be reconsidered, for Theodora's image meticulously parallels Justinian's and by no means suggests priority.[1]

The meaning of Theodora's figure within the apse is controversial, so interpreters of this scene have struggled to explain her fictive presence in the most sacred zone of the church where her actual presence would be forbidden, both as a layperson and as a woman. This seeming contradiction arises from how concretely one interprets the event portrayed, that is, to what extent does the viewer think of the imperial couple as actually "being" in the space where they are represented. A persuasive alternative is that they are more symbolically located, with an abstract significance that resists an attempt to reduce the image to a snapshot of a single ritual. Likewise the ivory consular diptych of Justinus also represents the imperial couple flanking the image of Christ—all three in the form of clipeate portraits.

By showing the emperor and empress presenting gifts to the church, these two prominent portraits reinforce themes of offering and kingship that appear elsewhere in the iconographic program of the Church of San Vitale.[2] Although Julianus Argentarius, a local banker, chiefly funded the church, the imperial couple appropriated the symbols of donation. Justinian holds a golden paten bearing the eucharistic bread; his wife, the chalice that contained the wine offered at the altar. Agnellus, the eighth-century author of the *Liber pontificalis ecclesiae Ravennatis,* provides the most information about the otherwise elusive Julianus Argentarius.[3] We learn that Julianus disbursed the remarkable figure of 26,000 gold solidi for this church.[4] Julianus Argentarius likely originated in the eastern part of the Byzantine Empire, because of his monogram form but also because such extensive private benefactions were unusual in the western regions.[5] This staggering expenditure for the Church of San Vitale coincides with four other church construction projects that Julianus supposedly funded both in Ravenna and the nearby port of Classe. As large as this

fig. 6.2. Empress Theodora and Court, Church of Saint Vitale, mosaics ca. A.D. 537–544, Ravenna, Italy.

amount is, Julianus' spending on the Ravenna churches is dwarfed by the outlay of the old senatorial aristocracy on consular games. Richard Lim compares it to the 144,000 solidi spent by Symmachus on games and the 288,000 solidi put out by Maximus.[6] It is not clear whether the banker numbers amongst Justinian's cohort in the mosaic, but Julianus' name appears in the Church of San Vitale in inscriptions and monograms. In contrast, these epigraphical sources omit mention of the emperor and empress. Ravenna's tradition of imperial portraiture continued after the sixth century. Agnellus reports in *De Reparato* "that at the time of Constantine (Constans II), the Bishop solicited and acquired funds from the emperor in Constantinople to have mosaic portraits made in Ravenna of three emperors: Constantine, Heraklios, and Tiberios."[7]

The scene of donation enacted by Justinian and Theodora is particularly appropriate to the apse mosaic, where the eucharistic offering was performed below. The imperial presence coherently reinforces the central theme of San Vitale's iconography, the eucharistic sacrifice. Maguire has taken the number of men in Justinian's cohort—twelve—as an emulation of Christ and his Apostles.[8] The Byzantine emperor traditionally possessed a privileged position in the performance of the Eucharist, just as the first Roman Emperor Augustus styled himself *pontifex maximus*. The Byzantine emperor, for example, gave an oblation at the altar long after he was forced to stop participating in Mass inside the sanctuary.[9] A pertinent antecedent to Ravenna's imperial sacrifice scene appears on Trajan's Arch from the second century. The Roman sacrifice depicts an idealized event that emphasized the emperor.[10] As in Ravenna, the Roman imperial monument conflates distinct scenes into one. The preliminary presentation by the chief sacrificant, Trajan, collapses with the dramatic moment of the ax about to fall upon the kneeling sacrificial victim. After considering several such imperial sacrificial scenes, Richard Gordon concludes that a central feature of Roman sacrificial imagery is "the massive domination of the emperor."[11] The overwhelming focus on the imperial presence in Ravenna perpetuates in a Christian context the same tenets of representation seen on Trajan's monument.

The classification of the imperial offering represented by the throng of courtiers in the Church of San Vitale has inspired a lively debate amongst scholars. An argument raged between André Grabar and Djordje Stričevič in the late 1950s and early 1960s in the journals *Felix Ravenna* and *Starinar*. Stričevič argued that the San Vitale mosaics depict a Great Entrance; Grabar, an *Apokombion*. Stričevič posits that mosaics very literally render an early part of the Eucharist ceremonies called the Great Entrance. Based on the customs described in Constantine Porphyrogennetos' tenth-century *Book of Ceremonies* and in Pseudo-Kodinos, Theodora would appear in the

fig. 6.3. Emperor Justinian and Court, Church of Saint Vitale, mosaics ca. A.D. 537–544, Ravenna, Italy.

prothesis of the Ravenna church in the act of preparing the gifts with her attendants.[12] Grabar's contrasting theory, also derived from the *Book of Ceremonies,* suggests that she participates in an offering ceremony by the church donors.[13] Deichmann likewise rejects the possibility of Great Entrance scene.[14] Thomas Mathews seized upon other aspects of the *Book of Ceremonies* and the San Vitale image to argue that the program depicts a Little (or First) Entrance, a ceremony which included the bishop, book, and cross.[15] Recent scholars such as Jaš Elsner seem at a momentary consensus that the mosaics render a First Entrance, when the Eucharist's celebration opens with the liturgical vessels being brought forward to the altar.[16]

These interpretations rely heavily on the *Book of Ceremonies* compiled in the tenth century, ostensibly by the Emperor Constantine Porphyrogennetos. As a primary source for the study of court practice, the detailed tenth-century compendium of rituals of courtly life drew from earlier ceremony manuals as well as contemporary practice.[17] His book claims both to revive old practices and document actual tenth-century ceremonial. His main mine for these rituals consisted of sixth-century Justinianic era texts, which four centuries later still loomed as a golden age in the Byzantine Empire's history. The sixth century's ongoing preeminence was assured by that era's wealth of literature compared to the relative paucity of texts from the seventh to the ninth centuries.

While parts of the *Book of Ceremonies* derive from the sixth century, attempts at a precise reconstruction, such as those applied to the imperial mosaics in the Church of San Vitale, remain specious. Court ceremonies could change even under one reign, for Prokopios denounces Justinian and Theodora for adopting practices from the Persian court, clearly a loaded accusation. Prokopios writes that *proskynesis,* wherein courtiers would greet the emperor and empress by falling prostrate, was now demanded by Justinian and, even more shockingly, Theodora.[18] While Prokopios' description forms part of his attack on the emperor and empress in the *Anekdota,* he may well register some degree of transformation occurring in the practices of the Byzantine court.

In this framework of interpretation by Mathews and Elsner, the two imperial mosaic panels serve as snapshots of discrete instances in the performance of the ceremony of the First Entrance. Justinian and his retinue precede his wife and her court, who lag behind in the narthex of the church with a fountain in the background. This haggling over the identification of the scene imbues our understanding of the representation with a false sense of specificity. Elsner's interpretation is firmly rooted in reception analysis, but any visitor to the Church of San Vitale observes that the imperial mosaics, parallel to the axis of the nave, are not even visible until one stands directly in front of the apse. Anyone besides a priest in an apse was afforded merely an awkward sidelong view even then, weakening his assertion that some generic "viewer's involvement is crucial."[19] Deichmann offers yet another hypothesis in his suggestion that they may be related to the ceremonial use of *laurata,* encaustic portraits of the rulers, in processions.[20] The image provokes this controversy precisely because it defies these systems of classification. While the mosaic does not document a specific court ceremony, as far as we can say based on our sources, it can perhaps be construed in a looser, more typological sense.[21]

The identification of many individuals rendered in the mosaic is thus also problematic. Their overriding meaning was, no doubt, as the generic constituents of the court. Theodora's privileged rank makes her the tallest of the ensemble, although she was actually rather short, according to Prokopios.[22] The discrepancy is typical of early Byzantine portraiture. In portraying the idealized vessels of imperial power, individual traits such as height are irrelevant. As the woman to Theodora's left is often identified as Antonina, the wife of Belisarios, perhaps the younger woman to Antonina's left is Joannina, her daughter.[23] One adventurous recent attribution identifies the woman closest to Theodora as Justinian's mother, who is not mentioned in any source or represented in any known image.[24] Anastasios, the grandson of Theodora, is possibly depicted to the right of another figure once identified as Belisarios in the Justinian panel. Anastasios was betrothed to Joannina in the spring of 544, forging another potential link amongst the figures in the two imperial portraits.[25] Byzantine sources attest to the eminence of Theodora's family that derived from her position, Justinian "gave Kometo, the Augusta Theodora's sister, to Tzitas in marriage."[26] However, the methodology behind such attributions comes down to poking around in sources for someone of the right age and gender and then affixing their name to the mosaic figure. These suggested identifications depend, therefore, on tenuous links and never seem very compelling.

These questions shape the discussion of the architectural features shown in the mosaic. Von Simson notes that the Justinian panel, in contrast to that of Theodora, lacks placement signifiers that would mark the emperor and his retinue as located outside of the apse.[27] There is, however, a Doric column on each side and the cornice strip above the courtiers, but representations of these architectural components are fairly common, so the men's location remains ambiguous. Theodora and her retinue, on the other hand, are solidly anchored with a conch-shaped apse that is framed by two porphyry Doric columns that are, in turn, bracketed by two much larger green marble Doric columns. Theodora's halo overlaps part of the depiction of the central conch. To the right of the empress stand two eunuchs, and one of these men hold back the ornately patterned curtain above a dark recess of a doorway. In front of the doorway stands a spurting fountain atop a

Corinthian base. To the left of Theodora, a cluster of her female courtiers await with a great swag of a colorful curtain above them, and this elaborate patterning of the draperies and the elegant architectural features bespeak the setting's richness. Heavily patterned Corinthian columns demarcate both mosaic panels and support the egg-and-dart cornice running along the top of both images. This architectural setting of the officiate is well known from other media; the imperial ivory panels in Vienna and Florence also render an empress framed by a conch, surrounded by copious drapery and ornate columns (see figures 7.6 and 7.9).

The fountain and curtains in the mosaic may indicate the women's location within the narthex of the church. Early Christian churches needed a fountain at the entrance to accommodate the frequent baptisms of the new religion. The form lingered in church planning, and a typical sixth-century church had a fountain west of the narthex in an oriented church. Paul Silentiarios mentions a fountain in the western end of the Church of Hagia Sophia in his poem celebrating the reconsecration of the church in 562, when the dome was rebuilt after its collapse in an earthquake, "Now on the western side of this divine church you will see a court encompassed by four aisles; one of these is joined to the narthex, while the others are open wide.... At the prized center of the wide court stands a spacious fountain, cleft from the Iasian peaks; from it a burbling stream of water, forced by a brazen pipe, leaps into the air—a stream that drives away all suffering."[28]

Theodora and her retinue's representation on the left side of the Christ mosaic in the apse connects with the mosaics' physical location. The female part of the congregation stood on the south side of a church during the Eucharistic service.[29] Rather than this parallel supporting the view that Theodora was meant to be considered inside the apse, more likely both cases result from a common cause: the tradition of privileging the right-hand side of Christ. This preference for the right would mandate that the emperor, not the empress, his inferior in Byzantine society, would be on the right side of the image of Christ in the apse mosaic. Galleries of churches were not proscribed for women in the fifth century, since some of the earliest Constantinopolitan examples with this feature were in monastic churches such as that of Saint John Stoudios. Zomer suggests that in the time of Justinian, the gallery of a church became associated with women and remained their unique zone, which perhaps influenced the design of the Church of Hagia Sophia.[30] Taft, in contrast, calls upon a fuller range of evidence to conclude that both the aisles and galleries were potential areas for the female congregation in both the Early and Middle Byzantine periods.[31]

Prokopios' account of the Church of Hagia Sophia indicates that one side of the building was specifically reserved for worship by women, "One of these colonnades is assigned to men for their devotions, while the other used by women for the same purpose. However, there is no difference or any distinction between the two, but their very equality and similarity contribute to the beauty and adornment of the church."[32] Paul Silentiarios confirms this arrangement in his description of the Church of Hagia Sophia in 562 after the reconstruction of its collapsed dome, "On either side are the bases of each arcade upheld on twin columns.... Here are the fair galleries for the women."[33] A glimpse of the Great Church enlivened by its sixth-century congregation appears a few lines later, "All the spaces between the Thessalian columns he fences with stone closures upon which the women may lean and rest their laborious elbows."[34] Another passage indicates that women might have used the galleries on both sides of the church, "And whoever mounts up will find that the women's aisles on either side are similar to those below."[35] A sixth-century rhetorician from the Empire's provinces, Chorikios, explains the existence of a women's gallery in the Church of Saint Stephen at Gaza in terms of considered preference and not necessity, "That the female congregation should not be mingled with the men, though there is room enough on the ground for both without crowding, you have constructed a double women's gallery, its length and width equal to those of the aisles below, but somewhat inferior in height."[36] These scraps of literary evidence confirm the boundaries between men and women in early Byzantine church worship. The sexual segregation of the imperial panels presents grandiosely a separation that was a fact of daily life in the more privileged classes.

The empress presided over a ritual life for the female elite of Constantinople that was both separate and distinct from that of male court culture. While the rituals and representation of the male world of Byzantine court ceremony has been examined at length by scholars, the life of the female court remains more elusive. The Church of San Vitale's mosaic magnificently represents the Byzantine empress leading the *sekreton ton gynaikon*, the female court based in the imperial palaces of Constantinople.[37] A pair of eunuchs and two upper-level female courtiers flank the empress. To the far right follow five more women, who lack sufficient rank to warrant the rich detailing lavished on the major figures in the scene. They are differentiated among themselves in several ways; formal qualities such as the degree of the appearance of plastic modeling correlate to their place within the court hierarchy, so those closest to the empress are rendered the most vividly. Other early Byzantine artworks display this gradation of naturalism to differentiate rank. An early icon of the Virgin Mary flanked by saints and angels now in Saint Catherine's Monastery at Mt. Sinai subtly registers degrees of presence by blurring and muting the coloration of the ethereal angels. Thus the images of Theodora, the two eunuchs, and the two women beside her are marked as more important, much as are the central five figures of the opposite panel depicting Justinian and his court. Individuating characteristics mark the most important figures as distinct from the group. This nuance articulates the court hierarchies that structured ceremonial life.

Sources such as the sixth-century text by Peter the Patrician included in the *Book of Ceremonies* suggest the presence of an empress' court during the reign of Justinian and Theodora.[38] As noted above, however, it is difficult to assess historical change in the *Book of Ceremonies*. Even specific ceremonies featuring the *sekreton ton gynaikon*, such as the marriage of the eighth-century Empress Irene the Athenian, are formulated in the present tense to signify the eternal persistence of court ceremony.[39] Whereas Book One of the *Book of Ceremonies* recaps courtly rituals that Constantine Porphyrogennetos found in other written sources, Book Two of the emperor's work moves into the uncharted territory of Byzantine court ceremonial he had heard about or had personally witnessed. The visit of the Russian Princess Olga to Constantinople in 957 fits into this rubric and shows a glimpse of the workings of the later, Middle Byzantine manifestation of the *sekreton ton gynaikon*. Unlike the ceremonies of the first book, described in the present tense, Olga's reception is firmly rooted in a precise moment in the past, specifically September 9, 957. In the palace's Triklinos of Justinian, dual thrones and silver organs were arrayed. Seven successive waves of Byzantine female officials entered in a strict hierarchy, followed by the procession of the Russian female nobility. An intricate waltz of entrances, movements within the palace, and multiple audiences then fill the emperor's account of Olga's visit.[40]

Other Byzantine sources attest to the tenacious tradition of the empress' entourage, but, again, they are largely Middle, rather than early, Byzantine. The tenth-century letters of the Patriarch Nicholas I focus on the role of the empress because of the problems that had arisen in the court when the Emperor Leo VI attempted to validate his fourth marriage. A serious argument for permitting Leo's questionable third marriage had been quite simply that the empress' important ceremonial role was being neglected; the patriarch wrote, "since there must be an Empress (Lady) in the Palace to manage ceremonies affecting the noblewomen, there is a condonation of the third marriage."[41] The women's court could not function without an empress, for key rituals could not happen in her absence. The necessity of maintaining these courtly rituals required occasional exceptions to the norm of the emperor's wife being crowned Augusta. Two Middle Byzantine examples offer further parallels. The Emperor Leo VI (emp. A.D. 886–912) crowned his daughter Anna Augusta during a period between two of his ill-fated marriages.[42] Other instances hint at some flexibility as well, for Theophilos' (emp. 829–42) daughters became Augustae and were rendered on coinage, too.

Ritual defines the *sekreton ton gynaikon*, since its hierarchies and existence as an institution flow from the stately patterns of court ceremony.[43] The way the institution evolved several centuries later reflects tendencies present in the sixth century. At the head of the Middle Byzantine female court was the *zoste patrikia*, Mistress of the Robes, who was appointed by the emperor, but was often related to the empress. Her functions were both ceremonial and practical. The *Book of Ceremonies* repeatedly mentions the *zoste patrikia* in the course of important imperial ceremonies; for example, after the coronation of an empress, she joined the first cohort of officials who greet the empress in her new role.[44] The new *zoste* was promoted in the Church of the Pharos within the imperial palace, and then she received the formulaic greetings of a succession of high dignitaries.[45] Her stature is also reflected in the fact that the *zoste patrikia* was one of six dignitaries who dined at the imperial table. While in exceptional circumstances a woman could be granted this title purely as an honor, usually the status entailed responsibility for the toilette of the empress.[46] Many of the titles of the women in the *sekreton ton gynaikon* correspond to those of the emperor's court, a practice that extends back to the Greek-speaking part of the Roman world.[47] In this way, the Byzantine empress' court diverges from other female institutions, such as the Ottoman harem, which were more defined by a series of relationships to the sultan.[48]

Lead seals record the prominence of some of the early Byzantine female courtiers. Women issued bilateral inscription seals in the sixth and seventh centuries: a seventh-century *hypatissa* named Anna, a sixth- or seventh-century *hypatissa* named Helen, and a sixth- or seventh-century *patrikia* named Domnikia.[49] The *patrikia* Anna issued a seal with an invocative monogram in the ninth or tenth century, and numerous inscribed cruciform monograms were issued by women of the court: a ninth-century Anastasia (imperial cubicularia and *parakoimae*), a ninth- or tenth-century Anna (*patrikia*), from 750–850 an Irene (*hegoumene*), and also from 750–850, Thekla (*protostraterina*).[50]

Knowledge of the funding for the *sekreton ton gynaikon* remains obscure, although a few textual references point to a separate stream of holdings and revenue from that of the emperor's court. In *De administrando imperio*, Constantine Porphyrogennetos mentions a change that made the master of the Augusta's barges the same as that of the Augustus, to avoid divided loyalties.[51] Likewise through the legislation of Justinian we know something of Theodora's holdings. Moving earlier several centuries, even the first Roman Imperial woman, Livia—the wife of Caesar Augustus—received special prerogatives that allowed her full control of her individual property, an authority that enabled her to pursue an independent program of patronage and beneficence.[52]

The dress of the empress and her female courtiers marked their special status. Ramsay MacMullen discussed the importance of rank-specific ostentatious costume as a hallmark of the court in late antiquity.[53] Insignia subtly calibrated office. Thus, in Ravenna, the Empress Theodora's chlamys, which initially functioned as a military cloak, had by the sixth century ossified into an expression of imperial rank.[54] Role, rather than gender, defined these accouterments in the eyes of the Byzantine beholder, so Theodora's chlamys is not as transgressive as Barber implies.[55] The empress on the two ivories in Florence and Vienna discussed in chapter seven also include a chlamys as part of an imperial woman's regalia, and empresses often wear the chlamys on coins. Justinian's chlamys in turn represents his civil, as opposed to military or consular, public identity.[56] Corippus offers a delightfully overwrought literary interpretation of this dress in his description of the Emperor Justin II,

> He stepped out and clothed his pious limbs in a tunic, covering himself with a gilded robe in which he shone out, white all over, and gave off light and dispersed the dusky shadows though the light from the heavens had not yet fully appeared. His calves resound with the shining purple boot. . . . for the royal feet with which the victorious Roman emperor tramples conquered kings and tames barbarian necks. Only emperors, under whose feet is the blood of kings, can adopt this attire. Indeed every mystery is revealed by some specific reasoning. And the sacred robe hung as far as the knee, fitting tightly, white, with a precious border. The chlamys, which was adorned with tawny gold and outdid the sun . . . covered the imperial shoulders in glowing purple.[57]

Likewise the image of the Magi on Theodora's chlamys was part of this shift to a preoccupation with the accouterments of hierarchy in late antiquity, which conforms to the widespread taste for wearing badge-type tokens of insignia.[58] The chlamys of Theodora—unlike that of Justinian—lacks the badge on the hem called a tablion. The tablion on the two empress ivories in Florence and Vienna likewise marks the Augusta's importance. On each ivory, the empress' cloak bears the image of the emperor as consul.

The Magi on the hem of Theodora's cloak show another aspect of imperial status. The meaning of the Magi is disputed in interpretations of the mosaics. Stričevič emphasizes the Magi's offertory nature; Grabar, the overriding imperial associations of the kings.[59] Early Byzantine sources and Coptic remains attest to Christian images on textiles worn by laity, but after Iconoclasm such imagery only appeared on liturgical vestments and cloths.[60] The eighth-century writer Agnellus comments at length on an image of the three Magi in his description of the nearby Church of San

Apollinare Nuovo in Ravenna, and offers an intricate explication of the Magi's robes. Whereas on the "men's side" of that church depictions of male martyrs and Christ are arrayed in mosaics, the other side is decorated with an image of the Virgin Mary, and a procession of holy Christian women and the Magi.[61] The royal connotations of the Magi are strengthened here by the fact that the procession of saints replaced an earlier procession of Theodoric's court. He mentions that his namesake, the sixth-century Bishop Agnellus of Ravenna, decorated the altar cloth with images of both himself and of the Magi, wrought "of marvelous needlework."[62] In the context of sixth-century visual culture in Ravenna, the image of the Magi on Theodora's garment seems all the more appropriate. Not only does the image contain desirable imperial connotations, but also in a local instance the Magi are associated with women.

The presence of eunuchs in the San Vitale mosaic also registers an important part of the *sekreton ton gynaikon*. As beardless, mature men, flaunting all of the marks of their high status, the two men almost certainly represent the elite group of eunuchs who helped administer the empire. One of the highest palace dignities, the position of Praepositus (High Chamberlain) was held by a eunuch, and the empress had her own chamberlain by the fifth century. After the sixth century and by 899, when a Philotheos wrote about court hierarchy, a whole series of offices and honorifics were exclusive to court eunuchs, with more positions open to eunuchs than uncastrated men.[63] Then after centuries in power, eunuchs were marginalized by the Komnenians.[64]

By the sixth century, eunuchs had functioned as an indispensable part of the court since the time of Diocletian. Hence, the two eunuchs in the Church of San Vitale mosaic possess high enough rank to be entitled to wear purple tablia and stand parallel to the female courtiers positioned to the right of Theodora.[65] With the elevation of the emperor and his family through the growing imperial cult, eunuchs established a firm niche as intermediaries between the ruler and the ruled, powerful yet incapable of usurping the throne because of their mutilation.[66] Kathryn Ringrose explored the complexities of eunuchs' status, encountering Byzantine authors such as Gregory of Nazianzos, who reckoned eunuchs a distinct third gender.[67] Other sources lump eunuchs with women into one conceptual category of the feminine gender defined by the absence of the masculine qualities of mental and physical fortitude.[68] Consistently eunuchs minded boundaries in Byzantine society by marshaling the *sekreton ton gynaikon* or in other liminal positions such as preparing cadavers for burial.[69] Most eunuchs were castrated before puberty, an emasculation that rendered them safe for tending the privileged class of medieval women who had slaves.[70] The same reasons of propriety propelled eunuchs to a central role in the education of Byzantine imperial women, and in the integration of foreign princesses into their new milieu, although many eunuchs themselves had foreign origins.[71] As Herrin noted in her study of the training of Byzantine imperial women, Byzantine eunuchs would be sent off to educate these young women destined for a future in the Byzantine court.[72] The existence of the later literary genre the *Mirror of Princes* bespeaks a serious interest in the formation of imperial men, but the training of imperial women to fulfill the rigors of their role seems more happenstance. Psellos fulminates against Basil II and Constantine VIII for their lack of attention to the training of Zoë and Theodora, which left the purple-born princesses inadequately prepared for their roles as empresses.[73] Eunuchs' ambiguous status as a "third sex" made them effective mediators between the two separate courts of the emperor and empress. This relationship signals the balance between the empress and her court and the emperor's retinue. The court life of the empress' women existed—as in the mosaics—parallel to that surrounding the emperor. The empress' court was not a shadow of a male institution, but possessed a distinct identity, representation, and ceremonial functions.

Although this tradition of the *sekreton ton gynaikon* is clearly important, the mosaics' meaning also depends on its specific context in Ravenna, a strategically crucial town. Within the tumultuous history of Ravenna during this period, the imperial portraits affirmed the newly regained Byzantine power in the city. Ravenna served as the Ostrogothic capital of Italy in the late fifth and early sixth centuries. Flourishing under the leadership of Odoacer, the city became an important intellectual and political center. In 540, Justinian's brilliant general, Belisarios, conquered Ravenna for the Byzantine Empire, and it subsequently served as a base for campaigns to reconquer the rest of Italy. The image of the emperor and empress carries juridical force, by bearing the imprimatur of imperial authority to the borders of the Empire.[74] Even little details such as the stubble on Justinian's face communicated this message, for "like the chlamys, it probably represented the idea that they were in service outside the capital-administration as *militia*."[75] In a similar way, the clipeate imperial images on consular diptychs legitimated the authority of the new consul. The mosaics chided the ambivalent population of Ravenna to remember their new status as Byzantine citizens.

Scholars previously assumed that these mosaics could be rather precisely dated between the appointment of Maximian to the episcopal see in 546 and the death of Theodora and the dedication of San Vitale in 548.[76] Maximian appears as an active cultural patron in Ravenna during his episcopate, and his throne still survives as a masterpiece of early Byzantine ivory carving. Maximian is the only figure within the two imperial panels whose name is included in the image, which has been thought to register his local eminence as the first archbishop of Ravenna. Later Agnellus copiously detailed Maximian's patronage at the Cathedral of Ravenna, and records both the church vessels and textiles that he commissioned. The churchman notes that the portrait of Maximian appeared in the cathedral "in two places: one is bigger and the other smaller, but there is no other difference between the two. By the smaller one is an inscription conceived like this: 'Glorify the Lord with me that He has raised me from the dung.'"[77]

Irina Andreescu-Treadgold and Warren Treadgold have now overturned this traditional dating with the discovery that the mosaic work of Maximian's head and the label above it are likely reworked.[78] Since the mosaic tesserae of the bishop's body were not reset, probably the bishop changed and the name was then added above a new portrait head. Therefore, the mosaics that were altered were probably made during the period of Maximian's predecessor, Victor (bishop 537/8–544/5). Victor's episcopal portrait was hardly the only one lost to the tides of fortune. An anecdote in John of Ephesus' *Ecclesiastical History,* tells of when the Bishop John Scholastikos, Patriarch of Constantinople from 565 to 577, "intoxicated and drunken with power, took down and erased all of the pictures of the orthodox fathers, and fixed up his own everywhere in their place."[79] No reshaping was detected in the Theodora mosaic, so her panel was probably made during the initial phase of manufacture as well. Sabine MacCormack suggested that the mosaic is actually a postmortem commemorative image of the empress, which would put its manufacture after 548.[80] This interpretation gives the architectural setting a different range of meanings than that discussed above. The curtained doorway would in this hypothesis represent the passage from the world of the living to that of the dead; the fountain, a fount of life like those in the Galla Placidia's Mausoleum.[81] MacCormack's innovative interpretation cannot be accepted, however, in light of the refinement in dating based on the Treadgold's technical analysis, which places the mosaic's creation several years before Theodora died.

Thus the Ravenna mosaic was made while the Empress Theodora still thrived far away in Constantinople. Just as in the case of the more generic steelyard weights, the crown of Theodora most clearly announces her imperial status. Her crown has long prependoulia as well as three jeweled projections on top. This elaborate headpiece originated in the snood surmounted by a diadem first worn by imperial women in the late antique period.[82] The mid-fifth-century solidi of Licinia Eudoxia show some of the San Vitale crown characteristics, for she wears a diadem with multiple projections and prependoulia that reach her shoulders (see figure 2.9). Jewels magnify Theodora's importance; her earrings and necklace complement the lavishness of her crown.

Furthermore, like Justinian, Theodora is honored with a halo in the imperial mosaics of the Church of San Vitale. Many examples survive from later Byzantine history of haloed empresses, the manuscript Paris gr. 510 and the image of John II Komnenos and Irene in the south galleries of Hagia Sophia are just a few well-known instances (see figure 6.4). The impression of her real presence is made abstract through the connotations of the halo, for "it signified that the haloed individual, person or place, participated also in a category of 'Time' which was different from the one determining the natural life on earth as the medieval mind understood it."[83] The medieval ruler was assumed to have two bodies, a mystical prototypic essence in addition to his or her earthly presence. The halo represented this concept of the imperial person as the incarnation of an eternal ideal of kingship descending from God. The official program of her representation both in textual and visual form asserted the disembodied, idealized presence of Theodora. These haloes evoke a liminal aspect to the role of the imperial beings represented, for they place the emperor and his consort firmly in the role of mediators between the viewer and the divine. Only incidentally do they depict the people named Justinian and Theodora, for, as Kantorowicz noted,

> The halo ... referred ... to the imperial power as such which was considered perpetual and sempiternal and, therewith, venerable and holy also in the Christian sense, regardless, of course, of the presence or absence of venerable or holy qualities in the individual bearer of the diadem. It indicated the bearer and executive of perpetual power derived from God and made the emperor the incarnation of some kind of 'prototype' which, being immortal, was *sanctus,* regardless of the personal character, *or even the sex,* of its constituent. (Author's italics)[84]

Individual attributes of the ruler were irrelevant, so that being female did not exclude Theodora from being marked as a mystical body.

Ceremony also played an inherent part of the promulgation of imperial ideology. The emperor and empress participated in an orderly cycle of rites that reflected the transcendent patterns and cycles of the cosmos. Repetitions of events such as the offering elevated its participants, so ritual served as a tool to enhance the "sacral" identity of the imperial person.[85] Reenactments affirmed *taxis,* the Byzantine sense of fundamental order to the world.[86] The disembodied, idealized presence of Theodora is asserted throughout the official program of her representation both in textual and visual form. The representation in San Vitale was heavily laden with traditional resonances of imperial authority, every detail magnifying her importance.

fig. 6.4. South gallery, mosaic of Emperor John II Komnenos and Empress Irene with the Virgin Mary and Child, A.D. 1118–34 Church of Hagia Sophia, Istanbul, Turkey.

This weight of tradition entailed that the imperial image was part of establishing identity and authority. Not surprisingly, then, Byzantine writers mention several prominent public images of the Empress Theodora in and near Constantinople, and possibly one or two sculpted representations of Theodora survive.[87] As we have seen, the stamp of her patronage filled a wide sweep and extended to the fringes of the sixth-century Byzantine Empire.

Theodora's image celebrated recent military triumphs in an elaborate mosaic on the Chalke Gate, the locus of a major artery in Constantinople in the sixth century. Elegantly rendered from the Greek name as the "Brazen House," this gate served as the main entrance to the imperial palace.[88] Like so much of this central area of the capital city, the existing structure built by the Emperor Anastasios was destroyed during the Nika Riot then rebuilt by Justinian. On the ceiling of the interior of the Chalke Gate, Prokopios describes:

> The Emperor and the Empress Theodora, both seeming to rejoice and to celebrate the victories over both the King of the Vandals and the King of the Goths, who approach them as prisoners of war to be led into bondage. Around them stands the Roman Senate, all in festal mood. This spirit is expressed by the cubes of the mosaic, which by their colors depict exultation on their very countenances.[89]

The presence of the vanquished Visigoths in this image puts its production squarely after 540.[90] Just as in the case of the imperial mosaic panels in Ravenna, its meaning both resonates with specific historical circumstances and conveys a broader message of eternally triumphant imperial power.[91] Thus in a secular context the empress Theodora could also be included as a joint emblem of imperial authority. The Chalke image descends from a tradition of imperial victory images that includes such monuments as the column of Arkadios.[92] Similar imperial victory images also covered the ceilings of the dome of Saint George in Thessalonike and the Orthodox Baptistery in Ravenna.[93]

Prokopios describes another official representation of Theodora slightly later in the *Buildings* at the conclusion of his discussion of the public bath called the Arkadianae. The historian renders an idyllic park located outside of the capital city. Marble pavements, columns, and statues lay along the seaside. Though he claims that the sculptures were all extraordinarily beautiful—so fine, in fact, that they could be mistaken for the work of Phidias, Lysippos, or Praxiteles—his flattery singles out for further comment only the statue of the empress: "There also the Empress Theodora stands upon a column, which the city in gratitude for the court dedicated to her. The statue is indeed beautiful, but still inferior to the beauty of the Empress... the column is purple, and it clearly declares even before one sees the statue that it bears an Empress."[94] Prokopios' description lingers on the sculpture's imperial marker, the fact that the column was purple, the color reserved for the Byzantine imperial house.

Further afield, the Church of Saint John at Selçuk near Ephesus, which was grandly rebuilt by Justinian, may have depicted Justinian and Theodora. All that survives is an inscription that describes an image of Saint John the Theologian crowning Justinian and Theodora: Ἰουστινιανόν τε καὶ ἠγαθέην Θεοδώρην στέψεν Ἰωάννης Χπισοῦ ἐφημοσύναις.[95]

The *Parastaseis Syntomoi Chronikai*, describes a statue of Theodora and Justinian next to the Baths of Zeuxippos in Constantinople. This mention crops up in a rambling catalog of the noteworthy sculpture of Constantinople, so it merely says: "When it was erected, Justinian was showered with praise, the Greens [a circus faction] chanting: 'Justinian and Constantine the new apostles.' Also there was Sophia his wife [*sic*] who received praise through the iambic verses of the philosopher Plumbas."[96] Due to contradictions within the text, however, the *Parastaseis* editors Judith Herrin and Averil Cameron suggest this reference may refer to an image of the Empress Sophia.[97]

A surviving fragment of sculpture in Milan's Castello Sforzesco may suggest the appearance of such a statue of Theodora (see figures 6.5 and 6.6).[98] Found inside the Milanese medieval wall, on stylistic grounds this piece is usually attributed to sixth-century Constantinople.[99] The face is quite slender, with relatively large, heavy-lidded eyes compared to the small rounded chin and little mouth. The distinctive crown comprises a pearl- and jewel-laden diadem encircling a snooded hairstyle. Within the study of comparable sculpture portraits of Byzantine empresses, the headdress type is not known to predate ca. 500 in any confirmed examples.[100] The lack of prependoulia has more recently been used to ascribe this piece to the early fifth century, since Licinia Eudoxia already has shoulder-length prependoulia in her numismatic depictions (see figures 2.9 and 2.10). Although not apparent in some published photographs, with first hand observation and in this book's figure one can see on the sides the circular indentations that indicate where prependoulia would have been attached. Diadem types cannot be used to date the sculpture with great precision, for, as Wessel noted, even within the cluster of representations of Ariadne from a few years on the consular diptychs we see different types of headpieces being worn by the empress.[101]

The identification of the Milan sculpture with the Empress Theodora remains uncertain; its foundation comes from the supposed likeness of the marble head with the empress' mosaic in San Vitale.[102] The image of the

fig 6.5. Front view, marble head, early Byzantine empress, found in Milan, Castello Sforzesco, Milan, Italy.

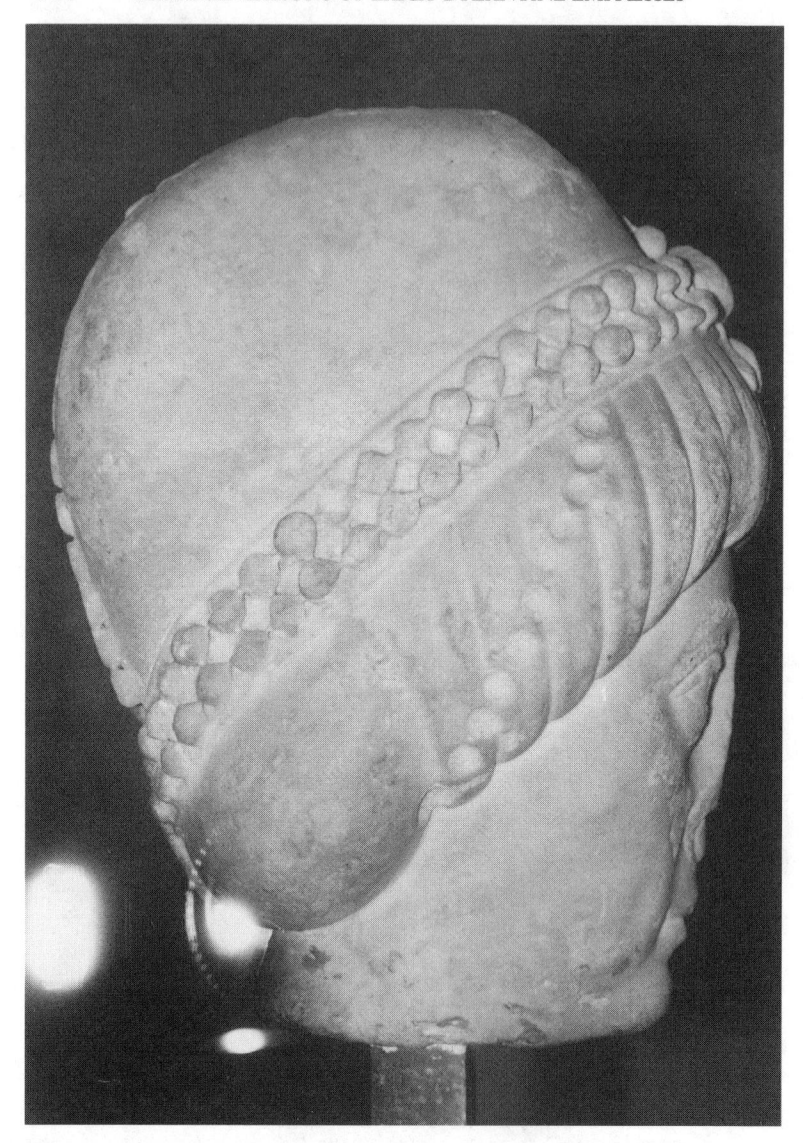

fig. 6.6. Side view, marble head, early Byzantine empress, found in Milan, Castello Sforzesco, Milan, Italy.

empress in Ravenna was not intended to be a precise portrait, for it bore a heavier weight in the iconographic program than the documentation of an individual's appearance. Given the idealized nature of both the marble sculpture and the mosaic, their superficial correspondence does not seem very conclusive. Despite the uncertainties of dealing with sculpture of this era in which attributions often range over one or two centuries, one author in his identification of the Milan head as Theodora went so far as to assert that it is "convincing not only as to physical similarity but psychological truth as well."[103] For lack of more substantive proof, it is difficult to maintain that it depicts Theodora instead of another eminent woman, such as Galla Placidia or one of the other identifications sometimes made for this work. Whereas in the Roman Imperial period a broader cross-section of women had marble portraits, in late antiquity very few non-imperial women had such an honor.[104] The Metropolitan Museum possesses one of the rare examples of such a sculpture of a woman without the trappings of office; this fine marble work dated to the Justinianic era represents a woman holding a scroll (see figure 2.14).[105]

Representations of the empress function emblematically rather than as portraits of an individual. Imperial images seem iconic and cultic as Gilbert Dagron has noted, "In contrast to an artistic portrait, a cult image is an image of consensus, a normalized image."[106] These "portraits" present a complex, and sometimes contradictory, sense of verisimilitude. Byzantine sources routinely compliment portraits for their strength of likeness to the individual represented. The portrait of Phillipikos in the ancient bath of Zeuxippos is extolled for its visual veracity, "As the story goes, it is just like its model. Painters greatly praised the artist, because he did not depart from the emperor's appearance with regard to the archetype."[107] The force of rhetoric propelling these statements, though, reflects a strong current from antiquity that undercuts the meaning, for Byzantine writers adopted some ancient conventions of ekphrasis in their insistence on the verism of an artwork.[108]

If the sculpture's attribution to Theodora is accepted, the statue presumably was installed in Milan during the early 540s, that is, fairly soon after the devastating massacre of its citizens in 539 performed by the Ostrogoths to punish the city for its allegiance to the Byzantine Empire. This timing coincides with the Ravenna mosaics, when newly won Byzantine rule in North Italy demanded visual articulation. Official statues of Byzantine emperors and empresses served as the actual embodiment of imperial authority in these distant reaches of the empire. For example, during the "Riot of the Statues" in Antioch in A.D. 387, mobs dragged statues of the imperial couple, Theodosios and Flaccilla, through the streets, "albeit not without elegance and their usual wit," Zosimos tells us.[109] The grave implications of this elegant insurrection were clear, and the emperor threatened to destroy the city entirely by burning as punishment. The custom of destroying honorific statues persists as long as they are still erected in the Empire.[110] During late antiquity imperial images could possess a very palpable link to the ruler. Saint Basil expresses the sense of identity between image and original, "The imperial image, too, is called the emperor, and yet there are not two emperors: neither is the power cut asunder nor is the glory divided."[111] During the Iconoclast controversy, Saint Theodore the Stoudite parallels the image of Christ and the image of the emperor,

> Take the example of a signet ring engraved with the imperial image, and let it be impressed upon wax, pitch and clay. The impression is one and the same and the several materials which, however, are different with respect to each other; yet it would not have remained identical unless it were entirely unconnected with the materials. . . . The same applies to the likeness of Christ, irrespective of the material upon which it is represented.[112]

No coins survive with the image of Theodora, although Justinian issued coins copiously. During the fourth and fifth centuries, the empress was often not depicted on coinage until she had given birth to an heir, but this generalization made by Grierson will be reconsidered in the next chapter.[113] A lead seal survives possibly issued by Empress Theodora.[114] A standing eagle encircled by a wreath border fills the obverse, and the reverse side has a cruciform monogram very similar to those appearing on the columns in the nave of the church of Hagia Sophia considered below. As noted above, other women at the time used lead seals in their correspondence and business transactions, so this lead seal may not belong to the Empress Theodora, but instead to another woman with the same popular name.

We have an example in the early seventh century that shows direct influence from the lofty world of the gold mosaics of the Church of San Vitale down to the world of ordinary coinage. A local mint, Ravenna, conformed the Empress Martina's representation to the ostentatious image of the Empress Theodora that loomed large in the local church. The Emperor Heraklios married Martina in 613/14. This second marriage of the emperor was wildly unpopular from the beginning, for his new bride was also his niece. Michael the Syrian inveighs: "Meanwhile Heraklios redoubled his acts of impiety. He married, while already an advanced age, Martina, the daughter of his brother, by which he had Heraklonas, child of iniquity."[115]

Martina appeared only on bronze coinage. An example from the capital shows the emperor standing in the center with his son, Heraklios Constantine, on the right and Martina on his right (see figure 6.7).[116] All three imperial figures carry a *globus cruciger* and wear a chlamys and a crown surmounted by a cross, but Martina's crown is slightly different from that worn by her male counterparts. The empress' crown has a loop on both sides of the cross on top as well as the characteristic prependoulia dropping down to her shoulders. Because of the more imprecise striking of bronze coinage as well as the more extensive wear it generally received, the subtle

fig. 6.7. Overstruck follis, bronze, Obverse: Heraklios (center), Heraklios Constantine (right), and Martina (left), Reverse: Denomination mark M, A.D. 615–24, Constantinople mint, Dumbarton Oaks, Washington, D.C. (DOC II, 1.96).

details of the regalia are no longer visible on many extant examples.[117] The common practice of overstriking magnifies the problem. When power shifted to a new ruler, the Byzantine mints would often reuse previously struck flans of the predecessor, casually imprinting the new die over that of his predecessor. Numerous examples of Heraklios' early follis overstrike those of Phokas, and these juxtaposed imprints on the metal create an often indecipherable mess.[118]

Regional mints sometimes strayed from the capital's norm. Thus at the mint of Ravenna, Martina's image is transformed by the local frame of reference. The Ravenna mint created a new obverse type for its Class 4 follis issued in 616/617–625/626 (see figure 6.8).[119] The familiar composition shows the two men in a loros and a crown with a cross. Martina, however, is depicted in a different manner than her image on coins issued by other mints. On the Ravennate coin, the empress bears a crown with three pinnacles and long prependoulia on each side. Her robe is clearly jeweled over a circular piece draping over her shoulders. Although Martina's crown and garment differ from her other numismatic representations, they have a close parallel—the image of the Empress Theodora at the nearby Church of San Vitale in Ravenna. The cramped surface of the coin with three busts squeezed onto the obverse does not allow for the level of detail permitted by the expansive apse wall, but to the extent that it was possible the local diecutter adapted the contemporary standard promulgated by Constantinople to the local sense of imperial representation based on the mosaic image from a century earlier. In addition to mimicking the three protuberances on the top, the seventh-century diecutter also graced the coin image with the same long prependoulia that also hang from the sixth-century empress' crown depicted in mosaic. Despite noting that "Martina's

fig. 6.8. Follis, bronze, Obverse: bust images of Heraklios (center), Heraklios Constantine (right), and Martina (left), Reverse: Denomination mark M, A.D. 616/17, Ravenna mint, Dumbarton Oaks, Washington, D.C. (DOC II, 1.289a2).

crown, with its long prependulia, is very carefully designed," Grierson (along with other numismatists) did not draw this parallel with the local mosaic depiction of an empress that influenced local artisans.[120] The bejeweled garment imitates Theodora's resplendent apparel, to the extent that three large jewels are similarly disposed across the upper sweep of her clothing. The mint of the coin is certain, for the reverse clearly bears the letters RAV for Ravenna in the exergue. In a roundabout way, a numismatic representation of Theodora was belatedly invented in the seventh century. The representation of the Empress Martina conveyed greater weight since no empresses were then represented on coinage until the ascendancy of the Empress Irene in the late eighth century.

This assimilation of imagery from a gold mosaic in a church to an ordinary bronze coin illustrates the degree of reciprocity amongst categories of the imperial image often kept separate by modern distinctions between "high culture" and the objects of everyday life. It is also important precisely because it is an example from the provinces, and gives us a rare glimpse of how the imperial imagery produced in Constantinople could be adapted in the hinterlands. Martina's shifting representation on bronze coinage underscores why numismatic imagery can help us understand the historical significance of two imperial representations on ivory plaques in the next chapter. Just as the die-cutters of Ravenna adjusted their representation of

fig. 6.9. Consular diptych of Justinus, A.D. 540, Staatliche Museen zu Berlin, Germany (6367).

the empress to conform to local expectations, the sixth-century imperial ivories utilize the same imagery as the official currency to articulate the unusual status of Sophia that warranted her enthronement.

This continuity is also illustrated by the consular diptych of Justinus in the Staatliche Museen in Berlin, which includes the image of Theodora following the tradition that represented Ariadne on official ivories (see figure 6.9).[121] Justinus was the son of Germanos, a nephew of Justinian, who rose to the office of *consul ordinarius* in 540.[122] The consular diptych of Justinus represents the final moment of this illustrious tradition of official arts—for with the end of the consulship the need for this particular kind of display disappeared in 541.[123] The role of the consul during these last years seems in flux, Justinian's Novel 105 from 536 grants consuls the right of silver largesse, though gold remained an imperial privilege. The Berlin ivory's length of 33.5 centimeters is shorter than many of the late diptychs, for, as Anthony Cutler has observed, the typical size range at this period was 38–40 centimeters.[124] Justinus' diptych is also slightly thicker than many comparable pieces, which may account for its worn surface.[125] A medallion portrait on the upper right-hand side of both panels depicts Theodora, wearing the regalia familiar from her image in the mosaic at the Church of San Vitale. Time has effaced the finer details, but her crown with side prependoulia is legible. On the left panel, her miniature ivory portrait also renders an ornate, broad band around her neck that is reminiscent of Theodora's bejeweled neckpiece in the San Vitale mosaic. Actual examples of such finery survive, such as the early seventh-century gold, pearl, emerald, and sapphire necklace in the Staatliche Museen in Berlin.[126]

Whereas this diptych in Berlin marks the end of the tradition of the diptychs, it also innovates. For between the clipeate portraits of Justinian and Theodora both panels depict Christ. André Grabar considers this unassuming cluster of three roundel portraits the beginning of the longstanding tradition in Byzantine art of depicting the imperial couple flanking Christ.[127] The apse of the Church of San Vitale, executed only a few years later, echoes this composition. A splendid Christ rules from the center of the apse, where he sits atop a blue orb; lower and obscurely placed, the two imperial panels flank the youthful god, the Byzantine court subordinated to its source of power.

CHAPTER 7

THE EMPRESS SOPHIA: AUTHORITY AND IMAGE IN AN ERA OF CONFLICT

> *When the Emperor Justin went out of his mind and was realized to be insane, the Empire was ruled by the Empress Sophia, who assumed sole power.*
>
> —Gregory of Tours, History of the Franks, v.19

Scholarship has largely bypassed the Empress Sophia, the wife of Justinian's successor, the Emperor Justin II. Although the most basic communication of the imperial house—the crudely struck bronze coins that circulated throughout the Empire—presented her with unprecedented force and distinction, these modest units lack the glamour of the lavish mosaics in the Church of San Vitale. Likewise the reign of Justin II and Sophia did not have the mixed blessing of a historian of genius such as Prokopios; their era was instead chronicled by an array of uninspiring courtiers such as Corippus. A far-flung assembly of other authors, such as John of Ephesus in the eastern end of the empire and Gregory of Tours remote in the west, contribute as well to our conception of the period. These writers mete out the basic outline of this reign, but our understanding lacks the vividness and depth of our sense of the Justinianic era. Averil Cameron, in pendant articles appearing in the journal *Byzantion*, produced the main overview, and Lynda Garland offers some coverage of the Empress Sophia, who has otherwise been neglected in scholarship to a surprising extent given her preeminence in the sixth century.[1]

We do not even know the precise dates bracketting Sophia's life, and are left with the vague assumption that she was born before A.D. 530 and died sometime after 601, when she disappears from the texts. Sophia was the niece of the Empress Theodora; her husband, the nephew of Justinian.[2] Her close familial ties to Justinian and Theodora probably enhanced Justin II's claim to the throne in addition to augmenting her credibility as a ruler during Justin's later illness, an eminence registered by her adoption of the by then old-fashioned prefix Aelia.[3] Justin II in fact succeeded his uncle Justinian in 565 through the efforts of court insiders, and retained office until his death in 578. In part because of her own strength and in part because of her husband's gradual debilitation through mental illness, Sophia emerged as the imperial decision maker later in the reign. Her political importance finds voice in the numismatic record as well as imperial commissions of the reign. After first analyzing the content and form of the textual record of Sophia's co-rule in light of the rich history of previous imperial women, we will consider her representation on coins, a votive cross now in the Vatican collections, and ivory.

The historical circumstances surrounding her ascent to the throne with Justin II and her reign frame subsequent events. The panegyric of Corippus praising the Emperor Justin II firmly plants Sophia at the center of court life as he describes the accession of Justin II and Sophia. The court rhetoric sketches a domestic scene punctuated with a theatrical interruption:

> The royal pair loved this place [the Sophiae palace];[4] from it they used to watch the waves in the strait and the curving ships carrying all the trade of two worlds. Here it was that the chosen emperor had risen from the soft bedcovers and was sitting in a remote corner telling his beloved wife what had been revealed to him. While he was speaking and turning over his anxiety with his pious wife, the senators entered the threshold with gloomy faces. Their appearance showed the state of affairs with the utmost clarity. Justin and Sophia rose quickly and leaving their conversation and their seats they came to the middle of the room.[5]

Justinian was dead. The flattery oozes forth, while Corippus claims that Justin "controlled the most important parts of the kingdom . . . [Justinian] achieved nothing without [Justin's] aid."[6]

After elaborate and insincere protestations, Justin assumes the throne. Sophia accompanied him, although "not this time accompanied by her usual crowd."[7] Sophia orchestrated part of the funeral proceedings, commissioning an elaborate funeral pall.[8] The Empress Sophia's preeminence in Corippus' poem may derive from a simple but important fact—she seems to be the patron of the work.[9] In the midst of Book Three, Corippus steps out of the narrative flow and directly addresses the empress: "Divine and propitious empress, holy and venerable name, immortal good, the wisdom of our tongue, I dedicate this to your auspices; look upon me as I sing your wishes...."[10] To curry his patron's favor, even the construction of the Church of Hagia Sophia (Holy Wisdom), comes to presage Sophia's reign: "Theodora was on the throne at the time when its founder established the holy citadel, and the citadel won the name of Sophia, who was not yet ruling; that was a sign that the sceptre would be hers.... We can see in vivid light that the empire was long ago promised to the pious Justin and Sophia by heavenly gift...."[11] This wordplay on the meaning of the Greek word "sophia" (wisdom) recalls the similar literary conceit deployed to honor the Theodosian Empress Eudokia. As mentioned in chapter one, Malalas recounts Eudokia similarly toying with the meaning of her name to proclaim her largesse. Corippus' elegant account of the coronation mirrors the honors and actions of the emperor and empress. Antiphonal chanting by the crowds echoed extravagant claims for the two rulers, so that the acclamations wishing Justin a long life are matched by "as many praises for the Empress Sophia."[12] Janet Nelson has discussed in a very incisive essay how this sense of election and consent, rather than coronation, were really the constitutive elements of Byzantine imperial inauguration.[13]

The accession of Justin and Sophia to the throne was not the seamless transition that Corippus is so eager to represent. No text indicates that Justinian had formally designated Justin as his successor, despite the intricate attempt by the panegyrist to suggest that appearance.[14] Rivals such as another Justin were supposedly eliminated by Sophia to clear the path for her husband.[15] Corippus recounts that Sophia was coronated the same day as Justin, indicating some parity from the beginning. Michael the Syrian attributes Monophysite beliefs to Sophia: "The Empress Sophia was raised in orthodoxy (Monophysitism) and took communion with Andrew, her priest. One time she undertook to come to a church of the partisans of Chalcedon and there, the Virgin appeared to her and said to her, 'My daughter, why have you abandoned me and come amongst heretics?'"[16] John of Ephesus furthermore claims that Sophia was an ardent Monophysite since her youth, and that her conversion to orthodoxy in the 560s was merely to expedite her husband's political aspirations.[17] The assertion seems like a bit of wishful thinking given Sophia's later enthusiasm for the persecution of Monophysites.[18] This pattern of suspect orthodoxy of imperial women repeats persistent rumors about Theodora's loyalty to the Monophysite cause. Likewise, in the period of Iconoclasm in the eighth and ninth centuries, a recurring motif in Iconoclast literature imputes that women were particularly susceptible to the heresy of icon-worship.[19] It is a commonplace even in the western medieval tradition that women and children were "more gullible and easily deceived by images."[20] In other accounts of her reign, such as—not surprisingly—the panegyric of Corippus, Sophia's orthodoxy remains incontestable, for she duly matches Justin's prayers at the Church of the Archangel with her worship at a church dedicated to the Virgin Mary.[21]

The toponymics of Constantinople also show Sophia's importance in the public image of the reign. Corippus' poem *De laudibus Iustini Minoris* advances the most information regarding the Sophiae palace, and it is the location of Sophia and Justin II when they heard the news of the Emperor Justinian's demise in 565.[22] This palace was built on the western shore of the Propontis. Theophanes also claims a new palace across the Bosporos honored Sophia in 568: "He began to build the palace of Sophianae, named after his wife Sophia, on the pretext that before he had become emperor and while he was still *curopalates* his son Justus had been buried there in the Church of the Archangel in that area. He decorated it with a variety of expensive marbles."[23] Theophanes the Confessor confuses the dating of the palace, for he later notes that "the emperor Tiberios built the palace that is by the harbour of Julian and named it after Sophia, the wife of Justin."[24] In addition to the Sophiae and the Sophianae, Cameron also distinguishes a third palace, which John of Ephesus records in the northwestern part of the city.[25] The palace on the Bosporos had been dated based on Theophanes to 568, but Cameron's slightly earlier date of this palace in 565 seems more plausible.[26] Theophanes notes, too, that Justin "restored the public bath of the Tauros and named it Sophianai after his wife Sophia."[27] The scale of high-profile commissions named after Sophia was unprecedented, although Pulcheria's palace, for example, seems to have given her name to an area of Constantinople, the Pulcherianiai. Reminders of Sophia's importance were pervasive, for her image blanketed the common coinage while her name echoed throughout the Byzantine capital's monuments. Just as her name marked these major constructions in Constantinople, statues of the empress formed part of the city's fabric. A gold statue of Sophia punctuated the Milion, the central artery of the city that linked the public areas. A poem by Agathias in the *Greek Anthology* refers to a portrait of the "divine Pair" in the palace built by Galla Placidia in Constantinople.[28] Because the life of Agathias (ca. 532–580) spanned two reigns, this could refer to a double portrait of Justinian and Theodora or one of Justin II and Sophia. The new port of Sophia also commemorated the imperial couple with a pair of statues linked to others of the imperial house, to name just a few examples of her public statuary. Her image was paralleled by inscriptions, for on the Mevlevihane Kapı (Rhesion Gate) Sophia is credited along with Justin II in the Gate's restoration early in their reign.[29]

An incident related by John of Ephesus bespeaks Sophia's capacities as a patron. Justin II initiated building a monumental pharos, a huge pillar, in the Baths of Zeuxippos, but died before it was finished. The question of its completion precipitated "a quarrel between Tiberios and Sophia: for she bade him to undertake it; but he said, 'I shall do nothing of the sort; for it is your duty to finish it.'"[30] Tiberios takes for granted that Sophia could and should undertake major building commissions in the capital.

In addition, Greek documentary papyri from Egypt consistently link Sophia with Justin II in their oath formulae Ἰουστίνου Νέου καὶ Αἰλίας Σοφίας τῶν αἰωνίων Αὐγούστων Αὐτοκρατόρων [To the Emperor Justin the Younger (Justinian) and Empress Sophia].[31] Five of the six papyri collected by Worp conjoin Sophia with Justin II in their texts, although neither Ariadne nor Theodora are mentioned in the oaths of Anastasios or Justinian.[32] After the precedent set by Sophia, imperial women such as Anastasia, Constantina, and Flavia continued to be routinely included in these documents.[33] Similarly legal Edicts and Novels were disseminated under the names of both Justin and Sophia.[34]

As one might expect given her high public profile, evidence survives of Sophia's influence in financial and political affairs. Sophia shaped financial policy by orchestrating a major remission of debt, according to Theophanes the Confessor: "Sophia, the most pious Augusta, summoned the bankers and money-lenders and ordered that the contracts and receipts of debtors be brought. Having read them, she took the receipts and handed them over to the debtors and repaid the amounts to their owners. For this she was greatly praised by the whole city."[35] Some scholars have suggested that Theophanes garbled his account at this point, and actually describes Justin II's settling of loans taken by Justinian.[36] Further anecdotal information about Sophia survives, such as the story of a spat between her and the eunuch general Narses.[37] When he was recalled from leadership in Italy, the Empress Sophia supposedly sent him a distaff with the churlish remark that he should now return to the women's quarters where he belonged.[38] This insult had far-reaching implications, for Narses was so infuriated that he thereupon invited the Lombards into Italy. Recent editors of Theophanes, however, discount this tale.[39] The nastiness of Sophia's insult derives from several layers of misogyny, but the notion that women, like eunuchs, were defective forms of men puts force behind the imputation.[40] Sophia also stepped into the complex negotiations of the Byzantine Empire with the Persians, and brokered a deal through her own emissary to the foreign court.

The most serious problem to arise during the reign of Justin and Sophia, however, was not the impending military crisis on the frontiers of the Empire, but the diminishing mental capacity of the Emperor Justin

II.[41] The most severe problems beset the emperor following the crushing loss to the Persians in November 573, yet Justin held the throne, at least in name, until his death in 578.[42] Theophanes the Confessor narrates a pathetic incident of the emperor's loss of faculty, when he "fell ill and became vexed with his own brother Badouarios, whom he insulted to the utmost, commanding the *cubicularii* to eject him during a *silentium* while pummeling him with their fists." Sophia cajoled the emperor to repent; finally the contrite emperor went to his brother, "who fled from corner to corner." The emperor's state was blamed on "the work of the devil."[43] News of Justin's impaired condition spread as far as Gaul, for Gregory of Tours matter-of-factly notes: "When the Emperor Justin went out of his mind and was realized to be insane, the Empire was ruled by the Empress Sophia, who assumed sole power."[44] Although scholars previously thought Gregory of Tours relied on ambassadors for his information, Averil Cameron argues persuasively that a written source, perhaps a Byzantine chronicle, inspired him here.[45]

John of Ephesus, our fullest source for Justin II's reign, recounts with frank delight the emperor's madness. His account is framed in the manner we have seen earlier in Prokopios, when that historian's story of the downfall of the ruler claimed to edify: "that those may fear who in future times shall be girt with high and princely power . . . that the dread judgment of God upon king Justin may be recorded."[46] John imputes the emperor in classic fashion with a long list of crimes: killing the innocent, harboring greed, and, most tellingly, persecuting the author's fellow Monophysites.[47] The wrath of God on the emperor was harsh, for our Syriac writer takes great pains to describe the emperor's many degradations from his illness. With his unsympathetic viewpoint, John dwells particularly on the behaviors that dehumanize the ruler or belittle him in the class structure. Thus Justin "uttered cries of various animals, and barked like a dog, and bleated like a goat; and then he would mew like a cat, and then again crow like a cock."[48] Likewise he portrays Justin standing at the window of the palace blaring out, "like those who go about hawking pottery, 'Who'll buy my pans?'"[49]

One of the most interesting aspects of John of Ephesus' account of Justin's madness is the way he describes Sophia's reaction to her husband's precipitous decline. Strangely he claims that rather than meet her husband's illness with dismay she "was rather elated, and said, 'The kingdom came through me, and it has come back to me: and as for him, he is chastised, and has fallen into this trial on my account, because he did not value me sufficiently, and vexed me.'"[50] The element of her statement concerning the transmission of power confirms the impression of Gregory of Tours, who spoke of Sophia as having "sole power." The rest of Sophia's statement also corroborates our sense (and apparently her sense) of her importance, although the claim that the empire came through her cannot be substantiated from our other surviving sources. If her claim had basis, it may explain why she was prominent on coinage from the beginning of their reign. John of Ephesus matches her explanation of the emperor's illness with a reiteration of his definition of the problem. In fact, others felt she had "spoken wickedly," for clearly Justin's problems had originated in his immoral behavior as ruler.[51]

The peculiar circumstances of a debilitated emperor created the need to appoint the young general Tiberios Caesar on 7 December 574. Although James has argued that early Byzantine empresses were the "vice-president" for the emperor, Sophia's authority was exceptional and the outcome of bizarre circumstances. The perceived need for Tiberios' appointment undercuts what would have been James' best example of the idea of an empress as a permanent understudy to the emperor.[52] Many of our references to Sophia relate to the difficulties with the transition to Tiberios. Gregory Abu'l-Faraj claims that during the last four years of Justin's enfeebled rule, Sophia would not allow Tiberios' wife to join her husband in Constantinople. The point of contention arose because only one Augusta was viable at a given time: "Justin blamed her, saying, 'Tiberios is a young man and his body cannot endure chastity, and yet thou keepest his wife from him,' Sophia said, 'My mind hath not perished like thine that I should give my sovereignty to another whilst I am still alive.'"[53] Sophia's tenacity reminds us of Theodora's purported declaration during the Nika Revolt, in which an empress stands resolute in the face of her wavering emperor.[54]

This transition of Byzantine rule from Justin II to Tiberios possessed momentous significance in sources such as Gregory Abu'l-Faraj. This thirteenth-century Syriac chronicler sees the reign of Tiberios as the end of the kingdom of the Romans, and the beginning of the kingdom of the Greeks:

> After Justinus Tiberios ruled three years. Up to this time all the kings had been Rhômâyê, that is to say Frangâyê, the first of whom was Augustus and the last Justinus. Although the tongue of the citizens and the men of law (or, scribes) was Greek, the kings and soldiers were Franks. But with this Tiberios, and onwards, the beginning of the Second Kingdom of the Greeks (Yâwnâyê) took place.[55]

With the passing of the triad of Justin I, Justinian, and Justin II—a solidly Latin-speaking lineage—an era ended for the Byzantine Empire.

The change in power following the death of Justin II tested the boundaries of a newly-widowed Sophia's authority. An incident in John of Ephesus' *Ecclesiastical History* indicates her extensive prerogatives. John relates that after the death of her husband Justin II,

Sophia gave no signs of changing her residence, and he [Tiberios] was unwilling to dispossess her, and she would not permit him to reside with her, he was in great difficulties, as the space allotted to him had always been of the narrowest description, and now that he was sole master, and had been joined by his wife and two daughters, was altogether inadequate to his wants. As he would not therefore oppose or annoy queen Sophia, by taking up residence in the palace itself, he was compelled to remodel the whole of the northern side.[56]

John of Ephesus also indicates that Sophia prevented the court of women from attending Tiberios' wife, Ino.[57] The way in which the incident is recounted makes clear that it contravened the expected protocols of Byzantine court life in the sixth century. The motivation for this supposedly peevish display is usually attributed to Sophia's jealousy arising from her unsuccessful attempt to have Tiberios divorce Ino and marry herself. Theophanes the Confessor reiterates the story of Sophia's supposed romantic interests in Tiberios: "She wanted to marry Tiberios and remain Augusta, but she did not know he had a wife. Some said that even during Justin's lifetime, she had taken Tiberios as her lover and had persuaded Justin to make him Caesar. But Tiberios brought in Anastasia.... He crowned her Augusta and distributed a large amount as consular largess."[58] Theophanes details Tiberios' subsequent care of the dowager queen: "He established her [in the Sophiai palace], granted her cubicularii for her own service, commanded that she be honored as his mother, built her a bath and every other amenity."[59] Although the romantic motif of the foolish older woman besotted by a younger man is often emphasized in recounting of the incident, Sophia's overriding priority most likely was maintaining the coveted status of Augusta. The literary piquancy of the situation constructed by these medieval authors undermines how seriously we can take the frivolous story of Sophia basing her actions on lust for a young courtier. A careful reading of Byzantine sources shows that Sophia's preeminent concern was more about the singularity of rank rather than a love interest, as she vowed, "I, as long as I live, will never give my kingdom and my crown to another, nor shall another enter here as long as I am alive."[60] The moment of conflict enriches our understanding of the potency of *basileía* for an Augusta, Sophia's prerogatives and privileges would be infringed by an interloper sharing the honors. The quixotic personal interpretation undervalues the importance of the institutional role of the empress.[61]

Michael the Syrian offers an account of the murky proceedings following the death of Justin II. Sophia seems to have designated Tiberios her husband's successor, and Michael fleshes out our understanding of Sophia's rejection of Ino: "The patriarch of Constantinople John counseled the emperor to repudiate his wife and marry the empress, 'For Sophia did not permit the entrance of his wife into the city.'"[62] Tiberios rebuked the patriarch for asking him to renounce his wife who had stood by him in poverty and given him three sons, before he chased the patriarch away.[63] This confrontation seemed to resolve the problem to Tiberios' and his loyal wife's satisfaction. Michael the Syrian then relates: "Sophia allowed entrance to the wife of Tiberios with great honors into the city, took her in with affection and gave her the name Helen."[64] The text's editor notes that this name Helen may have been the name given to Ino by the people of Constantinople, for Anastasia was the name she officially assumed.[65] The new name for an empress sometimes conveyed specific associations, such as the later popularity of the name Irene (peace) for foreign imperial brides.[66] Changing names upon coronation as empress parallels what happened at another important change of identity: a Byzantine would change his or her name upon entering a monastery or convent.

Theophanes the Confessor spins a different tale of Ino's renaming:

> When he became emperor, the factions chanted in the Hippodrome, "Let me know, let me know, the Augusta of the Romans." Tiberios sent a message saying, "What is the name of the church which is opposite the public baths of Dagistheus? The Augusta has the same name." The factions chanted, "Anastasia Augusta, *tu vincas*. Preserve, O Lord, those whom you have ordered to rule."[67]

John of Ephesus relates yet another version of this name change, and his account may clarify the confusion in the later sources.[68]

Sophia continued to hold strong and freely offered opinions on Byzantine governance after Tiberios and his family were ensconced on the throne. Gregory of Tours offers a lengthy anecdote in which Sophia chides Tiberios for overspending on charity, "What I have taken so many years to save . . . you are busy squandering in a prodigal way, and without losing much time about it, either."[69] Contemporary sources accuse Sophia of another form of interference, claiming that she participated in a failed coup by Justin II's nephew, Justinian.[70] Apparently this breach of faith did not permanently dislodge her from a position of influence, for Sophia also guided the appointment of Maurice as Tiberios' successor. When he fell ill, Tiberios sought Sophia's advice just before he died in 583. The same lurid motif reappears that was used to account for the choice of Tiberios, for when Sophia supposedly chose Maurice "she saw herself marrying Maurice as soon as Tiberios should be dead."[71] Just as Ariadne's and indeed Sophia's connection to the previous ruler had established her husband's claim to the throne, marriage to Tiberios' daughter was wrapped into the nomination of Maurice, "With this young woman . . . I give you my imperial power."[72] Our last trace of the Empress Sophia in the historical record appears in an incidental mention of a donation made on Easter of 601: "The Augusta Sophia, the wife of Justin, together with Constantina, the wife of Maurice, made a precious crown which they offered to the emperor."[73] Perhaps Sophia was another victim of Phokas, who slaughtered Maurice and others on his accession in 602.[74]

This historical record illuminates our understanding of the coinage of Justin and Sophia. Others have surveyed Sophia's numismatic depiction, but it deserves further attention within the context of the visual culture of the period.[75] The gold, silver, and bronze coins, destined for disparate audiences, rendered quite different images of the rulers. The gold coin issues of Justin II omit Sophia. Neither the standard solidus nor the lightweight solidus included the empress in the obverse side's depiction of the emperor (see figure 7.1).[76] Justin II is depicted in a bust portrait that faces forward, resplendent in military dress: a plumed helmet, cuirass, a shield bearing the horseman device, and a diminutive Victory personification alight the globe in his right hand. The reverse of the coin echoes reverse types popular in Late Roman coins; a seated personification of the Queen of Cities, Constantinople, looks to the right, and she wears the conventional helmet, tunic, and mantle.[77] The use of these blatantly pagan images on the coinage of Justin II is near the end of a numismatic tradition that began in the Roman Imperial era and lasted until the seventh century.

On certain silver issues, however, Sophia appeared prominently beside her husband from the beginning of their accession. On the obverse of the half siliqua minted in Constantinople, for example, the imperial couple sit together on a double throne, with their heads encircled by imperial halos.[78] They both hold an upright scroll, conveying a measure of their shared judicial/legislative authority.[79] Between the heads of the co-rulers is inscribed a cross. Another version also in the British Museum depicts the couple with tall diadems instead of nimbs, and with their hands raised to their chests.[80] The reverse of the half siliqua depicts a roughly etched half-length figure of the personification of Constantinople, wearing a helmet and tunic with an aegis on her right shoulder. In keeping with the general numismatic trends of the period, these silver issues were rare, and only a few mints issued any silver during their reign. The few double siliqua and siliqua that we have from this period do not represent Sophia.

Bronze coinage, in contrast, consistently depicts Sophia on equal footing with her husband Justin II. Although art historians in their discussion of medieval imperial representations more routinely consider the visually enticing gold and silver coinage, the modest bronze coinage would have

fig. 7.1. Justin II solidus, gold, Obverse: facing bust of Justin II, Reverse: personification of Constantinople seated looking right, holds globus cruciger, A.D. 566, Constantinople mint, Dumbarton Oaks, Washington, D.C. (DOC I, 1.1).

been one of the primary means by which the imperial image was disseminated to the population. The imperial image carried greater impact on bronze coinage, too, because only the obverse actually bore a figure. The reverse of early Byzantine bronze coins simply denoted the denomination of the coin with a letter. The primary bronze denomination, the follis, had a large M on the reverse with the mint of its origin indicated below the M and the year within the fifteen-year administrative indiction cycle shown on the right. Thus the obverse side with Sophia derived additional significance on these common issues, because of the lack of competing figural iconography on the reverse.

The typical obverse of Justin II's bronze coins, the follis and the half follis, shows Sophia reigning beside her husband on a double lyre-backed throne (figure 7.2).[81] The coin depicts the emperor and empress prominently nimbed, a practice in keeping with other noteworthy sixth-century imperial depictions such as the mosaics in the Church of San Vitale. The emperor holds in his right hand a *globus cruciger;* his empress, a cruciform scepter. Because of the roughness of the die impression on these bronze coins, subtleties of regalia are lost. Details of Sophia's crown, for example, are obscure. Her crown consistently includes three upright elements, but the headpiece can be either concave or straight.[82] Both the follis and half follis coins issued by Justin II from the major mint, Constantinople, render this double enthronement on the obverse. The closest precedent for this follis image suggests its impact, for Justin I represented himself with Justinian in a like manner on the solidus minted in Constantinople during their period of co-rule in 527 (see figure 7.3).[83] The coins communicate that Sophia and Justin ruled the Empire as a single unit. A jointly enthroned empress on ordinary issues is unprecedented. The Late Roman Augusta Galla Placidia was enthroned on the reverse of a gold medallion of which two survive in a hoard discovered in 1715, but that was from a special issue.[84] The reverse of a few other coin issues, for example Eudoxia's bronze of 403–404 or her grand-daughter Licinia Eudoxia's gold of 439

fig. 7.2. Justin II and Sophia follis, bronze, Obverse: Justin II and Sophia enthroned, Justin holds globus cruciger, Sophia holds cruciform scepter, Reverse: Denomination mark M, A.D. 567/8, Constantinople mint, Dumbarton Oaks, Washington, D.C. (DOC I 24c).

(see figure 2.9), also show an image of the empress on a throne. In any event, these fifth-century coins were brief issues that had limited exposure to the public and do not compare with the sizable, long-term promulgation of the follis including Sophia.

The two smaller and much less widely used bronze denominations issued by this mint do not show the Empress Sophia, probably because the limited size of the coin face scarcely allows space for one figure. Justin II's decanummium depicts the emperor dressed for battle as he leans on a spear. The pentanummium merely shows the monogram of the emperor on its small obverse face, although some examples utilize a monogram type that combines the names of Justin and Sophia.[85] Several of the regional mints initially issued a half follis with an obverse that looked much like the one used on his gold coins. After a few years, outlying centers of production, such as Thessalonike, also adopted this new obverse type for bronze issues of 568/69. Other local mints lagged only a year or two behind the central mint in following this change. The novelty combined with the inevitable delays in retooling regional mints contributed to this lag time. The

fig. 7.3. Justin I and Justinian solidus, gold, Obverse: Justin I (left) and Justinian (right), Reverse: angel, A.D. 4 April–1 August 527, Constantinople mint, Harvard University Art Museums, Cambridge, MA, Dumbarton Oaks, Washington, D.C. (DOC I 1a).

joint image of the emperor and empress was a radical departure from the coin imagery used by Justin II's predecessor Justinian. For all of the fulminations of Prokopios concerning Theodora's excessive power, she never appeared on the coinage of her time.

Although imperial lead seals represent a solitary Justin II, dated commercial seals may join Sophia with him in a bust pair above the inscription.[86] This evidence must be used cautiously, since lead seals are often dated loosely with only letterforms, style of decoration, and internal evidence as guides. The nimbed rulers wear similar imperial robes; however, their crowns differ along the usual gender lines, with elegant prependoulia on Sophia's headgear. Just as Sophia's depiction on coins prompted the emulation by her immediate successors on coins, Sophia's inclusion on lead seals led to later Augustae's sigillographic image. The imperial couple Maurice and Constantina (r. 582–602), who followed Tiberios and his wife to the throne, may be represented on a commercial lead seal.[87] Zacos and Veglery hesitate in their attribution, but they place the example in their catalog in the second half of the sixth century, indicating empress images on commercial seals in this period regardless of the precise identification. Much like the commercial weight attributed to the reign of Justin II and Sophia, the imperial couple are depicted in busts above the obverse inscription.[88] A third bust included on the left likely represents Theodosios.

Maurice perpetuated this iconographic type at the mint of Thessalonike, and a review of the evidence undermines a commonplace in numismatic literature—that imperial women were represented on coinage as a reward for bearing an heir. Maurice's marriage to the daughter of Tiberios cemented his hold on the imperial throne, and his numismatic iconography bespeaks his wife's central importance to his claims. The half follis has the now-established depiction of the emperor and empress enthroned together.[89] The most common formula represented in the Dumbarton Oaks collection mimics that of Tiberios II and Anastasia, in which the emperor bears the *globus cruciger* and his wife carries the royal scepter.

Maurice also introduced a similar standing type on the follis minted at Cherson.[90] This mint then continued to issue multiple variants in several denominations of bronze, altering a few details. Thus in the pentanummia series, the imperial couple is not nimbed and Constantina has no crown.[91] Grierson intriguingly labels this body of coins issued in Cherson as an "insurrectionary" coin type, suggesting that they arose from the counterforces against Phokas striving to put Theodosios on the throne after the death of his father Maurice in 602.[92] This series of coins minted by Maurice at Cherson is seen as the model for a series of coins minted in the east by Phokas that prominently include his wife Leontia.[93] In the capital city, the mint issued a follis with Leontia depicted standing next to Phokas.[94] The emperor wears a chlamys and a crown with prependoulia and carried the predictable *globus cruciger*. The crowned empress holds a cruciform scepter. This image was then superseded at the Constantinopolitan mint by an obverse image of Phokas in his consular robes.[95] At a mint such as Antioch, however, the obverse image of a standing Phokas and Leontia persisted almost until the year before the end of Phokas' reign in 610. Brubaker and Tobler see in this range of empresses' numismatic depictions, starting in 565 with Sophia, part of a loss of identity with the disappearance of "any individualising characteristics in the portraiture itself."[96] That shift characterizes numismatic imagery in general, though, and the same loss of individuation begins earlier and applies to emperors as well.

Philip Grierson proposes that Leontia's inclusion was "contrary to strict protocol, since she had not provided him with a male heir."[97] Although his widely consulted survey of Byzantine numismatics reiterates this claim, noteworthy exceptions undermine its value as a general principle.[98] While it may have applied earlier to some Late Roman coinage, the impressive political prowess of the women of the House of Theodosios overturned this distinction. While Justin I's wife Euphemia and Justinian I's wife Theodora were not represented on coinage, Sophia was represented with more authority than ever possible before, despite the loss of her one son before Justin and Sophia assumed the throne. Tiberios II's wife Anastasia was shown on coins in about the same limited degree as Maurice's wife Constantina, although Anastasia was childless and Constantina bore five sons and three daughters.[99] Likewise Phokas' wife Leontia was prominently shown on the coinage, although apparently she produced a daughter but no heir. Sophia's enthroned image is only one of the more glaring exceptions to this adage that mischaracterizes the place of women on one of the most important vehicles of imperial expression. Grierson makes an intelligent attempt to ascribe a consistent principle, the necessity of bearing an heir, to the representation of women on Late Roman and Byzantine coins, but then tries to account for the many deviations from this ideal on the basis of late antique hearsay. Grierson and Mays assert, "it can scarcely be an accident that each of these gaps in the series was immediately preceded by the coinage of an empress—Fausta, Verina, and Martina—whose personal and political reputation was a source of great scandal and scarcely calculated to encourage subsequent rulers to bring their consorts too conspicuously into public notice."[100] This theory all too readily falls prey to many of the stereotypes that we have seen shape the rhetoric used to represent Theodora. Perhaps Grierson and Mays confuse cause with effect, for it was most likely the eminence of particular women that inspired both their numismatic representations and vicious gossip.

As attractive as the maxim may be in its simplicity, it must be discarded and replaced with a model that acknowledges the fluidity of representation of the empress on early Byzantine coinage. This distinction allows us to recognize the dynamics of continuity and change specific to the political arena of the early Byzantine period.

The novel image on the bronze coinage of Sophia and Justin makes sense in these terms; Sophia co-ruled the Empire and her numismatic prominence bespeaks political importance and not heir-producing abilities.[101] The meaning of her depiction on the bronze coinage jointly enthroned with Justin cannot be ignored, for these coins translated into a visual form for the citizens of the Empire a more equal pairing from the beginning of their reign.

The preeminence of Sophia on the coins of the reign is matched by her joint depiction on a silver gilt cross now in the Sancta Sanctorum of the Vatican (see figures 7.4 and 7.5).[102] The lavishly bejeweled front side of the Crux Vaticana carries an inscription as well as a reliquary capsule. The reverse side is silver worked in repousée to depict the *Agnus Dei* at the center of the cross, the emperor and empress at the end of each crossbeam, and medallion images of Christ at the end of the top and bottom arms. The lower one, however, could render John the Baptist. This is one of the latest depictions of the symbolic lamb, for the Council of Trullo's prohibition of such symbols was soon to follow.

The dimensions of the medallions vary, for the imperial medallions are 5.1 centimeters wide compared with the central medallion of the lamb, which is 8 centimeters wide. Technical analysis indicates that the large medallion of the figure of the lamb at the center was cut out and rewelded onto the medallion face as part of a previous restoration of the cross.[103] The reverse side in relief consists of an alloy of silver and tin with one-millimeter-thick gold plating.[104] The cross is now a reliquary and both Elbern and Belting-Ihm rehearse the contours of the controversy regarding its original form as possibly a reliquary, a hanging cross,

fig. 7.4. Front, Crux Vaticana, gilt silver and precious stones, sixth century, Sancta Sanctorum, Vatican.

fig. 7.5. Back, Crux Vaticana, sixth century, repoussée silver, Sancta Sanctorum, Vatican.

or a processional cross.[105] An ornate vegetal motif occludes the area between the medallions. The inscription on the front names Justin:[106]

LIGNO QUO CHRISTUS HUMANUM/ SUBDIDIT HOSTEM DAT ROMAE
(Vertical Inscription)
IUSTINUS OPEM/ ET SOCIA DECOREM
(Horizontal Inscription)

[For the wood [of the cross] on which human Christ was overcome by the enemy, Justin (and his consort?) give Rome this wealth and decoration.]

The DAT as a singular verb form renders the relationship of the "SOCIA" uncertain, for DANT would be necessary to include the empress in the action of the verb. Justin II and Sophia seem more likely donors of the cross than Justin and Euphemia earlier in the sixth century.[107] Delbrueck held that the IUSTINUS referred to Justin I, which makes his "socia" the elusive figure of Euphemia, on the basis of an unconvincing comparison to consular diptych images of Ariadne.[108] Whereas de Linas also believed the "Iustinus" referred to Justin I, O. M. Dalton laconically changed the attribution to Justin II, which has since been generally accepted. De Linas based his argument on the assumption that the *Liber Pontificalis*' mention of a *gabata* given by the Emperor Justin I to Pope Hormisdas (514–25) referred to this object, but that term refers more to a votive cross than a reliquary cross.[109] SOCIA could render a misunderstanding of the Greek version of Sophia's name, in which the middle letter φ understood by a Western craftsman as the Latin letter C, but that is merely speculation unless one accepts that the inscription is a misconstrued later restoration of a sixth-century text. Part of what makes the precise dating of the cross tricky is that over the centuries since it was presented to the Pope it has received substantial alterations, with even the dimensions shortened to its current extent of 40 centimeters in length and 31 centimeters in width. The new proportions seem slightly squat and awkward. Its original form probably resembled other crosses extant from the period, such as the cross of the *globus cruciger* on the empress ivories in Vienna and Florence.[110] The current state of the object only dates from the time of Pope Pius IX (1846–78), when the front was retooled.[111] Furthermore, many stones on the front face have new settings. In contrast to the heavily reworked front, the reverse with the imperial medallions probably maintains to a greater extent its original appearance.[112]

The side medallions representing the imperial couple have been neglected in the previous scholarship of the Crux Vaticana. Both emperor and empress are bust-length figures in the *orans* position. The emperor wears a slender diadem with three elongated tear-shaped protrusions over his forehead, whereas on coins Justin II has a wide diadem with two prependoulia on each side. The emperor also possesses a jeweled collar. The empress wears a double-row pearl diadem with long prependoulia. Christa Belting-Ihm, who performed extensive technical analysis of the figures, notes that the seven protuberances on Sophia's diadem are quite difficult to define. In the middle are set three teardrop-shaped pearls, the four exterior points could be part of a crown bonnet, of which the faint line on the forehead is visible. The four-row pearl collar may belong to a dalmatic.[113] The representation of the pair on the Crux Vaticana does not offer a tidy match with contemporary imperial depictions, which prompted Belting-Ihm to speculate a provincial origin or perhaps a "freie mittelalterliche Nachahmungen frühbyzantinischer Typen" (a loose medieval imitation of early Byzantine models).[114] Sophia's crown does not conform precisely to the types of diadems worn by early Byzantine empresses on coins or ivory, but, according to this line of thinking, reflects a provincial manufacture for the silver piece that relied on cursory instructions to render the female imperial diadem with projections. Likewise the almost triangular facial shapes diverge from those on coins. Despite these anomalies, it seems unlikely for an imperial gift to be provincial but our lack of direct comparanda makes the matter difficult to assess. Probably as a result of wear, Justin's forehead and nose area seems pushed forward and flattened, and the most protruding areas on the *Agnus Dei* also look compressed. The hands raised in the *orans* pose are mechanically rendered with little modeling as they reach up and brush against the crosshatched border. This cross in formal aspects resembles other silver of the reign, including the Stuma and Riha patens and the Homs Vase.[115] Whereas art historians have sometimes assigned a provincial attribution to these objects, their stylistic peculiarities may represent a religious style that tried to affirm the more abstract nature of the subject matter.[116] The work of Dodds, for instance, suggests the complexity of connecting workshop to style. By looking at silver stamps, she concludes that the origin and date of purchase of the silver does not correlate with the time or place a silver object was crafted, making it difficult to posit regional silver styles.[117]

This early medieval gift to the Pope offers a unique survival from a common practice of the era, for our texts record that gifts were routinely exchanged to affirm the elaborate interconnections among courts and the papacy at the time. For example, we have record of a relic given to Saint Radegund at Poitiers by Justin and Sophia. Garland plausibly suggests that the Crux Vaticana may have been sent to the Pope ca. 568, when the imperial couple made their offering at Poitiers.[118] The poem by Venantius Fortunatus effuses over Sophia, comparing her to Helena, mother of Constantine the Great, and draws an extensive parallel between the lustre of both members of the imperial couple: "Of equal merit to him. . . . Behold, Augusti, you rival each other with like offerings; you ennoble your sex, as he does his; the man brings back Constantine, the godly woman Helena; as the honour is alike, so is the very love of the Cross. . . ."[119] This allusion corresponds to a material parallel for the Crux Vaticana—the Middle Byzantine cross of Adrianople that depicts in medallion bust images Helena and Constantine on its reverse side. This later processional cross depicts the Empress Helena in a cross-topped crown with prependoulia and carrying a globus and a cross in her hands.[120] The more unconventional images of the emperor and empress on the cross in the Vatican can be placed loosely into a tradition of the imperial image on these crosses. The *orans* pose on the Crux Vaticana also lacks parallels, but given the paucity of surviving imperial objects from this period, and the fact that this cross remains the sole extant example of this sort of imperial donation at the time, it could represent a standard form.

Now that we have looked at numismatic and votive representations of Sophia, we can return to the question of whether the imperial ivory plaques in Florence and Vienna might represent Sophia and not Ariadne, the empress to whom the ivories are usually attributed (see figures 7.6 and 7.7). Like other images of the early Byzantine empress, its overriding character is typological so the terms in which the distinction between the two women can be made rests on the particular ways the symbolism of rule was manipulated by each empress. In the Bargello collection in Florence, a deeply carved ivory panel depicts an early Byzantine empress in full regalia. The impressive figure of the woman stands on an ornamented pedestal, her right hand wields a *globus cruciger* and her left a scepter. We see other empresses balanced these two emblems of imperial power, as in Irene's late eighth-century numismatic portraits.[121] Prokopios, the foremost historian of Justinian's reign, describes an equestrian statue of Justinian in the guise of Achilles. The bronze statue gestured much like the ivory figure of the empress on the diptych, assuming the same potent symbolism:

> In his left hand he holds a globe, by which the sculptor signifies that the whole earth and sea are subject to him, yet he has neither sword nor spear nor any other weapon, but a cross stands upon the globe which he carries, the emblem by which alone he has obtained both his Empire and his victory in war. And stretching forth his right hand toward the rising sun and spreading out his fingers, he commands the barbarians.[122]

The *globus cruciger* has been called by the numismatist Philip Grierson "the most ubiquitous of Byzantine symbols of rule."[123] Other elements of im-

fig. 7.6. Enthroned empress, perhaps Sophia, ivory panel, early Byzantine period, Kunsthistorisches Museum, Vienna, Austria (ANSA X 39).

perial costume and regalia that are represented officially on coins and ivories were inspired by the actual accouterments of Byzantine emperors and empresses in the panoply of ceremonies over which they officiated. The *globus cruciger*, in contrast, was "purely notional," for there is no trace of reference to such an object used in court life.[124] Perhaps Pulcheria, the

fig. 7.7. Standing empress, perhaps Sophia, ivory panel, early Byzantine period, Bargello, Florence, Italy.

Theodosian Augusta studied in chapter one, first Christianized the globe form, and the connection between imperial women and the cross persists.[125] Its meaning can be construed from its form, so the globe depicts the world. The cross supplanted above it represents Christ's dominion over the world in whose authority the Byzantine emperor and empress ruled. In a fine example of life imitating art, after centuries of this abstract existence, in A.D. 1014 Pope Benedict ordered an actual *globus cruciger* made for the coronation of Henry II.[126]

The empress' carefully draped ceremonial cloak, the chlamys, covers most of her body on the Florence ivory. The later *Book of Ceremonies* evokes the central importance of the chlamys for imperial dress, for in this tenth-century compendium the empress receives the ceremonial cloak as part of the investiture to her new office, and other early Byzantine examples such as Theodora's chlamys in Ravenna confirm its long-standing significance.[127] Double rows of heavy half-orbs, perhaps depicting large pearls, line the cloak's edges, but its most ostentatious decoration is the large inset embroidered panel, the tablion, rendering the head of the emperor. In typical Byzantine ceremonial dress, another tablion would have been affixed to the opposite side so that it fell against the back of the official's body. Whereas earlier tablia were placed below the knee, from the sixth century they routinely were attached—as shown in this ivory—over the upper torso. These marks of honor were usually colored to contrast the main garment, and richly studded with jewels for emphasis. The wearer of this item embodied the imperial presence in a very palpable way, and the emperor's effigy born by the empress carried juridical resonances.[128]

The emperor shown in the tablion of the empress' cloak assumes his role as consul, and his right hand tightly grasps a *mappa*. This attribute links the ivory panel to the more common class of early Byzantine official ivory consular diptychs, since consular imagery for an emperor was long associated with imperial triumphal scenes.[129] The tablion on the Florence ivory encapsulates in miniature the main imagery of the consular diptychs—a seated consul with his arm lifted to toss the mappa, initiating the games.

Fluted columns flank the empress, and fanciful Corinthian capitals crown each post. From the rod running between them, two patterned curtains cascade down, and each wraps around a column in an elegant *tour de force* of ivory carving. Topping the space is the dome of a ciborium, an architectural form known primarily through ecclesiastical examples. Romans erected ciboria to protect important tombs, so key early Christian martyr graves received this covering. Medieval ciboria focused veneration on a religious or secular figure, such as a monarch. The imperial usage of the ciborium persisted in examples such as the eleventh-century manuscript of the Homilies of John Chrysostom in the Bibliothèque Nationale in Paris, in which the Emperor Nikephoros III Botaneiates is enthroned in front of the monk Sabas. Corinthian columns frame his throne; curtains and the canopy of the ciborium cover the emperor. An anonymous diptych of a patrician now in Novara offers a closer comparison, which depicts the official in a more austere version of the architectural setting of the imperial diptych in Florence.[130] Made about 425, the Northern Italian diptych frames the patrician with a Corinthian column and a tied curtain on each side of his head, and a grooved cupola above.

Atop the ciborium depicted on the Florence ivory perch two eagles, grasping laurel wreathes in their beaks.[131] While the eagle's imperial meaning from the Roman period is a commonplace, it has broader symbolism here. Returning again to the world of the hippodrome games, the eagle formed part of consular iconography, and was often depicted on top of the consul's scepter.[132] Other diptychs show a bust of an emperor atop the consul's scepter, visually equating the emperor's form and the eagle's.[133] On the diptych of the consul Basilius from 480 an eagle looms across the bottom of the recto face, wings outspread to support a Victory perched atop a globe.[134] The eagle on the large Anastasios missorium from the Sutton Hoo Burial was a distinctively imperial symbol, offering a tidy contemporary corollary.[135]

The curtains that drape down on both sides of the empress depicted on the ivory diptych may echo late antique court practices that mimicked the rites of mystery cults such as Mithraism.[136] The ruler would suddenly appear from behind elaborate drapery, staging a theophany of sorts to the audience, a moment within the "liturgie monarchique" in which the ruler presents himself as a revelation, a face-to-face confrontation with divinity.[137] Liz James nicely captured this aspect of these representations of the empress as "not only more than women, but as more than human."[138] The alternation between movement and stasis narrated in the *Book of Ceremonies* returns to the "iconic" mode in this ivory image, making a certain identification elusive.

An even more remarkable image of the Byzantine empress is now in the Kunsthistorisches Museum in Vienna.[139] In most ways the two ivories are similar. The primary, and rather stunning, difference is that the Vienna plaque depicts the empress as an enthroned ruler.[140] The empress on the ivory in the Kunsthistorisches Museum holds a *globus cruciger* in her left hand and her right arm is raised at elbow height so her palm extends forward. A snood covers her hair and a diadem rises above. The prependoulia hanging from the diadem, earrings, and an elaborate necklace enhance the empress' splendor. Her garments include a tunic and dalmatic as well as the chlamys. The tablion of her chlamys depicts a head on an inset panel, but the image is poorly preserved in an outline that renders quite different proportions than the head on the Florence ivory's tablion.[141] This more narrow silhouette, partially obfuscated by gold paint, does not seem to have an upraised hand, so it might not depict the emperor as consul.

The architectural frame of the Vienna ivory mimics that in Florence with the standing empress. A baldachino similar to the Florence ivory appears in the Vienna piece, just as an eagle also rests on each corner triumphantly. These architectural features are undercut to emphasize the empress' presence in the middle. The parallels between the two imperial plaques remind the viewer of the consular diptych panels of Boethius, consul of Rome in 487. A standing image of the consul on the *recto* side mirrors the enthroned consul on the *verso* panel. Because of the enthronement of the empress in Vienna, however, the body seems awkwardly contoured, for the chest leans forward to the same plane as the knees. Vestiges of the original color remain; the purple of the background and the black of the empress' pupils linger in faint traces.[142] More modern gold paint decorates robes and columns, and remnants of red and black survive on the instep of her right shoe and on the lower edging of the robe's jewels.

In another imperial panel, four ivory pieces flank the central piece with the imperial image. The five-part Barberini Diptych now in the Louvre shows an early Byzantine emperor carved in high relief astride a rearing horse (see figure 7.8). The left panel represents a military figure, but the corresponding right panel is missing. As in the case of some consular diptychs, a more narrative scene transpires in the lower panel. An elephant, a lion, and a tiger jostle with exotically clad barbarians and a personification of Earth as Terra. This image of the downtrodden vanquished beneath an emperor has many parallels, such as the eighth-century Victoria and Albert linen panel with its hapless Persian captives. The upper panel elevates the image into another realm. Two winged angels bear a clipeus with a beardless bust of Christ. By this time angels had assimilated the winged iconography of Victory figures, and the Christian status of these two flying creatures contrasts the winged Victory below.[143] A few tentative lines indicate the rising sun on Christ's right; the moon and stars, on His left. The iconography of the emperor bears rehearsing, for it suggests the appearance of the ivory panels that may have accompanied the empress plaques in Vienna and Florence. Further intact examples of five-part ivory diptychs survive in the Museo Nazionale in Ravenna and the Cathedral Treasury in Milan.[144] A cautionary note on the nomenclature of the "imperial diptychs" should be mentioned. We assume that these five-piece imperial ivories come from diptychs comparable in structure to the paired ivories of consular diptychs because three of the Christian five-piece ivories survive as pairs. No extant plaque of the imperial group has a corollary that could be its pair and furthermore no armature or fittings survive on these

fig. 7.8. Barberini Diptych, ivory panels, early sixth century, Louvre, Paris, France (OA. 9063).

ivories from a diptych arrangement.[145] James suggests that the two empress ivories may not render the same figure, but the distinctive iconography of the ivories is so similar that I think they should be linked.[146] Because Sophia's position was based on shared rule, and not sole rule as in the case of the Empress Irene two hundred years later, her ivory panels may have been paired with ones of the emperor. The dual composition would follow the precedent of similar ivory pairs rendering the Virgin Mary and Christ. Herrin has made the interesting point, though, that only when the western part of the Empire lost its imperial women with the loss of those territories, did the Maria Regina type gain prominence. Conversely, the images of the Virgin Mary in Byzantium lacked the splendid trappings of those in the west, in part, no doubt, because of the need to differentiate between her and the empress.[147]

Altogether twelve pieces from eight multi-part ivories survive, but the original use of these luxury objects remains disputed.[148] Because one imperial diptych was inscribed with the honorary title of a consul without his name, Dalton suggested that the consuls gave an imperial diptych to the emperor or empress as part of the gift giving on taking office.[149] In contrast, the gift exchange may have moved in the opposite direction, and perhaps the ruler bestowed the diptych on the new secular or ecclesiastical official upon ascent to the new rank.[150] In whichever direction the gift exchange occurred, these transactions incur a network of ties that knit the institutions of the court together. As Marcel Mauss averred in his classic anthropological study of gift exchange, "To refuse to give, or to fail to invite, is—like refusing to accept—the equivalent of a declaration of war; it is a refusal of friendship and intercourse."[151] Distribution patterns of late antique silver plate indicate that these objects too circulated as official gifts, not working capital.[152] It seems appropriate then that, just at the moment in history when the broader responsibilities of a consul were subsumed by the obligation to provide largesse in the form of elaborate public spectacles, his ascent to office would be marked by exquisite gift-tokens in ivory of his rank.

The identity of the empress on the two imperial ivories in Vienna and Florence has been disputed, for the two plaques lack inscriptions. Whereas mass-produced objects such as steelyard weights yielded a more generic meaning, luxury goods such as these were made for a particular individual. While not portraits in any modern sense, ivory and marble imperial sculpture was no doubt connected with a certain ruler despite the strong leanings to a normative type. The weight of scholarly opinion holds that both plaques depict the Empress Ariadne.[153] This identification derives mostly from the similarity of the Vienna and Florence ivories to the image of Ariadne on consular diptychs. Delbrueck instead considered the Florence ivory a depiction of the Empress Theodora.[154] Other suggestions include an Ostrogothic queen or the Empress Sophia.[155] The hypothesis that the ivories in Vienna and Florence depict Amalasuntha was first propounded by Graeven in 1898 but elaborated by Siegfried Fuchs in 1944.[156] The basis for this claim was the similarity of the facial type on the imperial diptych to that of

Amalasuntha on the diptych of Orestes, which Netzer subsequently demonstrated was a lightly recut image of Ariadne.[157] Fuchs' work in which this thesis was aired seems inflected by German nationalistic ideologies of the time, which predisposed the scholar to ascribe solidly Germanic origins to a variety of unlikely candidates.

The attribution to Sophia has to date been neglected. Sophia, like Ariadne decades earlier, possessed an independence and authority that found voice in official imagery, but she achieved the novel honor of joint enthronement with the emperor on coinage.[158] The numismatic image chosen by Justin II seized upon a vocabulary of imagery previously used to render co-emperors such as Justin I and his nephew Justinian (see figure 7.3), so the inclusion of Sophia carried a clear message of her importance. Sophia was the first empress to be rendered on coins with a *globus cruciger*. No image of Ariadne depicts her enthroned, and Sophia's numismatic enthronement was all the more riveting for its lack of compelling precedents. Although Ariadne was a politically important, she did not possess the full status of co-ruler that circumstances bequeathed to Sophia. Sophia fully shared the responsibilities and honors of Empire, and thereby the privilege of enthronement and wielding the *globus cruciger*.

Another indication that the two ivories might represent Sophia is that, with the reinstitution by Justin II of the consular office, he may have chosen to revive and aggrandize the discontinued tradition of consular diptychs. Justinian terminated the centuries-old consular office in 541 amid bitter rivalries in his court, but then Justin II resuscitated the position for himself with great pomp. If the empress ivories portray Sophia, they may represent a grander version of an earlier practice that emerged with Justin II's revival of the ancient office solely for himself. One reason scholars gravitated toward earlier datings was that the series of consular diptychs offered the comforting security of a dated range of comparisons. There is no reason to think that ivory carving suddenly stopped with Justinian's stifling of the consular office.

In addition, several important links tie the two empress ivories to other late sixth-century imperial images. The tablion image on the chlamys in Florence resembles that of the emperor on the consular medallion of Maurice Tiberios in the Metropolitan Museum of Art (see figure 7.9).[159] The gold medallion issued to commemorate Maurice Tiberios' consulship of either 583 or 602 depicts the emperor clutching the mappa in his right hand and bearing the consular eagle-headed scepter in his left. This medallion formed part of a belt with twelve solidi and four medallions, and eight of the twelve solidi and all four medallions celebrated the same consulship.[160] The reverse of the Metropolitan medallion depicts the emperor in military dress in command of a team of four horses. The obverse and reverse triumphantly resound the consular identity of the emperor.[161] Not

fig. 7.9. Gold belt of twelve solidi and four medallions, consular issues, A.D. 583 or 602, Metropolitan Museum of Art, New York (17.190.147).

only does the medallion obverse share iconography with the ivory representation, but the two images also iterate the same round facial type and similar crowns. This likeness gives weight to a later sixth-century date for the two empress plaques, for Maurice's depiction offers a closer comparison than imperial images of ca. 500, which would be from the same time frame if the Ariadne attribution is accepted. In addition, the coinage of Tiberios offers similar renderings of the emperor, the immediate successor of Justin II, who depicted himself as consul on his bronze coinage.[162] The emperor represented *en buste* proudly wears his consular robes and raises his right hand to hurl down the mappa. Only the coins of Tiberios and Maurice Tiberios render this form of imperial portrait that corresponds so closely with the empress ivories' tablion image.[163] Grabar, though, uses this fact to suggest that Constantina, the wife of Maurice Tiberios, is depicted on the two empress ivories, which is very unlikely both because of her historical insignificance and the fact that her numismatic image merely follows Sophia's cue. If Sophia is the empress honored on the two ivories, then the figure in the tablion is Emperor Justin II, which makes sense given what we have learned from the above consideration of the historical circumstances of their reign. The round face compares closely with the visage of the miniature emperor on the tablion of the imperial ivories.[164]

These considerations raise the strong possibility that the later date for the Florence and Vienna ivories may be viable and that the empress plaques render the singular authority of the Empress Sophia. Both the visual record and historical context clarified Sophia's representation. While the votive cross of the Vatican was brought back into the context of the textual record, the likelihood that the ivory plaques of the empress in Vienna and Florence depict Sophia was informed by numismatic comparanda. The importance of her depiction on the bronze coinage jointly enthroned with Justin cannot be ignored, for these coins translated the realities of power into a visual form for the citizens of the Empire, circulating the implications of Justin II's mental illness that propelled Sophia into authority. The message of her "sole power" reached as far away as Gaul in the account of Gregory of Tours. Furthermore, previous assumptions by scholars such as Grierson about the principles for the representation of imperial women on coins must be overturned; after reviewing a series of early Byzantine examples only a tenuous relationship exists between an empress producing an heir and her inclusion in numismatic iconography. The textual sources for the period have been distorted with the attention given to the rather muddled transition in power from Justin II to Tiberios. That focus obfuscates the more salient issues of who wielded authority during the reign of Justin II, and how this power structure was articulated in visual forms.

CONCLUSION

These chapters only begin a discussion about the representation of imperial women in this period of transition from Roman to medieval institutions. Rather than teaching eternal truths that dictated the lives of early Byzantine imperial women, each study yielded its own lessons, and the singularity of each woman's historical role and portrayal belies attempts to generalize. The institutional context of these images illuminates how generic forms were used and manipulated in the visual culture of the time.

One person held the rank of Augusta at any given time. She officiated over a particular sphere of palace life, but the flux over the early Byzantine period is marked by the adoption of the Greek term *basilissa* in preference for the Latin title Augusta.[1] The court, to the extent that we can use the term in the early Byzantine period, was based on an association with the palace, so that the empress' duties included aspects of maintaining the elaborate imperial household. Although usually held by a wife, the title Augusta could fall to a daughter.

While typology, here used in a more general, secular sense, is illuminating here, another sense of regularity, shaped by notions of a constitution, is not. Ideas of legitimacy seem flexible and, given that the early Byzantine society this book describes lacked a fixed aristocracy, there is not a very strong sense of "birthright" to the imperial throne.[2] Although the public image of the empress was not individualized, the particular roles a given empress had varied as part of this general fluidity. James' recent book, with its considerable merits, tends to underplay this range in an attempt to identify a uniform political role of the empress over almost five hundred years. Instances such as Ariadne's inordinate sway in determining a series of three emperors testify to a more local and individual kind of power.[3]

Patronage as well as representation is an important dimension of the empresses' role in early Byzantine visual culture. As much work in medieval art history in past decades has shown, during this era the patron often had the active, creative role in the patron-artist relationship. The choices that the empresses made carried even greater significance therefore. How does gender inflect these formulations both within and outside of the palace? Their specific brand of imperial patronage, for example, on some occasions was aimed at helping women, such as the convents established by the Empress Theodora. Likewise scholars such as Brubaker have demonstrated that Augustae consciously emulated the patronage of previous imperial women.[4]

The very fluidity of the imperial office and its retinue in the early Byzantine period may have actually strengthened this need for the appearance of continuity. No firmly delineated aristocracy existed at this time in the Empire; both the emperor and empress could well originate from obscurity. Evidence for this potential mobility is seen in the fact that family names are not regularly used until much later. Whereas surnames became standard among the elites of the Komnenian period in the eleventh and twelfth centuries, the key distinction in the early period seems to have been between officialdom and laborers. Unlike the early medieval west, which left behind silver hordes that testify to the wealth of a privileged elite, no comparably stable group existed in the east.[5] Thus Helena (d. between A.D. 330–336) was the first and perhaps most honored Christian imperial woman, although her origins were decidedly humble— to the point that she was accused of prostitution.

This parallel with the same imputations against the Empress Theodora in the sixth century is quite striking, for the pair of emperors, Justinian and Constantine, seen for centuries as models of kingship exemplified by the Middle Byzantine tympanum mosaic of Hagia Sophia with the pair. In a piquant display of medieval misogyny, the most prominent woman with whom each great emperor was associated was styled as a reformed courtesan. This trope had sprung up in attacks leveled against the first Roman imperial women by writers such as Seneca, for Julia, the daughter of Augustus, was also slandered with the charge of prostitution, we have seen.[6] In a Christian context, these lurid stories may be tinged with narrative patterns of redemption familiar from female saints' lives.[7] Just as in the case of Theodora two centuries later, what was probably merely an undistinguished background accrued scurrilous baggage through the never-idle machinations of court gossip. Such stories have remained popular and unscrutinized in much the same way that the *droit de cuissage,* the western medieval lord's first night, persisted as a convenient fixture in modern erotic imaginings placed in the medieval past.[8] The rumors do, however, bespeak that the court was to some degree a meritocracy instead of an aristocracy at this time, in the way the imperial couple, as well as members of the palace ranks around them, rose from obscurity in several noteworthy instances.[9] The weak place of hereditary rule ultimately is an echo of the republican ideology of the Roman state.[10]

CONCLUSION

Because of these anxieties about the chastity of imperial women, eunuchs had an indispensable part of palace life as in the San Vitale portrait of the *sekreton ton gynaikon*. Given the often precarious nature of the imperial office, eunuchs played an important role in providing continuity in the systems of the state; later, in the Middle Byzantine period, they seem largely responsible for maintaining ceremonial. Arguably one can describe a situation in which emperors and empresses may come and go, but eunuchs are forever in the Byzantine court.

Just as eunuchs mark boundaries, the dress of the empress and her female courtiers denote their exalted rank in social and political hierarchies. The world of the palace forced the fastidious observation of every distinction. The empress' garments flaunted her status, and details such as the tablion assert her unmatched rank among women. The other women held a place in their *sekreton* largely through marriage to male officials, though in the later period when our sources are better there are a few instances of positions detached from any male corollary.

The funding for the *sekreton ton gynaikon* remains obscure, although a few textual references point to a separate stream of holdings and revenue from those of the emperor, which funded this retinue. Thus the Empress Theodora could make a trek to the mineral springs of Pythia Therma with an entourage of 4,000. The number is surely inflated, but hints that a vast entourage accompanied the empress. Thus while the palace defines the *sekreton ton gynaikon,* it extends beyond the palace as a social reality.

The physical contours of the imperial palace in Constantinople are poorly understood because of the impossibility of extensive archeological study, because the Blue Mosque now sits upon much of the palace site. Unfortunately a later text, the *Book of Ceremonies,* is the major source on this building. Recently a few limited excavations have uncovered substructures, but so far have not illuminated the kind of questions asked here. The sixth-century past was palpably real for the tenth-century emperor/author, for he inhabited the same palace as his predecessors, a place modified only piecemeal in the intervening centuries. The sixth century's ongoing preeminence was further assured by that era's wealth of literature, compared to the relative paucity of texts from the seventh to the ninth centuries. Much as in the case of the ancient Greek house's "women's quarters," however, the location of the empress and her female courtiers within the palace seems to have been defined by changing needs rather than a physically located entity, for over time they shifted areas within the Great Palace complex. Alexander Kazhdan appears off the mark in his declaration that "Only if we find palpable traces of the Byzantine *gynaeceum* shall we be entitled to speak about the confinement of women in the empire of the Rhomaioi."[11] Our knowledge of Byzantine domestic architecture, imperial or otherwise, is so scanty that it is unlikely to yield such evidence, but it is hard to say what concrete monument Kazhdan expected to find. Gendered separation was a fact of life in the Byzantine imperial sphere, but was no doubt a prerogative of the wealthy as in imperial Rome, as a variety of conspicuous consumption. The already dicey task of reconstruction is further complicated by Prokopios' claim that court ceremonial fluctuated during Justinian's reign. The historian levels the charge that Justinian and Theodora innovated dangerously in this regard by introducing practices from the Persian court. The emperor, as well as the empress, now required their courtiers to humiliate themselves in a grovel before them. A later account of a ninth-century ceremony also dictates full obeisance to the empress.[12]

Sejunction structures the *Book of Ceremonies'* recounting of specific rituals of the *sekreton ton gynaikon,* such as the coronation and marriage of the Empress Irene the Athenian in the eighth century.[13] The document mainly recounts the movements from one area of the palace to another, with the dignitaries taking their place in this highly choreographed courtly dance of hierarchies and promenades. At one point in the narrative, we even learn that "it is important to know that the women at the coronation of the Augusta, do not wear a *propoloma* hair style," though what exactly is important to know about this regulation of coiffure is lost now in time.[14] Although the empress is carefully matched with the female courtiers throughout, it is the emperor, apparently, who designates which women are allowed to attend the actual marriage and ancillary ceremonies.

Standardized forms were likewise necessary for official representations of Byzantine emperors and empresses that served as the actual embodiment of imperial authority in distant reaches of the Empire. Just as we saw the San Vitale mosaic register to the Ravenna population a new reality of power, the imperial image conversely could be a means of registering disapproval of or at the state as the simulacrum for the body of the ruler in the midst of a riot. During late antiquity imperial images could possess a very palpable link to the ruler, and the public persona of the emperor or empress was expected at times to be frozen into the repose of a sculpture. We can recall Eusebios' praise for Constantine the Great's statue-like bearing—in this sense, the actual person of the Byzantine ruler was regarded as a likeness of an ideal type. This elision between the imperial image and personal identity is crucial for understanding the manner in which the imperial representations functioned. Modern notions of portraiture based on likeness are misleading here, and the demands of the public role of these images place them differently in society.

The modest army of empress-shaped counterpoises of commercial weights tucked away in museum storerooms balance our discussion of imperial representation made from more lavish materials. Scholarship on imperial art once gravitated toward the lavish adornments of the Constantinopolitan court, but the means of communication of imperial authority to ordinary people offers a new range of insights. As Arjun Appadurai notes, luxury goods can be usefully seen as a distinct "register" of consumption, rather than as entirely disparate from the realm of ordinary, useful commodities.[15] Furthermore looking at the archeological evidence proved that the steelyard weights should be dated to the sixth and seventh centuries rather than the period of the fourth and fifth centuries previously favored. The paucity of "Dark Ages" textual evidence led scholars to infer a corresponding loss in material culture that may not be fully true. The dwindling numbers of public statuary from the late sixth century on does not mean an end to imperial patronage and representation.[16] David Wright, for example, has illustrated that the ongoing renovation of the imperial palace continued into the reign of the seventh-century Emperor Justinian II.[17] Certainly the more quotidian purpose of the commercial weight would continue even through the diminished prosperity that began before the death of the sixth-century Emperor Justinian. Instead of viewing the weights as individual portraits attributable on the basis of numismatic corollaries, they depict the empress as a type, a pool of imagery linked closely to Athena and personifications. The generic meaning of the image of the empress in this context highlights the overvaluation granted to individual identity over typology in Byzantine imperial images. Even the figures on luxury goods have a generalized, emblematic sense that runs counter to the specific qualities of portraiture often ascribed to them. These banal objects open up the question, too, of the value of the semiotic bent of much interpretation of medieval art, when the specific categories into which we keep trying to corral these images seemed to have eluded even their original Byzantine audience. Although this topic is discussed most thoroughly in chapter two, Dan Sperber's interpretive model of the viewer's cognition of symbolism illustrates this ambiguity that applies more broadly to the imperial images studied here. Rather than a process of decoding to reach a finite answer, it seems to have worked more like an improvisation, with a number of acceptable conclusions in a kind of early Byzantine postmodernism. Classical antecedents in the realm of religious art are particularly telling in this regard. On the building records inscribed on the fifth-century B.C. Erectheum in Athens, frieze figures are identified by posture and not specific identity, just as our *Parastaseis* author seemed rather nonplussed on the topic of whether a Constantinopolitan statue represented the Empress Verina or the Goddess Athena.

Another intriguing part of Byzantine visuality appeared in texts such as Corippus that we have discussed earlier—a preoccupation with transient effects of light and the creation of these elusive layers of meaning. Like the concept of Baroque visuality sometimes tossed around in 1980s art historical literature, it emphasizes a "prior experience of a world of objects."[18] The most compelling comparison with Byzantium comes in the similarity of the perspective of the putative viewer, who also casts an "attentive eye on the fragmentary, detailed, and richly articulated surface of the world it is content to describe rather than explain."[19] Recent art history has developed an understanding of the faith put in the capacities of the Byzantine and Roman viewer, whose substantial interpretative abilities were taken for granted.[20] Others accept this notion, but emphasize that Byzantine texts on art reflect sensitivity to the artworks to render both their more abstract and realistic elements.[21] This framework means that images were formed not to be tersely decoded, but to be explored and completed in a way by the process of looking. Thus the viewer was expected to share a context of references that would richly evoke a range of associations. The mosaics of San Vitale share with steelyard weights the nuances that are integral to this mode of looking.

Just as the perceived documentary, or snapshot, quality of the mosaics of the Church of San Vitale in Ravenna requires reassessment, the interpretation of the textual record of the Empress Theodora warranted revision. The modern overemphasis on the *Anekdota*'s rendering of Theodora distorts our perception of the historical record. This book's textual analysis revised the standard reading of this text by focusing attention of the rhetorical nature of both the *Anekdota*'s structure and content. I used diachronic examples of political pornography to serve as methodological paradigms, but they do not elide the singular nature of early Byzantine culture. Prokopios' treatment of Theodora beguiles us into an odd cult of personality that feeds into preconceptions and anxieties about women in power. In an illusory way, we feel we know Theodora, for her contemporaries sketch her with such force and vividness. The palpability of these representations, though, does not bespeak their veracity, but shows the eloquence of a convention that now allows its continued acceptance. In these texts the woman is sketched by the male author resolutely as the "Other," but we lack sources from the early Byzantine period written by women.[22] The depiction of the Empress Theodora warrants more scrutiny for how she has been rendered over the centuries, and how Byzantine sources took on a new life and were reconstituted to express the interests of Enlightenment England, fin-de-siècle Paris, or contemporary American universities.

The Empress Sophia, long overshadowed by Theodora in modern accounts, wielded greater authority than her famous aunt did, for when her husband Justin II went insane she assumed "sole rule." Unprecedented numismatic iconography depicts the empress enthroned beside the emperor. Sophia's unparalleled status on these coins—as well as other factors dis-

CONCLUSION

cussed in chapter seven—suggests that the ivory plaques now in Florence and Vienna, the latter of which depicts the empress enthroned, may represent Sophia and not Ariadne. Because coinage is a medium with a continuous series of imperial representations, it permits a kind of comparison that the sporadic record of ivories or mosaics cannot. Thus Ariadne did not receive this honor, although her medallion portraits on consular diptychs indicate her importance; instead a woman decades later held a position in history that warranted enthronement. Thus it is striking that the main representation of the Empress Ariadne appears on ivory plaques that marked the accession of several new consuls. These consular diptychs advertise early medieval structures of urban power and control. The consul is precariously supported by the imperial endorsement of the rulers' medallion images above, as a carnival of raucous hippodrome imagery boils up from below. Consular diptychs render the volatile status of political authority, and these very uncertainties of rule required that the image of the ruler constantly reinforce the power structure. Thus mime shows and animal contests existed in tandem with the austere manifestation of imperial potency. The consul's main duty was to fund the urban games, which in turn could become a cauldron of subversion. The Nika Riot was only one instance of insurgency that broke out into the city from the hippodrome, where imperial authority could be freely challenged in the acclamations of the circus factions. The Empress Ariadne thus conferred legitimacy not only to her husband but also to the consul in these ivories.

The Empresses Ariadne and Sophia offer a compelling contrast with Theodora. Both Ariadne and Sophia appear on the coins of their reign, and Sophia achieved parity with the emperor on the bronze coins circulating throughout the Empire.

The numismatic record, though, has been misused in other circumstances, when—borrowing methodology from the study of Roman Imperial art—museum curators attributed the standardized empress steelyard weights to individual empresses of the Theodosian era. Even the imperial images of this period emphasize markings of rank over individual likeness, and these weights convey the authority of Empire in the more general language of an empress as a type rather than as an individual holder of that role.

We live in a culture transfixed by celebrities, which confuses our perception of a past not preoccupied with the same concerns. The empresses were not famous as individuals in the way that even a skillful hippodrome charioteer might capture the imagination of the populace of Constantinople. Athletes were probably the earliest heroes to be extolled as the stars of their age in antiquity.[23] In contrast, the force of the empresses' identity in the public eye was in their role as Augusta, in which the specific was subsumed into the general. Literary and artistic conventions obfuscated personal identity in the depiction of empresses. The steelyard weights with their generic rendering of the empress represent this feature of imperial publicity. Sources often transpose Byzantine empresses, for their individual identities sometimes eluded writers much closer to their time. In a typical example, Theophanes the Confessor incorrectly comments that Theodora—not Euphemia—was elevated to Augusta status almost immediately after Justin became emperor.[24]

Looking at the full spectrum of visual culture reminds us of the overwhelmingly typological status of the imperial image. In contrast to the Roman Imperial period, when there was a deep and persistent interest in imperial portraiture, in the late antique period that facet of representation shifted to a more generic image. Overturning the top-heavy focus of the appearance of the imperial image on sumptuary goods can change our perception of these exquisite objects, and here I have juxtaposed part of the wide range of the things that coexisted within medieval visual culture. The image of Sophia on a well-worn bronze coin expresses the same status quo as the ivory plaque in Vienna.

Empress Sophia's image on the follis illustrates the flexibility of Byzantine numismatic imagery, which was then stretched to its limit by the unprecedented ascent to power of the Empress Irene. During the Iconoclastic debates, the Augustae Irene, Theodora, and three daughters of the emperor Theophilos appeared on coinage.[25] Iconoclasm enflamed the Byzantine Empire during two long periods: from 726 to 787 and later from 815 to 843, and the role of imperial women in Iconoclasm illustrates how important the foundation of authority was that was established during the period considered in this book.[26]

The preeminence of women in the early Byzantine period started to shift in the Middle Byzantine period, and the law codes of the ninth-century Emperor Leo VI indicate their withdrawal from public life. In Novel 48, for example, women are prohibited from acting as witnesses to contracts.[27] These shifts evidenced in the legal codes over time become subsumed into a single state of existence for Byzantine women and flatten the field of historical difference in some studies.[28] We find the role of women legislated, but there is little in the codes that defines the position of the empress.[29] Then with the emergence of an aristocracy in the Middle Byzantine period, the mutability of status and power in the early period hardens into more rigidly proscribed roles.

Just as the position of empresses varied, the sources we have utilized range tremendously in content and type. The audience for literature such as Prokopios' writing was minuscule, yet its complexity and sophistication absorbs our attention until we forget how little of his vision of the era was shared by his contemporaries. The *Parastaseis* author's confusion about the statuary surrounding him likewise reveals the dissonance that exists between our categories and the modes of interpretation that were meaningful to a medieval audience.

The studies presented in this book emphasize the diversity of roles held by imperial women, yet also return to the typological nature of their representation. Whereas a figure such as Sophia deftly stepped into the lacuna caused by her husband's mental illness, her prestige was rendered in the stock terms of visual language that expressed the co-rule of Justin I and Justinian. Likewise the posthumous representation of Ariadne on the ivory consular diptychs emends previous iconography to legitimize Anastasios' rule. The representations of imperial women in this era provide insight into broader issues of imperial art as well as how notions of gender can frame the visualization of power. The enthroned image of the empress on ivory functioned within the same visual culture as the lowly commercial weights, and both defined the empress as a central and widely understood emblem of authority.

LIST OF ABBREVIATIONS

DOC	Catalogue of the Byzantine Coins in the Dumbarton Oaks Collection and in the Whittemore Collection
LCL	Loeb Classical Library
LRC	Catalogue of Late Roman Coins in the Dumbarton Oaks Collection and the Whittemore Collection
MGH	Monumenta Germaniae historica
ODB	*Oxford Dictionary of Byzantium,* ed. Alexander P. Kazhdan
PG	*Patrologiae cursus completus.* Series graeca, ed. J.-P. Migne, 161 vols. in 166 parts (Paris 1857–66)

NOTES

Introduction

1. Liutprand of Cremona, *Antapodosis,* 11, ed. Joseph Becker, *Die Werke Liudprands von Cremona,* MGH, Scriptores rerum Germanicarum (Hannover, Leipzig: Hahnsche, 1915); trans. F. A. Wright (London: Everyman's Library, 1993), pp. 10–11.
2. This characteristic of Byzantine letters has been described succinctly by Cyril Mango, *Byzantine Literature as a Distorting Mirror, An Inaugural Lecture* (Oxford: Clarendon Press, 1975).
3. Valentin Groebner, "Describing the Person, Reading the Signs in Late Medieval and Renaissance Europe: Identity Papers, Vested Figures, and the Limits of Identification," in *Documenting Individual Identity: The Development of State Practices in the Modern World,* ed. Jane Caplan and John Torpey (Princeton: Princeton University Press, 2001), pp. 25–26 [15–27].
4. Katerina Nikolaou, *Η θέοη της γυναίκας οτη βυζαντινη κοινωνία* (Athens: Hidryma Goulandre-Chorn, 1993), p. 48.
5. Barbara Hill develops this point further in her study of Middle Byzantine empresses, "Imperial Women and the Ideology of Womanhood in the Eleventh and Twelfth Centuries," in *Women, Men, and Eunuchs: Gender in Byzantium,* ed. Liz James (New York: Routledge, 1997), pp. 78–79 [76–99].
6. Elizabeth Bartman, *Portraits of Livia: Imaging Imperial Woman in Augustan Rome* (New York: Cambridge University Press, 1999), p. 13. Spatharakis' anachronistic criteria for a Byzantine portrait is basically that it be an image of a historical individual made during his or her lifetime. Iohannis Spatharakis, *The Portrait in Byzantine Illuminated Manuscripts* (Leiden: Brill, 1976), p. 3.
7. Susan E. Wood, *Imperial Women, A Study in Public Images, 40 B.C.-A.D. 68* (Leiden: Brill, 1999), p. 46.
8. Bartman, *Livia,* p. 26.
9. *Vita* of Saint Philaretos, trans. M.-H. Fourmy and M. Leroy, "La Vie de S. Philarète," *Byzantion* 9 (1934): 135.24–143.25.
10. Lynda Garland, *Byzantine Empresses: Women and Power in Byzantium A.D. 527–1204* (London: Routledge, 1999), p. 21. Reviewed by author, *The Medieval Review,* on-line, 5 July 2000.

11. Bartman discusses this in relationship to Livia's portraiture and modern norms of beauty, *Livia,* p. 28.
12. Susan Fischler, "Social Stereotypes and Historical Analysis: The Case of Imperial Women at Rome," in *Women in Ancient Societies: An Illusion of the Night,* ed. Léonie Archer, Susan Fischler, and Maria Wyke (New York: Routledge, 1994), pp. 127–29 [115–33].
13. Ernst H. Kantorowicz, *The King's Two Bodies: A Study in Mediaeval Political Theology* (Princeton: Princeton University Press, 1957).
14. Angeliki E. Laiou, "The Role of Women in Byzantine Society," *Jahrbuch der Österreichischen Byzantinistik* 31.1 (1981): 233 [233–60].
15. Charles Diehl, *Byzantine Empresses,* trans. Harold Bell and Theresa de Kerpely (New York: Knopf, 1963). This translation is an amalgam of two French works by Diehl, *Figures byzantines* (1906) and *Impératrices de Byzance* (1959); Donald Nicol, *The Byzantine Lady: Ten Portraits, 1250–1500* (New York: Cambridge University Press, 1994). The original work by Diehl is part of a flurry of interest in Byzantine empresses around the turn of the last century that parallels the current spate of scholarship. This enthusiam extended to less scholarly work as well, Paul Adam, *Princesses Byzantines* (Paris: Firmin-Didot, 1893).
16. Even early studies of the Byzantine empress that try to present a more continuous narrative are sidetracked by figures such as Theophano, as in Alfred Rambaud, "L'impératrice byzantine," *Revue des deux mondes* 130 (1891): 814–38.
17. André Grabar, *L'empereur dans l'art byzantin* (1936; repr. London: Variorum Reprints, 1971) and S. Lampros, Λεύχομα Βυζαντινών Αύτοχρατόρων (Athens: Eleftherodakis, 1930).
18. Grabar, *L'empereur,* p. 265.
19. Maria Delivorria, *Recherches sur l'iconographie d'impératrice byzantine,* Ph.D. diss. Sorbonne, 1966. I am grateful to Prof. Irina Andreescu-Treadgold for this reference.
20. Richard Delbrueck, "Portraets byzantinischer Kaiserinnen," *Mitteilungen des kaiserlich deutschen archäologischen Instituts, Römische Abteilung* 28 (1913): 310–52.
21. Garland, *Empresses.*
22. Liz James, *Empresses and Power in Early Byzantium* (London: Leicester University Press, 2001).
23. Henry Maguire, "Style and Ideology in Byzantine Imperial Art," *Gesta* 28 (1989): 217–31.
24. Leslie Brubaker, "Art and Byzantine Identity: Saints, Portraits, and the Lincoln College Typikon," in *Byzantium: Image, Identity, Influence,* XIX International Congress of Byzantine Studies, Major Papers (Copenhagen: Eventus Publishers, 1996), pp. 51–59.
25. Susan Bordo, "Feminism, Postmodernism, and Gender-Scepticism," in *Feminism / Postmodernism,* ed. N. Nicholson (New York: Routledge, 1990), p. 135 [133–56].

26. Angeliki Laiou justified such a study on these terms: "That gender is a factor which separated and distinguished the function of people in Byzantine society is a statement whose general validity is guaranteed by the legal provisions which relegated women to the private as opposed to the public life, and which imposed restrictions on some activities even in the private domain of the family." Angeliki Laiou, "Addendum to the Report on the Role of Women in Byzantine Society," *Jahrbuch der Österreichischen Byzantinistik* 32.1 (1982): 202 [198–204].
27. Gillian Clark, *Women in Late Antiquity: Pagan and Christian Life-styles* (Oxford: Clarendon Press, 1993).
28. Irmgard Hutter, "Das Bild der Frau in der byzantinischen Kunst," in ΒΥΖΑΝΤΙΟΣ: *Festschrift für Herbert Hunger,* ed. W. Hörander, et al. (Vienna: Ernst Becvar, 1984), pp. 163–70.
29. Liz James, ed. *Women, Men, and Eunuchs: Gender in Byzantium* (New York: Routledge, 1997).
30. Judith Herrin, *Women in Purple: Rulers of Medieval Byzantium* (London: Weidenfeld & Nicholson, 2001) and Barbara Hill, *Imperial Women in Byzantium, 1025–1204: power, patronage, and ideology* (New York: Longman, 1999).
31. Hill, *Imperial Women,* pp. 10–14, 18–28.
32. Joan Wallach Scott, "Gender: A Useful Category of Historical Analysis," in *Feminism and History,* ed. Joan Wallach Scott (New York: Oxford University Press, 1996), p. 156. This often-quoted essay originally appeared in *American Historical Review* 91.5 (1986): 1053–75.
33. Jill Dubisch, *In a Different Place: Pilgrimage, Gender and Politics at a Greek Island Shrine* (Princeton: Princeton University Press, 1995), p. 11.
34. Lucia Fischer-Papp, *Evita Peron: Empress Theodora Reincarnated* (Rockford, IL: Northwoods Press, 1983), p. 304.
35. Scott, "Gender" in *Feminism and History,* p. 165.
36. Gilbert Dagron, *Empereur et prêtre: étude sur le "césaropapisme" byzantin* (Paris: Gallimard, 1996), pp. 129–38.
37. St. Maslev, "Die staatsrechtliche Stellung der byzantinischen Kaiserinnen," *Byzantinoslavica* 27 (1966): 308–43.
38. Maslev, "Die staatsrechtliche," 316.
39. Garland, *Empresses,* p. 2.
40. Tacitus, *Annals,* I. 8, ed. and trans. John Jackson, LCL, vol. 2 (Cambridge, MA: Harvard University Press, 1962).
41. Maslev, "Die staatsrechtliche," 309.
42. José Grosdidier de Matons, "La femme dans l'empire byzantin," in *Histoire mondial de la femme,* ed. Pierre Grimal, 4 vols., (Paris: Nouvelle Librairie de France, 1967), 3: 21 [11–43].
43. Prokopios, *Anekdota,* 30.25–26, ed. J. Haury, *Procopii Caesariensis opera omnia* (Leipzig: Teubner, 1962). Liz James notes that of the twenty-two early Byzantine imperial women she considers, twelve or thirteen (depending on whose reckoning one follows) warranted the title Augusta. Liz James,

"Goddess, Whore, Wife, or Slave? Will the Real Byzantine Empress Please Stand Up?" in *Queens and Queenship in Medieval Europe,* ed. Anne J. Duggan (Woodbridge, U. K.: Boydell, 1997), p. 128 [123–40].

44. Steven Runcimann, "Some Notes on the Role of the Empress," *Eastern Churches Review* 4 (1972): 119 [119–24]. The most thorough discussion on the titulature of Byzantine empresses, a long article written by Elisabeth Bensammar, begins in the eighth century with the anomalous example of the Empress Irene. Elisabeth Bensammar, "La titulature de l'impératrice et sa signification," *Byzantion* 56 (1976): 243–91. Barbara Hill critiques Bensammar's use of sources, Barbara Hill, *Imperial Women,* p. 99.

45. Garland, *Empresses,* p. 5.

46. As we will see, a striking number of both positive and negative stereotypes that pervade the representation of the early Byzantine women were evident in Roman Imperial sources. Susan Fischler analyzes these precedents perceptively, Fischler, "Social Stereotypes," 115–33.

47. Suetonius praises the austerity of Augustus' household appurtenances and garments: "Except on special occasions he wore common clothes for the house, made by his sister, wife, daughter, or granddaughter." Suetonius, Augustus, *Lives of the Caesars,* 73, ed. and trans. J. C. Rolfe, LCL (Cambridge, MA: Harvard University Press, 1951).

48. Eve D'Ambra, *Private Lives, Imperial Virtues: The Frieze of the Forum Transitorium in Rome* (Princeton: Princeton University Press, 1993), pp. 100–103.

49. Laiou, "Role," 243–45.

50. Steven Runcimann, "The Empress Irene the Athenian," in *Medieval Women,* ed. Derek Baker (Oxford: Blackwell, 1978), p. 117 [101–18].

Chapter 1

1. Diana E. E. Kleiner, "Imperial Women as Patrons of the Arts in the Early Empire," in *I Claudia: Women in Ancient Rome,* ed. Diana E. E. Kleiner and Susan B. Matheson (New Haven: Yale University Art Gallery, 1996), p. 33 [28–41].

2. Kleiner, "Imperial Women," in *I Claudia: Women in Ancient Rome,* p. 36.

3. Eric Varner, "Domitia Longina and the Politics of Portraiture," *American Journal of Archaeology* 99 (1995): 187–206.

4. Simon Price, *Rituals and Power: The Roman Imperial Cult in Asia Minor* (New York: Cambridge University Press, 1984), p. 56.

5. Susan E. Wood, *Imperial Women, A Study in Public Images, 40 B.C.-A.D. 68* (Leiden: Brill, 1999), p. 41.

6. Price, *Rituals,* p. 75.

7. Price, *Rituals,* p. 227.

8. Kenneth M. Setton, *Christian Attitude Towards the Emperor in the Fourth Century* (New York: Columbia University Press, 1941), p. 198.

9. *Vita* of Saint Thekla, *Vie et Miracles de Sainte Thecle,* ed. and trans. Gilbert Dagron and Marie Dupre la Tour (Brussels: Societé des bollandistes, 1978).

NOTES TO PAGE 15

10. Not included in Eusebios, the first mention is over sixty years after her visit in the sermon by Ambrose, *De Obitu Theodosii,* ed. O. Faller, Corpus scriptorum ecclesiasticorum latinorum, vol. 73 (Vienna: Hoelder-Pichler-Tempsky, 1955). Drijvers contends that the cult of the cross began in Jerusalem in the 320's, and only in the late fourth century was Helena associated with it at the same time that narratives of discovery developed. Jan Willem Drijvers, *Helena Augusta* (Leiden: Brill, 1992), p. 93.
11. Liutprand of Cremona, *Antapodosis,* 4.25, ed. Joseph Becker, *Die Werke Liudprands von Cremona,* MGH, Scriptores rerum Germanicarum (Hannover: Hahnsche, 1915); *The Embassy to Constantinople and Other Writings,* trans. F. A. Wright (London: Everyman's Library, 1993).
12. Leslie Brubaker, "Memories of Helena: Patterns of Imperial Female Matronage in the Fourth and Fifth Centuries," in *Women, Men, and Eunuchs: Gender in Byzantium,* ed. Liz James (New York: Routledge, 1997), p. 59 [52–75].
13. Michael McCormick, *Eternal Victory: Triumphal Rulership in Late Antiquity, Byzantium, and the Early Medieval West* (New York: Cambridge University Press, 1986), p. 37.
14. Drijvers points out that although this trip became a model for later pilgrimage, it should not be considered a pilgrimage in the context of the situation at the time. Helena was motivated by a complex political agenda as well as religious concerns as she travelled. Drijvers, *Helena,* pp. 65–66.
15. *Oxford Dictionary of Byzantium,* "Helena," p. 909 and A. H. M. Jones, J. R. Martindale and J. Morris, *The Prosopography of the Later Roman Empire,* vol. 1 (New York: Cambridge University Press, 1971) delineate the sources for her life. Whether Helena was the wife or concubine of Constans, Late Roman authors make clear that Constans severed this tie when he became Caesar and married Theodora to cement his new status.
16. E. D. Hunt, *Holy Land Pilgrimage in the Later Roman Empire A.D. 312–460* (New York: Oxford University Press, 1982), p. 37.
17. Eusebios, *Vita Constantini,* 3.47, ed. F. Winkelmann, *Die griechischen christlichen Schriftsteller der ersten Jahrhunderte* (Berlin: Akademie-Verlag, 1975).
18. As Cooper states, "In an impasse between men, the introduction of a third, female element diffused the ever-present consciousness of ranking among males—a de-stabilizing move which favored the man who wished to undermine the status quo." Kate Cooper, "Insinuations of Womanly Influence: An aspect of the Christianization of the Roman Aristocracy," *Journal of Roman Studies* 82 (1992): 163 [150–64].
19. Eusebios, *Vita Constantini,* 3.43.
20. E. D. Hunt, *Holy Land Pilgrimage in the Later Roman Empire, A.D. 312–460* (Oxford: Clarendon, 1982), pp. 48 and 29.
21. Brubaker, "Memories," in *Women, Men, and Eunuchs: Gender in Byzantium,* p. 61.
22. Ambrose, "On Theodosius," 47, p. 328. This aspect of Helena's representation, in which "Helena is the mediator of grace for the imperial family and

the universal empire," is explored more fully by Lynda L. Coon, *Sacred Fictions: Holy Women and Hagiography in Late Antiquity* (Philadelphia: University of Pennsylvania Press, 1997), p. 101.

23. *Epistola synodica patriarcharum orientalium,* 7.8, ed. L. Duchesne, *Roma e l'Oriente* 5 (1912–1913).

24. Hiltje F. H. Zomer, "The So-Called Women's Gallery in the Medieval Church: An Import from Byzantium," in *The Empress Theophano: Byzantium and the West at the Turn of the First Millennium,* ed. Adelbert Davids (New York: Cambridge University Press, 1995), p. 296 [290–306].

25. Josef Vogt argues for Helena's Jewish heritage in "Helena Augusta, The Cross and the Jews: Some Enquiries about the Mother of Constantine the Great," *Classical Folia* 31 (1977): 141–49 [135–51]; Evelyn Waugh, *Helena* (London: Chapman and Hall, 1950).

26. After Constans arrived at an inn at Drepanum, "He announced his desire for intemperate pleasure to the guide, he, having observed his imperial bearing, since he had his young daughter Helena with him, a girl who was unitiated about the male sex. Constans took the girl and, having made love with her, gave her an embroidered mantle dyed in purple as an expression of his gratitude . . . a wonderful vision was revealed for just that night; for the sun that shines by day, having, contrary to nature, run backwards out of its bed which is beside Oceanus in the west, was unexpectedly directing its four-fold rays on the house where Constans was sleeping with the girl." "Anonymous Life of Constantine" (BHG 364), trans. Frank Beetham, et al, *From Constantine to Julian: Pagan and Byzantine Views,* ed. Samuel N. C. Lieu and Dominic Montserrat (New York: Routledge, 1996), Sect. 3, p. 108.

27. Mango surveys some of the problems in understanding the early Byzantine Augustaion, Cyril Mango, *The Brazen House. A Study of the Vestibule of the Imperial Palace of Constantinople* (Copenhagen: Arkaeologisk-kunsthistoriscke Meddelelser, 1959), pp. 45–46.

28. Some scholars such as A. P. Kazhdan view the *Parastaseis* as a document written to oppose the cult of Constantine the Great. He also reappraises the eighth-century dating given by the editors Cameron and Herrin and reascribes it roughly a century later. *ODB,* 1586 and *A History of Byzantine Literature, 650–850* (Athens: National Hellenic Research Foundation for Byzantine Research, 1999), p. 309. For an overview of recent discussion on the text, see Leslie Brubaker and John Haldon, *Byzantium in the Iconoclast Era (ca. 680–850): The Sources, An Annotated Survey* (Burlington, VT: Ashgate, 2001), p. 301.

29. *Parastaseis,* eds. and trans. Averil Cameron and Judith Herrin, *Constantinople in the Early Eighth Century: The Parastaseis Syntomoi Chronikai* (Leiden: E. J. Brill, 1984), sect. 11, p. 73.

30. *Parastaseis,* sect. 15, p. 79 and sect. 34, p. 95.

31. *Parastaseis,* sect. 43, pp. 120 and 122.

32. *Parastaseis,* sect. 53, p. 127.

33. *Parastaseis,* sect. 53, p. 129

34. *Parastaseis,* sect. 58, p. 135.
35. Brubaker, "Helena," in *Women, Men, and Eunuchs: Gender in Byzantium,* p. 59.
36. Dumbarton Oaks Collection, 70.37.
37. Andrew Carriker, "The Function and Importance of the Empress' Coinage, A.D. 241–404," Paper presented at the American Numismatic Society Summer 1993 Seminar, New York.
38. Vasiliki Limberis, *Divine Heiress: The Virgin Mary and the creation of Christian Constantinople* (New York: Routledge, 1994), p. 72. Text in Julian, "Oration to Eusebia," *The Works of Emperor Julian,* ed. and trans. Wilmer Cave Wright, 3 vols., LCL (London: William Heinemann, 1913), 1: 281.
39. Eusebios, *Letter to Constantia,* ed. F. Winkelmann, *Die griechischen christlichen Schriftsteller der ersten Jahrhunderte* (Berlin: Akademie-Verlag, 1975).
40. Sister Charles Murray, *Rebirth and Afterlife: A study of the transmutation of some pagan imagery in early Christian funerary art* (Oxford: B. A. R., 1981), pp. 25–26.
41. Marie-France Auzépy, "La destruction de l'icône du Christ de la Chalcé par Léon III: Propagande or réalité?" *Byzantion* 60 (1990): 445–92.
42. Kassia, "The Great-martyr Christina at the Orthos," *Kassia: The Legend, the Woman and Her Work,* trans. Antonia Tripolitis (New York: Garland, 1992), pp. 56–57, lines 1–4.
43. Kenneth G. Holum, *Theodosian Empresses: Women and Imperial Dominion in Late Antiquity* (Berkeley: University of California Press, 1982), p. 3. Dean A. Miller disputes his basic thesis, arguing for the development of this phenomenon much later, Dean A. Miller, "Byzantine Sovereignty and Feminine Potencies," in *Women and Sovereignity,* ed. Louise Olga Fradenburg (Edinburgh: Edinburgh University Press, 1992), p. 251 [250–63].
44. Holum, *Theodosian,* p. 27.
45. Agathias, *Greek Anthology,* 16.41.
46. Catia Galatariotou, "Holy Women and Witches: Aspects of Byzantine Conceptions of Gender," *Byzantine and Modern Greek Studies* 9 (1984–85): 62 [55–94].
47. Galatariotou, "Holy Women," 62.
48. Mark the Deacon, *Life of Porphyry,* 75, ed. and trans. Henri Grégoire and M. A. Kugener (Paris: Société d'Édition "Les Belles Lettres," 1930).
49. Mark the Deacon, *Life of Porphyry,* 76, trans. from Cyril Mango, *The Art of the Byzantine Empire 312–1453: Sources and Documents* (1972; repr. Toronto: University of Toronto Press, 1986), p. 31.
50. Mark the Deacon, *Life of Porphyry,* 84.
51. Jean-Pierre Sodini, "Images sculptées et propagande impériale du IVe au VIe siècle: recherches récentes sur les colonnes honorifiques et les reliefs politiques à Byzance," in *Byzance et les images,* ed. Andre Guillou and Jannic Durand (Paris: La documentation française, 1994), p. 64 [43–94].
52. *Parastaseis,* sect. 31, p. 93.
53. Maria Delivorria, *Recherches sur l'iconographie d'impératrice byzantine* (Ph.D. diss. Sorbonne, Paris, 1966), p. 6.

54. *The Life of Melania the Younger,* 58, trans. Elizabeth A. Clark (New York: Edwin Mellen Press, 1984).
55. A sixth-century source, Evagrius, assumed Eudokia hailed from Athens and that this declaration elliptically referred to Athenian colonists of Antioch, so this possibility should not be entirely discounted. As Festugière translates the text, "Elle était de race athénienne," Evagrius, *Ecclesiastical History,* 1.20, trans. A.-J. Festugière, in "Évagre: *Histoire Ecclesiastique,*" *Byzantion* 45 (1975): 228 [187–488].
56. Constantine VII Porphyrogennetos, *De administrando imperio, De administrando imperio,* Dumbarton Oaks Texts One, ed. Gy. Moravcsik, trans. R. J. H. Jenkins (Washington, D. C.: Dumbarton Oaks, 1967), p. 71.
57. John Malalas, *The Chronicle of John Malalas,* 14.8 [357], trans. Elizabeth Jeffreys, Michael Jeffreys, and Roger Scott (Melbourne: Australian Association for Byzantine Studies, 1986), pp. 194–95 n8.
58. Glanville Downey, *Ancient Antioch* (Princeton: Princeton University Press, 1963), p. 217.
59. Evagrius, *Ecclesiastical History,* 1.20.
60. *Parastaseis,* sect. 36, p. 97.
61. Malalas, *Chronicle,* 14.8 [356–57], p. 194. Zacharias of Mitylene merely says "Eudocia the queen, the wife of Theodosius, went to Jerusalem for prayer, and returned, and then died." *Syriac Chronicle,* 2.5, trans. F. J. Hamilton and E. W. Brooks (1899; repr. New York, 1979), p. 148.
62. Malalas, *Chronicle,* 14.8 [357–58], p. 195.
63. Yizhar Hirschfeld, *Judean Desert Monasteries in the Byzantine Period* (New Haven: Yale University Press, 1992), p. 242. Julia Burman points out some of the difficulties in precisely apprising her patronage. Julia Burman, "The Christian Empress Eudocia," in *Les Femmes et le Monochisme Byzantine,* ed. Jacques Y. Perreault, Canadian Archaeological Institute Athens no. 1 (Athens: Canadian Archaeological Institute, 1991), p. 57 [51–59].
64. Judith Herrin, "Public and Private Forms of Religious Commitment among Byzantine Women," in *Women in Ancient Societies: An Illusion of Night,* ed. Léonie J. Archer, Susan Fischler, and Maria Wyke (Basingstoke: Macmillan, 1994), p. 185.
65. Alan Cameron argues that Eudokia's classical pagan predilections have been exaggerated, "The Empress and the Poet: Paganism and Politics at the Court of Theodosius II," *Yale Classical Studies* 27 (1982): 217–90. Previous scholarship on the "University" allowed her influence as a possibility, Michael J. Kyriakis, "The University: Origin and Early Phases in Constantinople," *Byzantion* 41 (1971): 168 [161–82]; and Paul Lemerle, *Byzantine Humanism: The First Phase,* trans. Helen Lindsay and Ann Moffat (Canberra, Australia: Australian Association of Byzantine Studies, 1986), p. 66.
66. Lemerle, *Byzantine Humanism,* p. 127.
67. *Eudociae Augustae, Procli Lycii, Claudiani carminum graecorum reliquiae,* ed. Arthur Ludwich, Bibliotheca scriptorum Graecorum et Romanorum Teubneriana (Leipzig: Teubner, 1897), pp. 79–114. In this project Eudokia basically en-

larged and embellished the late fourth-century work of an otherwise unknown Bishop Patricius, Mark D. Usher, *Homeric Stitchings: The Homeric Centos of Empress Eudocia* (Lanham, MD: Rowman and Littlefield, 1998), p. 19.
68. Eudokia, *Carmen de S. Cypriano Antiocheno*, PG 85, 831–64; and Ephrat Habas, "A Poem by the Empress Eudocia: A Note on the Patriarch," *Israel Exploration Journal* 46 (1996): 108–19.
69. The *Chronicon Paschale* gives an account of the fifth-century events. *Chronicon Paschale*, Year 420, ed. Ludwig Dindorf (Bonn: Weber, 1932), p. 66. Chapter one in this book considers bride shows a little more fully.
70. Holum's overly-generous assessment of Pulcheria's precocious role in Constantinopolitan politics has been revised by Alan Cameron and Jacqueline Long, *Barbarians and Politics at the Court of Arcadius* (Berkeley: University of California Press, 1993), pp. 399–401.
71. W. Ensslin, "Pulcheria," *Paulys Real-Encyclopädie der classischen Altertumswissenschaft* 23 (1959): 1961.
72. Holum, *Theodosian*, p. 142.
73. Judith Herrin, "The Imperial Feminine in Byzantium," *Past and Present* 169 (2000): 14 [3–35].
74. *Parastaseis*, sect. 45, p. 123.
75. *Parastaseis*, sect. 33, p. 95.
76. Limberis, *Divine Heiress*, chapter three discusses this conflict of wills.
77. Limberis, *Divine Heiress*, p. 145; Ioli Kalavrezou has pursued this topic for the Middle Byzantine period effectively in "Images of the Mother: When the Virgin Mary Became *Meter Theou*," *Dumbarton Oaks Papers* 44 (1990): 165–72.
78. Kate Cooper, "Contesting the Nativity: Wives, Virgins, and Pulcheria's *imitatio Mariae*," *Scottish Journal of Religious Studies* 19 (1998): 41–42 [31–43].
79. Both the rendering of the building and the proximity of workman have antecedents even in late Flavian works such as the Tomb of Lucius Haterius. The Roman monument is discussed in Cornelius C. Vermeule, *Roman Art: Early Republic to Late Empire* (Boston: Department of Classical Art, Museum of Fine Arts, 1978), pp. 90–91, catalog no. 96.
80. Laurie Wilson, "The Trier Procession Ivory: A New Interpretation," *Byzantion* 54 (1984): 613 [602–14].
81. Josef Strzygowski, *Orient oder Rom. Beiträge zur Geschichte der Spätantike und frühchristlichen Kunst* (Leipzig: J. C. Hinrichs'sche Buchhandlung, 1901); Theodor Wiegand, Review of Delbrueck and Weitzmann, "Studien zur spätantiken Kunstgeschichte," in *Kritische Berichte*, Leipzig (1930.1): 57 [33–57]; and André Grabar, *Martyrium*, vol. 2, ch. 8, "Des reliques aux icones," (Paris: Collège de France, 1946), p. 352 n4.
82. Suzanne Spain, "The Translation of Relics Ivory, Trier," *Dumbarton Oaks Papers* 31 (1977): 279–304.
83. Kenneth G. Holum and Gary Vikan, "The Trier Ivory, Adventus Ceremonial, and the Relics of St. Stephen," *Dumbarton Oaks Papers* 33 (1979): 115–33.

84. Holum and Vikan, "Trier," 131. John Wortley points out, though, that the source for Theophanes on this point has never been determined, and thus our earliest source for this adventus is four centuries following the life of Pulcheria. If his skepticism is warranted, the events of 421 may be a later fiction, and if the ivory does represent them, the piece may have been made centuries later. "The Trier Ivory Reconsidered," *Greek, Roman, and Byzantine Studies* 21 (1980): 382 and 392 [381–94].
85. Wilson, "Trier," 602.
86. Wilson, "Trier," 603; and Saint John Chrysostom, Homily II, "Dicta postquam reliquiae Martyrum," ed. Migne, PG 63: 467–72.
87. Leslie Brubaker, " The Chalke Gate, the construction of the past, and the Trier ivory," *Byzantine and Modern Greek Studies* 23 (1999): 276–77 [258–85].
88. Liz James, *Empresses and Power in Early Byzantium* (London: Leicester University Press, 2001), p. 148.
89. Anonymous, *De rebus bellicis,* 3, ed. Robert I. Ireland (Leipzig: Teubner, 1984), p. 4, ed. and trans. E. A. Thompson (Oxford: Claredon, 1952), p. 111.
90. Eusebios, *Vita Constantini* 4.15, ed. F. Winkelmann, *Die griechischen christlichen Schriftsteller der ersten Jahrhunderte* (Berlin: Akademie-Verlag, 1975); *Life of Constantine,* trans. Averil Cameron and Stuart Hall (Oxford: Oxford University Press, 1999).
91. Susan Wood overviews the evidence for the possibility that Fulvia was the first Roman woman honored with a numismatic image and identifying inscription, *Imperial Women,* pp. 41–44.
92. Grierson and Mays, *LRC,* p. 7.
93. J. F. W. de Salis, "The Coins of the Two Eudoxias, Eudocia, Placidia, and Honoria, and of Theodosius II, Marcian, and Leo I Struck in Italy," *Numismatic Chronicle* 7 (1867): 203–15.
94. Grierson and Mays, *LRC,* nos. 273–94.
95. Grierson and Mays, *LRC,* p. 7. The relationship between the representation on coinage and bearing an heir is occasional and not predictive. Part of what is misleading are dramatic instances such as that of Faustina the Younger who was elevated to Augusta consequent to the birth of an heir or of Domitia Faustina, who had a new portrait type for each of her eleven births.
96. Fred Kleiner, catalog no. 17 entry in *I Claudia,* ed. Diana E. E. Kleiner and Susan B. Matheson, p. 64.

Chapter 2

1. K. Brown, in *Age of Spirituality: Late Antique and Early Christian Art, Third to Seventh Century,* ed. Kurt Weitzmann (New York: Metropolitan Museum of Art, 1977), p. 345.
2. R. Delbrueck, *Spätantike Kaiserporträts* (Berlin: Walter de Gruyter, 1933), pls. 122–23. Other scholars broadened the range to include women as late

as Ariadne; M. Tatic-Djuric, "L'archéologie byzantine au XIIe Congrès internationale des études byzantines d'Ochrid," *Byzantion* 31.2 (1961): 548 [548]. Delivorria's dissertation, though, which discusses these objects in a paragraph, questions this attribution, implying that the enterprise of ascribing these weights as portraits was somewhat dubious. Maria Delivorria, *Recherches sur l'iconographie d'impératrice byzantine* (Ph.D. diss. Sorbonne, Paris, 1966), p. 12.

3. Bartman has recently discussed some aspects of the over-reliance on numismatic imagery even for Roman early imperial imagery, in which the correlation between numismatics and sculpture is much stronger. Elizabeth Bartman, *Portraits of Livia: Imaging Imperial Woman in Augustan Rome* (New York: Cambridge University Press, 1999), p.13.
4. Christopher J. S. Entwistle and Michael Cowell, "A Note on a Middle Byzantine Silver Weight," in ΘΥΜΙΑΜΑ, vol. 1 (Athens: Benaki Museum, 1994), pp. 91–93.
5. Norbert Franken, *Aequipondia: Figürliche Laufgewichte römischer und frühbyzantinischer Schnellwaagen* (Diss. Rheinisch-Friedrich-Wilhelms-Universität, Bonn, 1994).
6. Marvin C. Ross, *Byzantine, Catalogue of the Byzantine and Early Mediaeval Antiquities in the Dumbarton Oaks Collections* (Washington, D. C.: Dumbarton Oaks, 1962), pp. 62–63.
7. Vera K. Ostoia, ed., *The Middle Ages: Treasures from the Cloister and the Metropolitan Museum of Art* (Los Angeles: Los Angeles County Museum of Art, 1970), catalog no. 46, p. 17.
8. Franken catalog no. CA 63.
9. Georgios Gounaris, "Kupfernes altchristliches 'Stathmion' (Gewicht) aus Philippi," *Makedonika* 20 (1980): 209–17; and "Chroniques des fouilles et découvertes archéologiques en Grèce en 1981," *Bulletin de correspondance hellénique* 106 (1982): 582 [582]. The ripple effect in the attributions to these figures is quite widespread, even Cornelius Vermeule adopts Eudokia in his discussion of a steelyard, *Roman Art: Early Republic to Late Empire* (Boston: Department of Classical Art, Museum of Fine Arts, 1978), p.180.
10. Franken, *Aequipondia*, p. 87.
11. Franken, *Aequipondia*, p. 91.
12. Franken, *Aequipondia*, p. 91.
13. Cornelius Vermeule, "New Near-Eastern, Greek and Roman Sculpture in the Museum of Fine Art, Boston," *The Classical Journal* 56 (1960): 13 [1–16].
14. Franken, *Aequipondia*, p. 88.
15. Franken, *Aequipondia*, p. 88.
16. Franken, *Aequipondia*, p. 83.
17. Franken catalog no. CA 7.
18. Franken catalog no. CA 36. This weight was first published in Rudolf Noll, *Von Altertum zum Mittelalter* (Vienna, Kunsthistorisches Museum, 1958), catalog no. 16, p. 14.

19. Franken catalog no. CA 22.Yildiz Meriçboyu and Sümer Atasoy, *Büst Seklinde Kantar Agirliklari: Steelyard Weights in the Form of a Bust* (Istanbul: Arkoloji Sanat Yayinlari, 1983).
20. Aelia Eudokia (Franken catalog nos. CA 7 and CA 1), Licinia Eudoxia (Franken catalog no. CA 22), Galla Placidia (Franken catalog nos. CA 16, CA 49, and CA 9), and Aelia Pulcheria (Franken catalog no. CA 45).
21. This steelyard weight from Kayseri is Istanbul Archeological Museum inventory no. 1333, which was later identified with Galla Placidia in the 1983 catalog cited above in n19. *Istanbul Müzeleri, Asariatika Müzesi Tunc Eserler Reheberi, Musée des Antiquités, Guide illustré des bronzes* (Istanbul: Devlet Basimevi, 1937), pl. 23.
22. Yildiz Meriçboyu, et al., *Büst,* p. 24. This attribution follows the precedent set by Delbrueck for an identification with Licinia Eudoxia on similar grounds, *Spätantike,* pl. 122B.
23. Bente Kiilerich, *Late Fourth Century Classicism in the Plastic Arts: Studies in the So-called Theodosian Renaissance* (Odense: Odense University Press, 1993), p. 83.
24. Franken catalog no. CA 6. Sheila D. Campbell, *The Malcove Collection: A Catalogue of the Objects in the Lillian Malcove Collection of the University of Toronto* (Toronto: University of Toronto Press, 1985), catalog no. 90.
25. Campbell, *Malcove,* p. 72.
26. Helen Evans claims of MMA 1980.416a, b, "Her dress and demeanor suggest she is an empresss of the Theodosian dynasty, which ruled between 379 and 450." Helen C. Evans, Melanie Holcomb, and Robert Hallman, *The Arts of Byzantium* (New York: Metropolitan Museum of Art, 2001), p. 16.
27. Weitzmann, ed., *Age of Spirituality,* catalog no. 272.
28. Elisabeth Alföldi-Rosenbaum, "Portrait Bust of a Young Lady of the Time of Justinian," *Metropolitan Museum Journal* 1 (1968): 25 [19–40].
29. John Klimax, *The Ladder of Divine Ascent,* 30, ed. Migne, PG 88: 632–1209. trans. Colm Luibheid and Norman Russell (NewYork: Paulist Press, 1982), p. 289; Paul Silentarius, "Descr. S. Sophiae," 664, *Johannes von Gaza und Paulus Silentiarios: Kunstbeschreibungen justinianischer Zeit,* ed. P. Friedländer (Leipzig, Berlin: Teubner, 1912).
30. Richard Brilliant, *Portraiture* (Cambridge: Harvard University Press, 1991), p. 104.
31. W. F. Volbach, *Geschichte des Kunstgewerbes,* ed. H. T. Bossert, 6 vols. (Berlin: Wasmuth, 1932) 5: 75.
32. Jens Fleischer, Øystein Hjort, and Mikael Bøgh Rasmussen, ed., *Byzantium: Late Antique and Byzantine Art in Scandinavian Collections* (Copenhagen: Ny Carlsberg Glyptothek, 1996), catalog no. 77.
33. The Athena weight found in the seventh-century Yassi Ada shipwreck, for example, is classified within the "Sofia Type," which was particularly popular during the fifth and sixth centuries." C. W. J. Eliot, "A Bronze Counterpoise of Athena," *Hesperia* 45 (1976): 168 [163–70].

34. Eliot, "Bronze," 163 n5.
35. Eliot, "Bronze," 170.
36. G. Kenneth Sams, "The Weighing Implements," in *Yassi Ada: A Seventh-Century Byzantine Shipwreck,* George F. Bass and Frederick H. Van Doorninck, Jr. (College Station: Texas A & M Press, 1982), p. 224 [202–30].
37. Franken, *Aequipondia,* catalog no. CA 70, p. 181
38. Liz James, *Empresses and Power in Early Byzantium* (London: Leicester University Press, 2001), p. 142; and Franken, *Aequipondia,* catalog nos. A106 and A107.
39. Franken, *Aequipondia,* catalog no. A208.
40. Franken, *Aequipondia,* catalog no. A209.
41. Franken, *Aequipondia,* catalog no. A210.
42. G. M. A. Richter, *Catalogue of Greek and Roman Antiquities in the Dumbarton Oaks Collection* (Cambridge, MA: Harvard University Press, 1956), catalog no. 22, pp. 40–42.
43. E. B. Thomas, "Eine frühbyzantinische Laufgewichtsbüste im germanischen Nationalmuseum," *Anzeiger der germanischen Nationalmuseum* (1987): 157 [151–59].
44. Corippus, the late sixth-century poet, describes a pall commissioned by the Empress Sophia that bore this type: "Old Roma holding out her arms and displaying her naked breast, her bosom bared, the ancient parent of empire and liberty." Corippus, *In laudem Iustini Augusti minoris,* 1. 285–90, ed. and trans. Averil Cameron (London: Athlone Press, 1976).
45. Ronald Mellor, "The Goddess Roma," ed. Hildegard Temporini and Wolfgang Haase, *Aufstieg und Niedergang der römischen Welt* 17.2 (1981): 1012.
46. Mellor, "Roma," 1013. Vienna, Kunsthistorisches Museum, Inv. nos. IX A 59 (chalcedony) and IX A 79 (Gemma Augustea). The dating of a related cameo, the Grand Camée in the Bibliothèque Nationale, has recently been shifted, though, to the fourth century. Elizabeth Mae Marlowe, "Repositioning the Grand Camée de France," *Archaeological Institute of American 2002 Annual Meeting,* Philadelphia.
47. The faces are strongly idealized on these pieces, on the Gemma Augustea. For instance, the faces of Roma and those of the Victory crowning Augustus and female charioteer are highly similar. Vermeule notes the numismatic corollaries of this representation, Cornelius Vermeule, *The Goddess Roma in the Art of the Roman Empire* (London: Spink, 1959), p. 84.
48. Gudrun Bühl, "Constantinopolis: Das Neue im Gewand des Alten," in *Innovation in der Spätantike,* ed. Beat Brenk (Wiesbaden: Reichert, 1996), p. 130 [115–36].
49. An example of an early dating (in this case to the second century) is found in G. Faider-Feytmans, "Antiquités gallo-romaines," in *Les antiquités égyptiennes, grecques, étrusques, romaines et gallo-romaines du Musée de Mariemont* (Brussels: Éditions de la librairie encyclopédique, 1952), p. 74, no. 379. Likewise Liz James incorrectly asserts that "After the third century, it seems that imperial personages are virtually the only image found in these

weights." James, "Goddess," in *Queens and Queenship in Medieval Europe*, p. 133. She reiterates this claim in *Empresses*, p. 115.
50. O. M. Dalton, *Catalogue of Early Christian Antiquities and Objects from the Christian East* (London: British Museum, 1901), p. 98.
51. Franken, *Aequipondia*, p. 93.
52. Franken, *Aequipondia*, p. 94.
53. Franken, *Aequipondia*, p. 92.
54. Franken, *Aequipondia*, p. 92.
55. Marvin C. Ross offers an early discussion of this type in his article on a steelyard weight he identifies with the goddess Minerva, "A Byzantine Bronze Weight," *American Journal of Archaeology* 50 (1946): 368–69.
56. Simon Price, *Rituals and Power: The Roman Imperial Cult in Asia Minor* (New York: Cambridge University Press, 1984), p. 217.
57. James Oliver, "Julia Domna as Athena Polias," *Athenian Studies Presented to William Scott Ferguson* (Cambridge, MA: Harvard University Press, 1940), p. 524.
58. Oliver, "Julia Domna," p. 527.
59. Oliver, "Julia Domna," p. 527.
60. Price, *Rituals,* p. 63.
61. Eve D'Ambra, *Private Lives, Imperial Virtues: The Frieze of the Forum Transitorium in Rome* (Princeton: Princeton University Press, 1993), p. 53.
62. Suetonius, *Lives of the Caesars,* Caligula 25, ed. and trans. J. C. Rolfe, LCL (Cambridge, MA: Harvard University Press, 1951).
63. The Corbridge lanx, *Age of Spirituality,* ed. Weitzmann, catalog no. 110; and the Metropolitan Museum Athena bracelet, *Age of Spirituality,* ed. Weitzmann, catalog no. 282, Metropolitan Museum 1917.17.190.2053.
64. Fulgentius the Mythographer, *The Mythologies,* 1, "Of Minerva," *Fulgentius the Mythographer,* trans. Leslie George Whitbread (Columbus, OH: Ohio State University Press, 1971), p. 65. I will discuss Athena/Minerva's range of meanings further in my essay in the anthology, *Art of Citizens, Soldiers, and Freedmen in the Roman World,* ed. Guy Métraux and Eve D'Ambra, forthcoming 2003.
65. Henning Wrede, *Consecratio in formam deorum: Vergöttlichte Privatpersonen in der römischen Kaiserzeit* (Mainz am Rhein: Philipp von Zabern, 1981).
66. Susan B. Matheson, "The Divine Claudia: Women as Goddesses in Roman Art," in *I Claudia,* ed. Kleiner and Matheson, p. 182.
67. Matheson, "Divine," in *I Claudia: Women in Ancient Rome,* p. 182.
68. Matheson, "Divine," in *I Claudia: Women in Ancient Rome,* p. 189. The location of this work is now unknown. Illustrated in Wrede, *Consecratio,* no. 234.
69. Franken catalog no. CB 28.
70. James Russell proposed an apotropaic meaning of these Athena-shaped objects in "The Archeological Context of Magic in the Early Byzantine Period," in *Byzantine Magic,* ed. Henry Maguire (Washington, D.C.: Dumbarton Oaks, 1995), p. 48. In conversation he speculates that the empress steelyard weights bear this association as well, but without the invo-

cation such as we have on the Athena counterpoise, the apotropaic function of the empress weights is less convincing.
71. Anna Gonosova and Christine Kondoleon, *Art of Late Rome and Byzantium* (Richmond: Virginia Museum of Fine Arts, 1994), catalog no. 83, pp. 242–45.
72. *Parastaseis,* sect. 61, p. 139.
73. Dan Sperber, *Rethinking Symbolism,* trans. Alice L. Morton (New York: Cambridge University Press, 1975), p. xi.
74. James Morton Paton, ed., *The Erectheum* (Cambridge, MA: Harvard University Press, 1927), inscription 17, col. 1, p. 389.
75. MFA 1984.222, Otis Norcross Fund. Vermeule and Comstock, *Sculpture in Stone and Bronze,* catalog no. 113, p. 90.
76. Catherine Johns and Roger Bland, "The Hoxne Late Roman Treasure," *Britannia* 25 (1994): 168 [165–74].
77. Johns and Bland, "Hoxne," 171.
78. Gonosova and Kondoleon, *Late Rome,* catalog no. 84, pp. 246–49.
79. Marvin C. Ross speculates these seated emperors were made in Rome and were based on the monumental statue of Constantine the Great erected there following his victory of the Milvian Bridge; Marvin C. Ross, "Bronze Statuettes of Constantine the Great," *Dumbarton Oaks Papers* 13 (1959): 179–83. Robert Calkins likewise discusses possible models, such as an enthroned Constantine in the Roman Basilica of Constantine, *A Medieval Treasury* (Ithaca, NY: Office of University Publications, Cornell University, 1968), p. 101. Another identification offered by Ross for the Dumbarton Oaks example is Theodosios II or Valentinian III (because of the weight's *globus cruciger,* which first appeared on the their coinage), but the thrust of his description is on the generic details that classify this object as an imperial representation: the diadem, orb, and throne. Ross, *Byzantine and Early Mediaeval Antiquities,* vol. 1, catalog no. 70, p. 60. In Ross' article on the group of "Constantine the Great" weights, he mentions other small-scale statues of seated men that might replicate large-scale works, commenting on a rough similarity between the small anonymous figures used as weights and long-destroyed monumental sculpture; "Bronze," 179–83. An earlier exploration of this topic, which follows many of the same arguments, is E. Schaffran, "Eine voelkerwanderungszeitliche Bronzstatuette eines christlichen Herrschers," *Rivista di Archeologica Cristiana* 32 (1956): 243–49.
80. Mary Comstock, Cornelius C. Vermeule, and Sandra Knudsen, *Romans and Barbarians,* catalog (Boston: Department of Classical Art, Museum of Fine Arts, 1976), catalog no. 135, p. 122.
81. Franken catalog no. CD 5.
82. David Buckton, ed., *Byzantium: Treasures of Byzantine Art and Culture* (London: British Museum Publications, 1994), catalog no. 110, p. 101.
83. Richard Gordon, "The Veil of Power: Emperors, Sacrificers and Benefactors," in *Pagan Priests: Religion and Power in the Ancient World,* ed. Mary

Beard and John North (Ithaca, NY: Cornell University Press, 1990), pp. 218–19.

Chapter 3

1. Theophanes gives the date as eight years earlier, Theophanes, *Chronographia*, AM 5951, A.D. 458/59, ed. C. de Boor, 2 vols. (Leipzig: Teubner, 1883–85), p. 111; *The Chronicle of Theophanes Confessor: Byzantine and Near Eastern History A.D. 284–813*, trans. Cyril Mango and Roger Scott (Oxford: Clarendon Press, 1997), p. 171. These particular circumstances opened the door for Ariadne to exert a strong voice in succession, but I would disagree that it "formalizes the empress's role in the choice of successor," as argued by James. Liz James, *Empresses and Power in Early Byzantium* (London: Leicester University Press, 2001), p. 52.
2. Cod. Paris gr. 1447, fols. 257–58, ed. A. Wenger, "Notes inédites sur les empereur Théodose I, Arcadius, Théodose II, Léon I," *Revue des études byzantines* 10 (1952): 54 [47–59], trans. Cyril Mango, in *The Art of the Byzantine Empire 312–1453: Sources and Documents* (1972; repr. Toronto: University of Toronto Press, 1986), p. 35.
3. Mango, *Sources*, p. 35 n57.
4. Simon Price, *Rituals and Power: The Roman Imperial Cult in Asia Minor* (New York: Cambridge University Press, 1984), catalog no. 28, p. 254.
5. Theophanes, *Chronicle*, AM 5965, A.D. 472/73, p. 119.
6. Zacharias of Mitylene, *The Syriac Chronicle*, 4.12, Zacharias, Bishop of Mitylene, eds. and trans. F. J. Hamilton and E. W. Brooks (1899; repr. New York, 1979).
7. Gregory Abu'l-Faraj, *Gregorii Barhebraei Chronicon syriacum*, 8.72, ed. P. Bedjian (Paris: Maison Neuve, 1890). *Chronicle*, trans. Ernest A. Wallis Budge (London: Oxford University Press, 1932), p. 69.
8. Gregory Abu'l-Faraj, 8.73, p. 69.
9. Anonymous, *Chronicon Paschale*, Year 477, ed. Ludwig Dindorf (Bonn: Weber, 1832); *Chronicon Paschale: 284–628 A.D.*, trans. Michael and Mary Whitby (Liverpool: Liverpool University Press, 1989), p. 600; and Gregory Abu'l-Faraj, 8.73, p. 69.
10. John of Nikiu, *The Chronicle of John, Bishop of Nikiu, Translated from Zotenberg's Ethiopic Text*, 88.41–42, trans. R. H. Charles (1916; repr. Amsterdam, 1982), p. 113.
11. John of Nikiu, 88.79–82, p. 119.
12. Theophanes, *Chronicle*, AM 5975, A.D. 482/83.
13. Theophanes, *Chronicle*, AM 5966, A.D. 473/74, pp. 186–87.
14. Theophanes, *Chronicle*, AM 5983, A.D. 490/91, p. 208.
15. "Anastasios was crowned in the Kathisma of the Hippodrome in the aforesaid 14th indiction on 14 April, it being Holy Thursday." Theophanes, *Chronicle*, AM 5983, A.D. 490/91, p. 209.

16. Cyril of Scythopolis, *Vita* of Saint Sabas, 51, ed. Eduard Schwartz (Leipzig: Hinrichs, 1939). *The Lives of the Monks of Palestine,* trans. R. M. Price (Kalamazoo, MI: Cistercian Publications, 1991).
17. *Chronicon Paschale,* Year 490, pp. 97–98. John of Nikiu also relates the same story of prophecy and mistaken interpretation, Sect. 88.92–94, p. 120.
18. *Chronicon Paschale,* Year 490, p. 98.
19. Zacharias of Mitylene, *Syriac Chronicle,* 7.1, p. 148.
20. Theophanes, *Chronicle,* AM 5983, A.D. 490/91, p. 208.
21. Theophanes, *Chronicle,* AM 6004, A.D. 511/12, p. 236. The conflict continued in this vein, until "Anastasius fled and hid in a suburban estate near Blachernai and was abused by Ariadne herself for having caused many evils to Christians." Theophanes, *Chronicle,* AM 6005, A.D. 512/13, p. 240.
22. John Lydus, *On Powers,* ed. and trans. Anastasius C. Bandy (Philadelphia: American Philosophical Society, 1983), p. 211.
23. Cyril of Scythopolis, *Vita* of Saint Sabas, 53.
24. The incident in Section 53 of the *Vita* of Saint Sabas contrasts with the preceeding sections' account of Sabas' interaction with Anastasios, Cyril of Scythopolis, *Life of Saint Sabas,* 51, 52, and 54.
25. Maria Delivorria, *Recherches sur l'iconographie d'impératrice byzantine* (Ph.D. diss. Sorbonne, Paris, 1966), p. 9.
26. Richard Delbrueck, *Die Consulardiptychen und verwandte Denkmäler,* 2 vols. (Berlin: Walter de Gruyter, 1929).
27. Wolfgang Fritz Volbach, *Elfenbeinarbeiten der spätantike und des frühen Mittelalters,* 3rd ed. (Mainz: Philipp von Zabern, 1976).
28. Roger S. Bagnall, Alan Cameron, Seth R. Schwartz, and Klaas A. Worp, *Consuls of the Later Roman Empire* (Atlanta: Scholar's Press, 1987), p. 7.
29. Bagnall, et al., *Consuls,* p. 23.
30. Corippus expounds,"When he [Justin II] reached the blessed threshold of the holy door where the path led to the middle of the city . . . he cast terror into the people by his appearance, and his eyes flashed. . . . When they saw the consul then the people rose to applaud and added voices to voices." 4. 250–62, p. 115.
31. Bagnall, *Consuls,* p. 87.
32. Bagnall, *Consuls,* p. 87.
33. Richard Lim, "People as Power: Games, Munificence, and Contested Topography," in *The Transformation of the Vrbs Roma in Late Antiquity,* ed. W. V. Harris, *Journal of Roman Archaeology, Supplemental Series* no. 33 (Portsmouth, RI: Journal of Roman Archaeology, 1999), 265–81.
34. Corippus, *In laudem Iustini Augusti minoris,* 4.9–13, ed. and trans. Averil Cameron (London: Athlone Press, 1976), p. 110.
35. John Lydus, *On Powers,* p. 95.

36. Anthony Cutler, "The Making of the Justinian Diptychs," *Byzantion* 54 (1984): 102 [75–115].
37. Delbrueck, *Consulardiptychen,* no. 16, pp.117–21; and Volbach, *Elfenbeinarbeiten,* no. 15, p. 35. For more recent scholarship on this ivory, see David Buckton, ed., *Byzantium: Treasures of Byzantine Art and Culture* (London: British Museum Publications, 1994), catalog no. 62, p. 71. The two panels are mounted in their current frame in reverse, Margaret Gibson, *The Liverpool Ivories* (London: HMSO, 1994), p. 19. The reverse of the ivories have an inscription probably made in Sicily in 732–33, Jean-Marie Sansterre, "Où le diptyque consulaire de Clemintinus fut-il remployé à une fin liturgique?," *Byzantion* 54 (1984): 645 [641–47].
38. Bagnall, et al., *Consuls,* p. 561.
39. George P. Galavaris, "The Symbolism of the Imperial Costume as Displayed on Byzantine Coins," *American Numismatic Society Museum Notes* 8 (1958): 101 [99–117].
40. Delbrueck, *Consulardiptychen,* vol. 2, no. 16, p. 120.
41. Prokopios, *History of the Wars,* 5.6.5, 5 vols., trans. H. B. Dewing, LCL (Cambridge, MA: Harvard University Press, 1919).
42. Anderson, *Age of Spirituality,* ed. Weitzmann, p. 48. In addition to the lack of positive evidence of such portraits in the consul box, other images, such as the icon of Saint Peter at Saint Catherine's Monastery on Mount Sinai, possess a similar composition without any such reference. This well-known early Byzantine icon depicts a young saint, Christ, and the Virgin Mary across the top of the panel above the haloed saint. The Roman tradition of *imagines clipeatae* in Italian funerary stelae extended to the Late Roman period; perhaps these offer one source for the medallion portraits on the consular diptychs. Scarpellini reports on a stele in Urbino, for example, that displays three medallions at the top above the traditional double door. Donatella Scarpellini, *Stele romane con imagines clipeatae in Italia* (Rome: Bretschneider, 1987), no. 25.
43. Delivorria, *Recherches,* pp. 52–53.
44. The consular throne descends from the *sella curulis.* Edward Capps, "The Style of the Consular Diptychs," *Art Bulletin* 10 (1927): 62 [61–101].
45. Kathleen J. Shelton, "Imperial Tyches," *Gesta* 18 (1979): 33 [27–38]. In the Liverpool piece, Rome is styled as an Amazon, whereas Constantinople bears the traditional Tyche's attributes of a cornucopia and a mural crown. The pairing of the personifications of Rome and Constantinople carried so much importance that a consular diptych now preserved in Vienna entirely omits the image of the new consul; instead, the two female figures consume the full face of each exterior side of the diptych panels. Stephen Zwirn, "The Vienna Ivories: The Consular Status of the Roma and the Constantinopolis Diptych," *Byzantine Studies Conference Abstracts* 26 (2000): 36–37.
46. Gudrun Bühl, "Constantinopolis: Das Neue im Gewand des Alten," in *Innovation in der Spätantike,* ed. Beat Brenk (Wiesbaden: Reichert, 1996), p. 131 [115–36].

47. Anthony Cutler, "'Roma' and 'Constantinopolis' in Vienna," in *Byzanz und der Westen, Studien zur Kunst des europaïschen Mittelalters* (Vienna: Österreichischen Akademie der Wissenschaften, 1984), pp. 60–61.
48. John Lydus, *On Powers*, p. 32.
49. Philip Grierson, *Byzantine Coins* (London: Methuen, 1982), p. 48.
50. Delbrueck, *Consulardiptychen*, vol. 2, no. 17, pp. 121–22; and Volbach, *Elfenbeinarbeiten*, no. 16, p. 35.
51. Bagnall, *Consuls*, p. 565.
52. Bagnall, *Consuls*, p. 569.
53. Delbrueck, *Consulardiptychen*, vol. 2, nos. 19–21, pp. 126–134; and Volbach, *Elfenbeinarbeiten*, nos. 20, 18, and 21, pp. 36–37.
54. Grierson, *Byzantine Coins*, p. 32.
55. Delbrueck, *Consulardiptychen*, vol. 2, no. 19, pp. 126–27; and Volbach, *Elfenbeinarbeiten*, no. 20, p. 36.
56. Delbrueck, *Consulardiptychen*, vol. 2, no. 20, pp. 127–31; and Volbach, *Elfenbeinarbeiten*, no. 17, pp. 35–36 (Berlin) and no. 18, p. 36 (London).
57. Shelton, "Imperial Tyches," 30. Singular statues of both Messalina and Claudia Octavia bear turreted crowns; Susan E. Wood, *Imperial Women, A Study in Public Images, 40 B.C.-A.D. 68* (Leiden: Brill, 1999), pp. 280 and 287–88.
58. Delbrueck, *Consulardiptychen*, no. 21, pp. 131–34; and Volbach, *Elfenbeinarbeiten*, no. 21, pp. 36–37.
59. Carolyn L. Connor, *The Color of Ivory* (Princeton: Princeton University Press, 1998), p. 16.
60. Shelton, "Imperial Tyches," 34.
61. Delbrueck, *Consulardiptychen*, p. 129.
62. Delbrueck, *Consulardiptychen*, p. 132. Lenormant's suggestion that this medallion represents Anastasia, the mother of the consul, is refuted by Delbrueck.
63. Delbrueck, *Consulardiptychen*, no. 32, pp. 148–50; and Volbach, *Elfenbeinarbeiten*, no. 31, pp. 40–41.
64. Marion Archibald, Michelle Brown, and Leslie Webster, "Heirs of Rome: The Shaping of Britain A.D. 400–900," in *The Transformation of the Roman World A.D. 400–900*, ed. Leslie Webster and Michelle Brown (Berkeley: University of California Press, 1997), p. 224 [208–48].
65. Delbrueck argues that the cap is specifically Gothic with "südrussisch-iranisch" origins, *Consulardiptychen*, p. 149.
66. Patrick Amory, *People and Identity in Ostrogothic Italy, 489–554* (New York: Cambridge University Press, 1997), p. 342.
67. Amory, *People*, p. 342.
68. Nancy Netzer, "Redating the consular ivory of Orestes," *Burlington Magazine* 125 (May 1983): 265–71. Capps had already noted the stylistic similarity of the diptychs of Clementinus and Orestes in 1927, but did not develop an explanation of this semblance. "Style," 99.
69. Netzer, "Redating," 269.

70. Netzer, "Redating," 270.
71. Pauline Allen, "Zachariah Scholasticus and the Historia Ecclesiastica of Evagrius Scholasticus," *The Journal of Theological Studies* 31 (1980): 473 [471–88].
72. Marcellinus, *The Chronicle of Marcellinus*, trans. Brian Croke (Sydney: Australian Association for Byzantine Studies, 1995), p. 38.
73. *Victoris Tonnennensis Episcopi Chronica*, ed. T. Mommsen, MGH, Auctorum Antiquissimorum, vol. 11, p. 195. *ODB*, "Victor Tonnensis," p. 2165.
74. Leslie Brubaker and John Haldon provide an incisive overview of the problems associated with using this text. Leslie Brubaker and John Haldon, *Byzantium in the Iconoclast Era (ca 680–850): The Sources* (Burlington, VT: Ashgate, 2001), pp. 168–70.
75. Diana E. E. Kleiner, "Imperial Women as Patrons of the Arts in the Early Empire," in *I Claudia: Women in Ancient Rome*, ed. Diana E. E. Kleiner and Susan B. Matheson, *I Claudia: Women in Ancient Rome* (New Haven: Yale University Art Gallery, 1996), p. 36.
76. Fittschen, "Courtly Portraits of Women," in *I Claudia: Women in Ancient Rome*, ed. Kleiner and Matheson, p. 65.
77. Marcellinus, *Chronicle*, Year 493.
78. Price, *Rituals*, p. 31.
79. Price, *Rituals*, p. 175.
80. Robin Cormack, "The Emperor at St. Sophia: Viewer and Viewed," in *Byzance et les images*, ed. Guillou and Durand (Paris: Documentation française, 1994), p. 234.
81. Vita of Saint Philaretos, 135.24–143.25. The questionable historicity of the Byzantine bride show has produced a mini-industry of scholarship. Because it largely falls outside of the chronological scope of this study, we must only glance on it here. A good account of the reasons for doubting the existence of bride shows can be found in Lennart Rydén, "The Bride-shows at the Byzantine Court—History or Fiction?" *Eranos* 83 (1985): 175–91. Unfortunately many of his objections could apply to any number of things reported in the often sketchy sources we have from this period. Warren Treadgold, therefore, argues the case for specific historical circumstances that led both to the ascendancy and decline of this odd exercise in imperial match-making. Warren Treadgold, "The Bride-Shows of the Byzantine Emperors," *Byzantion* 49 (1979): 395–413. The most important recent discussion of the question came in the Round table on "The Bride Shows at the Byzantine Court—History or Fiction?," moderated by Judith Herrin and Lennart Rydén, moderators, Round table, "The Bride Shows at the Byzantine Court—History or Fiction?," in *Byzantium: Image, Identity, Influence, XIX International Congress of Byzantine Studies*, Major Papers (Copenhagen: Eventus Publishers, 1996), pp. 506–07.
82. Gilbert Dagron, "L'image de culte et le portrait," in *Byzance et les images*, ed. Guillou and Durand (Paris: Documentation française, 1994), p. 131.
83. Elisabeth Alföldi-Rosenbaum, "Portrait Bust of a Young Lady of the Time of Justinian," *Metropolitan Museum Journal* 1 (1968): 29 [19–40].

84. Breckenridge, *Age of Spirituality,* ed. Weitzmann, catalog no. 24, p. 31.
85. Richard Delbrueck, "Portraets byzantinischer Kaiserinnen," *Mitteilungen des kaiserlich deutschen archäologischen Instituts, Römische Abteilung* 28 (1913): 323 [310–52]. Delivorria proposes that this head is slightly earlier than the Lateran or Louvre heads. Delivorria, *Recherches,* p. 14.
86. Siri Sande, "Zur Porträtplastik des sechsten nachchristlichen Jahrhunderts," *Acta ad archaeologiam et artium historiam pertinentia* 6 (1975): 67–81 [65–106].
87. Dagmar Stutzinger, "Das Bronzbildnis einer spätantiken Kaiserin aus Balajnac im Museum von Nis," *Jahrbuch für Antike und Christentum* 29 (1986): 146–65.
88. Stutzinger, "Das Bronzbildnis," 149. Other scholars such as Siri Sande agree with the general dating, but do not as quickly identify the head as a portrait of Ariadne; Sande, "Porträtplastik," 76. Rudolf Stichel, in contrast, adjusts the attribution to Euphemia in *Die römische Kaiserstatue am Ausgang der Antike* (Rome: Bretschneider, 1982), p. 63.
89. Stutzinger, "Bronzbildnis," 160.
90. Anonymous, *Parastaseis syntomoi chronikai Parastaseis,* sects. 32 and 80, eds. and trans. Averil Cameron and Judith Herrin, *Constantinople in the Early Eighth Century: The Parastaseis Syntomoi Chronikai* (Leiden: E. J. Brill, 1984), pp. 95 and 159 respectively.
91. *Parastaseis,* sect. 30, p. 93. This reference contradicts other sources that indicate that Anicia Juliana was more involved in the Church of Saint Euphemia.
92. First published by G. Zacos and A. Veglery, "An Unknown Solidus of Anastasios I," *The Numismatic Circular* 67.9 (1959): 154–55. This identification is questioned in Wolfgang Hahn, "Die Münzprägung für Aelia Ariadne," in *BYZANTIOΣ: Festschrift für Herbert Hunger,* ed. W. Hörander, et al. (Vienna: Ernst Becvar, 1984), p. 106 [101–06].
93. Zacos and Veglery, "Unknown," 154.
94. G. Zacos and A. Veglery, "Marriage Solidi of the Fifth Century," *Numismatic Circular* 68.4 (1960): 74 [73–74].
95. Jutta Meischner, "Der Hochzeitskameo des Honorius," *Archäologischer Anzeiger* 4 (1993): 613–19.
96. Philip Grierson and Melinda Mays, *Catalogue of Late Roman Coins in the Dumbarton Oaks Collection and in the Whittemore Collection* (Washington, D.C.: Dumbarton Oaks, 1992), p. 171.
97. Grierson and Mays, *LRC,* no. 594.
98. Ioli Kalavrezou, "Helping Hands for the Empire: Imperial Ceremonies and the Cult of Relics at the Byzantine Court," in *Byzantine Court Culture from 829 to 1204,* ed. Henry Maguire (Washington, D. C.: Dumbarton Oaks, 1997), pp. 63–64 [53–79].
99. Grierson and Mays, *LRC,* no. 606.
100. Hahn, "Die Münzprägung für Aelia Ariadne," pp. 104–05.
101. Grierson and Mays note, however, the authenticity of our few examples of these gold issues had been questioned because the obverse portrait side lacks the customary *Manus Dei* holding a crown coming down from above,

but the discovery of an example in a Scandinavian excavation dispelled those doubts. Grierson and Mays, *LRC,* p. 176.
102. Hahn, "Münzprägung," ills. 2 and 3.
103. Hahn, "Münzprägung," 105.
104. Grierson and Mays, *LRC,* p. 180.
105. Howard L. Adelson and George L. Kustas, "A Sixth-Century Hoard of Minimi from the Peloponnese," *American Numismatic Society Museum Notes* 11 (1964): 171 [159–205].
106. Zacharias of Mitylene, *Syriac Chronicle,* 7.13, p. 185.

Chapter 4

1. Michael Maas developes this contrast in his study, *John Lydus and the Roman Past: Antiquarianism and Politics in the Age of Justinian* (London: Routledge, 1992).
2. Inscription nos. 1, 2, 6, 8, 10, 11, 12,13, 14, 16, 17, 19, 20, and 21 include Theodora with Justinian. Jean Durliat, *Les dédicaces d'ouvrage de défense dans l'Afrique byzantine* (Rome: Ecole française de Rome, 1981).
3. Anonymous, *Chronicon Paschale,* Year 532, ed. Ludwig Dindorf (Bonn: Weber, 1832); *Chronicon Paschale: 284–628 A.D.,* trans. Michael and Mary Whitby (Liverpool: Liverpool University Press, 1989), p. 124.
4. *Fasti archaeologici* 20 (1969): 7128; Philippe Le Ba and W. H. Waddington, *Voyage archéologique en Grèce et en Asie Mineur* (Paris: Didot Frères, 1874): 1916a; Denis van Berchem, "Recherches sur la chronologie des enceintes de Syrie et de Mésopotamie," *Syria* 31 (1954): 267–68.
5. John Malalas, *Chronicle,* 18.31 [444], ed. Ioannes Thurn, *Ioannis Malalae Chronographia, Corpus fontium historiae Byzantinae,* 35 (Berlin: Walter de Gruyter, 2000); *The Chronicle of John Malalas,* trans. Elizabeth Jeffreys, Michael Jeffreys and Roger Scott (Melbourne: Australian Association for Byzantine Studies, 1986), p. 259.
6. Martin Harrison, *A Temple for Byzantium* (Austin: University of Texas Press, 1989), p. 36.
7. John of Nikiu, *The Chronicle of John, Bishop of Nikiu, Translated from Zotenberg's Ethiopic Text,* sect. 89.65, trans. R. H. Charles (1916; repr. Amsterdam, 1982), p. 129.
8. Anthony Cutler, "The Making of the Justinian Diptychs," *Byzantion* 54 (1984): 102 [75–115].
9. Harrison, *Temple,* p. 131.
10. Cyril Mango and Ihor Sevčenko, "Remains of the church of Saint Polyeuktos at Constantinople," *Dumbarton Oaks Papers* 15 (1961): 243–47.
11. Anonymous, *Greek Anthology,* 1.10.1–11, ed. H. Beckby, *Anthologia Graeca,* 4 vols. (Munich: Ernst Heimeran, 1965); trans. W. R. Paton, LCL (Cambridge, MA: Harvard University Press, 1916–27).
12. Leslie Brubaker, "Memories of Helena: Patterns of Imperial Matronage in the Fourth and Fifth Centuries," in *Women, Men, and Eunuchs: Gender in Byzantium,* ed. Liz James (New York: Routledge, 1997), p. 61 [52–75].

NOTES TO PAGES 96–99

13. Carolyn L. Connor, "The Epigram in the Church of Hagios Polyeuktos in Constantinople and its Byzantine Response," *Byzantion* 69 (1999): 514 [479–527].
14. Anonymous, *Greek Anthology*, 1.10.47–48.
15. Christine Milner, "The image of the rightful ruler: Anicia Juliana's Constantine mosaic in the church of Hagios Polyeuktos," in *New Constantines: The Rhythm of Imperial Renewal in Byzantium, 4th–13th Centuries*, ed. Paul Magdalino (Hampshire, U. K.: Variorum, 1994), pp. 76–77 [73–82].
16. Harrison, *Temple*, p.139.
17. Anonymous, *Greek Anthology*, 1.12.
18. Cyril of Scythopolis, *Vita* of Saint Sabas, 53 and 69, ed. Eduard Schwartz, *Kyrillos von Skythopolis* (Leipzig: Hinrichs, 1939); *The Lives of the Monks of Palestine*, trans. R. M. Price (Kalamazoo, MI: Cistercian Publications, 1991).
19. Theophanes, *Chronicle*, AM 6005, A.D. 512/13, ed. C. de Boor, 2 vols. (Leipzig: Teubner, 1883–85), p. 158; *The Chronicle of Theophanes Confessor: Byzantine and Near Eastern History A.D. 284–813*, trans. Cyril Mango and Roger Scott (Oxford: Clarendon Press, 1997), p. 239.
20. Codex Vindobonensis med. gr. 1, Vienna, Österreichische Nationalbibliothek, folio 6v. (Anicia Juliana).
21. Kurt Weitzmann, *Late Antique and Early Christian Book Illumination* (New York: George Braziller, 1977), p. 61.
22. Quoted in Anthony Cutler, "Uses of Luxury: On the Functions of Consumption and Symbolic Capital in Byzantine Culture," *Byzance et les images*, ed. André Guillou and Jannic Durrand (Paris: La documentation française, 1994), p. 298 [289–327].
23. Cutler, "Uses," in *Byzance*, p. 298. James implies that Anicia is the patron of this manuscript and that is the case only in the sense that the gift honored Anicia's patronage. Liz James, *Empresses and Power in Early Byzantium* (London: Leicester University Press, 2001), p. 149.
24. The date of the text is widely disputed, although its composition within the decade of the 550s seems fairly certain. For discussion see Averil Cameron, *Procopius and the Sixth Century* (Berkeley: University of California Press, 1985), p. 86.
25. Glanville Downey, "Notes on Procopius, *De aedifiis*, Book I," in *Studies Presented to David Moore Robinson on His Seventieth Birthday*, vol. 2, ed. George E. Mylonas and Doris Raymond (St. Louis, Missouri: Washington University Press, 1953), p. 722 [719–25]. George Kennedy discusses further the *Buildings* in the context of rhetorical education. George A. Kennedy, *Classical Rhetoric and Its Christian and Secular Tradition from Ancient to Modern Times*, 2nd ed. (Chapel Hill: University of North Carolina Press, 1999), p. 186.
26. Michael the Syrian, *Chronique de Michel le Syrien*, ed. and French trans. J.-B. Chabot (Paris: Ernest Leroux, 1901), 9.24 [287].
27. Prokopios, *Buildings*, ed. J. Haury, vol. 4, *Procopii Caesariensis opera omnia* (Leipzig: Teubner, 1964); trans. H. B. Dewing, *LCL* (Cambridge, MA: Harvard University Press, 1940), 1.2.17.
28. Prokopios, *Buildings*, 1.11.24–25.

29. J. B. Bury, *History of the Later Roman Empire*, 2 vols. (1923; repr. New York: Dover, 1958), 2: 31.
30. John of Ephesus, *Lives of the Eastern Saints*, ed. and trans. E. W. Brooks, *Patrologia Orientalis* 18, folio 4 (Paris: Firmin-Didot, 1924), p. 541. He bolsters this assertion with the stock quotation from Paul, "In Christ Jesus is no male or female, nor bond nor free," p. 542. Likewise his *Vita* of the Blessed Mary the Anchorite begins with "Therefore neither was the history of this holy Mary unworthy of admiration, a woman who by nature only bore the form of females, but herself also too bore in herself the character and soul and will not only of ordinary men, but of mighty and valiant men," p. 559.
31. Elizabeth A. Clark, "Ideology, History, and the Construction of 'Woman' in Late Ancient Christianity," *Journal of Early Christian Studies* 2.2 (1994): 166 [155–84].
32. John of Ephesus, *The Third Part of the Ecclesiastical History of John of Ephesus*, 3.1.1, ed. E. W. Brooks, *Iohannis Ephesini Historiae Ecclesiasticae Pars Tertia* (Paris: E typographeo reipublicae, 1935), trans. R. Payne Smith (Oxford: Oxford University Press, 1860).
33. "Syria and Armenia, Cappodocia and Cilicia, Isauria and Lycaonia, and Asia and Alexandria and Byzantium." John of Ephesus, *Lives of the Eastern Saints*, p. 677.
34. John of Ephesus, *Lives of the Eastern Saints*, pp. 676–84. He describes her in uniformly glowing terms although he makes a passing reference to her as "Theodora of the brothel." This comment can been seen as a vindication for the *Anekdota*.
35. It is commonly asserted that Theodora likely came from the eastern part of the Empire; this assumption is based both on her preference for Monophysitism, but also a lingering orientalism that conveniently locates the *femme fatale* in the east.
36. John of Ephesus, *Lives*, p. 677.
37. John of Ephesus, *Lives*, p. 678.
38. John of Ephesus, *Lives*, pp. 529, 533–36, 600.
39. John of Ephesus, *Lives*, p. 680.
40. John of Ephesus, *Lives*, p. 680.
41. Zacharias of Mitylene, *The Syriac Chronicle*, 9.15 and 9.19, eds. and trans. F. J. Hamilton and E. W. Brooks (1899; repr. New York, 1979), pp. 247 and 265.
42. Zacharias of Mitylene, *Syriac Chronicle*, 9.20, p. 270.
43. Gregory Abu'l-Faraj, 8.79, p. 74.
44. Jonathan Bardill, "The Church of Sts. Sergius and Bacchus in Constantinople and the Monophysite Refugees," *Dumbarton Oaks Papers* 54 (2000): 9 [1–11].
45. Cyril Mango, "The Church of Saints Sergius and Bacchus at Constantinople and the Alleged Tradition of Octagonal Palatine Churches," *Jahrbuch der Österreichischen Byzantinistik* 21 (1972): 190 [189–93]. Several of Mango's arguments were challenged in Thomas F. Mathews, "Architecture et

liturgie dans les premières églises palatiales de Constantinople," *Revue de l'Art* 24 (1974): 22–29; and by Richard Krautheimer in the same year, "Again Saints Sergius and Bacchus at Constantinople," *Jahrbuch der Österreichischen Byzantinistik* 23 (1974): 251–53. I believe Mango successfully refutes these issues in "The Church of Sts. Sergius and Bacchus Once Again," *Byzantinische Zeitschrift* 68 (1975): 385–92. Mango's view is also taken up in Wolfgang Müller-Wiener, "Küçük Aya Sofya Camii," in *Bildlexikon zur Topographie Istanbuls* (Tübingen: Ernst Wasmuth, 1977), p. 178 [177–83].

46. Mango, "Church," (1972), 192.
47. H. Swainson, "Monograms on the Capitals of S. Sergius at Constantinople," *Byzantinische Zeitschrift* 4 (1895): 106–08.
48. *Patria* 3.93; and Alexander van Millingen, *Byzantine Constantinople, The Walls of the City and Adjoining Historical Sites* (London: John Murray, 1899), p. 300.
49. The Church seems in other instances to be a refuge from the wrath of Justinian, despite its location within the Hormisdas Palace. The Pope Vergilius, for instance, hid there after annoying the emperor. Theophanes, *Chronicle*, AM 6039, A.D. 546/47.
50. John of Ephesus, *Lives*, pp. 680, 683.
51. John of Ephesus, *Lives*, p. 684.
52. John of Nikiu, 90.87, p. 144.
53. Gregory Abu'l-Faraj, 8.78, ed. P. Bedjian (Paris: Maison Neuve, 1890); *Chronicle*, trans. Ernest A. Wallis Budge (New York: Oxford University Press, 1932), pp. 73–74.
54. Michael the Syrian, *Chronicle,* 9.20 [277].
55. Michael the Syrian, *Chronicle*, 9.21 [278].
56. Harvey argues that, despite Theodora's initiative, the credit should go to Justinian for the protection of the Monophysites, although their amnesty was continued after her death, "because of his love for her and devotion to her memory." Susan Ashbrook Harvey, *Asceticism and Society in Crisis: John of Ephesus and the Lives of the Ancient Saints* (Berkeley: University of California Press, 1990), p. 82.
57. John Malalas, *Chronicle,* 18.61 [467], p. 272.
58. Marcelle Thiébaux translates the letter as follows:

> Since it is characteristic of our way of life to seek those things that are considered to pertain to the glory of pious princes, it is appropriate to venerate you in written words—you who all agree are continually enhaced in your virtues. Harmony exists not only between those who are in each others' presence; indeed, those joined together in the charity of the spirit have an even greater respect for each other. For this reason, rendering to the Augusta the affection of a reverent greeting, I hope that when our legates return— those whom we have sent to the most clement and glorious prince—you will make us rejoice in your safety. Your propitious

circumstances are as welcome to us as our own. It is essential to make your safety our heartfelt concern. It is well known that we hope for this unceasingly.

Letter of Queen Amalasuntha to Theodora Augusta, ed. and trans. Michelle Thiébaux, *The Writings of Medieval Women: An Anthology* (New York: Garland, 1994), pp. 82–83. This letter is particularly interesting given the accusations made in Prokopius that Theodora had the Gothic queen murdered out of jealousy.

59. John Lydus, *On Powers*, 2.69, ed. and trans. Anastasius C. Bandy (Philadelphia: American Philosophical Society, 1983). John Lydus' representation of Theodora is analyzed in Charles Pazdernik, "'Our Most Pious Consort Given Us by God': Dissident Reactions to the Partnership of Justinian and Theodora, A.D. 525–548," *Classical Antiquity* 13.2 (1994): 261–63.
60. Prokopios, *Anekdota*, 9.49, ed. J. Haury, vol. 2, *Procopii Caesariensis opera omnia* (Leipzig: Teubner, 1963); *Secret History*, ed. and trans. H. B. Dewing, LCL (Cambridge, MA: Harvard University Press, 1935).
61. Prokopios, *Anekdota*, 9.48.
62. Prokopios, *Anekdota*, 6.17.
63. Prokopios, *Anekdota*, 17.27.
64. Susan Fischler's comment regarding the Roman Imperial period holds true for the Byzantine era, "By definition, 'good emperors' had wives and mothers they can control, who never overstepped boundaries set by convention." Fischler, "Social Stereotypes," 127; and Kate Cooper, "Insinuations of Womanly Influence: An aspect of the Christinization of the Roman Aristocracy," *Journal of Roman Studies* 82 (1992): 163 [150–64].
65. Prokopios, *Anekdota*, 10.15.
66. For example, Justinian "wished to spare the men's lives; but he was not able to do so, so his consort was enraged . . . and adjured him to have the men put to death . . . and they were sent to the seashore and killed." Zacharias of Mitylene, *Syriac Chronicle*, 9.14, p. 246.
67. Prokopios, *Anekdota*, 10.16–17.
68. Prokopios, *Anekdota*, 10.23.
69. Kenneth G. Holum, *Theodosian Empresses: Women and Imperial Dominion in Late Antiquity* (Berkeley: University of California Press, 1982), p. 175.
70. Prokopios, *Buildings*, 1.9.5.
71. Roger Scott interprets Malalas' *Chronicle* as based on imperial propaganda and the *Anekdota* as within the tradition of emperor criticism. Roger D. Scott, "Malalas, the *Secret History*, and Justinian's Propaganda," *Dumbarton Oaks Papers* 39 (1985): 99–109.
72. Malalas, *Chronicle*, 18.24 [441], p. 255.
73. Simon Price, *Rituals and Power: The Roman Imperial Cult in Asia Minor* (New York: Cambridge University Press, 1984), p. 30.

74. Price, *Rituals*s, p. 32.
75. Barry Baldwin developes the argument in an elegant little study that Prokopios uses the term "obols" instead of the then-current coin, the "solidus," as a deliberate anachronism. Barry Baldwin, "Three Obol Girls in Procopius," *Hermes* 120 (1992): 255–57.
76. Prokopios, *Anekdota*, 17.5.
77. Prokopios, *Buildings*, 1.9.10.
78. Prokopios, *Buildings*, 1.9.2. The *Anekdota*, in contrast, tells us that the former prostitutes were so unhappy with their new life that "some of them threw themselves down from a height at night and thus escaped the unwelcome transformation." Prokopios, *Anekdota*, 17.6.
79. John of Nikiu, 93.3, p. 147. A later passage in John of Nikiu mentions a House of Theodore that the translator, R. H. Charles, speculates may refer to this convent. p. 167, n2.
80. Malalas, *Chronicle*, 18.19 [423], p. 243.
81. Malalas, *Chronicle*, 18.25 [441].
82. Glanville Downey, *Ancient Antioch* (Princeton: Princeton University Press, 1963), p. 254.
83. The verb rendered as "the columns were sent" is noted by the translators as being an active masculine participle, although it here clearly refers to the empress. The panegyrical form in this way seems to presuppose a male subject. Malalas, *Chronicle*, 17.19 [423], p. 243 n19.
84. Prokopios, *Buildings*, 2.10.19–25.
85. Prokopios, *Buildings*, 2.1.11–27.
86. Glanville Downey, "Procopius on Antioch: a Study of Method in the 'De Aedificiis,'" *Byzantion* 14 (1939): 369 [361–78].
87. Cameron, *Procopius*, p. 106.
88. I. Kawar, "Procopius and Arethas," *Byzantinische Zeitschrift* 50 (1957): 45 [39–67, 362–82].

Chapter 5

1. Scholars, notably Tinnefeld, have delineated the *Anekdota's* status in terms of rhetorical genre. Franz Hermann Tinnefeld, *Kategorien der Kaiserkritik in der byzantinischen Historiographie von Prokop bis Niketas Choniates* (Munich: Wilhelm Fink, 1971), pp. 29–36. Geoffrey Greatrex questions the very idea of *Kaiserkritik* in general, and in the specific instance of Prokopios he prefers to emphasize that criticism is present throughout his work, including the *Wars* and *Buildings*. Geoffrey Greatrex, "Procopius the Outsider?" in *Strangers to Themselves: The Byzantine Outsider* (Burlington: Ashgate, 2000), p. 221 [215–28].
2. Prokopios, *Anekdota*, 1.9, ed. J. Haury, vol. 2, *Procopii Caesariensis opera omnia* (Leipzig: Teubner, 1963); *Secret History*, ed. and trans. H. B. Dewing, *LCL* (Cambridge, MA: Harvard University Press, 1935).

3. John Lydus, *On Powers*, 2.58, ed. and trans. Anastasius C. Bandy (Philadelphia: American Philosophical Society, 1983).
4. Prokopios carefully crafts the appearance of historical rigor, so that in his account of the Persian Wars, he halts the narrative at one point to say: "I am unable to speak with accuracy. For the Persian accounts do not agree with each other, and for this reason I omit the narration of them." Prokopios, *Wars*, 1.6.9, ed. J. Haury, vols. 1–2, *Procopii Caesariensis opera omnia* (Leipzig: Teubner, 1962/1 and 1963/2); ed. and trans. H. B. Dewing, 5 vols., LCL (Cambridge, MA: Harvard University Press, 1919). This statement could also be read to suggest the untrustworthiness of historical accounts, implicitly including his own, although its presence in the *Wars* frames it differently than if it had been in the *Anekdota*.
5. J. A. S. Evans, *The Age of Justinian: The circumstances of imperial power* (New York: Routledge, 1996), p. 4.
6. Hans-Georg Beck, *Kaiserin Theodora und Prokop* (Munich: Piper, 1986), p. 93.
7. Prokopios, *Buildings*, 1.2, ed. J. Haury, vol. 4, *Procopii Caesariensis opera omnia* (Leipzig: Teubner, 1964); ed. and trans. H. B. Dewing, LCL (Cambridge, MA: Harvard University Press, 1940).
8. Suetonius, "Gaius (Caligula)," 20, *The Twelve Caesars*, trans. Robert Graves (New York: Viking Penguin, 1957), p. 163.
9. Averil Cameron, *Procopius and the Sixth Century* (Berkeley: University of California Press, 1985), p. 50.
10. The *Souda*'s prurient bent recurs in places such as its entry on Sappho, the first reference since the seventh century, in which this strange Middle Byzantine compendium relates that this ancient Greek poet from Lesbos is reported to have had shameful friendships with other women.
11. John of Nikiu, *The Chronicle of John, Bishop of Nikiu, Translated from Zotenberg's Ethiopic Text*, Sect. 92.20, trans. R. H. Charles (1916; repr. Amsterdam, 1982), p. 147.
12. The *Liber Pontificalis* relates the interchange between Theodora and Pope Vigilius, in which he refused her request to restore Anthimus to office. *Le Liber Pontificalis*, 1: 61.103–06, ed. L. Duchesne (Paris: Boccard, 1955).
13. Charles Diehl, *Théodora: Impératrice de Byzance* (Paris: Eugène Rey, 1904), pp. 289–304.
14. Cameron, *Procopius*, p. 49.
15. The many peculiarities of the *Anekdota* prompted one scholar, K. Adshead, recently to speculate that the text we currently consider one entity is actually an early tenth-century compilation of three distinct Prokopian texts. This provocative argument parses the *Anekdota* into an amalgam of literary genres. The first section, comprising chapters 1–5, revolves around Antonina and Belisarios, following the well-trodden narrative paths of an ancient novel, replete with the standard motifs of separation, an absurd love triangle, and travel. The second part, the locus of so much modern attention, is construed by Adshead as an aitiology, an examination of causes based specifically on Thucydides' renowned *Pathologia*. The final section, the cur-

rent chapters 19–30, follow the new structures of a financial pamphlet, representing "the increased awareness of economic factors as an independent dimension in the life of the state." Adshead posits that the patriographic literature of the intervening period from the sixth to tenth centuries had spawned a reading audience that was comfortable with this sort of textual potpourri. K. Adshead, "The Secret History of Procopius and Its Genesis," *Byzantion* 63 (1993): 18 and 23 [5–28].

16. Henry Maguire, *Art and Eloquence in Byzantium* (Princeton: Princeton University Press, 1981), p. 13.
17. Hans-Georg Beck, *Kaiserin Theodora und Prokop* (Munich: Piper, 1986), p. 18.
18. Plato, *Phaedrus*, trans. Harold North Fowler (with ed. of Schanz), Plato, vol. 1, LCL, 260 A (Cambridge, MA: Harvard University Press, 1914), p. 513.
19. Menander, *Menander Rhetor*, eds and trans. D. A. Russell and N. G. Wilson (New York: Oxford University Press, 1981), p. xi.
20. For example, Menander discusses how to laud with equal fervor the aristocratic or humble origins of an emperor. Menander, "Treatise II," p. 81.
21. Stanley Fish, "How to Recognize a Poem When You See One," *Is There a Text in This Class?* (Cambridge, MA: Harvard University Press, 1980), pp. 322–37.
22. John W. Barker, *Justinian and the Later Roman Empire* (Madison, WI: University of Wisconsin Press, 1966), p. 68.
23. Judith Herrin, "In Search of Byzantine Women: Three Avenues of Approach," in *Images of Women in Antiquity*, ed. Averil Cameron and Amélie Kuhrt (2nd. ed.; London: Routledge, 1993), p. 167 [167–89]. Judith Herrin likewise declares elsewhere that "part of this disreputable background is indubitably correct; Theodora was raised by Justinian from the position of a prostitute to occupy the imperial throne." Judith Herrin, "The Byzantine Secrets of Procopius," *History Today* 38 (1988): 40 [36–42].
24. Lynda Garland several times nods at the tradition of invective, but she does not to a large degree does not take the *Anekdota's* rhetorical structure into account in evaluating its assertions. Lynda Garland, *Byzantine Empresses: Women and Power in Byzantium A.D. 527–1204* (London: Routledge, 1999), p. 15.
25. Prokopios, *Buildings*, 1.11.9.
26. Lynda Garland, "'The Eye of the Beholder': Byzantine Imperial Women and their Public Image from Zoe Porphyrogenita to Euphrosyne Kamaterissa Doukaina (1028–1203)," *Byzantion* 64 (1994): 31 [19–39].
27. "Now Theodora was fair of face and in general attractive in appearance, but short of stature and lacking in color, being, however, not altogether pale but rather sallow, and her glance was always intense and made with contracted brows." Prokopios, *Anekdota*, 10.11–12.
28. Prokopios, *Anekdota*, 9.19. Having knowledge of birth control and methods of abortion would implicate a woman with low morals in early Byzantine literature. These issues are discussed further in Evelyne Patlagean,

"Birth Control in the Early Byzantine Empire," in *Biology of Man in History*, ed. Robert Forster and Orest Ranum (Baltimore: Johns Hopkins University Press, 1975), p. 10 [1–22] as well as a recent publication by the author. Anne McClanan, "'Weapons to Probe the Womb': The Material Culture of Abortion and Contraception in the Early Byzantine Period," in *The Material Culture of Sex, Procreation, and Marriage in Premodern Europe*, ed. Anne McClanan and Karen Encarnación (New York: St. Martin's Press/Palgrave, 2002), pp. 33–57.

29. Angeliki E. Laiou, "Observations on the Life and Ideology of Byzantine Women," *Byzantinische Forschungen* 9 (1985): 66–68 [59–102]; Gillian Clark likewise surveys the copious textual evidence from the late antique period that reflects this attitude, Clark, *Women in Late Antiquity*, pp. 46–48 and 86–87.
30. Prokopios, *Anekdota*, 17.16–23.
31. Even within the *Anekdota*, Prokopios refers to her grandson Anastasios. *Anekdota*, 5.18–21.
32. Peggy McCracken, *The Romance of Adultery: Queenship and Sexual Transgression in Old French Literature* (Philadelphia: University of Pennsylvania Press, 1998), p. 30.
33. Prokopios, *Anekdota*, 3.8. This description is similar to that of Saint John Chrysostom, who had a series of public arguments with the Theodosian Empress Eudokia: "You who are in the flesh make war against the incorporeal one. You who enjoy baths and perfumes and sex with a male do battle with the pure and untouched church." PG 52: 437, trans. in Holum, *Theodosian Empresses*, p. 77. Judith Herrin surprisingly finds Prokopios credible on the account: "She also tortured and probably killed several individuals whom she accused of serious crimes, trumped-up charges no doubt, but she was able to impose an arbitrary judgement." Judith Herrin, "The Imperial Feminine in Byzantium," *Past and Present* 169 (2000): 32 [3–35].
34. For example, Prokopios claimed that in a typical evening she would have sex with forty different men more than once. Prokopios, *Anekdota* 9.16.
35. Prokopios, *Anekdota*, 15.6–8.
36. John Lydus, *On Powers*, 2.65.
37. Anna Komnene, *Alexiad*, 3.3, eds. Diether R. Reinsch and Athanasios Kambylis, *Anna Comnenae Alexias, Corpus fontium historiae Byzantinae* 40, 2 vols. (Berlin: Walter de Gruyter, 2001); *The Alexiad of Anna Comnena*, trans. E. R. A. Sewter (New York: Penguin, 1969).
38. Anna Komnene, *Alexiad*, 3.3. Lynda Garland reminds us that Anna "is describing a paradigm of ideal behavior [and] not the canons of social reality." "Beholder," 373.
39. Prokopios, *Anekdota*, 9.14.
40. "And often even in the theatre, before the eyes of the whole people, she stripped off her clothing and moved about naked through their midst, having only a girdle about her private parts and her groins, not, however, that

she was ashamed to display these too to the populace, but because no person is permitted to enter there entirely naked." *Anekdota,* 9.20. These tropes appear in a wide range of literature, for Michael McCormick suggests, "it is not impossible that the modern notion of late Roman theater as a breeding ground for sensual depravity and civil disturbance is, to a large degree, the product of professional deformations of our ecclesiastical sources." McCormick, *Eternal Victory,* p. 98. Andrew White, in forthcoming work on the Byzantine theater, explores this question in greater detail than I can afford here.

41. Edward Gibbon with his inimitable elegance explains the social shift that had occured from ancient Greek civilization, "The most eminent of Greeks were actors, the Romans merely spectators, a senator, or even a citizen, conscious of his dignity, would have blushed to expose his person or his horses in the circus of Rome." Edward Gibbon, *The History of the Decline and Fall of the Roman Empire,* ed. J. B. Bury, 7 vols. (London: Methuen, 1909), 4: 233–34.

42. This class coding bore a heavy weight in laws going back to the Roman Imperial era, carefully meting out different appropriate relationships based on the the social class of each partner. Angeliki E. Laiou, "Sex, Consent, and Coercion in Byzantium," in *Consent and Coercion to Sex and Marriage in Ancient and Medieval Societies,* ed. Angeliki E. Laiou (Washington, D. C.: Dumbarton Oaks, 1993), pp. 114–16 [105–221]. Justinian's alteration in the legal status of actresses, particularly their marriageability into the senatorial class, is discussed in David Daube, "The Marriage of Justinian and Theodora. Legal and Theological Reflections," *Catholic University of America Law Review* 16 (1966): 380–99; and Dorothea R. French, "Maintaining Boundaries: The Status of Actresses in Early Christian Society," *Vigiliae Christianae* 52 (1998): 293–318. Constantine Tsirpanlis gives an overview of the changes made during Justinian's reign but does not connect them to Theodora. Constantine Tsirpanlis, "Marriage, Family Values and 'Ecumenical Vision' in the Legislation of Justinian the Great (527–565)," *The Patristic and Byzantine Review* 15 (1996–97): 59–69.

43. Seneca's charges against Julia have a rather familiar ring: "The deified Augustus banished his daughter, who was shameless beyond indictment of shamelessness, and made public the scandals of the imperial house—that she had been accessible to scores of paramours, that in nocturnal revels she had roamed about the city, that the very forum and the rostrum, from which her father had proposed a law against adultery, had been chosen by the daughter for her debaucheries, that she had daily resorted to the statue of Marsyas, and, laying aside the role of adulteress, there sold her favours, and sought the right to every indulgence with even an unknown paramour." Seneca, *De Beneficiis,* 6.32.1, trans. John W. Basore, *Seneca, Moral Essays,* 3 vols., *LCL* (Cambridge, MA: Harvard University Press, 1958), vol. 3. Fischler discusses these Roman antecedents more fully. Fischler, "Social," 121–27.

44. Laura Kipnis, "(Male) Desire and (Female) Disgust: Reading Hustler," in *Cultural Studies,* ed. Lawrence Grossberg, Cary Nelson, Paula A. Treichler, with Linda Baughman and assistance from John Macgregor Wise (New York: Routledge, 1992), p. 376. Kipnis continues this argument less effectively in *Bound and Gagged: Pornography and the Politics of Fantasy in America* (New York: Grove, 1996).
45. Prokopios, *Anekdota,* 9.18.
46. Mikhail Bakhtin, *Rabelais and His World,* trans. Hélène Iswolsky (Bloomington: Indiana University Press, 1984), p. 370.
47. Pauline Allen, "Contemporary Portrayals of the Byzantine Empress Theodora (AD 527–548)," in *Stereotypes of Women in Power: Historical Perspectives and Revisionist Views,* ed. Barbara Garlick, Suzanne Dixon, and Pauline Allen (New York: Greenwood Press, 1992), p. 96.
48. Lynn Hunt, "The Many Bodies of Marie Antoinette: Political Pornography and the Problem of the Feminine in the French Revolution," in *Eroticism and the Body Politic* (Baltimore: Johns Hopkins University Press, 1991), p. 111.
49. Sherry Ortner, "The Virgin and the State," *Feminist Studies* 4.3 (1978): 31 [19–36].
50. Prokopios, *Anekdota,* 10.2. While the modesty and chastity of a young bride had been a stock motif in ancient literature, these qualities become more prominent in the Byzantine period. Lynda Garland notes a divergence, too, in how sexual morality is depicted in different forms of Byzantine literature: "Whereas the learned romances specialise in erotic innuendo without the accompanying action, the popular romances in general prefer the action without the innuendo." Lynda Garland, "'Be Amorous, But Be Chaste . . . ': Sexual Morality in Byzantine Learned and Vernacular Romance," *Byzantine and Modern Greek Studies* 14 (1990): 103 [62–120].
51. Prokopios, *Anekdota,* 9.16. Martha Vinson has recently offered a convincing parallel to this rhetorical maneuver in her work on the topos of libido in the Roman Imperial representation of Julia Titi, the niece of Domitian. The consequences of these literary effects apply to the Justinianic era as well; Vinson concludes that these elaborate tales spun on the theme of the libido of imperial women ultimately serves as an attack aimed at the emperor Domitian, undermining his credibility as a good ruler. Martha Vinson, "Domitia Longina, Julia Titi, and the Literary Tradition," *Historia* 38 (1989): 431 and 444 [431–50].
52. Asterius of Amaseia, *Description of a painting of the martyrdom of St. Euphemia,* trans. Cyril Mango, in *The Art of the Byzantine Empire 312–1453: Sources and Documents* (1972; repr. Toronto: University of Toronto Press, 1986), p. 37. Text in *Euphémie de Chalcédoine,* Subsidia hagiographica, 41, ed. François Halkin (Brussels: Société des Bollandistes, 1965).
53. Janet Fairweather, "Fiction in the Biographies of Ancient Writers," *Ancient Society* 5 (1974): 237 [231–75].

54. Fairweather, "Fiction," 237.
55. Fairweather, "Fiction," 247.
56. Form rather than content dictated genre in this milieu. Holt Parker, "Love's Body Anatomized: The Ancient Erotic Handbooks and the Rhetoric of Sexuality," in *Pornography and Representation in Greece and Rome*, ed. Amy Richlin (New York: Oxford University Press, 1992), p. 91 [90–111].
57. Prokopios, *Anekdota*, 9.25–26.
58. Hermogenes, *On Types of Style*, trans. Cecil W. Wooten (Chapel Hill: University of North Carolina Press, 1987), p. 31.
59. Elizabeth A. Fisher, "Thedora and Antonina in the Historia Arcana: History and/or Fiction?" in *Women in the Ancient World: The Arethusa Papers*, ed. John Peradotto and J. P. Sullivan (Albany: State University of New York Press, 1984), p. 310 [287–313].
60. Cameron, *Procopius*, p. 60.
61. Michel Foucault, *The History of Sexuality*, 3 vols., trans. Robert Hurley (New York: Random House, 1978), 1:35.
62. Monica Green has a forthcoming anthology that explores the association of secrecy with women in the late Middle Ages. I am grateful to Professor Kathryn Park for her discussions of this material with me as well as this reference.
63. Gibbon, *Decline*, 4: 226.
64. Gibbon, *Decline*, 4: 228.
65. Gibbon, *Decline*, 4: 225–26.
66. Gibbon, *Decline*, 4: 227.
67. Gibbon, *Decline*, 5: 241.
68. Gibbon, *Decline*, 5: 241.
69. Averil Cameron, "Gibbon and Justinian," in *Edward Gibbon and Empire*, ed. Rosamond McKitterick and Roland Quinault (New York: Cambridge University Press, 1997), p. 38 [34–52].
70. Gibbon's classicism was hardly without ambivalence; he wrote to his father from Rome, "Whatever ideas books may have given us of the greatness of that people, their accounts of the most flourishing state of Rome fall infinitely short of the picture of its ruins. I am convinced that there never existed such a nation and I hope for the happiness of mankind that there never will again." Gibbon to Edward Gibbon, Sr., Rome, 9 October 1764, in *Letters*, I, p. 184.
71. Diehl, *Théodora*, pp. 113–22.
72. Plays continue to be written and produced about Theodora. *Theodora, She-Bitch of Byzantium*, which ran off-Broadway in the 1980s, offers a drag send-up of Sarah Bernhardt's performance as Theodora in the Sardou play. Charles Busch, *Theodora, She-Bitch of Byzantium* (Garden City, NY: Fireside Theater, 1992) and Victorien Sardou, *Théodora, drame en cinq actes et sept tableaux* (Paris: L'Illustration, 1907).
73. "Tandis que Justinien, né dans les rudes montagnes de la haute Macédoine, était profondément pénétré de l'esprit romain, Théodora demeura toujours

une pure Orientale, imbue de toutes les idées, de toutes les croyances, de toutes les préjugés de sa race." Diehl, *Théodora*, p. 14. Diehl's representation of Theodora is still worth noting because it reached a relatively wide audience in his biography about the empress and in its abbreviated form in *Byzantine Portraits* and *Byzantine Empresses*.

74. Some of the clearest instances of this are, "Mais Théodora était femme, partant mobile autant que passionnée," "très femme avec cela, toujours coquette et désireuse de plaire," and "Sous ses qualités d'homme d'Etat, Théodora en effet restait femme, et par là, par la violence de ses passions et l'ardeur de ses haines, souvent elle agita assez inutilement la monarchie." Diehl, *Théodora*, pp. 43, 84, 155. The sense that the *Anekdota's* representation of Theodora as prostitute-turned-empress embodies the quintessential Woman is also demonstrated by the plan in 1955 to make a movie about her simply entitled *The Female*. Steven Runciman was offered the job of expert consultant on *The Female*, and in his autobiography he wryly comments, "I felt greatly flattered to be considered a specialist on such an important subject till I remembered that there had appeared recently a book under that name which concerned the life of the great Byzantine empress Theodora." The film was never made, in part because when Ava Gardner, cast as Theodora, read the script "she pronounced it to be lousy." Steven Runciman, *A Traveller's Alphabet* (NewYork:Thames and Hudson, 1991), p. 83. Other films about the imperial couple have been made, such as Robert Siodmak's *Der Kampf um Rom* from 1968, released in the United States as *The Last Roman*.

75. Gustave Flaubert, *The Dictionary of Received Ideas*, trans. Geoffrey Wall (New York: Penguin, 1994), p. 21.

76. Bram Dijkstra, *Idols of Perversity: Fantasies of Feminine Evil in Fin-de-Siècle Culture* (NewYork: Oxford University Press, 1986), p. 387. This is a longstanding stereotype noted by art historians as well, "The so-called Oriental woman has often been conflated with the erotic in the European imagination." Anna C. Chave, "New Encounters with *Les Demoiselles d'Avignon*: Gender, Race, and the Origins of Cubism," *Art Bulletin* 76 (1994): 600 [596–611].

77. Anonymous author quoted in Dijkstra, *Idols*, p. 387.

78. Dijkstra, *Idols*, p. 397.

79. Dijkstra, *Idols*, p. 396.

80. Paul I. Wellman, *The Female: A Novel of Another Time* (NewYork: Doubleday, 1953); John W. Vandercook, *Empress of the Dusk: a life of Theodora of Byzantium* (NewYork: Reynal and Hitchcock, ca. 1940); and Gillian Bradshaw, *The Bearkeeper's Daughter* (Boston: Houghton Mifflin, 1987). Liz James notes that in these novels "sex is ever present but prurient." Liz James, "'As the actress said to the bishop . . .': the portrayal of Byzantine women in English-language fiction," in *Through the Looking Glass: Byzantium Through British Eyes*, ed. Robin Cormack and Elizabeth Jeffreys (Burlington: Ashgate, 2000), p. 244 [237–50].

81. Michael the Syrian, 11.17 [450].
82. Martha Vinson offers a helpful introduction to this sainted empress to accompany her recent translation of the *Vita*. *Vita* of Saint Theodora, trans. Martha Vinson, in *Byzantine Defenders of Images: Eight Saints' Lives in English Translation,* ed. Alice-Mary Talbot (Washington, D. C.: Dumbarton Oaks, 1998), pp. 353–82; and in "The Life of Theodora and the Rhetoric of the Byzantine Brideshow," *Jahrbuch der Österreichischen Byzantinistik* 49 (1999): 31–60. Warren Treadgold discusses the circumstances of this bride show. Warren Treadgold, "The Problem of the Marriage of the Emperor Theophilus," *Greek, Roman, and Byzantine Studies* 16 (1975): 325–41. Even the Empress Irene, of course, became a saint, although an apparently less likely candidate for such honors, François Halkin, "Deux Impératrices de Byzance," *Analecta Bollandiana* 106 (1998): 5 [5–34].

Chapter 6

1. Robin Cormack, "The Emperor at St. Sophia: Viewer and Viewed," in *Byzance et les images,* ed. Guillou and Durand, p. 235 [223–53].
2. Otto G. von Simson, *Sacred Fortress,* (1948; repr. Princeton Princeton University Press, 1987), p. 29.
3. A recent article by Deborah Mauskopf Deliyannis looks at Agnellus in his eighth-century context, in which the Ravennate exarchs never quite managed to enforce the imperial directive from Constantinople to impose Iconoclasm. The main counterforce was the contingent of local archbishops, who were unwavering in their support of the Pope's iconophile position. Deliyannis posits Agnellus' "many detailed descriptions of images may . . . be intended to emphasize their theological and didactic value." Deborah Mauskopf Deliyannis, "Agnellus of Ravenna and Iconoclasm: Theology and Politics in a Ninth-Century Historical Text," *Speculum* 71 (1996): 575 [559–76].
4. Agnellus, *De Sancto Ecclesio,* 23, *Codex pontificalis ecclesiae Ravennatis,* 59, ed. O. Holder-Egger, MGH, *Scriptores rerum Langobardicarum et italicarum saec. VI-IX* (1878; repr. Hannover: Hahnsche Buchhandlung, 1988), p. 319.
5. S. J. B. Barnish, "The Wealth of Julianus Argentarius: Late Antique Banking and the Mediterranean Economy," *Byzantion* 55 (1985): 8 [5–38]. His monogram and other evidence for patronage are discussed in Friedrich Wilhelm Deichmann, "Giuliano Argentario," *Felix Ravenna* 56 (1951): 5–26.
6. Richard Lim, "People as Power: Games, Munificence, and Contested Topography," in *The Transformation of the Vrbs Roma in Late Antiquity.* ed. W. V. Harris, *Journal of Roman Archaeology,* Supplemental Series No. 33 (Portsmouth, RI: Journal of Roman Archaeology, 1999), p. 277 [265–81].
7. Agnellus, *De Reparato,* 25.115, ed. O. Holder-Egger, MGH, *Scriptores rerum Langobardicarum et italicarum saec.* VI-IX (1878; repr. Hannover: Hannsche Buchhandlung, 1988), pp. 353–54 [265–391].

8. Henry Maguire, *Earth and Ocean: The Terrestrial World in Early Byzantine Art* (University Park, PA: Penn State University Press, 1987), p. 80.
9. Otto G. von Simson, *Sacred Fortress* (1948; repr. Princeton: Princeton University Press, 1987), p. 30.
10. Richard Gordon, "The Veil of Power: Emperors, Sacrificers and Benefactors," in *Pagan Priests: Religion and Power in the Ancient World*, ed. Mary Beard and John North (Ithaca, NY: Cornell University Press, 1990), p. 203 [199–232]. Jaš Elsner recently made a strong argument for continuity in the imperial image in the Late Roman period in *Imperial Art and Christian Triumph* (Oxford: Oxford University Press, 1998), see especially chapter 3.
11. Gordon, "Veil," in *Pagan Priests: Religion and Power in the Ancient World*, p. 205.
12. Djordje Stričević, "The Iconography of the Compositions Containing Imperial Portraits in San Vitale," *Starinar* 9–10 (1958–59): 75 [67–76]; and Djordje Stričević, "Sur le problème de l'iconographie des mosaïques imperiales de Saint-Vital," *Felix Ravenna* 34 (1962): 80–100.
13. André Grabar, *L'empereur dans l'art byzantin* (1936; repr. of Strasbourg ed. London: Variorum Reprints, 1971), pp. 106–107; and André Grabar, "Quel est le sens de l'offrande de Justinien et de Théodora sur les mosaïques de Saint-Vital?," *Felix Ravenna* 81 (1960): 75 [63–77]. An example of the *Apokombion* is in the *Book of Ceremonies*, 1.1.
14. Friedrich Wilhelm Deichmann, *Ravenna: Hauptstadt des spätantiken Abendlandes*, vol. 2, Commentary, part 2, (Wiesbaden: Franz Steiner, 1976), p. 1980.
15. Thomas F. Mathews, *The Early Churches of Constantinople: Architecture and Liturgy* (University Park: Penn State University Press, 1971), pp. 146–47.
16. Jaš Elsner, *Art and the Roman Viewer* (New York: Cambridge University Press, 1995), p. 187.
17. Michael McCormick rightly observes that "the value placed in public appearance and the extent to which social standing was gauged by one's presence and precise position in imperial ceremonies help explain ceremonial writer's insistence on the rigor with which their proscriptions must be observed, as well as allusion to 'disorder' in ceremonies." Michael McCormick, "Analyzing Imperial Ceremonies," *Jahrbuch der Österreichischen Byzantinistik* 35 (1985): 5 [1–20].
18. Prokopios, *Anekdota*, 30.21–26, ed. J. Haury, vol. 2, *Procopii Caesariensis opera omnia* (Leipzig: Teubner, 1963); *Secret History*, ed. and trans. H. B. Dewing, LCL (Cambridge, MA: Harvard University Press, 1935).
19. Elsner, *Viewer*, p. 184.
20. Deichmann, *Ravenna*, vol. 2, Commentary, part 2, p. 181.
21. As Franses noted in his dissertation on Byzantine donor portraits, "Their debate is really about the mixture in the panels of the representational (in terms of correspondence to a ceremony) and the symbolic (items that do not correspond to the specifics of the ceremony). . . . But as there is no criterion provided by the scene itself by which to judge just what this

mixture is (why, for example, should the crowns be symbolic for Mathews, but the cross not?), these are hardly claims which can be made with any certainty or conviction." Henri Franses, *Symbols, Meaning, Belief: Donor Portraits in Byzantine Art* (Ph.D. diss., Courtauld Institute of Art, 1992), pp. 210–11.
22. Prokopios, *Anekdota*, 10.11.
23. Irina Andreescu-Treadgold and Warren Treadgold, "Dates and Identities in the Imperial Panels in San Vitale," *Byzantine Studies Conference Abstract of Papers* 16 (1990): 52 [52].
24. Gerhard Steigerwald, "Ein Bild der Mutter des Kaisers Justinian in San Vitale zu Ravenna?" in *Vom Orient bis an den Rhein: Begegnungen mit der Christlichen Archäologie; Peter Poscharsky zum 65. Geburtstag*, ed. Ulrike Lange and Reiner Sörries (Dettelbach: Röll, 1997), p. 140 [123–46].
25. Andreescu-Treadgold, "Dates," 52.
26. Theophanes, *Chronicle*, AM 6020, A.D. 527/28, ed. C. de Boor, 2 vols. (Leipzig: Teubner, 1883–85), p. 175; *The Chronicle of Theophanes Confessor: Byzantine and Near Eastern History A.D. 284–813*, trans. Cyril Mango and Roger Scott (Oxford: Clarendon Press, 1997), p. 266.
27. von Simson, *Sacred*, p. 30.
28. Paul Silentarios, *Description of Hagia Sophia*, 590, ed. P. Friedländer, *Johannes von Gaza und Paulus Silentiarios: Kunstbeschreibungen justinianischer Zeit* (Leipzig: Teubner, 1912); trans. from Cyril Mango, in *The Art of the Byzantine Empire 312–1453: Sources and Documents* (1972; repr. Toronto: University of Toronto Press, 1986), p. 85.
29. von Simson, *Sacred*, p. 30.
30. Hiltje F. H. Zomer, "The So-called Women's Gallery in the Medieval Church: An Import from Byzantium," in *The Empress Theophano: Byzantium and the West at the Turn of the First Millenium*, ed. Adelbert Davids (New York: Cambridge University Press, 1995), p. 298 [290–306].
31. Robert F. Taft, S. J., "Women at Church in Byzantium: Where, When—and Why?," *Dumbarton Oaks Papers* 52 (1998): 27–87.
32. Prokopios, *Buildings*, 1.1, ed. J. Haury, vol. 4, *Procopii Caesariensis opera omnia* (Leipzig: Teubner, 1964); ed. and trans. H. B. Dewing, LCL (Cambridge, MA: Harvard University Press, 1940).
33. Paul Silentiarios, *Description of Hagia Sophia*, p. 237.
34. Paul Silentiarios, *Description of Hagia Sophia*, p. 237.
35. Paul Silentiarios, *Description of Hagia Sophia*, p. 244.
36. Chorikios, Laudatio Marciani, 2.47, *Choricii Gazaei Opera*, ed. R. Foerster and E. Richtsteig (Leipzig: Teubner, 1929), p. 40, trans. from Mango, in *Sources*, p. 71.
37. Michael McCormick, *Eternal Victory: Triumphal Rulership in Late Antiquity, Byzantium, and the Early Medieval West* (New York: Cambridge University Press, 1986), pp. 203–04.
38. J. B. Bury, "The Ceremonial Book of Constantine Porphyrogennetos," *The English Historical Review* 22(1907): 212–13. Peter was *Magister Officiorum* in

542 and 565, but whether this was a continuous period in office is unknown. Panayotis T. Antonopoulos, "Petrus Patricius, Some Aspects of His Life and Career," in *From Late Antiquity to Early Byzantium*, ed. Vladimir Vavrinek (Prague: Academia, 1985), 49 [49–53].
39. *Oxfoed Dictionary of Byzantium*, ed. Kazhdan, "De ceremoniis" (New York: Oxford University Press, 1991), p. 596.
40. Jeffrey Featherstone translates this text in his article, "Ol'ga's Visit to Constantinople," *Harvard Ukrainian Studies* 14 (1990): 293–312.
41. Nicholas I Patriarch of Constantinople, *Letters*, 32, eds. and trans. R. J. H. Jenkins and L. G. Westerink (Washington, D. C.: Dumbarton Oaks, 1973), p. 221.
42. Steven Runcimann, "Women in Byzantine Aristocratic Society," in *The Byzantine Aristocracy IX to XIII Centuries*, ed. Michael Angold (Oxford: B. A. R. International Series, 1984), p. 12 [10–22].
43. Runcimann, "Women in Byzantine Aristocratic Society," in *The Byzantine Aristocracy*, p. 11.
44. Constantine Porphyrogennetos, *De cerimoniis aulae Byzantinae*, 1.49 (40), ed. Reiske, 2 vols. (Bonn: Corpus Scriptorum Historiae Byzantinae, 1829–30); Partial translation in *Le Livres des cérémonies*, ed. and trans. Albert Vogt, 2 vols. in 4 parts with commentary (Paris: Les Belles Lettres, 1967).
45. Constantine Porphyrogennetos, *De Cer.*, 1.59 (50).
46. Rodolphe Guilland, "Patricienne à ceinture," *Byzantinoslavica* 32 (1971): 270 [181–238].
47. Ramsay MacMullen, "Women in Public in the Roman Empire," *Historia* 29 (1980): 214–15 [208–18].
48. Leslie P. Peirce, *The Imperial Harem: Women and Sovereignity in the Ottoman Empire* (New York: Oxford University Press, 1993).
49. G. Zacos and A. Veglery, *Byzantine Lead Seals* (Basel: Augustin, 1972–85), vol. 1, nos. 744, 793, and 843.
50. All five lead seals are in Zacos and Veglery, vol. 1, part 2: no. 1412 Anna (the *patrikia*), no. 1699 Anastasia (the imperial *cubicularia* and *parakoimae*), no. 1718 Anna (the *patrikia*), no. 1864 Eirene (the *hegoumene*), and no. 2409 Thekla (the *protostraterina*).
51. Constantine Porphyrogennetos, *De administrando imperio*, 255–56.
52. Diana E. E. Kleiner, "Imperial Women as Patrons of the Arts in the Early Empire," in *I Claudia: Women in Ancient Rome*, ed. Kleiner and Matheson, p. 28 [28–41].
53. Ramsey MacMullen, "Some Pictures in Ammianus Marcellinus," *Art Bulletin* 46 (1964): 435–55.
54. R. R. R. Smith, "Late Antique Portraits in a Public Context: Honorific Statuary at Aphrodisias in Caria, A.D. 300–600," *Journal of Roman Studies* 89 (1999): 177 [153–89].
55. Charles Barber, "The Imperial Panels at San Vitale: A Reconsideration," *Byzantine and Modern Greek Studies* 14 (1990): 36 [19–42].

NOTES TO PAGES 133–135   229

56. Ann M. Stout, "Jewelry as a Symbol of Status in the Roman Empire," in *The World of Roman Costume,* ed. Judith Lynn Sebesta and Larissa Bonfante (Madison: University of Wisconsin Press, 1994), p. 83 [77–100].
57. Corippus, *In laudem Iustini Augusti minoris,* 2.98–120, ed. and trans. Averil Cameron (London: Athlone Press, 1976).
58. MacMullen, "Some Pictures," 448.
59. Stričevič, "Iconography," 75; Grabar, "Quel," 67.
60. Henry Maguire, "Magic and the Christian Image," in *Byzantine Magic,* ed. Henry Maguire (Washington, D. C.: Dumbarton Oaks, 1995), pp. 55–56 [51–71].
61. Agnellus rhetorically proposes a question and its answer, "Why is it, however, that they (the Magi) are depicted in different garments, and not all in the same kind? Becaused the painter has followed divine Scripture. Now, Caspar is offering gold and is wearing a blue garment, and by his garment he denotes matrimony. Balthasar is offering frankincense and wears a yellow garment, and by his garment denotes virginity. Melchior is offering myrrh and wears a variegated garment, and by his garment he denotes penitence." Agnellus, *De Agnello,* 28, trans. from Mango, in *Sources,* p. 106.
62. Agnellus, *De Agnello,* 28; trans. from Mango, in *Sources,* p. 108.
63. Shaun F. Tougher, "Images of Effeminate Men: the Case of Byzantine Eunuchs," in *Masculinity in Medieval Europe,* ed. D. M. Hadley (London: Longman, 1999), p. 90; and Michael McCormick, "Emperors," in *The Byzantines,* ed. Guglielmo Cavallo (Chicago and London: University of Chicago Press, 1997), p. 237 [230–54].
64. Kathryn M. Ringrose, "Eunuchs as Cultural Mediators," *Byzantinische Forschungen* 23 (1996): 75.
65. Shaun F. Tougher, "Byzantine Eunuchs: An Overview, with a Special Reference to Their Creation and Origin," in *Women, Men, and Eunuchs: Gender in Byzantium,* ed. Liz James (New York: Routledge, 1997), p. 169 [168–84].
66. Keith Hopkins, *Conquerors and Slaves* (New York: Cambridge University Press, 1978), p. 187.
67. Gregory of Nazianzos, PG 35: 1106. Saint Basil likewise describes "the dishonest race of detestable eunuchs, neither men nor women . . ." letter 115, trans. from Hopkins, *Conquerors,* p. 195.
68. Alpha-privative forms were used to describe the state of eunuchs in opposition to adult men; Kathryn M. Ringrose, "Living in the Shadows: Eunuchs and Gender in Byzantium," in *Third Sex, Third Gender: Beyond Sexual Dimorphism in Culture and History,* ed. Gilbert Herdt (New York: Zone, 1994), p. 93 [85–109], translating and summarizing Aretaeus Medicus, *De Causis et signis acutorum morborum,* ed. K. Hude, *Corpus Medicorum Graecorum,* vol. 2 (Berlin: Akademie, 1958).
69. Ringrose, "Eunuchs," in *Third Sex, Third Gender,* p. 97.
70. Hopkins, *Conquerors,* p. 194.
71. Tougher, "Eunuchs," in *Women, Men, and Eunuchs,* p. 178.

72. Judith Herrin, "Theophano: considerations on the education of a Byzantine princess," in *The Empress Theophano: Byzantium and the West at the turn of the first millenium*, ed. Adelbert Davids (New York: Cambridge University Press, 1995), p. 71 [64–85].
73. Psellos writes, "Their uncle, the Emperor Basil, died without making any plans for their subsequent promotion, and as for their father, even he, when he acceded to the throne, failed to reach any wise decision about their future, except in the case of the second sister, the one who was most like an empress." Michael Psellos, *Chronography*, 2.4, ed. S. Impellizzeri, *Imperatori di Bisanzio* (Milan: Fondazione L. Valla, A. Mondadori, 1984); *Fourteen Byzantine Rulers: The Chronographia of Psellus*, trans. E. R. A. Sewter (Baltimore: Penguin, 1966), pp. 55–56.
74. Franses discussed the juridical aspect of imperial portraiture, Henri Franses, *Symbols, Meaning, Belief: Donor Portraits in Byzantine Art*, (Ph.D. diss., Courtauld Institute of Art, London, 1992), p. 19, calling upon the earlier analysis of Grabar, André Grabar, *L'empereur dans l'art byzantin* (1936; repr. of Strasbourg ed. London: Variorum Reprints, 1971), pp. 6–7.
75. Smith, "Late Antique Portraits," 183.
76. von Simson, *Sacred*, p. 24. Michael the Syrian notes the death of Theodora, 9.29 [310]. James Fitton calls into question the common assumption that Theodora died of cancer, "The Death of Theodora," *Byzantion* 46 (1976): 119. The sole source for this piece of information is Victor Tonnensis, who uses terminology to chronicle the cause of her death that could apply to maladies as diverse as gangrene and ulcerations as well as cancer. *Victoris Tonnennensis Episcopi Chronica*, Year 549, p. 202. Körbler offers the suggestion that her demise was caused by syphilis, though his main inspiration is an uncritical reading of the *Anekdota*, Juraj Körbler, "Die Krebskrankung der byzantinischen Kaiserin Theodora (Ein Beitrag zur Geschichte der Syphilis)," *Janus* 61 (1974): 15–21.
77. Agnellus, *De Maximiano*, 26.
78. Andreescu-Treadgold and Treadgold, "Dates and Identities," 52; and "Procopius and the Imperial Panels of S. Vitale," *Art Bulletin* 79 (1997): 708–23.
79. John of Ephesus, *Ecclesiastical History*, 3.2.27, ed. E.W. Brooks (Paris: E typographeo reipublicae, 1935; Latin trans.: Louvain: Ex officina et scientifica, 1936); *The Third Part of the Ecclesiastical History of John of Ephesus*, trans. R. Payne Smith (Oxford: Oxford University Press, 1860).
80. Sabine G. MacCormack, *Art and Ceremony in Late Antiquity* (Berkeley: University of California Press, 1981), p. 264.
81. MacCormack, *Art*, p. 263. Molinier likens the styling of the empress in this setting to that of the wife Serena in the diptych in Monza Cathedral Treasury. Émile Molinier, "La coiffure des femmes dans quelques monuments byzantins," in *Études d'histoire de Moyen Age dédiées à Gabriel Monod* (Paris: Leopold Cerf, 1896), p. 63.
82. Ann M. Stout, "Jewelry as a Symbol of Status in the Roman Empire," in *The World of Roman Costume*, ed. Judith Lynn Sebesta and Larissa Bonfante (Madison: University of Wisconsin Press, 1994), p. 85 [77–100].

83. Ernst H. Kantorowicz, *The King's Two Bodies: A Study in Mediaeval Political Theology* (Princeton: Princeton University Press, 1957), p. 84.
84. Kantorowicz, *King's*, p. 80.
85. Alexander Kazhdan, "Certain Traits of Imperial Propaganda in the Byzantine Empire from the Eight to the Fifteenth Centuries," in *Prédication et propagande au Moyen Age: Islam, Byzance, Occident*, Dumbarton Oaks Colloquia 3 (Paris: Presses Universitaires de France, 1983), pp. 15–16 [13–27].
86. Henry Maguire, "Images of the Court," in *Glory of Byzantium: Art and Culture of the Middle Byzantine Era A.D. 843–1261*, ed. Helen C. Evans and William D. Wixom (New York: Metropolitan Museum of Art, 1997), p. 184 [183–91].
87. Gladys Amad unconvincingly proposes that a mosaic in Carthage also depicts Theodora, but the woman in the Tunisian image does not possess any distinctive insignia that identifies her as an empress. Gladys Amad, *Qui est la mysterieuse figure de Carthage?* (Beyrouth: Dar el-Machreq, 1978).
88. Cyril Mango, *The Brazen House: A Study of the Vestibule of the Imperial Palace of Constantinople* (Copenhagen: Arkaeologisk-kunsthistoriske Meddelelser, 1959).
89. Prokopios, *Buildings*, 1.10.17.
90. Mango, *Brazen House*, p. 34.
91. McCormick, "Analyzing," 9. Philip Rousseau recently made the subtle argument that Prokopios wished to emphasize Justinian's hubris in this and other desciptions. Phillip Rousseau, "Procopius's *Buildings* and Justinian's Pride," *Byzantion* 68 (1998): 125–26 [121–30].
92. Grabar, *L'empereur*, p. 82.
93. Mango, *Brazen House*, p. 33.
94. Prokopios, *Buildings*, 1.11.9.
95. Henri Grégoire, *Inscriptions grecques chretienne d'Asie Mineure* (Paris: Ernest Leroux, 1922), no. 100 ter, p. 31.
96. Anonymous, *Parastaseis*, sect. 81, eds. and trans. Averil Cameron and Judith Herrin, *Constantinople in the Early Eighth Century: The Parastaseis Syntomoi Chronikai* (Leiden: E. J. Brill, 1984), p. 159.
97. *Parastaseis*, Commentary, Cameron and Herrin, p. 272.
98. Kurt Weitzmann, ed., *Age of Spirituality: Late Antique and Early Christian Art, Third to Seventh Century* (New York: Metropolitan Museum of Art, 1977), catalog no. 27.
99. James D. Breckenridge, *Age of Spirituality*, ed. Weitzmann, p. 33.
100. Siri Sande, "Zur Porträtplastik des sechsten nachchristlichen Jahrhunderts," *Acta ad archaeologiam et artium historiam pertinentia* 6 (1975): 95 [65–106]. Other scholars such as Heintze attribute the head in Milan to 400–25, an attribution discounted by Bente Kiilerich, *Late fourth century classicism in the plastic arts: Studies in the so-called Theodosian renaissance* (Odense: Odense University Press, 1993), p. 117.
101. Klaus Wessel, "Das kaiserinnenporträt im Castello Sforzesco zu Mailand," *Jahrbuch des deutschen archäologischen Instituts und Archäologischer Anzeiger* 77 (1962): 243 [240–55].

102. For example, Delbrueck attributed the Milan head to Theodora on these terms although he leaves open the question of where it was produced. Richard Delbrueck, "Portraets byzantinischer Kaiserinnen," *Mitteilungen des kaiserlich deutschen archäologischen Instituts, Römische Abteilung* 28 (1913): 349 [310–52].
103. Breckenridge, *Age of Spirituality,* ed. Weitzmann, p. 33. We already see in Meischner's account of the head attributed to Galla Placidia in Rome's Museo dell'Alto Medioevo the suggestion that it was one of the last Roman individual portraits in the classical sense. Jutta Meischner, "Das Porträt der Galla Placidia im Museo dell'Alto Medioevo, Rom," *Latomus* 50 (1991): 864.
104. Kiilerich, *Late,* p. 118.
105. Cornelius V. Vermeule, *Greek and Roman Sculpture in America: Masterpieces in Public Collections in the United States and Canada* (Berkeley: University of California Press, 1981), p. 378. A very similar piece of just a snooded woman's head exists as well in the Musée Saint Raymond of Toulouse, but Alföldi-Rosenbaum dates it to no later than 400 A.D., despite its similarity to the sixth-century Metropolitan Museum head. This disparity in dating seems untenable; perhaps the Metropolitan sculpture warrants a slightly earlier dating, as the Toulouse head may belong more squarely to the fifth century. Technical aspects, such as the similarity of the eye carving techniques between the Metropolitan and the three marble Ariadne heads as was noted by Alföldi-Rosenbaum, support this thesis. Elisabeth Alföldi-Rosenbaum, "Portrait Bust of a Young Lady of the Time of Justinian," *Metropolitan Museum Journal* 1 (1968): 28 [19–40].
106. "Contrairement au portrait d'artiste, l'image de culte est une image de consensus, une image normalisée . . . ," Gilbert Dagron, "L'image de culte et le portrait," in *Byzance et les images,* ed. Guillou and Durand, p. 125 [121–50].
107. *Parastaseis,* sect. 82, p. 161.
108. The topic of ekphrasis in Byzantine art has received assiduous attention. Henry Maguire set the terms of recent discussion in *Art and Eloquence in Byzantium* (Princeton: Princeton University Press, 1981). In addition, Liz James and Ruth Webb offer a useful overview in "'To Understand Ultimate Things and Enter Secret Places': Ekphrasis and Art in Byzantium," *Art History* 14 (1991): 1–17.
109. Zosimos, *New History,* 4.41, ed. L. Mendelssohn (Leipzig: Teubner, 1887), Partial ed.: *Histoire nouvelle,* ed. F. Paschoud (Paris: Les Belles Lettres, 1971–86); trans. R.T. Ridley, *New History* (Sidney: Australian Association for Byzantine Studies, 1982). John of Nikiu claims it was actually a coffin with the body of Flacilla that was insulted by the Antiochenes. John of Nikiu, *Chronicle,* 83.46, John of Nikiu, trans. R. H. Charles (1916; repr. Amsterdam, 1982).
110. Peter Stewart, "The Destruction of Statues in Late Antiquity," in *Constructing Identities in Late Antiquity,* ed. Richard Miles (London and NewYork: Routledge, 1999): 182 [159–89].

111. Saint Basil, *De Spiritu Sancto*, 18.45, PG 32: 149 [67–218].
112. Saint Theodore the Stoudite, *Epistola ad Platonem*, PG 99:501 [499–506].
113. Philip Grierson, *Byzantine Coins* (London: Methuen, 1982), p. 44.
114. Zacos and Veglery, *Byzantine Lead Seals*, I, 1 no. 696 (Basel: Augustin, 1972–85).
115. Michael the Syrian, 11.3 [410].
116. *DOC* II, 1 Heraklios type 90a1. A less popular variant also survives of this follis type in which Martina is shown to the right and her son to the left. *DOC* II, 1, Heraklios type 92.
117. *DOC* II, 2, p. 288.
118. In two examples of the misstruck half follis included by Grierson in his catalog, he suggests that they are the half follis corollary to the Class III follis issued by Heraklios, but that Martina is simply off flan (*DOC* II, 1, p. 291). Wroth in his catalog of the British Museum collection of Byzantine coins classifies these bronzes as issues of the Emperor Constans II, but Grierson seems right in arguing that the fact that the larger emperor wears a chlamys instead of the characteristic armor in which Constans II is represented probably puts the coins much more firmly in the range of types propagated by Heraklios. A very similar follis type was the next series of large denomination bronze issued by Heraklios; it is labeled Class 4 by Grierson (*DOC* II, 1, Heraklios type 99a.1). Issued beginning in 624/25, this coin type differs from its numismatic predecessor in the reverse, in which ANNO is inscribed above the large denomination mark M, instead of to the left of the M as was the case in the earlier Class III.
119. *DOC* II, 1, Heraklios type 289 ff.
120. *DOC* II, 1, p. 240.
121. Richard Delbrueck, *Die Consulardiptychen und verwandte Denkmäler* (Berlin: Walter de Gruyter, 1929), no. 34; Wolfgang Fritz Volbach, *Elfenbeinarbeiten der spätantike und des frühen Mittelalters*, 3rd edn. (Mainz: Philipp von Zabern, 1976), no. 33, p. 41. Its catalog entry provides an overview of previous scholarship on this piece: Arne Effenberger and Hans-Georg Severin, *Das Museum für spätantike und byzantinische Kunst* (Berlin: Staatliche Museen zu Berlin, 1992), pp. 140–41.
122. Roger Bagnall, Alan Cameron, Seth R. Schwartz, and Klaas A. Worp, *Consuls of the Later Roman Empire* (Atlanta: Scholar's Press, 1987), p. 615.
123. Alan Cameron and Diane Schauer analyze the abrupt termination of this institution in "The Last Consul: Basilius and his Diptych," *Journal of Roman Studies* 72 (1982): 126–45.
124. Anthony Cutler, "The Making of the Justinian Diptychs," *Byzantion* 54 (1984): 77–78 [75–115].
125. Cutler, "Making," 82.
126. Weitzmann, ed., *Age of Spirituality*, catalog no. 284.
127. André Grabar, *L'iconoclasme byzantin; dossier archeologique* (Paris: Collège de France, 1957), pp. 24–26.

Chapter 7

1. Averil Cameron, "Notes on the Sophiae, the Sophianae, and the Harbor of Sophia," *Byzantion* 37 (1967): 11–20; and "The Empress Sophia," *Byzantion* 45 (1975): 5–21; and Lynda Garland, *Byzantine Empresses: Women and Power in Byzantium A.D. 527–1204* (London: Routledge, 1999), pp. 40–57.
2. Thus Sophia was the daughter of Comito or Anastasia (sisters of Theodora) and Justin, the son of Vigilantia (sister of Justinian). Garland cites this as one of the "prime examples of the dynastic marriages that Theodora orchestrated to the advantage of her family." Garland, *Empresses,* p. 40.
3. Garland, *Empresses,* p. 40.
4. Cameron, "Notes," 13 for this identification.
5. Corippus, *In laudem Iustini Augusti minoris,* 1.108–17, ed. and trans. Averil Cameron (London: Athlone Press, 1976).
6. Corippus, 1.138–41.
7. Corippus, 1.188.
8. "No less did his glorious consort weep for the beloved father of the empire, and piously grieve for the human lot. She added more gifts than was usual for her father's funeral, and told the people to file past in a close packed line. And she brought a pall interwoven with precious purple, where the whole series of Justinian's achievements was picked out in woven gold and glittered with gems. On one side the artist had cleverly depicted with his sharp needle barbarian phalanxes bending their necks, slaughtered kings and subject peoples in order. And he had made the yellow gold stand out from the colours, so that everyone looking at it thought that they were real bodies. The faces were in gold, the blood in purple. And Justinian himself he had depicted as a victor in the midst of his court, trampling on the bold neck of the Vandal king, and Libya, applauding, bearing fruit and laurel: he added old Rome ..." Corippus, 1.271–90.
9. Cameron argues that "Sophia's importance is very clear from Corippus' poem," but her probable patronage of the work contravenes that straightforward meaning. Cameron, "Empress," 9.
10. Corippus, 3.145–50.
11. Corippus, 3.270–77.
12. Corippus, 1.168–69.
13. Janet Nelson, "Symbols in Context: Rulers' Inauguration Rituals in Byzantium and the West in the Early Middle Ages," in *Orthodox Churches and the West,* ed. Derek Baker (Oxford: Blackwell, 1976), p. 106.
14. Cameron, "Empress," 6.
15. John of Biclar notes "Justin, son of the patrician Germanus and cousin of the emperor Justin, was killed in Alexandria by a faction loyal to the empress Sophia." *Chronicle,* Year 568.5, ed. Julio Campos (Madrid: Consejo Superior de Investigaciones Científicas, 1960), p. 79.
16. Michael the Syrian, *Chronique de Michel le Syrien,* ed. and French trans. J.-B. Chabot (Paris: Ernest Leroux, 1901), 10.7 [345].

17. "She was a Monophysite from childhood but is said to have transferred her support to the Chalcedonians some three years before her husband became emperor, in order to facilitate his accession." John of Ephesus, *Ecclesiastical History,* 3.2.10, ed. E. W. Brooks (Paris: E typographeo reipublicae, 1935; Latin trans.: Louvain: Ex officina et scientifica, 1936); *The Third Part of the Ecclesiastical History of John of Ephesus,* trans. R. Payne Smith (Oxford: Oxford University Press, 1860); and Michael the Syrian, 10.7 [345].
18. Cameron, "Empress," 7.
19. Robin Cormack recently reinterpeted this trope, by suggesting that women were rendered as deviants in these debates to undermine the credibility of the iconophiles, and thus the association of women with iconophiliais as overdetermined as the clichés hurled at the iconoclasts likening them to Jews. Robin Cormack, "Women and Icons, and Women in Icons," in *Women, Men, and Eunuchs: Gender in Byzantium,* ed. Liz James (New York: Routledge, 1997), p. 27 [24–51]. This interpretation is based on the revelation yielded by Auzépy's research; Auzépy thinks that there is some reality to women being more attached to icons. Auzépy, "La destruction de l'icône du Christ de la Chalcé," 481–82.
20. Michael Camille, *The Gothic Idol: Ideology and Image-Making in Medieval Art* (New York: Cambridge University Press, 1989), pp. 117–18.
21. Corippus gives a lengthy account of her ministrations: "And the chaste consort in his mighty rule went too to the lofty temple of the Virgin Mother. She blessed its holy threshold and entered with joy and stood dressed in white before the pious face, holding out her hands and with her face cast down began this supplication." 2.45–50.
22. Cameron, "Notes," 13.
23. Theophanes, *Chronicle,* AM 6061, A.D. 568/69, ed. C. de Boor, 2 vols. (Leipzig: Teubner, 1883–85), p. 243; *The Chronicle of Theophanes Confessor: Byzantine and Near Eastern History A.D. 284–813,* trans. Cyril Mango and Roger Scott (Oxford: Clarendon Press, 1997), p. 358.
24. Theophanes, *Chronicle,* AM 6072, A.D. 579/80, quotation from p. 371, Mango and Scott trans. The harbor of Julian disappears from the topography of Constantinople after the reign of Justin II. Rodolphe Guilland, "Les ports de Byzance sur la Propontide," *Byzantion* 23 (1953): 183.
25. John of Ephesus states "Justin had also busied himself in building, even when engaged in persecution. . . . For having formed the idea of erecting a palace upon the site of his former dwelling in the north-western suburb of the city, he razed a great number of houses there to the ground, and built a hippodrome, and laid out extensive gardens and pleasure-grounds, which he planted with trees of all kinds: and gave orders for the erection of two magnificent statues of brass in honor of himself and Sophia." John of Ephesus, *Ecclesiastical History,* 3.3.24.
26. Cameron, "Notes," 12.
27. Theophanes, *Chronicle,* AM 6062, A.D. 569/70, p. 359.

28. "Those who are entering on the new office dedicated Thomas, the universal Emperor's blameless Curator, close to the sacred Pair, that by his very portrait also he may have a place near Majesty. For he raised higher the thrones of the divine Palace by increasing their wealth . . ." Agathias, *Greek Anthology,* 16.41, ed. H. Beckby, *Anthologia Graeca,* 4 vols. (Munich: Ernst Heimeran, 1965); trans. W. R. Paton, *LCL* (Cambridge, MA: Harvard University Press, 1916–27).
29. Ihor Sevčenko, "The Inscription of Justin II's Tme on the Mevlevihane (Rhesion) Gate at Istanbul," *Beograd* 12 (1970): 3 and 7.
30. John of Ephesus, *Ecclesiastical History,* 3.3.24.
31. Syene papyrus no. 574. K. A. Worp, "Byzantine Imperial Titulature in the Greek Documentary Papyri: The Oath Formulas," *Zeitschrift für Papyrologie und Epigraphik* 45 (1982): 211 [199–226].
32. Worp, "Byzantine," 209–11.
33. Worp, "Byzantine," 212–14.
34. Maria Delivorria, *Recherches sur l'iconographie d'impératrice byzantine* (Ph.D. diss. Sorbonne, Paris, 1966), p. 64.
35. Theophanes, *Chronicle,* AM 6060, A.D. 567/68, p. 357.
36. Cameron, "Empress," 9–10; and Mango and Scott commentary to Theophanes, *Chronicle,* pp. 357–58.
37. The *Liber Pontificalis* offers a viewpoint of his recall much more sympathetic to Narses. 63.110–11 (John), ed. L. Duchesne, 2 vols. (2nd edn.; Paris: Boccard, 1955–57); *The Book of Pontiffs (Liber Pontificalis): The Ancient Biographies of the First Ninety Roman Bishops to A.D. 715,* trans. Raymond Davis (Liverpool: Liverpool University Press, 1989).
38. Believing the insinuations of Narses' rivals, Justin and Sophia sent Longinus to replace his command of Italy, "But Narses, when he knew these things, feared greatly, and so much was he alarmed, especially by the same empress Sophia, that he did not dare to return again to Constantinople. Among other things, because he was a eunuch, she is said to have sent him this message, that she would make him portion out to the girls in the women's chamber the daily tasks of wool. To these words Narses is said to have given this answer, that he would begin to weave her such a web as she could not lay down as long as she lived. Therefore, greatly wracked by hate and fear, he withdrew to Neapolis (Naples), a city of Campania, and soon sent messengers to the nation of the Langobards, urging them to abandon the barren fields of Pannonia and come and take possession of Italy." Paul the Deacon, *History of the Lombards,* 2.5, ed. L. Bethmann and G. Waitz, MGH, Scriptores rerum Langobardicarum et italicarum saec. VI-IX (Hannover: Hahnsche Buchhandlung, 1878), p. 75.
39. Cyril Mango and Roger Scott, ed. and trans., Theophanes, *Chronicle,* n360. In *De administrando imperio* by Constantine Porphyrogennetos the same story is told in brief about Narses, although the name of the empress in this tenth-century account is Irene. *De administrando imperio,* 27.

40. Ruth Webb, "Salome's Sisters: The Rhetoric and Realities of Dance in Late Antiquity and Byzantium," in *Women, Men, and Eunuchs: Gender in Byzantium*, ed. Liz James (New York: Routledge, 1997), p. 127 [119–48].
41. Ewald Kislinger,"Der Kranke Justin II. und die ärztliche Haftung bei Operationen in Byzanz," *Jahrbuch der Österreichischen Byzantinistik* 36 (1986): 39–44.
42. Garland, *Empresses*, p. 50.
43. Theophanes, *Chronicle*, AM 6065, A.D. 572/73, p. 364. Badouarios was actually the emperor's son-in-law, not brother, for he was married to Sophia's daughter Arabia, adding more weight to Sophia's intervention on his behalf.
44. Gregory of Tours, *History of the Franks*, 5.19.
45. Averil Cameron, "The Byzantine Sources of Gregory of Tours," *Journal of Theological Studies* 26 (1975): 422 [421–26].
46. John of Ephesus, *Ecclesiastical History*, 3.3.1. Averil Cameron points out, however, that despite John's vitriol he is still more balanced than Evagrius. Averil Cameron, "Early Byzantine *Kaiserkritik:* Two Case Histories," *Byzantine and Modern Greek Studies* 3 (1977): 10 [1–17].
47. John of Ephesus, *Ecclesiastical History*, 3.3.2.
48. John of Ephesus, *Ecclesiastical History*, 3.3.2.
49. John of Ephesus, *Ecclesiastical History*, 3.3.3.
50. John of Ephesus, *Ecclesiastical History*, 3.3.4. The Novels of Leo VI give some indication of the rights and responsibilities of a wife when her husband becomes insane, for Novel 112 indicates that after five years of insanity the wife was permitted to divorce her husband, albeit with a reasoning that emphasizes the consequences of the man's mental illness for procreation of the couple. Karsten Fledelius, "Woman's Position and Possibilities in Byzantine Society, with Particular Reference to the Novels of Leo VI," *Jahrbuch der Österreichischen Byzantinistik* 32.2 (1982): 427[425–32]. The full legal text is translated in *Les Novelles de Léon VI le Sage*, 112, trans. P. Noailles and A. Dain (Paris: Société d'Édition "Les Belles Lettres," 1944), 366–73.
51. John of Ephesus, *Ecclesiastical History*, 3.3.4.
52. Despite the latitude of Sophia in this crisis, the empresses' role was not institutionalized as a kind of second in command of the Empire. The evidence simply does not yield a consistent sense that empresses had a kind of vice-presidential role, but rather that the specific confluence of circumstances permitted this situation. Liz James, *Empresses and Power in Early Byzantium* (London: Leicester University Press, 2001), p. 83.
53. Gregory Abu'l-Faraj, 9.87, p. 81.
54. As Prokopios relates of the Nika Riot,"The emperor and his court were deliberating as to whether it would be better for them if they remained or if they took flight in the ships. And many opinions were expressed favouring either course. And the Empress Theodora also spoke to the following effect: 'As to the belief that a woman ought not to be daring

among men or to assert herself boldly among those who are holding back from fear, I consider that the present crisis most certainly does not permit us to discuss whether the matter should be regarded in this or in some other way. . . . My opinion then is that the present time, above all others, is inopportune for flight, even though it bring safety. For while it is impossible for a man who has seen the light not also to die, for one who has been an emperor it is unendurable to be a fugitive. May I never be separated from the purple, and may I not live that day on which those who meet me shall not address me as mistress [δέσποιναν]. . . . For as myself, I approve a certain ancient saying that royalty is a good burial-shroud." Prokopios, *Wars*, I.24.32–37. Although this scene taps into rhetorical traditions and may be all or partially fictional, it confirms the empress' insider status in these deliberations. Judith Herrin, "The Imperial Feminine in Byzantium," *Past and Present* 169 (2000): 31–32 [3–35].

55. Gregory Abu'l-Faraj, Chronicle, 9.86–87, ed. P. Bedjian (Paris: Maison Neuve, 1890); *Chronicle,* trans. Ernest A. Wallis Budge (New York: Oxford University Press, 1932), p. 81.
56. John of Ephesus, *Ecclesiastical History,* 3.3.23.
57. John of Ephesus, *Ecclesiastical History,* 3.3.7.
58. Theophanes, *Chronicle,* AM 6071, A.D. 578/79, p. 370.
59. Theophanes, *Chronicle,* AM 6072, A.D. 579/80, p. 371.
60. John of Ephesus, *Ecclesiastical History,* 3.3.7.
61. Cameron well exemplifies this interpretation in modern scholarship, framing the situation in the terms of a romance novel, "Tiberios was tall, handsome, kindhearted, and charitable. No surprise, then, that Sophia, not yet ready to take back seat, should be attracted to him." Cameron, "Empress," 16.
62. Michael the Syrian, 10.17 [369]; and Gregory Abu'l-Faraj's account is consistent, 9.87, p. 81.
63. Michael the Syrian, 10.17 [369].
64. Michael the Syrian, 10.17 [370].
65. Victor Langlois mentions Gregory Abu'l-Faraj as a historical source for this double naming (IX.88, p. 82), Michael the Syrian, *Chronique de Michel le Grand,* ed. and trans. Victor Langlois (Venice: Académie de Saint-Lazare, 1868), p. 210 n1.
66. Ruth Macrides, "Dynastic marriages and political kinship," in *Byzantine Diplomacy,* ed. Jonathan Shepard and Simon Franklin (London: Variorum, 1992), p. 276 [263–80].
67. Theophanes, *Chronicle,* AM 6071, A.D. 578/79, p. 370.
68. John of Ephesus narrates "From the palace she proceeded in a covered litter to the church, attended by the senate and her chamberlains, while the blue and green factions stood prepared each to greet her, the blue naming her Anastasia, while the green shouted Helena; and so fiercely did they

contend with rival shouts for the honour of naming her, that a great and terrible riot ensued, and all the people were in confusion. She meanwhile entered the church, and made adoration, and returned to the palace as queen," *Ecclesiastical History,* 3.3.9.
69. Gregory of Tours, *History of the Franks,* 5.19.
70. Gregory of Tours, *History of the Franks,* 5.30.
71. Gregory of Tours, *History of the Franks,* 6.30.
72. Gregory of Tours, *History of the Franks,* 6.30.
73. Theophanes, *Chronicle,* AM 6093, A.D. 600/01, p. 406.
74. Garland, *Empresses,* p. 56.
75. Garland, *Empresses,* pp. 50–51; moreover Brubaker and Tobler's recent article and James' book put these issues in the context of other empresses' numismatic imagery.
76. Justin II gold issues as published in *DOC* I, Constantinople mint: types 1–15, pp. 198–202; Antioch types 138-(142), pp. 240–41; Alexandria types (190a)–190g, pp. 250–52; Ravenna types 210a–212, pp. 259–60.
77. All of Justin II's gold issues listed above have a personification of Constantinople or of Victory on the reverse.
78. W. Wroth, *Catalogue of the Imperial Byzantine Coins In The British Museum,* 2 vols. (London: Longmans, 1908), 1: Justin II, type 26.
79. Bellinger, in *DOC* I, p. 204, reads the object represented on the image as a scroll, whereas the catalog of Wroth describes the object in each sovereign's hand as a book. Wroth, *Catalogue,* p. 77.
80. Wroth, *Catalogue,* Justin II, type 27.
81. *DOC* I, Justin II type 24c. The only exception to this is the rare issue of the mint of Carthage, in which the follis, half follis, and decannumium of 572/3 represent the emperor and empress *en buste. DOC* I, Justin II types 198.1–201. The inscription on the follis below the exergue line proclaims VITA.
82. Most of the *DOC* examples have the concave sides, such as *DOC* I, Justin II type 22 a.1, but *DOC* I, Justin II type 23c has straight sides.
83. *DOC* I, Justin I type 1a ff.
84. Philip Grierson and Melinda Mays, *Catalogue of Late Roman Coins in the Dumbarton Oaks Collection and in the Whittemore Collection* (Washington, D.C.: Dumbarton Oaks, 1992), p. 230. These two 1 1/2 solidi weight issues render the empress in the familiar form of the seated image of Roma used on the reverse types of Honorius.
85. Cécile Morrisson, *Catalogue des monnaies byzantines de la Bibliothèque Nationale* (Paris: Bibliothèque Nationale, 1970), p. 125.
86. G. Zacos and A. Veglery, *Byzantine Lead Seals* (Basel: Augustin, 1972–85), vol. I, 1 no. 130.
87. Zacos and Veglery, *Byzantine,* I, 1 no. 130bis. Olster also holds that this kind of numismatic emulation occurred, theorizing that the double portrait established a image of legitimacy. David Olster, "The Dynastic Iconography of Heraclius' Early Coinage," *XVI. Internationaler Byzantinistenkongress,*

Akten 2.2 (Vienna: Der Österreichischen Akademie der Wissenschaften, 1982), p. 400.
88. Zacos and Veglery, *Byzantine*, I, 1 no. 130.
89. *DOC* I, Maurice type 71.1.
90. *DOC* I, Maurice type 297.1.
91. *DOC* I, Maurice type 300, p. 374.
92. Philip Grierson, *Byzantine Coins* (London: Methuen, 1982), p. 45.
93. *DOC* II, 1, p. 147. Although it is not clear why Phokas would choose to emulate this coin type if indeed it was the product of an "insurrectionary" movement of a former (and very likely more legitimate) rival for power.
94. *DOC* II, Phokas 24b1.
95. *DOC* II, 1, Phokas follis Class 2, pp. 163–65.
96. Leslie Brubaker and Helen Tobler, "The Gender of Money: Byzantine Empresses on Coins (324–802)," *Gender and History* 12 (2000): 590 [572–94].
97. Grierson, *DOC* II, 1, p. 147.
98. Grierson phrases this claim in survey text as "The old tradition had been that coins might only be struck in the name of the empress after she had provided an heir to the throne." Grierson, *Byzantine Coins*, p. 44.
99. Grierson, *Byzantine Coins*, p. 45.
100. Grierson and Mays, *LRC*, p. 8.
101. Morrison likewise attributes this anomaly to "l'ambition de Sophia," although she puzzles over the lack of comparable representations of Theodora. Morrisson, *Catalogue*, p. 125.
102. Elbern gives a useful overview of early scholarship on the cross beginning in the eighteenth century; Victor H. Elbern, "Zum Justinuskreuz im Schatz von Sankt Peter zu Rom," *Jahrbuch der Berliner Museen* 6 (1964): 25–38.
103. Elbern, "Justinuskreuz," 33. Anna Kartsonis in her recent mention of the "Crux Vaticana" emphasizes the preeminence of the *Agnus Dei* over the two images of Christ. Anna Kartsonis, "Emancipation of the Crucifixion," in *Byzance et les images*, ed. Guillou and Durrand (Paris: La Documentation française, 1994), pp. 153–87.
104. Belting-Ihm, "Justinuskreuz," 147.
105. Elbern, "Justinuskreuz," 30; and Belting-Ihm, "Justinuskreuz," 142–44.
106. Charles de Linas, *Les origines de l'orfévrerie*, vol. 1 (Paris: E. Didron, 1877), p. 305, attributes the lettering to the sixth century but Bergman represents current opinion in his placement of the inscription paleographically to the tenth or eleventh centuries, when the original inscription was replaced. Robert Bergman, *The Vatican Treasures* (Cleveland: Cleveland Museum of Art, 1998), p. 22.
107. de Linas, *Les origines de l'orfévrerie*, vol. 1 (Paris: Edouard Didron, 1877), pp. 305–07; and O. M. Dalton, *Byzantine Art and Archaeology* (Oxford: Clarendon, 1911), p. 548.
108. Richard Delbrueck, "Portraets byzantinischer Kaiserinnen," *Mitteilungen des kaiserlich deutschen archäologischen Instituts, Römische Abteilung* 28 (1913): 340 [310–52].

109. *Liber Pontificalis,* 54.85.
110. Belting-Ihm, "Justinuskreuz," 158–59.
111. Belting-Ihm, "Justinuskreuz," 151.
112. David Talbot Rice, *Art of the Byzantine Era* (1963; repr. New York: Thames and Hudson, 1986), p. 63.
113. Belting-Ihm, "Justinuskreuz," 147. She suggests that this crown may be an amalgam of an earlier type of women's crown with *mitrella* and later forms with rigid protrusions, underdeveloped *mitrella* and *cataseistae* beginning at eye height, 160.
114. Belting-Ihm, "Justinuskreuz," 160.
115. Beckwith characterizes this mode of representation as a specifically religious style. John Beckwith, *The Art of Constantinople* (London: Phaidon, 1961), p. 46; and Bergman, *Vatican,* p. 125.
116. Beckwith, *Art,* p. 47.
117. Erica Cruikshank Dodd, "The Question of Workshop: Evidence of the Stamps on the Sion Treasure," in *Ecclesiastical Silver Plate in Sixth-Century Byzantium,* ed. Susan A. Boyd and Marlia Mundell Mango (Washington, D.C.: Dumbarton Oaks, 1992), pp. 62–63 [57–63].
118. Garland, *Empresses,* p. 45. Averil Cameron interprets both gifts as attempts early in the reign to assure orthodoxy. Averil Cameron, "The Artistic Patronage of Justin II," *Byzantion* 50 (1980): 67–68 [62–84].
119. Venantius Fortunatus in "To Justin and Sophia, the August," in *Venantius Fortunatus: Personal and Political Poems,* trans. Judith George (Liverpool: Liverpool University Press, 1995), pp. 114–15. Venantius Fortunatus, MGH, Auctores Antiquissimi, 4.1, ed. F. Leo (1881; repr. Munich; MGH, 1981), App. 2, pp. 275–78. The historical context of this gift is discussed in Judith W. George, *Venantius Fortunatus A Latin Poet in Merovingian Gaul* (Oxford: Clarendon Press, 1992), pp. 62–64. Although it has been suggested that Radegund was the actual author of the poem, a *gratiarum actio,* Brennan convincingly argues for maintaining the attribution to Fortunatus. Brian Brennan, "The Disputed Authorship of Fortunatus' Byzantine Poems," *Byzantion* 66 (1996): 340–43 [335–45].
120. Laskarina Bouras, *The Cross of Adrianople: A Silver Processional Cross of the Middle Byzantine Period* (Athens: Benaki, 1979), p. 23.
121. For example, *DOC* III, 1, Class 1 gold solidus from the period of Irene's regency.
122. Prokopios, *Buildings,* I.2.11–12, ed. J. Haury, vol. 4, *Procopii Caesariensis opera omnia* (Leipzig: Teubner, 1964); ed. and trans. H. B. Dewing, LCL (Cambridge, MA: Harvard University Press, 1940).
123. Grierson, *DOC* III,1, 131.
124. Grierson, *DOC* III,1, 131.
125. Grierson and Mays, *Late Roman Coins,* p. 152. Brubaker and Tobler, "Gender of Money," 580.
126. Grierson, *Byzantine Coins,* p. 30.
127. Constantine VII Porphyrogennetos, *De cerimoniis aulae Byzantinae,* 1.49 (40), ed. Reiske, 2 vols. (Bonn: Corpus Scriptorum Historiae Byzantinae,

1829); Partial translation in *Le Livres des Cérémonies,* ed. and trans. Albert Vogt, 2 vols. in 4 parts with commentary (Paris: Les Belles Lettres, 1967).
128. André Grabar, *L'empereur dans l'art byzantin* (1936; repr. of Strasbourg ed. London: Variorum Reprints, 1971), p. 6.
129. Grabar, *L'empereur,* p. 12.
130. Richard Delbrueck, *Die Consulardiptychen und verwandte Denkmäler* (Berlin: Walter de Gruyter, 1929), no. 65; and Volbach, *Elfenbeinarbeiten,* no. 64.
131. Delbrueck speculates that the eagle to the viewer's right is masculine, and his companion is female. Delbrueck, *Consulardiptychen,* no. 51, p. 204.
132. *ODB,* "Eagle," p. 669. A diptych of the Western consul Boethius, now in Brescia, from A.D. 487 depicts the consul clutching an eagle-topped scepter in one hand and a mappa in the other.
133. An unidentified Constantinopolitan diptych now in Novara represents the half-length consul in a central medallion holding a mappa and a scepter with the bust of an emperor on top. Delbrueck, *Consulardiptychen,* no. 42; and Wolfgang Fritz Volbach, *Elfenbeinarbeiten der spätantike und des frühen Mittelalters,* 3rd ed. (Mainz: Philipp von Zabern, 1976), no. 42.
134. Delbrueck, *Consulardiptychen,* no. 6; and Volbach, *Elfenbeinarbeiten,* no. 5.
135. Josef Engemann, "Ein Missorium des Anastasius, Überlegungen zum ikonographischen Programm der 'Anastasius'-Platte aus dem Sutton Hoo Ship-Burial," in *Festschrift für Klaus Wessel* (Munich: Editio Maris, 1988), p. 115 [103–15].
136. André Grabar, "Une fresque visigothique et l'iconographie du silence," *Cahiers archéologiques* 1 (1945): 125 [124–28].
137. Grabar, "fresque," 125.
138. Liz James, "Goddess, Whore, Wife, or Slave? Will the Real Byzantine Empress Please Stand Up?" in *Queens and Queenship in Medieval Europe,* ed. Anne J. Duggan (Woodbridge, U. K.: Boydell, 1997), p. 131 [123–40].
139. Delbrueck, *Consulardiptychen,* no. 52; and Volbach, *Elfenbeinarbeiten,* no. 52.
140. The throne type is discussed in Edmund Wiegand, "Zum Denkmälerkreis des Christogrammnimbus," *Byzantinische Zeitschrift* 31 (1932), 67 [63–81].
141. Even during first-hand examination the author could not discern any details in the tablion that would support Volbach's suggestion that the tablion bore the image of Roma or Constantinopolis.
142. Breckenridge, in *Age of Spirituality: Late Antique and Early Christian Art, Third to Seventh Century* (New York: Metropolitan Museum of Art, 1977), p. 31.
143. Glenn Peers offers an intriguing account of this development in *Subtle Bodies: Representing Angels in Byzantium* (Berkeley: University of California Press, 2001), pp. 23–25.
144. *Age of Spirituality,* ed. Weitzmann, figs. 59 and 64.
145. David H. Wright, "Ivories for the Emperor," in *Third Annual Byzantine Studies Conference Abstracts of Papers,* 1977, p. 7 [6–9].
146. James, *Empresses,* p. 139.

NOTES TO PAGES 175–179

147. Herrin, "Imperial Feminine," 16 n38 on that page continues with the argument that Maria Regina iconography developed in the West in response to this lacuna.
148. *ODB*, "Diptych," p. 637.
149. Dalton, *Byzantine Art and Archaeology*, pp. 197–99.
150. H. G. Thümmel, "Kaiserbild und Christusikone: Zur Bestimmung der fünfteiligen Elfenbeindiptychen," *Byzantinoslavica* 39 (1978): 196–206.
151. Marcel Mauss, *The Gift: Forms and Functions of Exchange in Archaic Societies*, trans. Ian Cunnison (New York: Norton, 1967), p. 11.
152. Kenneth S. Painter, "Roman Silver Hoards: Ownership and Status," in *Argenterie romaine et byzantine*, ed. François Baratte (Paris: De Boccard, 1988), p. 105 [97–105].
153. A solid articulation of this attribution is Breckenridge, *Age of Spirituality*, ed. Weitzmann, catalog no. 25, p. 31.
154. Delbrueck, "Portraets," 341.
155. Delivorria, *Recherches*, pp. 67–68.
156. Hans Graeven, "Elfenbeinportraits der Königin Amalasuintha," *Jahrbuch der königlich preussischen Kunstsammlungen* 19 (1898): 82–88; and Siegfried Fuchs, *Kunst der Ostgotenzeit* (Berlin: Walter de Gruyter, 1944), pp. 64–70.
157. Nancy Netzer, "Redating the Consular Ivory of Orestes," *Burlington Magazine* 125 (May 1983): 265–71.
158. Delivorria proposed this identification in her unpublished dissertation of 1966, and this suggestion has not received adequate consideration. Delivorria, *Recherches*, pp. 67–68.
159. Weitzmann, ed., *Age of Spirituality*, p. 72, catalog no. 61.
160. Zwirn, *Age of Spirituality*, ed. Weitzmann, p. 72.
161. George P. Galavaris, "The Symbolism of the Imperial Costume as Displayed on Byzantine Coins," *American Numismatic Society Museum Notes* 8 (1958): 103 [99–117].
162. *DOC* I, Tiberius II type 11a. Galavaris notes that it is on the coinage of Tiberios that consular dress becomes preferred over military dress for the emperor. Galavaris, "Imperial," 104.
163. Grabar, *L'empereur*, p. 13.
164. Delivorria suggested that it represents Tiberios II in consular dress, *Recherches*, p. 70.

Conclusion

1. Liz James offers a very useful table of individual empresses and the surviving sources for their titles, Liz James, *Empresses and Power in Early Byzantium* (London: Leicester University Press, 2001), pp. 120–22.
2. Alexander Kazhdan and Michael McCormick, "The Social World of the Byzantine Court," in *Byzantine Court Culture from 829 to 1204* (Washington, D. C.: Dumbarton Oaks, 1997), p. 170 [167–97].

3. Ensslin, for example, discusses the elective principle behind successsion, though much thinking about the issues of succession and legitimacy in Byzantium seems concentrated in the early twentieth century in the work of scholars such as Bury. Wilhelm Ensslin, "The Emperor and Imperial Administration," in *Byzantium: An Introduction to East Roman Civilization*, ed. Norman H. Baynes and H. St. L. B. Moss (1948; repr. New York: Oxford University Press, 1961), p. 270.
4. Leslie Brubaker, "Memories of Helena: Patterns of Imperial Matronage in the Fourth and Fifth Centuries," in *Women, Men, and Eunuchs: Gender in Byzantium*, ed. Liz James, pp. 52–75.
5. Ernst Kitzinger, "Artistic Patronage in Early Byzantium," in *Committenti e produzione artistico-letteraria nell'alto medioevo occidentale* (Spoleto: Presso la sede del centro, 1992), p. 43 [33–55].
6. Seneca, *De Beneficiis*, 6.32.1, ed. and trans. John W. Basore, LCL, 3 vols. (Cambridge, MA: Harvard University Press, 1958).
7. Sister Benedicta Ward, *Harlots of the Desert: A Study of Repentance in Early Byzantine Monastic Sources* (Kalamazoo, MI: Cistercian Publications, 1987).
8. Alain Boureau has deftly dismantled the myth of the *droit de cuissage* in his work, *The Lord's First Night: The Myth of the Droit de Cuissage*, trans. Lydia G. Cochrane (Chicago: University of Chicago Press, 1998, French ed. in 1995).
9. Kazhdan and McCormick, "The Social World," in *Byzantine Court Culture*, p. 170.
10. Michael McCormick, "Emperors," in *The Byzantines*, ed. Guglielmo Cavallo (Chicago and London: University of Chicago Press, 1997), p. 232 [230–54].
11. Alexander Kazhdan, "Women at Home," *Dumbarton Oaks Papers* 52 (1998): 5 [1–17].
12. Constantine VII Porphyrogennetos, *De cerimoniis aulae Byzantinae*, 50 (41).1.24, ed. Reiske (Bonn: Corpus Scriptorum Historiae Byzantinae, 1829–30); Partial translation in *Le Livres des cérémonies*, ed. and trans. Albert Vogt (Paris: Les Belles Lettres, 1967).
13. *ODB*, ed. Kazhdan, "De ceremoniis," p. 596.
14. De Cer, 50(41), vol. 2, p. 21, lines 25–26.
15. Arjun Appadurai, *The Social Life of Things: Commodities in Cultural Perspective* (New York: Cambridge University Press, 1986), p. 38.
16. The evidence from Aphrodisias, for example, shows slowed artistic production. Whereas there were 140 individual bases for honorific statues from the first through third centuries AD, from A.D. 300–600 there are merely thirty-four with none at all from the late sixth century onward. R. R. R Smith, "Late Antique Portraits in a Public Context: Honorific Statuary at Aphrodisias in Caria, A.D. 300–600," *Journal of Roman Studies* 89 (1999): 173 [153–89].
17. David H. Wright, "The Shape of the Seventh Century in Byzantine Art," *First Annual Byzantine Studies Conference Abstracts of Papers* (1975): 24–25 [9–28].

18. Martin Jay, "Scopic Regimes of Modernity," *Vision and Visuality,* ed. Hal Foster (Seattle: Bay Press, 1988), p. 12 [3–28].
19. Jay, "Scopic," 13.
20. James Trilling, "The Image Not Made by Hands and the Byzantine Way of Seeing," in *The Holy Face and the Paradox of Representation,* ed. Herbert L. Kessler and Gerhard Wolf (Bologna: Nuova Alfa Editoriale, 1998), pp. 109–27; and R. L. Gordon, "The Real and the Imaginary: Production and Religion in the Graeco-Roman World," *Art History* 2.1 (1979): 5–34.
21. Henry Maguire, "Originality in Byzantine Art Criticism," in *Originality in Byzantine Literature, Art and Music,* ed. A. R. Littlewood (Oxford: Oxbow, 1995), pp. 101–14.
22. Dion C. Smythe explores this theme in an essay largely concerned with the Middle Byzantine *Alexiad* by Anna Komnene, "Women as Outsiders," in *Women, Men, and Eunuchs: Gender in Byzantium,* ed. Liz James (New York: Routledge, 1997), pp. 149–67.
23. Leo Braudy, *The Frenzy of Renown: Fame and Its History* (New York: Oxford University Press, 1986), p. 41 n7.
24. Theophanes, *Chronicle,* AM 6016, A.D. 523/24, ed. C. de Boor (Leipzig: Teubner, 1883–85), p. 170; *The Chronicle of Theophanes Confessor: Byzantine and Near Eastern History A.D. 284–813,* trans. Cyril Mango and Roger Scott (Oxford: Clarendon Press, 1997), p. 260.
25. *DOC* III, 1, 130.
26. Judith Herrin maps out this terrain in her new book, *Women in Purple: Rulers of Medieval Byzantium* (London: Weidenfeld & Nicholson, 2001).
27. Nevra Necipoğlu, "Byzantine Women," in *Woman in Anatolia: 9000 Years of the Anatolian Woman,* ed. Günsel Renda (Istanbul: Turkish Republic Ministry of Culture, 1993), p. 127 [125–31].
28. A good example of this practice is Despina White, "Property Rights of Women: The Changes in the Justinian Legislation Regarding the Dowry and the Parapherna," *Jahrbuch der Österreichischen Byzantinistik* 32.2 (1982): 539–48. Some scholars, however, such as Joëlle Beaucamp, have been much more sensitive to tracking change over time. Joëlle Beaucamp, *Le statut de la femme à Byzance,* 2 vols. (Paris: Boccard, 1990).
29. Liz James and Barbara Hill, "Women and Politics in the Byzantine Empire: Imperial Women," in *Women in Medieval Western European Culture,* ed. Linda E. Mitchell (New York: Garland, 1999), p. 163 n4 [157–78].

BIBLIOGRAPHY

For convenience I have included a reference to a modern translation when possible.

Primary Sources

Agathias Scholastikos, ed. Giovanni Viansino, *Epigrammi, Agazio Scolastico* (Milan: Casa Editrice Luigi Trevisini, 1967); *Greek Anthology,* trans. W. R. Paton, LCL (Cambridge, MA: Harvard University Press, 1979).

Agnellus, *Codex pontificalis ecclesiae Ravennatis,* ed. O. Holder-Egger, MGH, *Scriptores rerum Langobardicarum et italicarum saec.* VI–IX (1878; repr. Hannover: Hannsche Buchhandlung, 1988), pp. 265–391.

Amalasuntha's Letter to Theodora Augusta, ed. and trans. Michelle Thiébaux, in *The Writings of Medieval Women: An Anthology* (New York: Garland, 1994).

Ambrose, *De Obitu Theodosii,* ed. O. Faller, Corpus scriptorum ecclesiasticorum latinorum, vol. 73 (Vienna: Hoelder-Pichler-Tempsky, 1955); *Funeral Orations by Saint Gregory Nazianzen and Saint Ambrose,* trans. Roy J. Deferrari (New York: Fathers of the Church, 1953).

(Anonymous works are listed by title.)

Anna Komnene, *Alexiad,* eds. Diether R. Reinsch and Athanasios Kambylis, *Anna Comnenae Alexias,* Corpus fontium historiae Byzantinae, 40, 2 vols. (Berlin: Walter de Gruyter, 2001); *The Alexiad of Anna Comnena,* trans. E. R. A. Sewter (New York: Penguin, 1969).

Asterius of Amaseia, ed. François Halkin, *Euphémie de Chalcédoine,* Subsidia hagiographica, 41 (Brussels: Société des Bollandistes, 1965); *Description of a painting of the martyrdom of St. Euphemia,* trans. Cyril Mango, in *The Art of the Byzantine Empire 312–1453: Sources and Documents* (1972; repr. Toronto: University of Toronto Press, 1986), p. 37.

Chorikios, Laudatio Marciani, *Choricii Gazaei Opera,* eds. R. Foerster and E. Richtsteig, *Corpus scriptorum historiae byzantinae* (Leipzig: Teubner, 1929); partial trans. Mango, in *Sources,* pp. 68–72.

Chronicon Paschale [Easter Chronicle], Anonymous, ed. Ludwig Dindorf (Bonn: Weber, 1832); *Chronicon Paschale: 284–628 A.D.,* trans. Michael and Mary Whitby (Liverpool: Liverpool University Press, 1989).

de Clavijo, Ruy González, ed. Francisco López Estrada, *Embajada a Tamorlán* (Madrid: Consejo superior de investigaciones científicas, 1943); *Embassy to Tamerlane, 1403–1406*, trans. Guy le Strange (New York: Harper, 1928).

Cod. Paris gr. 1447, fols. 257–58, Anonymous, ed. A. Wenger, "Notes inédites sur les empereur Théodose I, Arcadius, Théodose II, Léon I," *Revue des études byzantines* 10 (1952): 47–59; trans. Mango, in *Sources,* p. 35.

Constantine VII Porphyrogennetos, *De administrando imperio,* Dumbarton Oaks Texts, 1, ed. Gy. Moravcsik, trans. R. J. H. Jenkins (Washington, D.C.: Dumbarton Oaks, 1967).

———, *De cerimoniis aulae Byzantinae,* ed. Reiske, 2 vols. (Bonn: Corpus Scriptorum Historiae Byzantinae, 1829–30); Partial translation in *Le Livres des Cérémonies,* ed. and trans. Albert Vogt, 2 vols. in 4 parts with commentary (Paris: Les Belles Lettres, 1967).

Constantine, Anonymous Life (BHG 364), trans. Frank Beetham, et al, *From Constantine to Julian: Pagan and Byzantine Views,* eds. Samuel N. C. Lieu and Dominic Montserrat (New York: Routledge, 1996).

Corippus, *In laudem Iustini Augusti minoris,* ed. and trans. Averil Cameron (London: Athlone Press, 1976).

Cyril of Scythopolis, *Vita* of Saint Sabas, ed. Eduard Schwartz, *Kyrillos von Skythopolis* (Leipzig: Hinrichs, 1939); *The Lives of the Monks of Palestine,* trans. R. M. Price (Kalamazoo, MI: Cistercian Publications, 1991).

De rebus bellicis, Anonymous, ed. Robert I. Ireland (Leipzig: Teubner, 1984); *A Roman Reformer and Inventor: Being a New Text of the Treatise* De rebus bellicis, ed. and trans. E. A. Thompson (Oxford: Claredon, 1952).

Epistola synodica patriarcharum orientalium, ed. L. Duchesne, *Roma e l'Oriente* 5 (1912–13); trans. Mango, in *Sources,* p. 114.

Eudokia, *Carmen de S. Cypriano Antiocheno,* PG 85: 831–64.

———, *Eudociae Augustae, Procli Lycii, Claudiani carminum graecorum reliquiae,* ed. Arthur Ludwich, Bibliotheca scriptorum Graecorum et Romanorum Teubneriana (Leipzig: Teubner, 1897).

Eudoxia and the Holy Sepulchre: A Constantinian Legend in Coptic, ed. Tito Orlandi, trans. Birger A. Pearson (Milan: Cisalpino-Goliardica, 1980).

Eusebios, *Letter to Constantia,* ed. F. Winkelmann, *Die griechischen christlichen Schriftsteller der ersten Jahrhunderte* (Berlin: Akademie-Verlag, 1975); partial trans. Mango, in *Sources,* pp. 16–18.

———, *Vita Constantini,* ed. F. Winkelmann, *Die griechischen christlichen Schriftsteller der ersten Jahrhunderte* (Berlin: Akademie-Verlag, 1975); *Life of Constantine,* trans. Averil Cameron and Stuart Hall (Oxford: Oxford University Press, 1999).

Evagrius Scholasticus, *Ecclesiastical History,* eds. J. Bidez and L. Parmentier (1898; repr. Amsterdam, 1964); Fr. trans. A.-J. Festugière, in "Évagre: *Histoire Ecclesiastique,*" *Byzantion* 45 (1975): 187–488.

Fulgentius, *Opera,* ed. Rudolfus Helm (1898, repr. Stuttgart: Teubner, 1970); *Fulgentius the Mythographer,* trans. Leslie George Whitbread (Columbus, OH: Ohio State University Press, 1971).

Greek Anthology, ed. H. Beckby, *Anthologia Graeca,* 4 vols. (Munich: Ernst Heimeran, 1965); trans. W. R. Paton, LCL (Cambridge, MA: Harvard University Press, 1916–27).

Gregory Abu'l-Faraj, *Gregorii Barhebraei Chronicon syriacum,* ed. P. Bedjian (Paris: Maison Neuve, 1890); *Chronicle,* trans. Ernest A. Wallis Budge (New York: Oxford University Press, 1932).

Gregory of Tours, *The History of the Franks,* vol. 1.1 : eds. Bruno Krusch and Wilhelm Levison, MGH, *Scriptorum rerum Merovingicarum* (1885; repr. Stuttgart, 1951), vol. 1.2: ed. Bruno Krusch, MGH, *Scriptorum rerum Merovingicarum* (1888; repr. Stuttgart, 1951); *Gregory of Tours: The History of the Franks,* trans. Lewis Thorpe (New York: Penguin, 1974).

Hermogenes, *Hermogenis opera,* ed. Hugo Rabe (Leipzig: Teubner, 1913); *On Types of Style,* trans. Cecil W. Wooten (Chapel Hill: University of North Carolina Press, 1987).

(Saint) John Chrysostom, Homily II, "Cum imperatrix," ed. Migne, PG 63: 467–72.

John of Biclar, *Chronicle,* ed. Julio Campos, *Juan de Biclaro Obispo de Gerona, Su vida y su obra* (Madrid: Consejo Superior de Investigaciones Científicas, 1960); trans. Kenneth Baxter Wolf, in *Conquerors and Chroniclers of Early Medieval Spain* (Liverpool: Liverpool University Press, 1990).

John of Ephesus, *Iohannis Ephesini Historiae Ecclesiasticae Pars Tertia,* ed. E. W. Brooks (Paris: E typographeo reipublicae, 1935; Latin trans.: Louvain: Ex officina et scientifica, 1936); *The Third Part of the Ecclesiastical History of John of Ephesus,* trans. R. Payne Smith (Oxford: Oxford University Press, 1860).

―――, *Lives of the Eastern Saints,* trans. and ed. E. W. Brooks, *Patrologia Orientalis* (Paris: Firmin-Didot): 17 (1923) 1–307, 18 (1924): 513–698, 19 (1926): 153–285.

John Klimax, *Scala paradisi,* PG 88: 632–1209; *The Ladder of Divine Ascent,* trans. Colm Luibheid and Norman Russell, *The Classics of Western Spirituality* (New York: Paulist Press, 1982).

John Lydus, *On Powers,* ed. and trans. Anastasius C. Bandy (Philadelphia: American Philosophical Society, 1983).

John Malalas, *Chronographia,* ed. Ioannes Thurn, *Ioannis Malalae Chronographia, Corpus fontium historiae Byzantinae,* 35 (Berlin: Walter de Gruyter, 2000); *The Chronicle of John Malalas,* trans. Elizabeth Jeffreys, Michael Jeffreys and Roger Scott (Melbourne: Australian Association for Byzantine Studies, 1986).

John of Nikiu, *The Chronicle of John, Bishop of Nikiu, Translated from Zotenberg's Ethiopic Text,* trans. R. H. Charles (1916; repr. Amsterdam, 1982).

Julian, *The Works of Emperor Julian,* ed. and trans. Wilmer Cave Wright, 3 vols., LCL (London, William Heinemann, 1913).

Kassia, ed. K. Krumbacher, "Kassia," *Sitzungsberichte der Bayerischen Akademie der Wissenschaften* 1 (1897): 305–70; *Kassia: The Legend, the Woman and Her Work,* trans. Antonia Tripolitis (New York: Garland, 1992).

Leo VI, Novels, ed. J.-P. Migne, PG 107: 419–660; ed. and French trans.: *Les Novelles de Léon VI le Sage,* trans. P. Noailles and A. Dain (Paris: Société d'Édition "Les Belles Lettres," 1944).

Le Liber Pontificalis, ed. L. Duchesne, 2 vols. (2nd ed.; Paris: Boccard, 1955–57); *The Book of Pontiffs (Liber Pontificalis): The Ancient Biographies of the First Ninety Roman Bishops to A.D. 715,* trans. Raymond Davis (Liverpool: Liverpool University Press, 1989).

Liutprand of Cremona, *Antapodosis,* ed. Joseph Becker, *Die Werke Liudprands von Cremona,* MGH, Scriptores rerum Germanicarum (Hannover: Hahnsche, 1915); *The Embassy to Constantinople and Other Writings,* trans. F. A. Wright (London: Everyman's Library, 1993).

Marcellinus, ed. T. Mommsen, MGH, Auctorum antiquissimorum, 11: 37–108 (1892; repr. Berlin: Weidman, 1961); *The Chronicle of Marcellinus,* trans. Brian Croke (Sydney: Australian Association for Byzantine Studies, 1995).

Mark the Deacon, *Life of Porphyry,* eds. and French trans. Henri Grégoire and M.-A. Kugener (Paris: Société d'Édition, "Les Belles Lettres," 1930); partial trans. Mango, in *Sources,* pp. 30–32.

Vita Melania, (Greek text), ed. Denys Gorce (Paris: Les Éditions du Cerf, 1962); *The Life of Melania the Younger,* trans. Elizabeth A. Clark (New York: Edwin Mellen Press, 1984).

Menander, *Menander Rhetor,* eds. and trans. D. A. Russell and N. G. Wilson (New York: Oxford University Press, 1981).

Michael the Syrian, *Chronique de Michel le Syrien,* ed. and French trans. J.-B. Chabot (Paris: Ernest Leroux, 1901).

Nicholas I, Patriarch of Constantinople, *Letters,* eds. and trans. R. J. H. Jenkins and L. G. Westerink (Washington, D.C.: Dumbarton Oaks, 1973).

Niketas Choniates, *Annals,* ed. I. A. van Dieten, *Nicetae Choniatae Historia* (Berlin: Walter de Gruyter, 1975); *O City of Byzantium, Annals of Niketas Choniates,* trans. Harry J. Magoulias (Detroit: Wayne State University Press, 1984).

Parastaseis syntomoi chronikai, Anonymous, eds. and trans. Averil Cameron and Judith Herrin, *Constantinople in the Early Eighth Century: The Parastaseis Syntomoi Chronikai* (Leiden: E. J. Brill, 1984).

Paul the Deacon, *Historiae Langobardorum,* eds. L. Bethmann and G. Waitz, MGH, *Scriptores rerum Langobardicarum et italicarum saec. VI-IX.* (1878; repr. Hannover: Hahnsche Buchhandlung, 1988); *History of the Lombards,* trans. William Dudley Foulke, ed. Edward Peters (1907; repr. Philadelphia: University of Pennsylvania Press, 1974).

Paul Silentiarios, *Description of Hagia Sophia,* ed. P. Friedländer, *Johannes von Gaza und Paulus Silentiarios: Kunstbeschreibungen justinianischer Zeit* (Leipzig: Teubner, 1912); partial trans. Mango, in *Sources,* pp. 80–91.

Vita of Saint Philaretos, eds. and French trans. M.-H. Fourmy and M. Leroy, "La Vie de S. Philarète," *Byzantion* 9 (1934): 135.24–143.25.

Plato, *Phaedrus,* trans. Harold North Fowler (with ed. of Schanz), *Plato: Euthyphro, Apology, Crito, Phaedo, Phaedrus,* LCL (Cambridge, MA: Harvard University Press, 1914).

Prokopios, *The Anekdota,* ed. J. Haury, vol. 2, *Procopii Caesariensis opera omnia* (Leipzig: Teubner, 1963); *Secret History,* ed. and trans. H. B. Dewing, LCL (Cambridge, MA: Harvard University Press, 1935).

―――, *Buildings,* ed. J. Haury, vol. 4, *Procopii Caesariensis opera omnia* (Leipzig: Teubner, 1964); ed. and trans. H. B. Dewing, LCL (Cambridge, MA: Harvard University Press, 1940).

―――, *History of the Wars,* ed. J. Haury, vols. 1–2, *Procopii Caesariensis opera omnia* (Leipzig: Teubner, 1: 1962 and 2: 1963); ed. and trans. H. B. Dewing, 5 vols., LCL (Cambridge, MA: Harvard University Press, 1919).

Psellos, Michael. *Chronography,* ed. S. Impellizzeri, *Imperatori di Bisanzio* (Milan: Fondazione L.Valla, A. Mondadori, 1984); *Fourteen Byzantine Rulers: The Chronographia of Psellus,* trans. E. R. A. Sewter (Baltimore: Penguin, 1966).

Seneca, ed. and trans. John W. Basore, LCL, 3 vols. (Cambridge, MA: Harvard University Press, 1958).

Simokattes, Theophylaktos, *The History of Theophylact Simokatta,* ed. C. de Boor, rev. Peter Wirth, *Theophylacti Simocattae Historiae* (Stuttgart: Teubner, 1972); trans. Michael and Mary Whitby (Oxford: Clarendon Press, 1986).

Souda, Anonymous, *Suidae Lexicon,* ed. Ada Adler, 5 vols. (1928–38; Stuttgart, 1967–71).

Suetonius, *Lives of the Caesars,* ed. and trans. J. C. Rolfe, LCL (Cambridge, MA: Harvard University Press, 1951).

Tacitus, *Annals,* ed. and trans. John Jackson, LCL (Cambridge, MA: Harvard University Press, 1962).

Vita Thekla, *Vie et Miracles de Sainte Thecle,* eds. and French trans. Gilbert Dagron and Marie Dupre la Tour (Brussels: Societé des bollandistes, 1978).

Vita Theodora, ed. A. Markopoulos, "Bios tes autokrateiras Theodoras (BHG 1731)," *Symmeikta* 5 (1983): 249–85; trans. Martha Vinson, in *Byzantine Defenders of Images,* ed. Alice-Mary Talbot (Washington, D.C.: Dumbarton Oaks, 1998), pp. 353–82.

Theodore the Stoudite, *Epistola ad Platonem,* ed. J.-P. Migne, PG 99: 499–506.

Theophanes the Confessor, *Chronographia,* ed. C. de Boor, 2 vols. (Leipzig: Teubner, 1883–85); *The Chronicle of Theophanes Confessor: Byzantine and Near Eastern History A.D. 284–813,* trans. Cyril Mango and Roger Scott (Oxford: Clarendon Press, 1997).

Venantius Fortuntatus, "To Justin and Sophia, the August," ed. F. Leo, MGH, Auctores Antiquissimi, 4.1, (1881; repr. Munich; MGH, 1981), App. 2, pp. 275–78; trans. Judith George in *Venantius Forunatus: Personal and Political Poems,* trans. (Liverpool: Liverpool University Press, 1995), pp. 111–15.

Victor Tonnensis, *Victoris Tonnennensis Episcopi Chronica,* ed T. Mommsen, MGH, Auctores Antiquissimi, vol. 11 (Berlin: Wiedmann, 1894).

Zacharias, Bishop of Mitylene, *The Syriac Chronicle known as that of Zachariah of Mitylene,* eds. and trans. F. J. Hamilton and E. W. Brooks (1899; repr. New York, 1979).

Zosimos, *Historia nova,* ed. L. Mendelssohn (Leipzig: Teubner, 1887), Partial ed.: *Histoire nouvelle,* ed. François Paschoud (Paris: Les Belles Lettres, 1971–86); trans. R. T. Ridley, *New History* (Sidney: Australian Association for Byzantine Studies, 1982).

Secondary Sources

Adam, Paul, *Princesses Byzantines* (Paris: Firmin-Didot, 1893).
Adelson, Howard L. and George L. Kustas, "A Sixth Century Hoard of Minimi from the Western Peloponnese," *American Numismatic Society Museum Notes* 11 (1964): 159–205.
Adshead, K., "The Secret History of Procopius and Its Genesis," *Byzantion* 63 (1993): 5–28.
Allen, Pauline, "Contemporary Portrayals of the Byzantine Empress Theodora (A.D. 527–548)," in *Stereotypes of Women in Power: historical perspectives and Revisionist Views,* ed. Barbara Garlick, Suzanne Dixon, and Pauline Allen (New York: Greenwood Press, 1992), pp. 93–103.
———, "Zachariah Scholasticus and the Historia Ecclesiastica of Evagrius Scholasticus," *The Journal of Theological Studies* 31 (1980): 471–88.
Amad, Gladys, *Qui est la mystérieuse figure de Carthage?* (Beirut: Dar el-Machreq, 1978).
Amory, Patrick, *People and Identity in Ostrogothic Italy, 489–554* (New York: Cambridge University Press, 1997).
Andreescu-Treadgold, Irina and Warren Treadgold, "Dates and Identities in the Imperial Panels in San Vitale" *Byzantine Studies Conference Abstract of Papers* 16 (1990): 52.
———, "Procopius and the Imperial Panels of S. Vitale," *Art Bulletin* 79 (1997): 708–23.
Antonopoulos, Panayotis T., "Petrus Patricius, Some Aspects of His Life and Career," in *From Late Antiquity to Early Byzantium,* ed. Vladimir Vavrinek (Prague: Academia, 1985), pp. 49–53.
Appadurai, Arjun, *The Social Life of Things: Commodities in Cultural Perspective* (New York: Cambridge University Press, 1986).
Archibald, Marion, Michelle Brown, and Leslie Webster, "Heirs of Rome: The Shaping of Britain A.D. 400–900," in *The Transformation of the Roman World A.D. 400–900,* ed. Leslie Webster and Michelle Brown (Berkeley: University of California Press, 1997), pp. 208–48.
Atasoy, Yildiz and Sümer Meriçboyu, *Istanbul Arkeoloji Muzesindeki Büst Seklinde Kantar Agirliklari; Steelyard Weights in the Form of Busts in the Archeological Museum of Istanbul* (Istanbul: Arkeoloji ve Sanat Yayinlari, 1983).
Auzépy, Marie-France, "La destruction de l'icône du Christ de la Chalcé par Léon III: Propagande ou réalité?," *Byzantion* 60 (1990): 445–92.
Bagnall, Roger, Alan Cameron, Seth R. Schwartz, and Klaas A. Worp, *Consuls of the Later Roman Empire* (Atlanta, GA: Scholar's Press, 1987).
Bakhtin, Mikhail, *Rabelais and His World,* trans. Hélène Iswolsky (Bloomington, IN: Indiana University Press, 1984).
Baldwin, Barry, "Three Obol Girls in Procopius," *Hermes* 120 (1992): 255–57.
Barber, Charles, "The Imperial Panels at San Vitale: A Reconsideration," *Byzantine and Modern Greek Studies* 14 (1990): 19–42.
Bardill, Jonathan, "The Church of Sts. Sergius and Bacchus in Constantinople and the Monophysite Refugees," *Dumbarton Oaks Papers* 54 (2000): 1–11.

Barker, John W., *Justinian and the Later Roman Empire* (Madison, WI: University of Wisconsin Press, 1966).

Barnish, S. J. B., "The Wealth of Julianus Argentarius: Late Antique Banking and the Mediterranean Economy," *Byzantion* 55 (1985): 5–38.

Bartman, Elizabeth, *Portraits of Livia: Imaging Imperial Woman in Augustan Rome* (New York: Cambridge University Press, 1999).

Bass, George F. and Frederick H. Van Doorninck, Jr., *Yassi Ada: A Seventh-Century Byzantine Shipwreck*, vol. 1 (College Station, TX: Texas A & M Press, 1982).

Beaucamp, Joëlle, *Le statut de la femme à Byzance*, 2 vols. (Paris: Boccard, 1990).

Beck, Hans-Georg, *Kaiserin Theodora und Prokop* (Munich: Piper, 1986).

Beckwith, John, *Art of Constantinople* (London: Phaidon, 1961).

———, *Early Christian and Byzantine Art* (New York: Penguin, 1979).

Bellinger, Alfred R. and Philip Grierson, *Catalogue of the Byzantine Coins in the Dumbarton Oaks Collection and in the Whittemore Collection* (Washington, D.C.: Dumbarton Oaks, 1966–99).

Belting-Ihm, Christa, "Das Justinuskreuz in der Schatzkammer der Peterskirche zu Rom," *Jahrbuch des römisch-germanischen Zentralmuseums Mainz* 12 (1965): 142–66.

Bensammar, Elisabeth, "La titulature de l'impératrice et sa signification," *Byzantion* 56 (1976): 243–91.

Berchem, Denis van, "Recherches sur la chronologie des enceintes de Syrie et de Mésopotamie," *Syria* 31 (1954): 267–68.

Bergman, Robert, *The Vatican Treasures* (Cleveland, OH: Cleveland Museum of Art, 1998).

Bordo, Susan, "Feminism, Postmodernism, and Gender-Scepticism," in *Feminism/Postmodernism*, ed. Linda N. Nicholson (New York: Routledge, 1990), pp. 133–56.

Bosch, Ursula Victoria, "Fragen zum Frauenkaisertum," *Jahrbuch der Österreichischen Byzantinistik* 32.2 (1982): 499–505.

Boureau, Alain, *The Lord's First Night: The Myth of the Droit de Cuissage*, trans. Lydia G. Cochrane (Chicago: University of Chicago Press, 1998, French ed. in 1995).

Bouras, Laskarina, *The Cross of Adrianople: A Silver Processional Cross of the Middle Byzantine Period* (Athens: Benaki, 1979).

Bradshaw, Gillian, *The Bearkeeper's Daughter* (Boston: Houghton Mifflin, 1987).

Braudy, Leo, *The Frenzy of Renown: Fame and Its History* (New York: Oxford University Press, 1986).

Brennan, Brian, "The Disputed Authorship of Fortunatus' Byzantine Poems," *Byzantion* 66 (1996): 335–45.

Brilliant, Richard, *Portraiture* (Cambridge, MA: Harvard University Press, 1991).

Brubaker, Leslie and Helen Tobler, "The Gender of Money: Byzantine Empresses on Coins (324–802)," *Gender and History* 12 (2000): 572–94.

Brubaker, Leslie, "Art and Byzantine Identity: Saints, Portraits, and the Lincoln College Typikon," in *Byzantium: Image, Identity, Influence*, 19th International Congress of Byzantine Studies, Major Papers (Copenhagen: Eventus Publishers, 1996), pp. 51–59.

———, "The Chalke Gate, the construction of the past, and the Trier ivory," *Byzantine and Modern Greek Studies* 23 (1999): 258–85.

———, "Memories of Helena: Patterns of Imperial Matronage in the Fourth and Fifth Centuries," in *Women, Men, and Eunuchs: Gender in Byzantium*, ed. Liz James, pp. 52–75.

Brubaker, Leslie and John Haldon, *Byzantium in the Iconoclast Era (ca. 680–850): The Sources, An Annotated Survey* (Burlington, VT: Ashgate, 2001).

Bryson, Norman, *Vision and Painting: The Logic of the Gaze* (New Haven: Yale University Press, 1983).

Buckton, David, ed., *Byzantium: Treasures of Byzantine Art and Culture* (London: British Museum Publications, 1994).

Bühl, Gudrun, "Constantinopolis: Das Neue im Gewand des Alten," in *Innovation in der Spätantike*, ed. Beat Brenk (Wiesbaden: Reichert, 1996), pp. 115–36.

Burman, Julia, "The Christian Empress Eudocia," in *Les Femmes et le Monochisme Byzantine*, ed. Jacques Y. Perreault, Canadian Archaeological Institute Athens, no. 1 (Athens: Canadian Archaeological Institute, 1991), pp. 51–59.

Bury, J. B., "The Ceremonial Book of Constantine Porphyrogennetos," *The English Historical Review* 22 (1907): issue 86: 209–227; issue 87: 417–39.

———, *History of the Later Roman Empire*, 2 vols. (1923; repr. New York: Dover, 1958).

———, "Justa Grata Honoria," *Journal of Roman Studies* 9 (1919): 1–13.

Busch, Charles, *Theodora, She-Bitch of Byzantium* (Garden City, NY: Fireside Theater, 1992).

Calkins, Robert G., *A Medieval Treasury* (Ithaca, NY: Office of University Publications, Cornell University, 1968).

Cameron, Alan, "The empress and the poet: paganism and politics at the court of Theodosius II," *Yale Classical Studies* 27 (1982): 217–89.

Cameron, Alan and Jacqueline Long, *Barbarians and Politics at the Court of Arcadius* (Berkeley: University of California Press, 1993).

Cameron, Alan and Diane Schauer, "The Last Consul: Basilius and His Diptych," *Journal of Roman Studies* 72 (1982): 126–45.

Cameron, Averil, "The Artistic Patronage of Justin II," *Byzantion* 50 (1980): 62–84.

———, "The Byzantine Sources of Gregory of Tours," *Journal of Theological Studies* 26 (1975): 421–26.

———, "Early Byzantine *Kaiserkritik*: Two Case Histories," *Byzantine and Modern Greek Studies* 3 (1977): 1–17.

———, "The Empress Sophia," *Byzantion* 45 (1975): 5–21.

———, "Gibbon and Justinian," in *Edward Gibbon and Empire*, ed. Rosamond McKitterick and Roland Quinault (New York: Cambridge University Press, 1997), pp. 34–52.

———, "Notes on the Sophiae, the Sophianae and the Harbor of Sophia," *Byzantion* 37 (1967): 11–20.

———, *Procopius and the Sixth Century* (Berkeley: University of California Press, 1985).

Camille, Michael, *The Gothic Idol: Ideology and Image-Making in Medieval Art* (New York: Cambridge University Press, 1989).

Campbell, Shiela D., *The Malcove Collection: A Catalogue of the Objects in the Lillian Malcove Collection of the University of Toronto* (Toronto: University of Toronto Press, 1985).

Capps, Edward, "The Style of the Consular Diptychs," *Art Bulletin* 10 (1927): 61–101.

Carriker, Andrew, "The Function and Importance of the Empress' Coinage, A.D. 241- 404," Paper presented at the American Numismatic Society Summer 1993 Seminar, New York.

Chave, Anna C., "New Encounters with *Les Demoiselles d'Avignon*: Gender, Race, and the Origins of Cubism," *Art Bulletin* 76 (1994): 596–611.

Cigaar, K., "Theophano: an empress reconsidered," in *The Empress Theophano: Byzantium and the West at the turn of the first millennium*, ed. Adelbert Davids (New York: Cambridge University Press, 1995), pp. 49–63.

Clark, Elizabeth A., "Ideology, History, and the Construction of 'Woman' in Late Ancient Christianity," *Journal of Early Christian Studies* 2.2 (1994): 155–84.

Clark, Gillian, *Women in Late Antiquity: Pagan and Christian Life-Styles* (Oxford: Clarendon, 1993).

Comstock, Mary, Cornelius C. Vermeule, and Sandra Knudsen, *Romans and Barbarians*, catalog (Boston: Department of Classical Art, Museum of Fine Arts, 1976).

Connor, Carolyn L., *The Color of Ivory* (Princeton: Princeton University Press, 1998).

———, "The Epigram in the Church of Hagios Polyeuktos in Constantinople and its Byzantine Response," *Byzantion* 69 (1999): 479–527.

Coon, Lynda L., *Sacred Fictions: Holy Women and Hagiography in Late Antiquity* (Philadelphia: University of Pennsylvania Press, 1997).

Cooper, Kate, "Contesting the Nativity: Wives, Virgins, and Pulcheria's *imitatio Mariae*," *Scottish Journal of Religious Studies* 19.1 (1998): 31–43.

———, "Insinuations of Womanly Influence: An aspect of the Christianization of the Roman Aristocracy," *Journal of Roman Studies* 82 (1992): 150–64.

Cormack, Robin, "The Emperor at St. Sophia: Viewer and Viewed," in *Byzance et les images*, ed. Guillou and Durand, pp. 223–53.

———, "Women and Icons, and Women in Icons," in *Women, Men, and Eunuchs: Gender in Byzantium*, ed. Liz James, pp. 24–51.

Cutler, Anthony, "The Making of the Justinian Diptychs," *Byzantion* 54 (1984): 75–115.

———, "'Roma' and 'Constantinopolis' in Vienna," in *Byzanz und der Westen, Studien zur Kunst des europäischen Mittelalters*, ed. Herbert Hunger (Vienna: Österreichischen Akademie der Wissenschaften, 1984), pp. 43–64.

———, "Uses of Luxury: On the Functions of Consumption and Symbolic Capital in Byzantine Culture," ed. Guillou and Durrand, in *Byzance et les images*, pp. 289–327.

Dagron, Gilbert, *Empereur et prêtre: étude sur le "césaropapisme" byzantin* (Paris: Gallimard, 1996).

———, "L'image de culte et le portrait," in *Byzance et les images*, ed. Guillou and Durand, pp. 121–50.

Dalton, O. M., *Byzantine Art and Archaeology* (Oxford: Clarendon, 1911).

———, *Catalogue of Early Christian Antiquities and Objects from the Christian East in the Department of British and Mediaeval Antiquities and Ethnography of the British Museum* (London: British Museum, 1901).

D'Ambra, Eve, *Private Lives, Imperial Virtues: The Frieze of the Forum Transitorium in Rome* (Princeton: Princeton University Press, 1993).

Daube, David, "The Marriage of Justinian and Theodora. Legal and Theological Reflections," *Catholic University of America Law Review* 16 (1966): 380–99.

Deichmann, Friedrich Wilhelm, "Giuliano Argentario," *Felix Ravenna* 56 (1951): 5–26.

———, *Ravenna: Hauptstadt des spätantiken Abendlandes* (Wiesbaden: Franz Steiner, 1976).

Delbrueck, Richard, *Die Consulardiptychen und verwandte Denkmäler* (Berlin: Walter de Gruyter, 1929).

———, "Portraets byzantinischer Kaiserinnen," *Mitteilungen des kaiserlich deutschen archäologischen Instituts, Römische Abteilung* 28 (1913): 310–52.

———, *Spätantike Kaiserporträts* (Berlin: Walter de Gruyter, 1933).

Delivorria, Maria, *Recherches sur l'iconographie d'impératrice byzantine* (Ph.D. diss. Sorbonne, Paris, 1966).

Deliyannis, Deborah Mauskopf, "Agnellus of Ravenna and Iconoclasm: Theology and Politics in a Ninth-Century Historical Text," *Speculum* 71 (1996): 559–76.

Diehl, Charles, *Byzantine Empresses*, trans. Harold Bell and Theresa de Kerpely (New York: Knopf, 1963).

———, *Byzantine Portraits*, trans. Harold Bell (New York: Knopf, 1927).

———, *Figures byzantines*, series 1–2 (Paris: Librairie Armand, 1906–08).

———, *Impératrices de Byzance* (Paris: Colin, 1959).

———, *Théodora: Impératrice de Byzance* (Paris: Eugène Rey, 1904).

Dijkstra, Bram, *Idols of Perversity: Fantasies of Feminine Evil in Fin-de-Siècle Culture* (New York: Oxford University Press, 1986).

Dodd, Erica Cruikshank, "The Question of Workshop: Evidence of the Stamps on the Sion Treasure," in *Ecclesiastical Silver Plate in Sixth-Century Byzantium*, ed. Susan A. Boyd and Marlia Mundell Mango (Washington, D.C.: Dumbarton Oaks, 1992), pp. 57–63.

Downey, Glanville, *Ancient Antioch* (Princeton: Princeton University Press, 1963).

———, "Notes on Procopius, De Aedificiis, Book I," in *Studies Presented to David Moore Robinson on His Seventieth Birthday*, ed. George E. Mylonas and Doris Raymond, vol. 2 (Saint Louis, Missouri: Washington University, 1953), pp. 719–25.

———, "Procopius on Antioch: a Study of Method in the 'De Aedificiis'," *Byzantion* 14 (1939): 361–78.

Drijvers, Jan Willem, *Helena Augusta* (Leiden: Brill, 1992).

Dubisch, Jill, *In a Different Place: Pilgrimage, Gender, and Politics at a Greek Island Shrine* (Princeton: Princeton University Press, 1995).

Durliat, Jean, *Les dédicaces d'ouvrage de défense dans l'Afrique byzantine* (Rome: École française de Rome, 1981).

Effenberger, Arne and Hans-Georg Severin, *Das Museum für spätantike und byzantinische Kunst* (Berlin: Staatliche Museen zu Berlin, 1992).

Elbern, Victor H., "Zum Justinuskreuz im Schatz von Sankt Peter zu Rom," *Jahrbuch der Berliner Museen* 6 (1964): 25–38.

Eliot, C. W. J., "A Bronze Counterpoise of Athena," *Hesperia* (1976): 163–70.

Elsner, Jaś, *Art and the Roman Viewer* (New York: Cambridge University Press, 1995).

———, *Imperial Art and Christian Triumph* (Oxford: Oxford University Press, 1998).

Engemann, Josef, "Ein Missorium des Anastasius: Überlegungen zum ikonographischen Programm der 'Anastasius'-Platte aus dem Sutton Hoo Ship-Burial," in *Festschrift für Klaus Wessel zum 70. Geburtstag*, ed. Marcell Restle (Munich: Editio Mars, 1988), pp. 103–15.

Ensslin, Wilhelm, "The Emperor and Imperial Administration," in *Byzantium: An Introduction to East Roman Civilization*, ed. Norman H. Baynes and H. St. L.B. Moss (1948; repr. New York: Oxford University Press, 1961), pp. 268–307.

———, "Pulcheria," *Paulys Real-Encyclopädie der classischen Altertumswissenschaft* 23 (1959): 1954–64.

Entwistle, Christopher J. S., and Michael Cowell, "A Note on a Middle Byzantine Silver Weight," in *ΘΥΜΙΑΜΑ στη μνήμη της Λασκαρίνας Μπούρα*, vol. 1 (Athens: Benaki Museum, 1994), pp. 91–93.

Evans, Helen C., Melanie Holcomb, and Robert Hallman, *The Arts of Byzantium* (New York: Metropolitan Museum of Art, 2001).

Evans, Helen C. and William D. Wixom, ed., *Glory of Byzantium: Art and Culture of the Middle Byzantine Era A.D. 843–1261* (New York: Metropolitan Museum of Art, 1997).

Evans, J.A.S., *The Age of Justinian: The circumstances of imperial power* (New York: Routledge, 1996).

Faider-Feytmans, G., "Antiquités gallo-romaines," in *Les antiquités égyptiennes, grecques, étrusques, romaines et gallo-romaines du Musée de Mariemont* (Brussels: Éditions de la librairie encyclopédique, 1952), pp. 163–81.

Fairweather, Janet, "Fiction in the Biographies of Ancient Writers," *Ancient Society* 5 (1974): 231–75.

Featherstone, Jeffrey, "Ol'ga's Visit to Constantinople," *Harvard Ukrainian Studies* 14 (1990): 293–312.

Fischer-Papp, Lucia, *Evita Peron: Empress Theodora Reincarnated* (Rockford, IL: Northwoods Press, 1983).

Fischler, Susan, "Social Stereotypes and Historical Analysis: The Case of Imperial Women at Rome," in *Women in Ancient Societies: An Illusion of the Night*, ed. Léonie Archer, Susan Fischler, and Maria Wyke (New York: Routledge, 1994), pp. 115–33.

Fish, Stanley, *Is There a Text in this Class?: The Authority of Interpretive Communities* (Cambridge, MA: Harvard University Press, 1980).

Fisher, Elizabeth A., "Theodora and Antonina in the Historia Arcana: History and/or Fiction?," in *Women in the Ancient World: The Arethusa Papers*, ed. John Peradotto and J. P. Sullivan (Albany, NY: State University of New York Press, 1984), pp. 287–313.

Fitton, James, "The Death of Theodora," *Byzantion* (1976): 119.
Fittschen, Klaus, "Courtly Portraits of Women in the Era of the Adoptive Emperors (AD 98–180) and their Reception in Roman Society," ed. Kleiner and Matheson, in *I Claudia: Women in Ancient Rome*, pp. 42–51.
Flaubert, Gustave, *The Dictionary of Received Ideas*, trans. Geoffrey Wall (1913; New York: Penguin, 1994).
Fledelius, Karsten, "Woman's Position and Possibilities in Byzantine Society, with Particular Reference to the Novels of Leo VI," *Jahrbuch der Österreichischen Byzantinistik* 32 (1982): 425–32.
Fleischer, Jens, Øystein Hjort, and Mikael Bøgh Rasmussen, ed., *Byzantium: Late Antique and Byzantine Art in Scandinavian Collections* (Copenhagen: Ny Carlsberg Glyptothek, 1996).
Foucault, Michel, *The History of Sexuality: An Introduction*, vol. 1, trans. Robert Hurley (New York: Random House, 1978).
Franken, Norbert, *Aequipondia: Figürliche Laufgewichte römischer und frühbyzantinscher Schnellwaagen* (Ph.D. diss., Rheinisch-Friedrich-Wilhelms-Universität, Bonn, 1994).
Franses, Henri, *Symbols, Meaning, Belief: Donor Portraits in Byzantine Art*, (Ph.D. diss., Courtauld Institute of Art, London, 1992).
French, Dorothea R., "Maintaining Boundaries: The Status of Actresses in Early Christian Society," *Vigiliae Christianae* 52 (1998): 293–318.
Fuchs, Siegfried, *Kunst der Ostgotenzeit* (Berlin: Walter de Gruyter, 1944).
Galatariotou, Catia S., "Holy Women and Witches: Aspects of Byzantine Conceptions of Gender," *Byzantine and Modern Greek Studies* 9 (1984–85): 55–94.
Galavaris, George P., "The Symbolism of the Imperial Costume as Displayed on Byzantine Coins," *American Numismatic Society Museum Notes* 8 (1958): 99–117.
Garland, Lynda, "'Be Amorous, But Be Chaste . . . ': Sexual morality in Byzantine learned and vernacular romance," *Byzantine and Modern Greek Studies* 14 (1990): 62–120.
———, *Byzantine Empresses: Women and Power in Byzantium A.D. 527–1204* (London: Routledge, 1999).
———, "'The Eye of the Beholder': Byzantine Imperial Women and their Public Image from Zoe Porphyrogenita to Euphrosyne Kamaterissa Doukaina (1028–1203)," *Byzantion* 64 (1994): 19–39.
George, Judith W. *Venantius Fortunatus, A Latin Poet in Merovingian Gaul* (Oxford: Clarendon Press, 1992).
Gibbon, Edward, *The History of the Decline and Fall of the Roman Empire*, ed. J. B. Bury, 7 vols. (London: Methuen, 1909).
Gibson, Margaret, *The Liverpool Ivories: Late Antique and Medieval Ivory and Bone Carving in Liverpool Museum and the Walker Art Gallery* (London: HMSO, 1994).
Gonosova, Anna and Christine Kondoleon, *Art of Late Rome and Byzantium* (Richmond: Virginia Museum of Fine Arts, 1994).
Gordon, Richard, "The Real and the Imaginary: Production and Religion in the Graeco-Roman World," *Art History* 2.1 (1979): 5–34.

———, "The Veil of Power: Emperors, Sacrificers and Benefactors," in *Pagan Priests: Religion and Power in the Ancient World*, ed. Mary Beard and John North (Ithaca, NY: Cornell University Press, 1990), pp. 199–232.

Gounaris, Georgios, "Chroniques des fouilles et découvertes archéologiques en Grèce en 1981," *Bulletin de correspondance hellénique* 106 (1982): 582.

———, "Kupfernes altchristliches 'Stathmion' (Gewicht) aus Philippi," *Makedonika* 20 (1980): 209–17.

Grabar, André, *L'empereur dans l'art byzantin* (1936; repr. of Strasbourg ed. London: Variorum Reprints, 1971).

———, "Une fresque visigothique et l'iconographie du silence," *Cahiers archéologiques* 1 (1945): 124–28.

———, *L'iconoclasme byzantin; dossier archelogique* (Paris: Collège de France, 1957).

———, *Martyrium* (Paris: Collège de France, 1946).

———, "Quel est le sens de l'offrande de Justinien et de Théodora sur les mosaïques de Saint-Vital?," *Felix Ravenna* 81 (1960): 63–77.

———, "Une couronne du début du XIIIe siècle et les coiffures d'apparat féminines," *Cahiers archéologiques* 8 (1956): 265–73.

Graeven, Hans, "Elfenbeinportraits der Königin Amalasuintha," *Jahrbuch der königlich preussischen Kunstsammlungen* 19 (1898): 82–88.

Greatrex, Geoffrey, "Procopius the Outsider?," in *Strangers to Themselves: The Byzantine Outsider* (Burlington, VT: Ashgate, 2000), pp. 215–28.

Grégoire, Henri, *Inscriptions grecques chretienne d'Asie Mineure* (Paris: Ernest Leroux, 1922).

Groebner, Valentin, "Describing the Person, Reading the Signs in Late Medieval and Renaissance Europe: Identity Papers, Vested Figures, and the Limits of Identification," in *Documenting Individual Identity: The Development of State Practices in the Modern World*, ed. Jane Caplan and John Torpey (Princeton: Princeton University Press, 2001), pp. 15–27.

Grierson, Philip, *Byzantine Coins* (London: Methuen, 1982).

Grierson, Philip and Melinda Mays, *Catalogue of Late Roman Coins in the Dumbarton Oaks Collection and in the Whittemore Collection* (Washington, D.C.: Dumbarton Oaks, 1992).

Grosdidier de Matons, José, "La femme dans l'empire byzantin," in *Histoire mondial de la femme*, ed. Pierre Grimal, 4 vols. (Paris: Nouvelle Librairie de France, 1967), 3:11–43.

Guilland, Rodolphe, "Patricienne à ceinture," *Byzantinoslavica* 32 (1971): 269–75.

———, "Les ports de Byzance sur la Propontide," *Byzantion* 23 (1953): 181–238.

Guillou, André and Jannic Durrand, ed., in *Byzance et les images* (Paris: La documentation française, 1994).

Habas, Ephrat, "A Poem by the Empress Eudocia: A Note on the Patriarch," *Israel Exploration Journal* 46 (1996): 108–19.

Hahn, Wolfgang, "Die Münzprägung für Aelia Ariadne," in *ΒΥΖΑΝΤΙΟΣ: Festschrift für Herbert Hunger*, ed. W. Hörander, et al. (Vienna: Ernst Becvar, 1984), pp. 101–06.

Halkin, François, "Deux Impératrices de Byzance," *Analecta Bollandiana* 106 (1998): 5–34.

Harrison, Martin, *A Temple for Byzantium* (Austin, TX: University of Texas Press, 1989).

Harvey, Susan Ashbrook, *Asceticism and Society in Crisis: John of Ephesus and the Lives of the Eastern Saints* (Berkeley: University of California Press, 1990).

Herrin, Judith, "The Byzantine Secrets of Procopius," *History Today* 38 (1988): 36–42.

———, "The Imperial Feminine in Byzantium," *Past and Present* 169 (2000): 3–35.

———, "In Search of Byzantine Women: Three Avenues of Approach," in *Images of Women in Antiquity*, ed. Averil Cameron and Amélie Kuhrt (2nd ed.; London: Routledge, 1993), pp. 167–89.

———, "Public and Private Forms of Religious Commitment among Byzantine Women," in *Women in Ancient Societies: An Illusion of Night*, ed. Léonie J. Archer, Susan Fischler and Maria Wyke (Basingstoke: Macmillan, 1994), pp. 181–203.

———, "Theophano: considerations on the education of a Byzantine princess," in *The Empress Theophano: Byzantium and the West at the Turn of the First Millenium*, ed. Adelbert Davids (New York: Cambridge University Press, 1995), pp. 64–85.

———, "Women and Faith in Icons in Early Christianity," in *Culture, Ideology, and Politics: Essays for Eric Hobsbawn*, ed. Raphael Samuel and Gareth Stedman Jones (London: Routledge & Kegan Paul, 1982), pp. 56–83.

———, *Women in Purple: Rulers of Medieval Byzantium* (London: Weidenfeld & Nicholson, 2001).

———, and Lennart Rydén, moderators, Round table, "The Bride Shows at the Byzantine Court—History or Fiction?," in *Byzantium: Image, Identity, Influence*, XIX International Congress of Byzantine Studies, Major Papers (Copenhagen: Eventus Publishers, 1996), pp. 506–07.

Hill, Barbara, "Imperial Women and the Ideology of Womanhood in the Eleventh and Twelfth Centuries," in *Women, Men, and Eunuchs: Gender in Byzantium*, ed. Liz James, pp. 76–99.

———, *Imperial women in Byzantium, 1025–1204: power, patronage, and ideology* (New York: Longman, 1999).

Hirschfeld, Yizhar, *Judean Desert Monasteries in the Byzantine Period* (New Haven: Yale University Press, 1992).

Holum, Kenneth G., *Theodosian Empresses: Women and Imperial Dominion in Late Antiquity* (Berkeley: University of California Press, 1982).

Holum, Kenneth G. and Gary Vikan, "The Trier Ivory, Adventus Ceremonial, and the Relics of St. Stephen," *Dumbarton Oaks Papers* 33 (1979): 115–33.

Hopkins, Keith, *Conquerors and Slaves* (New York: Cambridge University Press, 1978).

Hunger, Herbert, "Die Schönheitskonkurrenz in 'Belthandros und Chrysantza' und die Brautschau am byzantinischen Kaiserhof," *Byzantion* 35 (1965): 150–58.

Hunt, E. D., *Holy Land Pilgrimage in the Later Roman Empire, A.D. 312–460* (Oxford: Clarendon, 1982).

Hunt, Lynn, "The Many Bodies of Marie Antoinette: Political Pornography and the Problem of the Feminine in the French Revolution," in *Eroticism and the Body Politic*, ed. Lynn Hunt (Baltimore: Johns Hopkins University Press, 1991), pp. 108–30.

Hutter, Irmgard, "Das Bild der Frau in der byzantinschen Kunst,"in *BYZANTIOΣ: Festschrift für Herbert Hunger*, ed.W. Hörander, et al. (Vienna: Ernst Becvar, 1984), pp. 163–70.

Istanbul Archeological Museum, *Istanbul Müzeleri, Asariatika Müzesi Tunc Eserler Reheberi, Musée des Antiquités, Guide illustré des bronzes* (Istanbul: Devlet Basimevi, 1937).

James, Liz, "'As the actress said to the bishop . . .': the portrayal of Byzantine women in English-language fiction,"in *Through the Looking Glass: Byzantium Through British Eyes*, ed. Robin Cormack and Elizabeth Jeffreys (Burlington, VT: Ashgate, 2000), pp. 237–250.

―――, *Empresses and Power in Early Byzantium* (London: Leicester University Press, 2001).

―――, "Goddess, Whore, Wife, or Slave? Will the Real Byzantine Empress Please Stand Up?"in *Queens and Queenship in Medieval Europe*, ed. Anne J. Duggan (Woodbridge, U. K.: Boydell, 1997), pp. 123–40.

―――, ed. *Women, Men and Eunuchs: Gender in Byzantium* (NewYork: Routledge, 1997).

James, Liz and Barbara Hill, "Women and Politics in the Byzantine Empire: Imperial Women," in *Women in Medieval Western European Culture*, ed. Linda E. Mitchell (New York: Garland, 1999), pp.157–78.

James, Liz and Ruth Webb, "'To Understand Ultimate Things and Enter Secret Places': Ekphrasis and Art in Byzantium,"*Art History* 14 (1991): 1–17.

Jay, Martin, "Scopic Regimes of Modernity,"in *Vision and Visuality*, ed. Hal Foster (Seattle: Bay Press, 1988).

Johns, Catherine and Roger Bland, "The Hoxne Late Roman Treasure," *Britannia* 25 (1994): 165–74.

Jones, A. H. M., J. R. Martindale, and J. Morris, *The Prosopography of the Later Roman Empire*, vol. 1 (NewYork: Cambridge University Press, 1971).

Kalavrezou, Ioli, "Eudokia Makrembolitissa and the Romanos Ivory," *Dumbarton Oaks Papers* 31 (1977): 307–25.

―――, "Helping Hands for the Empire: Imperial Ceremonies and the Cult of Relics at the Byzantine Court,"in *Byzantine Court Culture from 829 to 1204*, ed. Henry Maguire (Washington, D.C.: Dumbarton Oaks), pp. 53–79.

―――, "Images of the Mother: When the Virgin Mary Became *Meter Theou*," *Dumbarton Oaks Papers* 44 (1990): 165–72.

Kantorowicz, Ernst H. *The King's Two Bodies: A Study in Mediaeval Political Theology* (Princeton: Princeton University Press, 1957).

Kartsonis, Anna, "Emancipation of the Crucifixion," in *Byzance et les images*, ed. Guillou and Durrand, pp. 153–87.

Kawar, I., "Procopius and Arethas," *Byzantinische Zeitschrift* 50 (1957): 39–67, 362–82.

Kazhdan, Alexander, *A History of Byzantine Literature, 650–850* (Athens: National Hellenic Research Foundation for Byzantine Research, 1999).

―――, "Certain Traits of Imperial Propaganda in the Byzantine Empire from the Eigthth to the Fifteenth Centuries," in *Prédication et propagande au Moyen Age: Islam, Byzance, Occident* (Paris: Presses Universitaires de France, 1983), pp. 13–27.

———, ed., *Oxford Dictionary of Byzantium* (New York: Oxford University Press, 1991).

———, "Women at Home," *Dumbarton Oaks Papers* 52 (1998): 1–17.

———, and Michael McCormick, "The Social World of the Byzantine Court," in *Byzantine Court Culture from 829 to 1204* (Washington, D.C.: Dumbarton Oaks, 1997), pp.167–97.

Kennedy, George A., *Classical Rhetoric and Its Christian and Secular Tradition from Ancient to Modern Times* (2nd ed.; Chapel Hill: University of North Carolina Press, 1999).

Kiilerich, Bente, *Late fourth century classicism in the plastic arts: Studies in the so-called Theodosian renaissance* (Odense: Odense University Press, 1993).

Kipnis, Laura, *Bound and Gagged: Pornography and the Politics of Fantasy in America* (New York: Grove, 1996).

———, "(Male) Desire and (Female) Disgust: Reading Hustler," in *Cultural Studies,* ed. Lawrence Grossberg, Cary Nelson, Paula A. Treichler, with Linda Baughman and assistance from John Macgregor Wise (New York: Routledge, 1992), pp. 373–91.

Kislinger, Ewald, "Der Kranke Justin II. und die ärztliche Haftung bei Operationen in Byzanz,"*Jahrbuch der Österreichischen Byzantinistik* 36 (1986): 39–44.

Kitzinger, Ernst, "Artistic Patronage in Early Byzantium," in *Committenti e produzione artistico-letteraria nell'alto medioevo occidentale* (Spoleto: Presso la sede del centro, 1992), pp. 33–55.

Kleiner, Diana E. E., "Imperial Women as Patrons of the Arts in the Early Empire," in *I Claudia: Women in Ancient Rome,* ed. Kleiner and Matheson, pp. 28–41.

Kleiner, Diana E. E. and Susan B. Matheson, ed. *I Claudia: Women in Ancient Rome* (New Haven: Yale University Art Gallery, 1996).

Körbler, Juraj, "Die Krebskrankung der byzantinischen Kaiserin Theodora (Ein Beitrag zur Geschichte der Syphilis)," *Janus* 61 (1974): 15–21.

Krautheimer, Richard, "Again Saints Sergius and Bacchus at Constantinople," *Jahrbuch der Österreichischen Byzantinistik* 23 (1974): 251–53.

Kyriakis, Michael J., "The University: Origin and Early Phases in Constantinople," *Byzantion* 41 (1971): 161–82.

Laiou, Angeliki, "Addendum to the Report on the Role of Women in Byzantine Society," *Jahrbuch der Österreichischen Byzantinistik* 32.1 (1982): 198–204.

———, "Observations on the Life and Ideology of Byzantine Women," *Byzantinische Forschungen* 9 (1985): 59–102.

———, "The Role of Women in Byzantine Society," *Jahrbuch der Österreichischen Byzantinistik* 31.1 (1981): 233–60.

———, "Sex, Consent, and Coercion in Byzantium," in *Consent and Coercion to Sex and Marriage in Ancient and Medieval Societies,* ed. Angeliki E. Laiou (Washington, D.C.: Dumbarton Oaks, 1993), pp. 105–221.

Le Ba, Philippe and W. H. Waddington, *Voyage archéologique en Grèce et en Asie Mineur* (Paris: Didot Frères, 1874).

Lemerle, Paul, *Byzantine Humanism: The First Phase,* trans. Helen Lindsay and Ann Moffat (Canberra, Australia: Australian Association of Byzantine Studies, 1986).

BIBLIOGRAPHY

Lieu, Samuel N.C. and Dominic Montserrat, ed., *From Constantine to Julian: Pagan and Byzantine Views* (New York: Routledge, 1996).

Lim, Richard, "People as Power: Games, Munificence, and Contested Topography," in *The Transformation of the Vrbs Roma in Late Antiquity,* ed. W.V. Harris, *Journal of Roman Archaeology, Supplemental Series No. 33* (Portsmouth, RI: Journal of Roman Archaeology, 1999), pp. 265–81.

Limberis, Vasiliki, *Divine Heiress: The Virgin Mary and the creation of Christian Constantinople* (New York: Routledge, 1994).

de Linas, Charles, *Les origines de l'orfévrerie,* vol. 1 (Paris: E. Didron, 1877).

Maas, Michael, *John Lydus and the Roman Past: Antiquarianism and Politics in the Age of Justinian* (London: Routledge, 1992).

MacCormack, Sabine G., *Art and Ceremony in Late Antiquity* (Berkeley: University of California Press, 1981).

MacMullen, Ramsey, "Some Pictures in Ammianus Marcellinus," *Art Bulletin* 46 (1964): 435–55.

———, "Women in Public in the Roman Empire," *Historia* 29 (1980): 208–18.

Macrides, Ruth, "Dynastic Marriages and Political Kinship," in *Byzantine Diplomacy,* ed. Jonathan Shepard and Simon Franklin (London: Variorum, 1992), pp. 263–80.

Maguire, Henry, *Art and Eloquence in Byzantium* (Princeton: Princeton University Press, 1981).

———, ed., *Byzantine Magic* (Washington, D.C.: Dumbarton Oaks, 1995).

———, *Earth and Ocean: The Terrestrial World in Early Byzantine Art* (University Park, PA: Penn State University Press, 1987).

———, "Images of the Court," in *Glory of Byzantium: Art and Culture of the Middle Byzantine Era A.D. 843–1261,* ed. Helen C. Evans and William D. Wixom (New York: Metropolitan Museum of Art, 1997), pp. 183–91.

———, "Magic and the Christian Image," in *Byzantine Magic,* ed. Henry Maguire (Washington, D.C.: Dumbarton Oaks, 1995), pp. 51–71.

———, "Originality in Byzantine Art Criticism," in *Originality in Byzantine Literature, Art and Music,* ed. A. R. Littlewood (Oxford: Oxbow, 1995), pp. 101–14.

———, "Style and Ideology in Byzantine Imperial Art," *Gesta* 28.2 (1989): 217–31.

Mango, Cyril, *The Art of the Byzantine Empire 312–1453: Sources and Documents* (1972; repr. Toronto: University of Toronto Press, 1986).

———, *The Brazen House. A Study of the Vestibule of the Imperial Palace of Constantinople* (Copenhagen: Arkaeologisk-kunsthistoriscke Meddelelser, 1959).

———, *Byzantine Literature as a Distorting Mirror, An Inaugural Lecture* (Oxford: Clarendon Press, 1975).

———, "The Church of Saints Sergius and Bacchus at Constantinople and the Alleged Tradition of Octagonal Palatine Churches," *Jahrbuch der Österreichischen Byzantinistik* 21 (1972): 189–93.

———, "The Church of Sts. Sergius and Bacchus Once Again," *Byzantinische Zeitschrift* 68 (1975): 385–92.

Mango, Cyril and Ihor Ševčenko, "Remains of the Church of Saint Polyeuktos at Constantinople," *Dumbarton Oaks Papers* 15 (1961): 243–47.

Marlowe, Elizabeth Mae, "Repositioning the Grand Camée de France," *Archaeological Institute of American 2002 Annual Meeting*, Philadelphia.

Maslev, St., "Die staatsrechtliche Stellung der byzantinischen Kaiserinnen," *Byzantinoslavica* 27 (1966): 308–43.

Matheson, Susan B., "The Divine Claudia: Women as Goddesses in Roman Art," in *I Claudia: Women in Ancient Rome*, ed. Kleiner and Matheson, pp. 182–93.

Mathews, Thomas F., "Architecture et liturgie dans les premières palatiales de Constantinople," *Revue de l'Art* 24 (1974): 22–29.

———, *The Clash of the Gods*, rev. ed. (Princeton: Princeton University Press, 1999).

———, *The Early Churches of Constantinople: Architecture and Liturgy* (University Park, PA: Penn State University Press, 1971).

Mauss, Marcel, *The Gift: Forms and Functions of Exchange in Archaic Societies*, trans. Ian Cunnison (New York: Norton, 1967).

McClanan, Anne, "'Weapons to Probe the Womb': The Material Culture of Abortion and Contraception in the Early Byzantine Period," in *The Material Culture of Sex, Procreation, and Marriage in Premodern Europe*, ed. Anne McClanan and Karen Encarnación (New York: St. Martin's Press/Palgrave, 2002), pp. 33–57.

———, Review of Lynda Garland, *Byzantine Empresses*, on-line, *The Medieval Review*, 5 July 2000.

McCormick, Michael, "Analyzing Imperial Ceremonies," *Jahrbuch der Österreichischen Byzantinistik* 35 (1985): 1–20.

———, "Emperors," in *The Byzantines*, ed. Guglielmo Cavallo (Chicago: University of Chicago Press, 1997), pp. 230–54.

———, *Eternal Victory: Triumphal Rulership in Late Antiquity, Byzantium, and the Early Medieval West* (New York: Cambridge University Press, 1986).

McCracken, Peggy, *The Romance of Adultery: Queenship and Sexual Transgression in Old French Literature* (Philadelphia: University of Pennsylvania Press, 1998).

McKitterick, Rosamond and Roland Quinault, ed. *Edward Gibbon and Empire* (New York: Cambridge University Press, 1997).

Meischner, Jutta, "Das Porträt der Galla Placidia im Museo dell'Alto Medioevo, Rom," *Latomus* 50 (1991): 861–64.

———, "Der Hochzeitskameo des Honorius," *Archäologischer Anzeiger* 4 (1993): 613–19.

Mellor, Ronald, "The Goddess Roma," ed. Hildegard Temporini and Wolfgang Haase, *Aufstieg und Niedergang der römischen Welt* 17.2 (1981): 952–1030.

Meriçboyu, Yildiz and Sümer Atasoy, *Büst Seklinde Kantar Agirliklari: Steelyard Weights in the Form of a Bust* (Istanbul: Arkoloji Sanat Yayinlari, 1983).

Miller, Dean A., "Byzantine Sovereignty and Feminine Potencies," in *Women and Sovereignty*, ed. Louise Olga Fradenburg (Edinburgh: Edinburgh University Press, 1992), pp. 250–63.

van Millingen, Alexander, *Byzantine Constantinople, The Walls of the City and Adjoining Historical Sites* (London: John Murray, 1899).

Milner, Christine,"The image of the rightful ruler: Anicia Juliana's Constantine mosaic in the church of Hagios Polyeuktos," in *New Constantines: The Rhythm of Imperial Renewal in Byzantium, 4th–13th Centuries,* ed. Paul Magdalino (Hampshire, U. K.: Variorum, 1994), pp. 73–82.

Molinier, Émile, "La coiffure des femmes dans quelques monuments byzantins," in *Études d'histoire du Moyen Age dédiées à Gabriel Monod* (Paris: Léopold Cerf & Félix Alcan, 1896), pp. 61–76.

Morrisson, Cécile, *Catalogue des monnaies byzantines de la Bibliothèque Nationale* (Paris: Bibliothèque Nationale, 1970).

Müller-Wiener, Wolfgang, "Küçük Aya Sofya Camii," in *Bildlexikon zur Topographie Istanbuls* (Tübingen: Ernst Wasmuth, 1977), pp. 177–83.

Murray, Sister Charles, *Rebirth and Afterlife: A study of the transmutation of some pagan imagery in early Christian funerary art* (Oxford: B. A. R., 1981).

Necipoglu, Nevra, "Byzantine Women," in *Woman in Anatolia: 9000 Years of the Anatolian Woman,* ed. Günsel Renda (Istanbul: Turkish Republic Ministry of Culture, 1993), pp. 125–31.

Nelson, Janet, "Symbols in Context: Rulers' Inauguration Rituals in Byzantium and the West in the Early Middle Ages," in *Orthodox Churches and the West,* ed. Derek Baker (Oxford: Blackwell, 1976), pp. 97–119.

Netzer, Nancy, "Redating the Consular Ivory of Orestes," *Burlington Magazine* 125 (May 1983): 265–71.

Nicol, Donald M., *The Byzantine Lady: Ten Portraits, 1250–1500* (New York: Cambridge University Press, 1994).

Nikolaou, Katerina, *Η θέση της γυναικας στη βυζαντινη χοινωνία,* He these tes gynaikas ste Vyzantine koinonia (Athens: Hidryma Goulandre-Chorn, 1993).

Noll, Rudolf, *Von Altertum zum Mittelalter* (Vienna: Kunsthistorisches Museum, 1958).

Oikonomides, Nicolas, "Le serment de l'impératrice Eudocie (1067)," *Revue des études byzantines* 21 (1963): 101–28.

———, "The Mosaic Panel of Constantine IX and Zoe in Saint Sophia," *Revue des études byzantines* 36 (1978): 219–36.

Oliver, James H., "Julia Domna as Athena Polias," in *Athenian Studies Presented to William Scott Ferguson* (Cambridge, MA: Harvard University Press, 1940), pp. 521–30.

Olster, David, "The Dynastic Iconography of Heraclius' Early Coinage," in *XVI. Internationaler Byzantinistenkongress,* Akten 2.2 (Vienna: Der Österreichischen Akademie der Wissenschaften, 1982), pp. 399–408.

Ortner, Sherry, "The Virgin and the State," *Feminist Studies* 4 (3 1978): 19–36.

Ostoia, Vera K., ed., *The Middle Ages: Treasures from the Cloisters and the Metropolitan Museum of Art* (Los Angeles: Los Angeles County Museum of Art, 1970).

Painter, Kenneth S., "Roman Silver Hoards: Ownership and Status," in *Argenterie romaine et byzantine,* ed. François Baratte (Paris: De Boccard, 1988), pp. 97–105.

Parker, Holt, "Love's Body Anatomized: The Ancient Erotic Handbooks and the Rhetoric of Sexuality," in *Pornography and Representation in Greece and Rome,* ed. Amy Richlin (New York: Oxford University Press, 1992), pp. 90–111.

Patlagean, Evelyne,"Birth Control in the Early Byzantine Empire," in *Biology of Man in History,* ed. Robert Forster and Orest Ranum (Baltimore: Johns Hopkins University Press, 1975), pp. 1–22.

Paton, James Morton, ed., *The Erectheum* (Cambridge, MA: Harvard University Press, 1927).

Pazdernik, Charles, "'Our Most Pious Consort Given Us by God': Dissident Reactions to the Partnership of Justinian and Theodora, A.D. 525–548," *Classical Antiquity* 13.2 (1994): 256–81.

Peers, Glenn, *Subtle Bodies: Representing Angels in Byzantium* (Berkeley: University of California Press, 2001).

Peirce, Leslie P., *The Imperial Harem: Women and Sovereignity in the Ottoman Empire* (New York: Oxford University Press, 1993).

Price, Simon, *Rituals and Power: The Roman Imperial Cult in Asia Minor* (New York: Cambridge University Press, 1984).

Puff, Helmut, "The Sodomite's Clothes: Gift-Giving and Sexual Excess in Early Modern Germany and Switzerland," in *The Material Culture of Sex, Procreation, and Marriage in Premodern Europe,* ed. Anne McClanan and Karen Encarnación (New York: Palgrave, 2002), pp. 251–72.

Rambaud, Alfred, "L'impératrice byzantine," *Revue des deux mondes* 130 (1891): 814–38.

Rice, David Talbot, *Art of the Byzantine Era* (1963; repr. London: Thames and Hudson, 1986).

Richter, G. M. A., *Catalogue of Greek and Roman Antiquities in the Dumbarton Oaks Collection* (Cambridge, MA: Harvard University Press, 1956).

Ringrose, Kathryn M. "Eunuchs as Cultural Mediators," *Byzantinische Forschungen* 23 (1996): 75–93.

———, "Living in the Shadows: Eunuchs and Gender in Byzantium," in *Third Sex, Third Gender: Beyond Sexual Dimorphism in Culture and History,* ed. Gilbert Herdt (New York: Zone, 1994), pp. 85–109.

Ross, Marvin C., "Bronze Statuettes of Constantine the Great," *Dumbarton Oaks Papers* 13 (1959): 179–83.

———, "A Byzantine Bronze Weight," *American Journal of Archaeology* 50 (1946): 368–69.

———, *Catalogue of the Byzantine and Early Mediaeval Antiquities in the Dumbarton Oaks Collections,* 3 vols. (Washington, D. C.: Dumbarton Oaks, 1962).

Rousseau, Phillip, "Procopius's *Buildings* and Justinian's Pride," *Byzantion* 68 (1998): 121–30.

Runcimann, Steven, "The Empress Irene the Athenian," in *Medieval Women,* ed. Derek Baker (Oxford: Blackwell, 1978), pp. 101–18.

———, "Some Notes on the Role of the Empress," *Eastern Churches Review* 4 (1972): 119–24.

———, *A Traveller's Alphabet* (New York: Thames and Hudson, 1991).

———, "Women in Byzantine Aristocratic Society," in *The Byzantine Aristocracy IX to XIII Centuries,* ed. Michael Angold (Oxford: B. A. R. International Series, 1984), pp. 10–22.

Russell, James, "The Archeological Context of Magic in the Early Byzantine Period," in *Byzantine Magic*, ed. Henry Maguire (Washington, D. C.: Dumbarton Oaks, 1995), pp. 35–50.

Rydén, Lennart, "The Bride-shows at the Byzantine Court—History or Fiction?," *Eranos* 83 (1985): 175–91.

de Salis, J. F. W., "The Coins of the Two Eudoxias, Eudocia, Placidia, and Honoria, and of Theodosius II, Marcian, and Leo I Struck in Italy," *Numismatic Chronicle* 7 (1867): 203–15.

Sams, G. Kenneth, "The Weighing Implements," in *Yassi Ada: A Seventh-Century Byzantine Shipwreck.*, ed. George F. Bass and Frederick H. Van Doorninck, Jr. (College Station, TX: Texas A & M Press, 1982), pp. 202–30.

Sande, Siri, "Zur Porträtplastik des sechsten nachchristlichen Jahrhunderts," *Acta ad archaeologiam et artium historiam pertinentia* 6 (1975): 65–106.

Sansterre, Jean-Marie, "Où le diptyque consulaire de Clemintinus fut-il remployé à une fin liturgique?," *Byzantion* 54 (1984): 641–47.

Sardou, Victorien, *Theodora, drame en cinq actes et sept tableaux* (Paris, L'Illustration, 1907).

Scarpellini, Donatella, *Stele romane con imagines clipeatae in Italia* (Rome: Bretschneider, 1987).

Schaffran, E., "Eine Voelkerwanderungszeitliche Bronzstatuette eines christlichen Herrschers," *Rivista di Archeologica Cristiana* 32 (1956): 243–49.

Scott, Joan Wallach, "Gender: A Useful Category of Historical Analysis," in *Feminism and History*, ed. Joan Wallach Scott (New York: Oxford University Press, 1996).

Scott, Roger D., "Malalas, *the Secret History*, and Justinian's Propaganda," *Dumbarton Oaks Papers* 39 (1985): 99–109.

Setton, Kenneth M., *Christian Attitude Towards the Emperor in the Fourth Century* (New York: Columbia University Press, 1941).

Ševčenko, Ihor, "The Inscription of Justin II's Time on the Mevlevihane (Rhesion) Gate at Istanbul," *Beograd* 12 (1970): 1–8.

Shelton, Kathleen J., "Imperial Tyches," *Gesta* 18 (1979): 27–38.

von Simson, Otto G., *Sacred Fortress* (1948; repr. Princeton: Princeton University Press, 1987).

Smith, R. R. R., "Late Antique Portraits in a Public Context: Honorific Statuary at Aphrodisias in Caria, A.D. 300–600," *Journal of Roman Studies* 89 (1999): 153–89.

Smythe, Dion C., "Women as Outsiders," in *Women, Men, and Eunuchs: Gender in Byzantium*, ed. Liz James, pp. 149–67.

Sodini, Jean-Pierre, "Images sculptées et propagande impériale du IVe au VIe siècle: recherches récentes sur les colonnes honorifiques et les reliefs politiques à Byzance," in *Byzance et les images*, ed. Guillou and Durand, pp. 43–94.

Spain, Suzanne, "The Translation of Relics Ivory, Trier," *Dumbarton Oaks Papers* 31 (1977): 279–304.

Spatharakis, Iohannis, *The Portrait in Byzantine Illuminated Manuscripts* (Leiden: Brill, 1976).

Sperber, Dan, *Rethinking Symbolism,* trans. Alice L. Morton (New York: Cambridge University Press, 1975).

Steigerwald, Gerhard, "Ein Bild der Mutter des Kaisers Justinianin San Vitale zu Ravenna?" in *Vom Orient bis an den Rhein: Begegnungen mit der Christlichen Archäologie; Peter Poscharsky zum 65. Geburtstag,* ed. Ulrike Lange and Reiner Sörries (Dettelbach: Röll, 1997), pp. 123–46.

Stewart, Peter, "The Destruction of Statues in Late Antiquity," in *Constructing Identities in Late Antiquity,* ed. Richard Miles (London: Routledge, 1999): 159–89.

Stichel, Rudolf, *Die römische Kaiserstatue am Ausgang der Antike* (Rome: Bretschneider, 1982).

Stout, Ann M., "Jewelry as a Symbol of Status in the Roman Empire," in *The World of Roman Costume,* ed. Judith Lynn Sebesta and Larissa Bonfante (Madison: University of Wisconsin Press, 1994), pp. 77–100.

Stričević, Djordje, "The Iconography of the Compositions Containing Imperial Portraits in San Vitale," *Starinar* 9–10 (1958–9): 67–76.

———, "Sur le problème de l'iconographie des mosaïques imperiales de Saint-Vital," *Felix Ravenna* 34 (1962): 80–100.

Strzygowski, Josef, *Orient oder Rom. Beiträge zur Geschichte der Spätantike und frühchristlichen Kunst* (Leipzig: J.C. Hinrichs'sche Buchhandlung, 1901).

Stutzinger, Dagmar, "Das Bronzebildnis einer spätantiken Kaiserin aus Balajnac im Museum von Niš," *Jahrbuch für Antike und Christentum* 29 (1986): 146–65.

Swainson, H., "Monograms on the Capitals of S. Sergius at Constantinople," *Byzantinische Zeitschrift* 4 (1895): 106–08.

Taft, S. J., Robert F., "Women at Church in Byzantium: Where, When—and Why?," *Dumbarton Oaks Papers* 52 (1998): 27–87.

Tatic-Djuric, M., "L'archéologie byzantine au XIIe Congrès internationale des études byzantines d'Ochrid," *Byzantion* 31.2 (1961): 548.

Thomas, Edit B., "Eine frühbyzantische Laufgewichtsbüste im Germanischen Nationalmuseum," *Anzeiger des Germanischen Nationalmuseums* (1987): 151–59.

Thümmel, H.G., "Kaiserbild und Christusikone: Zur Bestimmung der fünfteiligen Elfenbeindiptychen," *Byzantinoslavica* 39 (1978): 196–206.

Tinnefeld, Franz Hermann, *Kategorien der Kaiserkritik in der byzantinischen Historiographie von Prokop bis Niketas Choniates* (Munich: Wilhelm Fink, 1971).

Tougher, Shaun F., "Byzantine Eunuchs: An Overview, with a Special Reference to Their Creation and Origin," in *Women, Men, and Eunuchs: Gender in Byzantium,* ed. Liz James, pp. 168–84.

———, "Images of Effeminate Men: the Case of Byzantine Eunuchs," in *Masculinity in Medieval Europe,* ed. D. M. Hadley (London: Longman, 1999), pp. 89–100.

Treadgold, Warren T., "The Problem of the Marriage of the Emperor Theophilus," *Greek, Roman, and Byzantine Studies* 16 (1975): 325–41.

———, "The Bride-Shows of the Byzantine Emperors," *Byzantion* 49 (1979): 395–413.

Trilling, James, "The Image Not Made by Hands and the Byzantine Way of Seeing," in *The Holy Face and the Paradox of Representation,* ed. Herbert L. Kessler and Gerhard Wolf (Bologna: Nuova Alfa Editoriale, 1998), pp.109–27.

Tsirpanlis, Constantine, "Marriage, Family Values and 'Ecumenical Vision' in the Legislation of Justinian the Great (527–565)," *The Patristic and Byzantine Review* 15 (1996–97): 59–69.

Usher, Mark D. *Homeric Stitchings: The Homeric Centos of Empress Eudocia* (Lanham, MD: Rowman and Littlefield, 1998).

Vandercook, John W., *Empress of the Dusk: a life of Theodora of Byzantium* (New York: Reynal and Hitchcock, c.1940).

Varner, Eric, "Domitia Longina and the Politics of Portraiture," *American Journal of Archaeology* 99 (1995): 187–206.

Vermeule, Cornelius C., *The Goddess Roma in the Art of the Roman Empire* (London: Spink, 1959).

———, *Greek and Roman Sculpture in America: Masterpieces in Public Collections in the United States and Canada* (Berkeley: University of California Press, 1981).

———, "New Near Eastern, Greek and Roman Sculpture," *The Classical Journal* 56 (1960): 1–16.

———, *Roman Art: Early Republic to Late Empire* (Boston, Department of Classical Art, Museum of Fine Arts, 1978).

Vermeule, Cornelius (Catalogue) and Mary Comstock, *Sculpture in Stone and Bronze, Additions to the Collections of Greek, Etruscan, and Roman Art, 1971–1988* (Boston: Museum of Fine Arts, 1988).

Vinson, Martha, "Domitia Longina, Julia Titi, and the Literary Tradition," *Historia* 38 (1989): 431–50.

———, "The Life of Theodora and the Rhetoric of the Byzantine Brideshow," *Jahrbuch der Österreichischen Byzantinistik* 49 (1999): 31–60.

———, trans. *Vita Theodora*, in *Byzantine Defenders of Images*, ed. Alice-Mary Talbot (Washington, D. C.: Dumbarton Oaks, 1998), pp. 353–82.

Vogt, Josef, "Helena Augusta, The Cross and the Jews: Some Enquiries about the Mother of Constantine the Great," *Classical Folia* 31 (1977): 135–51.

Volbach, Wolfgang Fritz, *Geschichte des Kunstgewerbes*, ed. H. Th. Bossert, 6 vols. (Berlin: Wasmuth, 1932), vol. 5.

———, *Elfenbeinarbeiten der spätantike und des frühen Mittelalters*, 3rd ed. (Mainz: Philipp von Zabern, 1976).

Waagé, Frederick O., "Bronze Objects from Old Corinth, Greece," *American Journal of Archaeology* 39 (1935): 79–86.

Ward, Sister Benedicta, *Harlots of the Desert: A Study of Repentance in Early Byzantine Monastic Sources* (Kalamazoo, MI: Cistercian Publications, 1987).

Waugh, Evelyn, *Helena* (London: Chapman & Hall, 1950).

Webb, Ruth, "Salome's Sisters: The Rhetoric and Realities of Dance in Late Antiquity and Byzantium," in *Women, Men, and Eunuchs: Gender in Byzantium*, ed. Liz James, pp. 119–48.

Weber, Max, *Economy and Society: An Outline of Interpretive Sociology*, ed. Guenther Roth and Claus Wittich, multiple trans. (Berkeley: University of California Press, 1978).

Webster, Leslie and Michelle Brown, ed., *The Transformation of the Roman World A.D. 400–900* (Berkeley: University of California Press, 1997).

Weitzmann, Kurt, ed., *Age of Spirituality: Late Antique and Early Christian Art, Third to Seventh Century* (New York: Metropolitan Museum of Art, 1977).

——, *Late Antique and Early Christian Book Illumination* (New York: George Braziller, 1977).

Wellman, Paul I., *The Female: A Novel of Another Time* (New York: Doubleday, 1953).

Wessel, Klaus, "Das kaiserinnenporträt im Castello Sforzesco zu Mailand," *Jahrbuch des deutschen archäologischen Instituts und Archäologischer Anzeiger* 77 (1962): 240–55.

——, "Wer ist der Consul auf der Florentiner Kaiserinnen-Tafel?," *Byzantinische Zeitschrift* 57 (1964): 374–79.

White, Despina, "Property Rights of Women: The Changes in the Justinian Legislation Regarding the Dowry and the Parapherna," *Jahrbuch der Österreichischen Byzantinistik* 32.2 (1982): 539–548.

Wiegand, Edmund, "Zum Denkmälerkreis des Christogrammnimbus," *Byzantinische Zeitschrift* 31 (1932): 63–81.

Wiegand, Theodor, review of Delbrueck and Weitzmann, "Studien zur spätantiken Kunstgeschichte," *Kritische Berichte*, Leipzig (1930/31): 33–57.

Williams, Gordon, "Representations of Roman Women in Literature," in *I Claudia: Women in Ancient Rome*, ed. Kleiner and Matheson, pp. 126–38.

Wilson, Laurie, "The Trier Procession Ivory: A New Interpretation," *Byzantion* 54 (1984): 602–14.

Wood, Susan E., *Imperial Women, A Study in Public Images, 40 B.C.-A.D. 68* (Leiden: Brill, 1999).

Worp, K. A., "Byzantine Imperial Titulature in the Greek Documentary Papyri: The Oath Formulas," *Zeitschrift für Papyrologie und Epigraphik* 45 (1982): 199–226.

Wortley, John, "The Trier Ivory Reconsidered," *Greek, Roman, and Byzantine Studies* 21 (1980): 381–94.

Wrede, Henning, *Consecratio in formam deorum: Vergöttlichte Privatpersonen in der römischen Kaiserzeit* (Mainz am Rhein: Philipp von Zabern, 1981).

Wright, David H., "Ivories for the Emperor," *Third Annual Byzantine Studies Conference Abstracts of Papers* (1977): 6–9.

——, "The Shape of the Seventh Century in Byzantine Art," *First Annual Byzantine Studies Conference Abstracts of Papers* (1975): 9–28.

Wroth, W., *Catalogue of the Imperial Byzantine Coins in The British Museum*, 2 vols. (London: Longmans, 1908).

Zacos, G. and A. Veglery, *Byzantine Lead Seals*, 2 vols. in 6 parts (Basel: Augustin, 1972–85).

——, "Marriage Solidi of the Fifth Century," *The Numismatic Circular* 68.4 (1960): 73–74.

——, "An Unknown Solidus of Anastasios I," *The Numismatic Circular* 67.9 (1959): 154–55.

Zomer, Hiltje F. H., "The So-called Women's Gallery in the Medieval Church: An Import from Byzantium," in *The Empress Theophano: Byzantium and the West at the turn of the first millenium*, ed. Adelbert Davids (New York: Cambridge University Press, 1995), pp. 290–306.

Zwirn, Stephen, "The Vienna Ivories: The Consular Status of the Roma and the Constantinopolis Diptych," *Byzantine Studies Conference Abstracts* 26 (2000): 36–37.

INDEX

Note on the index: buildings are listed under the city of their location.

abortion 111
acclamations 69, 70n30, 94, 140, 151, 157, 185
actresses and actors 14, 113n40–42, see also Constantinople (hippodrome), Theodora
Agathias 152
Agnellus 123, 125, 133–34, 135
Akathistos hymn 22
Amalasuntha 80, 102, 175
Ambrose 15
Ammianus Marcellinus 118
Anastasia (Ino), empress, 155–57, 162, see also renaming, Tiberios, Sophia
Anastasios, emperor, 68, 78, 82, 90–92, 139, 153, 172
Anekdota (Prokopios) 5, 93, 100n34, 103, 104, 107–08, 108n4, 109, 111–14, 115n15, 116, 118, 120, 154
  dating 108–09
  manuscript survival 109, 117, 120
  see also Buildings, invective, political pornography, *Wars*
Anemourion 47
Angel 130, 152
Anicia Juliana 20, 94–98
  see also inscription, Constantinople (Church of Saint Polyeuktos), manuscript, Vienna Diskorides
animal, see cattle, dog, eagle, horse, pig
Antioch 20, 76, 105, 143

Antoinette, Marie 114, see also political pornography
Antopodosis, see Liutprand of Cremona
apotheosis 14
apotropaic elements 58, 58n70
apple 21
Areobindus 70, 96
Argentarius, see Julianus Argentarius
Ariadne, empress, 65–92, 153, 168, 175, 178
  coinage 5, 90–92
  consular diptychs 69–82, 140, 147, 166, 184
  death 81–82
  imperial succession 65, 82, 157, 179
  sculpture 30, 82–90
aristocracy, Byzantine, 179–80, 186, see also class
Arkadios, emperor, 19, 52, see also Eudoxia
Asterios of Amaseia 116
Atalarich 80
Athena
  iconography 57–58, 183
  worship of 55–58
Athenaïs, see Eudokia
Athens 20, Erectheum 60, 183
Augusta, use of title 10, 10n43, 15, 27, 120, 131, 155, 156, 179, 185
Augustus 50, 125, 132, see also Julia, Livia

Bakhtin, Mikhail 113, 114
Bar Hebraeus, *see* Gregory Abu'l-Faraj
Barberini Diptych (fig. 7.8) 173–74
basileía 18, 20, 21, 103, 106, 156
Basiliskos 67
basilissa 10, 179
bathing 112, 112n33, 156, *see also* Constantinople (Baths)
beauty, convention in description of empresses 3–4, 111, 115, 119, *see also* symmetry
Belisarios 110, 112, 128, 135
Bethlehem 15
biography, conventions in 116
Blues, *see* circus factions
Book of Ceremonies, *see* Constantine Porphyrogennetos
Bosporos 150, 152
brass 152n25
bride show 3, 21, 83, 120n82
bronze sculpture, imperial statuary 16, 19, 71, 87, *see also* steelyard weights
Buildings (Prokopios) 93, 98, 99, 103, 104, 105, 108, 109, 111, 118, 120, 139, 168
burial 24, 25, 134, 143n109, 150n8, 155n54, 171

cake molds 63–64
Caligula, emperor, 27, 57, 109
cattle 19
celibacy, *see* chastity
ceremony, court, *see* Book of Ceremonies, circus factions, Peter the Patrician, Trier ivory, Ravenna (Church of San Vitale), *sekreton ton gynaikon*
charioteers 14, *see also* Constantinople (Hippodrome)
chastity 21, 115n50, 181
Chi-Rho 27
chiton, *see* clothing
chlamys, *see* clothing
Chorikios 130

Christ, representations of 16, 24, 71, 71n42, 123, 129, 134, 144, 148, 163, 167, 173, 175
Christianity, conversion to 15
Christianization of pagan culture 7, 14, 58, 168, 169–71, 172, *see also* Athena, personifications
Chronicon Paschale 66, 67, 68, 93
ciborium 171–72, 173
circus factions 20, 103, 140, 157, 185, *see also* acclamations, Constantinople (hippodrome), Nika Riot
class divisions 2, 14, 74, 113, 113n42, 114, 116, 133, 134, 146, 154, 158, 182, 183
Clementinus diptych (fig. 3.1) 70–71, 80
Cleopatra 3
Clinton, Hillary Rodham (fig. 5.1) 113, *see also* political pornography
clothing 2, 133
   boot 133
   chiton 40
   chlamys 25, 133, 135, 144, 162, 171, 172, 176
   dalmatic 167, 172
   loros 74, 145
   palla 42
   tunic 76, 133, 158, 172
   see belt, imperial insignia, nakedness, snood
coinage 104n75, 133, 158–62, 167
   as adornment 17, 176–78
   circumstances of empress issues 26–27, 131, 144, 162–63, 175, 178, 184
   consular imagery 72, 133, 162, 176
   hoards 92, 180
   and imperial sculpture 26, 30n3
   numismatic reform 5
   overstriking 145
   as propaganda 26, 57, 133
   regional mints 144–46, 160

INDEX

see also Ariadne, Eudokia, Eudoxia, follis, Honoria, Licinia Eudoxia, Martina, medallions, minimus, Pulcheria, solidus, Sophia, steelyard weights, Theodora, Verina
commercial enterprises of empresses 132
conservatism of female representations 7
Constantia, daughter of Constantine the Great, 17
Constantina, empress, 162, 178, see also Maurice
Constantine Porphyrogennetos, emperor, 20, 125, 131–32, 153n39, 171, 181, 182
Constantine the Great (Constantine I), emperor, 15, 16, 16n28, 17, 20, 22, 26, 52, 61–62, 140, 168, 180
Constantinople (Istanbul)
Augustaion 16, 19
Baths of Arkadianae 139
Baths of Dagistheus 157
Baths of the Tauros (Sophianai) 152
Baths of Zeuxippus 140, 143, 153
Chalke Gate (Brazen House) 17, 22, 24, 87, 139
Church of the Archangel 152
Church of the Forty Martyrs 25
Church of Hagia Irene 99
Church of Hagia Sophia (fig. 6.4) 16, 45, 66–67, 96, 97, 101, 129–30, 151, 180, see also gallery (church), Paul Silentiarios
Church of Saint Euphemia 88, 98
Church of Saint John Stoudios 129
Church of Saints Sergios and Bakchos 100–02
Church of Saint Polyeuktos (fig. 4.1) 20, 94–98
Convent of Repentance 104, 104n79, 180
Forum Bovis 16
Forum of Constantine 58

Gate of the Philadelphion 16
Hippodrome 68n15, 110, 113, 152n25, 157, 172, 184
Hormisdas Palace 99–100, 102
Milion 16, 152
mint for coinage 41, 159, 162
Propontis 152
Pulcherianiai district 152
Rhesion gate 152
Sophiae Palace 150, 152, 156
Sophianae Palace 152
see also Bosporos
Constantinopolis, see personifications
Constantius II, emperor, 17
constitutional role of empresses 9–10
consul, office of 43, 67, 69–70, 72, 81, 133, 147–48, 171, 175, 185, see also coinage, consular diptychs, mappa
consular diptychs, 69–82, 96, 123, 135, 140, 146–48, 172, 173, 176, 184, see also Ariadne, consul, personifications, and Theodora
Corbridge lanx (fig. 2.17) 57
Corippus 50n44, 70, 133, 149, 150, 151, 152, 183
coronation, imperial 10, 151, 157, 171, 182, see also succession
Council of Ephesus 21
Crispus 17
cross 25, 71, 104, 144, 158, 159, 171, see Crux Vaticana and Helena
crown, see coronation and diadem
Crux Vaticana (figs. 7.4 and 7.5) 150, 163–68, 178
cult, imperial 14, 16n28, 55, 58, 82, 172, see also King's two bodies
Cyril of Scythopolis, see Vita of Saint Sabas

damnatio memoriae 17
debt remission 153
Demosthenes 116
diadem 37, 45, 60, 62n79, 76–78, 80, 136, 140, 144, 145, 158, 159,

161, 162, 167, 172, *see also* prependoulia
dining 132, *see also* gluttony
Dioskorides, *see* manuscript
diplomacy, *see* Sophia and Theodora
dog 19, 154

eagle 144, 172, 176
earrings, *see* jewelry
education 133–34
ekphrasis 143, *see also* Paul Silentiarios
empress as literary trope 45
empress-looking, concept of 5, 9, 58
encomium 108–09
enthronement, representation of 62n79, 71n42, 158–60, 172, 173, 175, 184
epilepsy 67
Erectheum, *see* Athens
Eucharist 125, 127
Eudokia (Athenaïs), empress, 20–21, 112n33
    coinage 26
    literary output 21
    patronage 21, 151
    pilgrimage 20, 22
    sculpture 20, 40
    see also Homeric Centos
Eudoxia, empress, 19–20
    coinage 26–27, 159
    patronage 19, 25
    pilgrimage 19–20
    sculpture 19, 25, 33
    see also Arkadios
eunuch 128, 129–30, 134–35, 181
Euphemia, empress, 22, 87–88, 102–03, 162, *see also* Constantinople (Church of Saint Euphemia), Justin I
Eusebia, empress, 17, literary patronage 17
Eusebios 15, 17, 26
Evagrius 20n55
Eve 15

Fausta, empress, 15, 16, 17, 163
feather 76
fecundity of empresses 111
films about empresses, *see* Theodora
Flaccilla, Aelia Flavia, empress, 18–19, 21, 143
Flaubert, Gustave 119
follis (pl. folles) 6, 91, 145, 158–60, 162–63, 186
fortune telling 68, *see also* witchcraft
Foucault, Michel 117
Franks 20, *see also* Gregory of Tours
Fulgentius 57

Galla Placidia, empress, 19, 40, 96, 136, 143, 152, 159
gallery, church 129–30, 134
    see also Ravenna (Church of San Vitale)
games 74, 76, 125, *see also* consul and Constantinople (hippodrome)
garden, Byzantine 152n25
Gaza
    Church of Saint Stephen 130
    Temple of Zeus Marnas 19
gems, engraved 50
gender, methodological implications of 8–9
Gibbon, Edward 107, 117–20
gift exchange 98, 123, 167, 175
globus cruciger 62n79, 144, 159, 161, 166, 168–71, 172, 175
gluttony, topos of 112
goddesses and empresses 55–58, *see also* Athena
gold sculpture 55, 152
Goths, *see* Amalasuntha, Atalarich, Orestes, Theodatus, Visigoths
greed, topos of 154
Greece, classical 3
Greek Anthology 19, 96, 98, 152
Greens, *see* circus factions
Gregory Abu'l-Faraj 67, 101, 155
Gregory of Nazianzos 134
Gregory of Nyssa 19

INDEX

Gregory of Tours 149, 154, 157, 178
grotesque 112, 114

hair 77–78, 182, *see also* snood
halo 114, 128, 137, 158, 159, 161, 162, *see also* light
Hammat Gader 21
Helena 14–17, 87, 180
   coinage 17
   Discovery of True Cross 14–15
   legacy 15, 119, 168, 180
   novel about 16
   patronage 15, 17, 21
   pilgrimage 15, 20
   sculpture 16–17
helmet 48, 50, 52, 57, 158
Heraklios (Heraclius) 20, 125, 144, 145
hierarchy, *see* precedence
hippodrome, *see* Constantinople (hippodrome)
Homeric Centos 21, *see also* Eudokia
Honoria 27
horse 74, 76, 176
hospices, *see* hostels
hospitals 13, 22
hostels 22, 99
Hoxne treasure pepper pot (fig. 2.22) 60
Hustler magazine, 113, *see also* political pornography

Iconoclasm 123n3, 144
   destruction of imperial image 14, 82, 143, 182
   women and 17–18, 120, 151–52, 186
   see also textiles
icons 17, 21, 120, 130, *see also* Christ, Iconoclasm and Virgin Mary
identity, individual 2, 142–44, 182, 186, *see also* portraiture
imperial insignia 2, 133, *see also* diadem, globus cruciger, mappa, prependoulia, scepter, tablion
Ino, *see* Anastasia

insanity 149, 153–55, 178
inscriptions, 87, 93–94, 96, 125, 140, 152, 166, 175, *see also* Athens (Erectheum), steelyard weights, Theodora
invective 110n24, 118
Irene (Empress) 10n44, 25, 120n82, 131, 146, 153n39, 168, 175, 182, 186
Istanbul, *see* Constantinople
ivory, 168–78
   painting on 76, 173
   see also Barberini Diptych, consular diptychs, Sophia, Theodora, Trier ivory

Jerusalem 15, 20, 21, 104
   Church of the Holy Sepulcher 15
   Mount of Olives 15
jewelry 37, 40–42, 57, 136, 146, 148, 172
John of Biclar 151n15
John of Cappadocia 102, 108, 114
John of Ephesus 93, 99, 100, 101, 102, 108, 136, 149, 152, 154–55, 157
John of Nikiu 94, 101, 104, 109, 143n109
John Klimax (John Climmachus) 45
John Lydos (John the Lydian) 68, 70, 71, 93, 102, 108
John Malalas 20, 21, 93, 94, 102, 103, 104, 105–06, 108
John the Baptist 163
juggling 74, *see also* actresses and actors, Constantinople (hippodrome)
Julia, daughter of Augustus 113, 180, *see also* Augustus, political pornography
Julia Domna 55
Julian the Apostate 52
Julianus Argentarius 123–25, *see also* Ravenna (Church of San Vitale)
Justin I, emperor, 94, 96, 100, 153, 159, 166, 175

Justin II, emperor, 69, 70, 120, 133, 149, 150, 152, 153–55, 158–61, 167, 175, 178
  see also Crux Vaticana, insanity, Sophia
Justin (Justinus), the consul 147–48
Justinian, emperor, 16, 19, 69, 98–99, 105, 125, 128, 132, 133, 135, 137, 139, 140, 147, 150, 151, 152, 159, 168, 175, 180, see also Ravenna (Church of San Vitale), Theodora
Justinian II, emperor, 20, 183

Kantorowicz, Ernst, see King's two bodies
Kassia 17
Kayseri 40n21
Kedrenos, George 25
King's Two Bodies, notion of 6, 114, 137
Komnene, Anna 111, 112, 113, 118
Kontorniate 71

lamp 60
law
  imperial representation 14, 71
  mention of empresses in 132, 153
  status of consuls 148
  status of women 8n26, 113n42, 154n50, 186
lead seals 132, 144, 161
Leo the Great (Leo I), emperor, 22, 58, 65, 66, 67
Leo II, emperor, 67, 82
Leo III, emperor, 17
Leontia empress, 67, 162
Liber Pontificalis 166
Licinia Eudoxia, empress,
  coinage 26, 136, 140, 159
  and steelyard weights 40
Licinius, emperor, 15
Life of Constantine (Anonymous) 16
light 133, 183, see also halo
Liutprand of Cremona 1, 3
Livia, empress, 13, 14, 50, 57, 132

Lydos, see John of Lydos
loros, see clothing

Magi, representation of 133–34
Malalas, see John Malalas
Manus Dei 27, 90
manuscript, illuminated 98, 137, 171–72
mappa 43, 71, 72, 171, 176
marble, sculpture 41, 83–87, 141–43, 175, see also sculpture (architectural)
Marcellinus 81, 82
Marcian 22, 24
Maria Regina 175, see also Virgin Mary
Mark the Deacon 19
marriage 10, 20, 90, 99, 102, 111, 114, 120, 131, 144, 158, 161, 181, 182, see also bride show, renaming, solidus (marriage)
marriage solidus, see solidus
Martina, empress, 144–46, 163
Maurice Tiberios, emperor, 157, 161, 162, 175–78
Maximian 135, 136
Menander Rhetor 110
metalwork 17, 135, see also Crux Vaticana, jewelry, silver wares
Michael the Syrian 67, 99, 102, 120, 144, 151, 156
Milan, Castello Sforzesco (Sforza), sculpture of empress (figs. 6.5 and 6.6) 140–43
misogyny 99, 153, 180
monograms, 125, see also Theodora
Monophysite heresy 68, 99–100, 101, 102, 109, 151, 154
mosaic, see Constantinople (Chalke Gate), Constantinople (Church of Hagia Sophia), Ravenna (Church of San Vitale)
motherhood, see fecundity, procreation, succession
music 74, 131

nakedness 113
Narses 153
necklace, see jewelry
Nero, emperor, 71, 108
Nestorios 22
Nika Riot 94, 98–99, 103, 139, 155, 184, see also revolt
Nikephoros Kallistos 25
Nikiu, see John of Nikiu
novels about empresses, see Helena and Theodora
numismatics, see coinage

oath 153
Onassis, Jacqueline Kennedy 113, see also political pornography
Orestes diptych (fig. 3.5) 80–81, 176
Orientalism 100n35, 118–19, 119n73, 119n76
Ostrogoths 143, 175
Ottoman Empire 132

palaces, imperial 19, 90, 132, 152n25, 181, see also Constantinople for palaces
papyri evidence, see Sophia
Parastaseis Syntomoi Chronikai 16, 19, 20, 22, 58, 87, 88, 140, 183, 186
Patriarch 157
patriographic literature
  see Parastaseis Syntomoi Chronikai
patronage, see Anicia Juliana, Eudoxia, Helena, hospitals, hostels, poorhouses, Theodora
Paul Silentiarios 45, 129–30
Paulinus of Nola 15
pearls 40, 41, 45, 76, 78, 104, 140, 148, 167, 171, see also jewelry
pepper pot, see Hoxne treasure
Persians 153, 154, 182
personal hygiene, see bathing
personifications 27, 47, 76, 98, 183
  Constantinopolis 50, 52, 71, 158, 173n141
  Roma 50, 50n44, 52, 71, 173n141

Sophia 50
Victory 27, 74, 76, 91, 158, 172, 173
Peter the Patrician 131
philanthropia 13, 99, 101, 103, 105, 106
Phokas 63, 145, 162
pig 19
pilgrimage, 15, see also Helena
poorhouses 13, 22, 104
Pope 101n49, 123n3, 166–67, 171, see also Liber Pontificalis and Vatican
pornography, political 6, 87, 94, 113–15
porphyry 16, 22, 139
portraiture, Byzantine notion of 3, 3n6, 45–7, 128–29, 131,142–43, 162, 175, 183–84
pottery 154
precedence, rules of 71, 74
prependoulia (pendules) 40, 47, 63, 76, 136, 140, 144, 145, 161, 162, 167, 172, see also diadem
procreation, see abortion, fecundity, and succession
Prokopios (Procopius)
  see Anekdota, antiencomium, Buildings, political pornography, Wars
proskynesis 127
prostitution 15, 104, 113n43, 116, 119n74
Psellos, Michael 135
Pulcheria 21–24, 169–71
  coinage 27, 90
  palace 152
  patronage 22, 99
  sculpture 19, 22, 33, 40
  and succession 22
  and Virgin Mary 22
  see also celibacy, globus cruciger, succession
purple 16n26, 133, 139, 150n8, 155n54, see also porphyry
Pythia Therma, springs 104–05, 181

Ravenna, Church of Saint Vitale 121–37
    ceremony 123, 125–28
    Church of San Apollinare Nuovo
        133
    dating 135–36
    identification of figures 128–29,
        135–36
    Justinian and court (fig. 6.3) 123,
        125, 127, 136, 159
    patronage 123–25, 135
    Theodora and court (fig. 6.2) 108,
        120, 121–23, 128–29, 133, 137,
        140, 144–46, 148, 159, 171,
        181, 184
    see Agnellus, halo, Justinian,
        Theodora
Ravenna, reconquest of 135, 143, 182
relics 22, 163, *see also* Trier ivory
renaming of empresses 20, 120, 157
Republican Rome 13, 82
revolt 82, 143, 182
    see also Iconoclasm and Nika Riot
rhetoric, critique of 110
riot, *see* revolt
Roma, *see* personifications

Saint Basil 143–44
Saint John Chrysostom 19, 25, 112n33
Saint Melania the Younger 20
Saint Neophytos 19
Saint Sabas 172, *see also Vita* of Saint
    Sabas
Saint Theodore the Stoudite 144
scepter 151, 159, 161, 168, 172, 176
scholarship, previous, on Byzantine
    empresses 7–10
scroll 45, 60, 158
sculpture, architecture 19, 96, 105, 130,
    152
seclusion of women 113, 129–30, 134,
    153, 181–82
secrecy, topos of 117
Secret History, *see Anekdota*, secrecy
sekreton ton gynaikon 10, 69, 134, 135,
    150, 156

ceremony 131–32
empresss, importance of 131
funding 132
representation 130–31, 181
titulature 132, 134, 181
see also eunuch, lead seals, *zoste
    patrikia*
Selçuk, Church of Saint John 101,
    140
Senate 68, 113n42, 125, 150
Seneca 113n43, 180
sexual excess 112, 114, 116, 116n51,
    see also political pornography
siliqua 158
silver sculpture 19, *see also* Crux
    Vaticana
silver wares 60, 71, 167, 172, 175, *see
    also* Hoxne treasure
Simmokattes, Theophylaktos
Sirmium 17
slavery 103, 104, 134, *see also* eunuch
snood 83, 87, 140, 172
solidus (pl. solidi) 17, 90–91, 104n75,
    125, 158, 159, 176, 178;
    marriage solidus (fig. 1.3) 27,
        90–91
Sophia 6, 140, 149–78, 184
    coinage 6, 45, 63, 82, 149, 150,
        155, 158–61, 162–63, 186
    dates 150
    diplomacy 153
    family ties 6, 150, 154n43
    financial affairs 153, 157
    inscription 152
    ivory 129, 133, 146–47, 150,
        168–78, 184
    lead seal 161
    Monophysitism 151
    palace construction 152, 157
    papyri 153
    patronage 50n44, 150–51, 152–53,
        166
    sculpture 152, 152n25
    succession, imperial 10, 150,
        154–55, 156, 157, 162–63

see also Anastasia, Constantinople (Sophiae Palace), Crux Vaticana, enthronement, Justin II, law, Maurice, succession
Souda 109, 117
Sperber, Dan 58
steelyard weights, early Byzantine 29–64, 175, 182–83
   ambiguity 57–60
   chronology 47, 52–55
   geographic distribution 30–34, 47
   inscriptions 58
   male types 60–63
   manufacture 34–35
   origin of term 30
   pagan imagery, meaning of 48, 55–60
   see also Anemourion, jewelry, personifications, Yassi Ada
steelyard weights, Roman 48–50, 60
stylites 100
succession, imperial 10, 22, 82, 150, 151, 157, 161, 179n3, 180
Suetonius 11
symmetry, as notion of beauty 4

tablion 133, 171, 172, 173n141, 176, 178
textiles 11, 16n26, 50n44, 129, 133, 134, 135, 150n8, 153, 155n54, 171–72
theater 76, see also actresses and actors
Theodatus 71
Theodora, empress, 87, 93–106, 107–120, 121–48, 133, 137, 139n87, 144, 151, 153, 161, 162, 171, 184
   body 112, 113–14, 137
   charity to women 11, 104
   consular diptych (fig. 6.9) 82, 123, 147–48
   diplomacy 102
   disagreements with Justinian 103
   family 100, 101–02, 109, 111, 128, 150, 180
   income 99
   inscriptions 101
   lead seal 144
   legacy in Byzantium 120–21
   monograms 101
   novels about 6, 119
   plays and films about 102, 118, 119n74
   religious patronage 11, 25, 100, 101, 102, 103–06, 108–09, 139, 151, 180
   sculpture 139, 140, 152, 175
   also see abortion, basileia, bathing, beauty, halo, Monophysite heresy, Nika Riot, political pornography, prostitution, and also see these buildings: Constantinople (Chalke Gate), Constantinople (Church of Hagia Sophia) Constantinople (Convent of Repentance), Constantinople (hippodrome), Pythia Therma, springs, Ravenna (Church of San Vitale)
Theodoric 134
Theodosios I, emperor, 18, 94, 143
Theodosios II, emperor, 20, 21
Theophanes the Confessor 25, 66n1, 67, 81, 98, 101n49, 105, 152, 153, 154, 156, 157, 186
Theophilos, emperor, 120, 131
throne, see enthronement
Tiberios, emperor, 125, 153, 155, 156–58, 178, see also Anastasia, Justin II, Sophia, succession
titulature 10n44, see also Augusta and basilissa
torture 111–12
treasury, imperial 68
tremissis (pl. tremisses) 90–91
Trier ivory (fig. 1.2) 24–26
triumphal imagery 139
typological, discussion of term 2, 179

urban space 9, 14, 16, 87, 113, 139, 152, see also Constantinople

Vandals 139, 150n8
Venantius Fortunatus 167–68
Verina, empress, 58, 65, 66, 183
   coinage 26, 90–2, 163
   revolt, participation in 67
Victor Tonnensis 81, 93
Victory, *see* personification
Vienna Dioskorides (fig. 4.2) 98, *see also* manuscript
Virgin Mary
   church dedications 16, 22, 152
   patron of Constantinople 22
   relics 66
   representations of 16, 21, 71, 71n42, 130, 134, 175
   and empresses 15, 22, 151
   see also Council of Ephesus, Maria Regina, Pucheria
Visigoths 139
visuality, Byzantine 183–84

Vita of Saint Philaretos, *see* bride show
Vita of Saint Sabas 68, 69, 98
Vita of Saint Stephen 17
Vita of Saint Thekla 14

Wars (Prokopios) 105, 108, 108n4, 109, 118, 120
weaving, *see* textiles
weight 161, *see also* steelyard weights
widowhood 80, 155
witchcraft 19, *see also* fortune telling

Yassi Ada 47, 52, 53

Zacharias of Mitylene 21n61, 66, 67, 68, 81, 92, 93, 100, 103
Zeno 66, 81–82, 87, 90–92
Zosimos 143
zoste patrikia 132